CW01466975

PAN

Great God of Nature

PAN

Great God of Nature

Leo Vinci

Neptune Press
49a, Museum Street, London WC1A 1LY

First published in 1993

© Leo Vinci

All rights reserved. No portion of this book may be reproduced or utilised in any form or by any means, electromechanical, including photocopying, recording or retrieval system, without the prior permission in writing of the publisher. Nor it is to be otherwise circulated in any form or binding or cover other than that in which it is published.

ISBN 0 9505001 8 6

Made and printed in Great Britain by Booksprint, Bristol, England

For Pan
Amicus humani generis

Decicated with love to
Patricia Arthy

To the warmth that
accompanies the light.

CONTENTS

Detail, drawn from an early fifteenth century woodcut, showing Pan resting outside his cave in the early evening.

Introduction

THIS work has had a somewhat chequered history. Chapter Two was written first and not for this manuscript but another. It came of its own free will when I was making the first draft of a book concerning the flora of the planet, which made many references to Pan. It was thought, by those who read my pre-publication thoughts, that it should be extracted from the original work and sent out on its own to fend for itself; that has been done in this work. The reader should not make too much of the statement that it 'came of its own free will,' even though it did. I was sitting with a clean screen on the computer and fresh notepaper for the project I had in mind and I wanted to see how it would work out in principle. It was then it began to flow of its own free will accompanied by very strong visual images that concurred with what was being dictated.

I am not sure I like the word 'dictated' but there is little doubt I was merely a witness to what was happening. I would be delighted to be able to write that there were angelic choirs, seraphic trumpets and the heavens opened...but it wasn't so. There was very strong imagery with a form of commentary added. This seems rather cold when seen in print but it was very pleasant at the time and, when it ceased on the first night, it was obviously not complete. I presented myself at the same time the next night and, taking the telephone off the hook, to my delight it picked up where it had stopped the night before. I suspended all intellectual criticism and accepted what was being presented without judgement.

On the final night, when I could see it was drawing to a conclusion, 'intellect' broke through and demanded to know why it had been banished these past few nights and no more came. Whatever it was, whatever its worth, it had gone. I (metaphorically) lambasted 'intellect' for putting its oar in when it hadn't been invited to the feast and banished it again, and it went. Half-an-hour and two or three glasses of Auslese later, the 'story' picked up where it had stopped and the exercise was concluded.

I was undecided what to do when it was finished, whether it should stay in the new manuscript and form the closing chapter of the work. It seemed very personal and I thought perhaps it should be omitted completely, as being of little interest to others. It was the dedicatee who suggested perhaps it should form the basis of a book of Pan. This was followed by Karl Duncan asking for such a book for the Neptune Press imprint. I started to write it up to see how it would work out and look, which is my way of working, and from there it went its own way until it was finished.

Pan has been close to my heart and a 'presence' in my affairs for a long time now. I have always felt he is a greatly neglected and misunderstood deity. For me personally Pan has always appeared in my life at the last minute when all seemed to be lost, which after all, is when you need him most. When Pan 'panicked the Persians laying siege' to my door, and made my personal 'Athens' secure, he would leave with my thanks ringing in his ears.

I am sure I am not the first to entertain the thought, but I have long believed that Greece is often a state of mind, that you do not have to be born Greek to be 'Greek.' I felt at home the moment I landed there and I am sure the world is filled with such 'Greeks,' all wanting to go back. I have always wanted to write an introduction to Pan but I have side-stepped the issue for quite some time, fearing I might not do him justice. Every now and then things seem to come of their own accord and take over; I think this is one of those occasions, and when this does happen I just get on with it.

There seems little point in labouring the mistakes being made regarding the planet on which we live, which is Pan's kingdom; but you sometimes feel obliged, in the current climate, to write something. To relieve me of the burden of trying to find something new or original to say, I was sent a newspaper clipping from The Guardian, dated the 11th of March 1993. It tells how Greek environmentalists are fighting to try save **Homer's** 'Achelous, the Father of All Rivers.'

I will not quote the full report, but it seems that the Greek government is completing plans to divert the Achelous from its course, which will threaten an ecological catastrophe in an area which is one of Europe's richest regions of flora and fauna.

If the plans go ahead, and it seems likely they will at the time of writing, Greece's largest river will be diverted from one side of the country to the other, to provide irrigation and hydroelectric power which, it is claimed, is not needed there. The report claims that the interested parties are 'concealing impact reports that show catastrophic consequences for all forms of animal life in the area and on the lagoons, wet meadows and riverine forests at Messalongi.' It was at Messalongi that Lord Byron succumbed to fever in 1824.

The report implies, again at the time of writing, that the case may already be lost for when the contract goes to Parliament for debate 'it will be passed easily.' It seems approximately forty miles of the river would stay in its original bed and the environment it supports will be destroyed for ever. The legend of Achelous and his daughters, the Sirens, are discussed in the main text. It seems superfluous to try and add anything to the above.

Finally I would like to tender my sincere thanks to Steve Moore. In the final stage of the manuscript he did sterling work to help the book on its way. He gave the work a good burnishing and removed those embarrassing 'trip-wires' missed because of familiarity with the page.

Adsit Anglis Sanctus Georgius

Leo Vinci.

September 23rd 1993

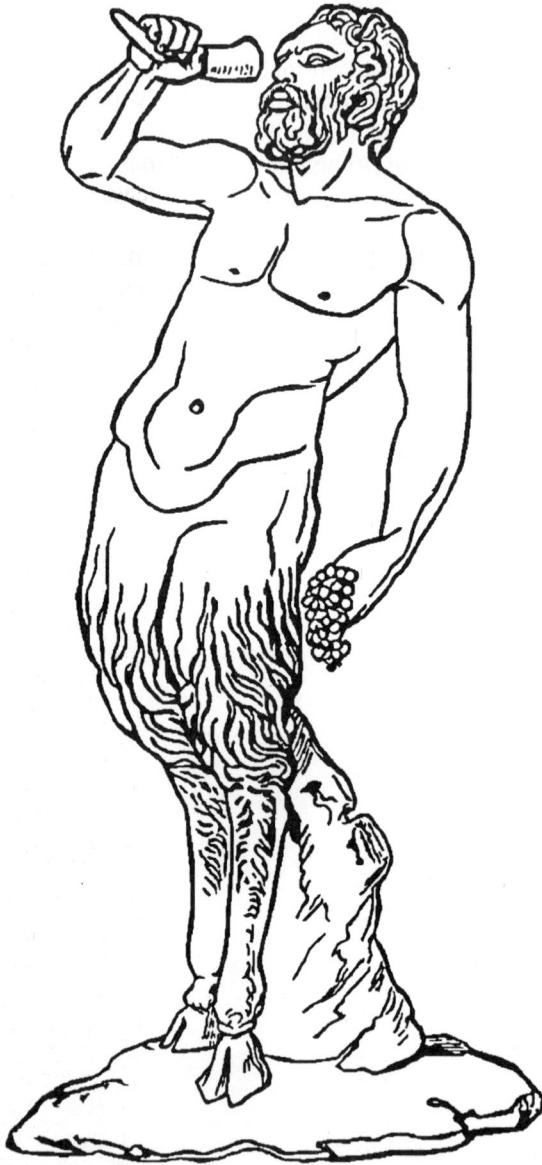

Drawing, taken from
a statue of Pan.
(Florence)

THE GREAT GOD PAN

from '*The Rite of Pan.*'
'Half a man and half a beast,
Pan is greatest, Pan is least.
Pan is all, and all is Pan;
Look for him in every-man
Goat-hoof swift and shaggy thigh
Follow him to Arcady.'
The Goat-Foot God: **Dion Fortune**.

THIS first section deals with the Greek god Pan and contains the usually mentioned myths of him and his birth. However, it does not insist that Pan was sired by Hermes and that Pan's mother, according to the **Homeric Hymn to Pan,** was 'the rich-tressed daughter of Dryops,' who is not named, as if that were the only story. It is the most popular one, but there are other accounts of his birth and his parentage, it is said there are around twenty claimants to Pan's birth, and some of them have excellent credentials. The mystery of Pan is greater than most people realize and he has hardly begun to be mastered by us, but his day is coming. Pan is a mystery that needs unravelling badly, but this short introduction to Pan is not the place to attempt such a monumental task. It would be a daunting one to undertake.

These sections on Pan are followed by the other Roman and Greek deities of nature. Those of cave and grotto, wood and glade, field and forest. The writer has always felt a great affinity with the Greek and Roman Gods and in particular with Pan. This naturally includes those countries where Pan and these gods were worshipped. I also have a great love of the Celtic Gods, for they are the gods of the country where I was born. My affinity with the British and Celtic Gods is not only great, but inborn. I count myself lucky to have such a great wealth in my coffers and feel no dichotomy in this.

One way of starting is to get to know as much as we can about Pan the Goat-god of nature. We must become at one with Nature that is to be found all around us, and our nature within. We should read about Pan from the sources available to us. It would be to advantage to imbue ourselves with his myth, legend, folklore, fable and the fictional stories that are based upon these. Take note of how Pan is regarded in literature and novel, by poets such as **Elizabeth B. Browning,** and the quotations given later of Greek epigrams and lyrics collected over the years from old books. Read writers such as **Algernon Blackwood,** for example his short story, *A Touch of Pan.* 'He (Pan) sanctioned every natural joy in them and blessed each passion with his power of creation.' Similarly read of Pan in **Dion Fortune's** tale, **The Goat-Foot God.** 'When Hugh had asserted to himself the Divine Right of Nature, he had evoked Pan quite effectually. Each time he had renewed the assertion, Pan had answered. Each time he had doubted the natural divinity, the god had withdrawn.'

Let us take a short example from **Kenneth Graham's** beautifully evocative work *The Wind in the Willows.* 'This is the place of my song-dream, the place the music played to me,' whispered the Rat, as if in a trance. 'Here, in this holy place, here if anywhere, surely we will find Him!' Incidentally, **Dion Fortune** thought the chapter on Pan in this work inspired and considered it a 'direct contact' with the god. I could not dissent in any way with that opinion.

Finally, although this has hardly exhausted the subject or the authors, let us take a novel by **Stephen McKenna** called **The Oldest God** (1926). I have deliberately saved this book until the last. Long out of print and hard to obtain, this novel now needs the reprint it is worthy of having. The professor in the story tells us of Christ and Pan. 'No compromise in that war! No saint's halo for a Pan artfully made respectable. The two could not coexist. Wild nature, everywhere the enemy of Christ, was made the enemy of all who were being won to Christ's side. He became the embodiment and symbol of evil...'

Another character says, 'When you come to a god who runs in the blood of his people, so to say, it's no mean thing to get him repudiated and dethroned.' The professor replies (condensed to main arguments), 'It would never have happened in a straight fight. Pan was betrayed by his own followers...you may express the conflict between them as a conflict between asceticism and nature...it was one of the greatest conflicts in history; the oldest god fighting for his life on the oldest battlefield, the meeting place of religion and morals...Christ was not himself an ascetic, he was abused for gluttony and wine-bibbing; but those who came after him believed that the shortest way to the higher life which he preached was by mortifying the flesh till it lay dead to Pan's enticement...they made asceticism an end in itself instead of a means to the life which Christ had preached as something nobler than wild nature. One sometimes doubts whether Christ, at any time in the last nineteen hundred years would have recognised the faith called Christianity.'

This tale concerns a guest who brings with him someone whom they know only as 'Mr Stranger.' The guest himself is not quite sure how Mr Stranger arrived but he has a remarkable effect upon the guests at the party merely by his presence and on the veneer of civilization they all thought they securely possessed. Finally the strange guest leaves the house at Nateby but he leaves a note simply signed 'Stranger.' The last part of the letter written by him (in the novel) I will quote. Why should I let Pytheas make the accusation my writing 'smells of the lamp?' If others have written better, then stand aside and let them speak. '...I wish our discussion last night had not been interrupted. I fancy you share my love for theorising; you probably feel, with me, that we have too few opportunities to test our theories. And here, so far as I have been able to piece together the events of the last four days, came the proof of a conviction which we hold in common: the world is too weak for Christianity. It is too timid, we must add, for paganism; and so mankind remains suspended in mid-air, higher than the beasts and lower than the angels, miserable in the void between animal satisfaction and celestial bliss. Before you and your friends made that strange choice between Christ and Pan, did any but you and the professor - confirmed and universal sceptics! - reflect that the one was no more practical than the other? You, indeed, voted against paganism on the ground that civilisation was the less uncomfortable: a confusion of issue, surely? Or perhaps a simplification, since you left god out of both scales. Is that, secretly, your solution to the riddle? The form of Christ and the spirit of Pan? It has a long history to recommend it: nearly two thousand years.

Curiosity has almost prevailed over natural diffidence in one respect: I would give much to read the next chapter in the lives of those who abandoned one misunderstood allegiance for another that they comprehended no better. To see that, I nearly resolved to stay. What is to be the mental, moral, the material position of those who followed freedom when they thought nature ordained it, but picked up their chains when they fancied it was a devil's mutter? Heaven is closed to them; and they have closed the earth against themselves for fear of a hell which they imagine to lie under the earth! My compliments to the professor: he has established his ingenious hypothesis. The rule of Pan came to an end on the day when a fanatic preached that the kindly, joyous, savage Pan was in truth the embodiment of original sin! And now, if I am to attend his service, I must waste no time.'

Here the letter ends. After the 'Stranger' had departed one of the main characters noticed that in the hall 'the smell was a familiar one...the reek of powder and tobacco...the baffling animal-scent had departed. I wondered if I had imagined it! Then I realized that, if I began to wonder about anything, I should lose my few remaining wits.'

We must try to piece together all we can about Pan, much as we would do about someone we do not know: from the reports given about him by others, by gathering all the information we can. The early sources are rich veins to work with, such as **Artemidorus the Dream-Interpreter** who was born at Ephesus late in the 2nd century A.D. His work on dreams seems to assume Pan is seen and heard most frequently at night. **Artemidorus** tells us of goats seen in dreams, they 'do not predict marriages or friendships or partnerships nor do they assure those that exist, for such goats do not run in a flock, but rather pasture separately from one another.' In the **Homeric** hymn, Pan is a 'lonely god.' (**H.Hom.** *Pan* 14-15)

Horace wrote with great warmth of the protection the gods afforded him and especially that of Pan, who attended to the well-being of his country farm. Although **Horace** never met Pan face to face, he said that Pan visited him often. In the pastoral romance of *Daphnis and Chloe* by **Longus**, written in the 3rd century A.D., Pan is heard and felt more than seen. Scattered throughout will be found quotations from the works of Ovid Homer, Pindar, Herodotus, Dio Chrysostomus, Pausanias, etc. to name but a few. The reader is well served for these writers should they seek other sources.

Pan loved the poet Pindar and he sang and danced to his lyric songs; and in return for honour Pan afforded him, Pindar built Pan a sanctuary in front of his house. However, sadly, we cannot receive all the tales of Pan as historical fact. Yet it is most important to know the general beliefs the Greeks and Romans held regarding Pan at the time. Often it is very difficult to find out the original form of a legend. Poets, on the one hand, embellish it with the creations of their own fancy. Historians, on the other, omit many of its more marvellous incidents, to reduce it to the form of probable history. We, the searchers, are generally set down somewhere in the middle, between the two camps without a foot in either, when what we seek is a foothold in both.

If possible we should go to the places where these sources tell us Pan could once be found. Although obviously desirable, it does not necessarily have to be Greece. It must be admitted that to stand on a site where Pan was honoured or reputed to have been, never leaves you, even when you leave the place. These places are no longer words in a guide book or a few lines in history. Go out into the glades and forests, the rivers and streams, the caves and grottoes, mountains and peaks. Seek out 'the lonely places and caves obscure,' though they are getting harder to find by the minute today. Partially empty yourself to make room to invite the god to come and stay a while. Make a space in your home and garden for Pan, leave some untilled ground on the edge of your garden at the rear, if you can, 'in thanks' for him, and invite him in. Read part of the 6th century A.D. epigram by the scholar **Agathias,** who knew his Pan:

'Pan of the crags, Stratonicus the plowman
In thanks sets aside for you this unsown place...
... no longer cut with bronze
You'll find this station fortunate...'

Ask Pan to teach you his ways, his lore, his personal magic if he will, so long neglected but gathering impetus. If ever the epithet from the Delphic Oracle and written over Jung's doorway at Kusnacht - VOCATUS ATQUE NON VOCATUS DEUS ADERIT (*'Bidden or unbidden the gods are here'*) - is justified, it is regarding Pan, he never left, he is always here.

He is our constant companion whether we will it or no. In its positive aspect Pan's love can sometimes be like a form of possession. It would be difficult, almost impossible, to divorce ourselves from Pan, to attempt to destroy or try to escape from him. Though who in their right mind would want to, I can't tell. However, I have declared my interest and I am biased. We would have to sever ourselves from our nature to attempt to divorce ourselves from Pan, to lay waste instinct and everything that is natural within us. To try to destroy him we would virtually have to obliterate the planet and such a course would be foolish.

The results of such an attempt do not bear thinking about. The destruction, havoc and panic of such an action would be great and in the end, we would be the only ones to suffer. Pan would simply withdraw and wait to see if there was anything left to come back to. Take such a course of action too far or make the exile permanent and there would not be. Learn from the canon of early Judaeo-Christianity, which appears to condemn and suppress most of the natural and joyful aspects of life as sins marked out for punishment or retribution. This creed seems to have created far more problems than it was ever intended to solve.

When you say 'I don't know what came over me' because you seemed to act out of character, Pan came over you and the reader will find this phrase occurring often in this work I am sure, for which I make no apology. However, do not think this gives you a convenient scapegoat for your life and the actions you chose to take. Pan is not your personal Azazel. Pan has been bearing that burden for many centuries in the name of the Christian Devil and it is time it was taken from his shoulders and placed where it belongs: put back on the shoulders of the medieval monsters who invented it in the first place to protect their own interests and power. You are, have always been and will always be, responsible for your life and your actions.

You are responsible, not this ridiculous charade of Pan as the Christian Devil who tempted you. 'The Devil is, historically, the god of any people that one personally dislikes.' **Aleister Crowley**. The Devil may have tempted you, but even if tempted you accepted the offer to do something you wanted to do really, instead of refusing it. What you lacked was a scapegoat, someone to shoulder the blame if you are found out or it goes wrong, a personal whipping boy. Someone to whom you can point and say they made me do it. Often this is why so many fortune-tellers flourish like the green bay tree. We need someone to blame when things go wrong, occult sanction for the responsibility people should take for their own lives, and for things they know they shouldn't have done in the first place. How you make use of Pan is your responsibility, not his. What he gives is as natural as breathing, eating and drinking. What you choose to breathe, eat and drink is your choice; choose wrongly and you will suffer accordingly.

Do not blame Pan if your choice is faulty; you made the choice, not him. So many seem to make a problem concerning the things they do, no matter how natural they are or should be. Sex, as the great fertilizing power in nature, is one prime aspect of Pan: it is a perfectly normal, healthy appetite and should simply be regarded as such. If you are thirsty you drink, you make little fuss about it and that is how it should be with Pan, for he is just as natural. Listen with your inner ear away from the towns, cities and the infernal, ever present television; away from all the things that vie for an all-inclusive and jealous attention to their demands. They seem to know instinctively that if we start to hear other voices, their tyranny and power could weaken, perhaps even broken. Many more, perhaps, may start thinking instead of regurgitating last night's received and ready digested televised pap in the name of thought. Do not misunderstand me, I do not dislike all television, but some of it, at times, is little more than an open sewer; nor do I condemn it to create an effect on paper. However, I do know where the off switch is and use it a lot of the time. Of Pan, **Oscar Wilde** wrote reflectively. 'O goat-footed god of Arcady! This modern world hath need of thee.'

THE PLACE

It may seem strange to begin a book about the Greek god Pan with what appears to be a geography lesson, but my research has shown it would be to advantage. Naturally, very few people had trouble in placing Greece, or even Athens. It was when we began to narrow the focus that the trouble began. The areas that caused the most problems were in the Peloponnese: the Isthmus of Corinth, Arcadia, Sparta, Mycenae and the other parts of Greece where Pan was found.

On the map, the Peloponnese is the lowest part of Greece. It is shaped like the leaf of a plane tree and has thus long been affectionately known as 'The Leaf.' It is a peninsula, the largest in Greece, and in turn forms the southern extremity of the Balkan peninsula as it extends south-west from the Isthmus of Corinth, a narrow neck of land some three miles wide. As far back as Agamemnon and the Trojan War there were suggestions that a canal should be cut across the Isthmus, joining the Gulf of Corinth and Saronic Gulf and shortening the sea passage from east to west. The canal was finally cut in 1893. The civil service never really changes, the actors change but the play remains the same, and the cry of being short of money is hardly a new device of civil servants or governments, from Agamemnon to today.

The Peloponnese is mountainous in the north, levelling out to alluvial plains at the inlets around the coast as it falls away from the mainland. This country attracted people of differing origins, though some of the tribes were related to each other. Even so their customs and cultures were extremely varied and their intermingling produced a new civilization. The peninsula is divided into seven prefectures or nomes (= a province or political district, especially in (modern) Greece and Egypt, from Gr. *nomos*= a district, from *nemo*= to assign by lot) and these preserve roughly the same boundaries and names as the ancient territories of the Peloponnese. The seven nomes are the Argolid (= eastern), Corinthia (= north-east), Archaea (= north), Elis (= north-west), Messenia (= south-west), Laconia (= south-east) and Arcadia (= central). Part of Corinthia extends into Central Greece across the Isthmus, which is regarded today as the boundary between the Peloponnese and northern Greece. Far to the north of the Isthmus lies Mount Olympus, the home of the high gods of Greece. This important site is in the nome of Pieria, the capital of which Katerini, is located near the coast, between Mount Olympus and the Gulf of Thermaikos.

Let us now move back to that all-important nome, Arcadia, which occupies the central area of the Peloponnese, a very mountainous region.

Arcadia's boundaries still abut those of the other provinces, as of old, but today it extends eastwards to the coast of the Gulf of Argolis. I bought my statue of Pan in Nauplion, in what are now the Arcadian foothills, though the sellers were sure it was either Priapus or a Satyr - not Pan! I was surprised and aggrieved at the neglect Pan is still suffering in the land of his birth, compared to the other deities. I was amazed to find that some shops did not even know of his existence. Yet for some time Nauplion was the capital of Greece, until its place was taken by Athens in 1834.

In antiquity Arcadia possessed no littoral: Kynouria, now in Arcadia, was then part of the Argolid, although the Spartans said it was theirs and fought over it. The modern capital of Arcadia is Tripolis, which was completely rebuilt after its destruction by the army of Ibrahim Pasha in 1827. The first reference to the town occurs in 1467 when it was called Drobliza, but the Arcadians are said to be the oldest inhabitants of the Peloponnese.

Now we must leave this theme before it becomes a history lesson of the Peloponnese in particular and Greece in general. If that is required, the reader is well served elsewhere on the subject.

THE GOD PAN ...

'et ego in Arcadia vixi'

'Beloved PAN, and all the gods who haunt this place, give me beauty in the inward soul; and may the outward and inward man be one.' *Phaedrus*. **Plato**.

'Muse, tell me about Pan, the dear son of Hermes, with his goat's feet and horns - a lover of merry noise.' from: *Homeric Hymn to Pan*.

Pan is the pasturer, having the same root as the Latin pastor, literally 'the feeder'; and panis, for he is a herdsman, especially a shepherd. *Panis*= coarse bread, a loaf. From the root *pa*= *pabulum*, fodder, food of animals, especially those that graze; and *pabulor*= to feed, graze or forage. In many religious philosophies, diverse All-father Gods have bread as one of their symbols and bread was often combined with wine. The bread represented the body of the god with the wine exemplifying the blood. These two symbols also represented life and wisdom. When Pan and the nymphs were worshipped together, wine was never offered to the nymphs, only to Pan. Athenian custom prohibited offering wine to the nymphs so if any wine was left with the sacrifice, it was for Pan.

Pan in Greek means *all*, god-in-Nature, everything you see. He is shown as an Arcadian god of the hills and woods. The protecting deity of the flocks both domestic and wild, god of herdsmen and hunters, the *President of the Mountains*, he himself is a hunter. He is *Hylaeos* or a forest god. In literature he became the patron of pastoral poets.

'Pan himself,
The simple shepherd's awe-inspiring god!'
The Excursion. Wordsworth.

The origins of Pan are given to many progenitors. The usual myth tells us he was born on Mount Lycaeum in Arcadia. Lycaeum is the epithet of certain deities worshipped on Mount Lycaeum and Zeus had a sanctuary there, in which the festival of the Lycaea was celebrated. None were allowed to enter the temple and if anyone forced an entrance he was believed to stay within one year and he lost his shadow in consequence. According to others those who entered it were stoned to death by the Arcadians or they were called 'stags' and obliged to take flight to save their lives. Pan was called *Lycaean* because he was born and had a sanctuary on Mount Lycaeum, Lycaeus is also an epithet of Apollo.

As an oracular god one of Pan's main sanctuaries was built here, from which he gave his prognostications. As with many gods of the past, his parentage is a mystery, though Pan's origins are deeper and more mysterious than most. According to **Homer** Pan is the son of Hermes, who appeared in the guise of a ram to his mother, who was a daughter of Dryops (= *woody*). Hermes abandoned Olympus and took service as a shepherd in Arcadia, where he succeeded in gaining the heart of the 'well tressed' nymph. Dryops was the son of the river god Spercheius. This is the most frequently quoted birth and parentage. However, **Graves** and others tell us 'Pan was the foster-brother of Zeus and therefore was far older than Hermes,' more of which later. See also the section referring to the Orphic mysteries.

Perhaps the most famous sandals are those of Hermes or Mercury. In art and myth the sandals of Hermes are winged. Sandals are consecrated to Aphrodite and Hermes. 'In art and myth the sandals of Hermes are winged and "carry him over the sea and the boundless earth, with the blasts of the winds".' Homer, Il. xxiv. The next sentence tells us 'Perseus and Pan had winged sandals.' No reference is supplied for the Perseus and Pan entry, so this is given without comment. We meet the symbolism of winged sandals frequently, often as the seven-leagued boots in fairy tales that do much the same for the wearer.

Let us stay a little longer with Hermes and Arcadia. The seven Pleiades, the daughters of Atlas and the Oceanid nymph Pleione, were born on Mount Cyllene in Arcadia. The eldest and most beautiful of these was Maia who became the mother of Hermes by Zeus, and Hermes was the father of Pan. This would make her Pan's grandmother and the remainder of the Pleiades his aunts. There are two main stories of the fate of these seven sisters called the Pleiades. In the first they killed themselves, either because of the fate of their father Atlas at the hands of Zeus in the latters battle with the Titans, or the death of their sisters, the Hyades. Atlas is called 'the bearer' or 'endurer' though **Homer** calls him 'the thinker of mischief' who knows the depths of the whole sea, and has under his care the pillars which, hold heaven and earth asunder. In **Hesiod** he stands at the western end of the earth, near where the Hesperides dwell, holding the broad heaven on his head and unweared hands, not the earth as often shown.

The Hyades - *'the raining ones'* - whose number varies from two to seven. They were nymphs, daughters of Atlas and Aethra, and sisters of the Pleiades. It was the Hyades who supplied nourishment by means of moisture. The were worshipped in Dodona as the nurses of Zeus or of the infant Dionysus, one story tells us that as a reward for this they were placed in the stars. The constellation of the Hyades, when arising simultaneously with the sun, announced rainy and stormy weather. Their grief at the death of their brother Hyas, who had been killed in Libya by a wild beast, was so great that they pined away and died or, Jupiter was so moved by their grief he changed them into stars. The Pleiades were afterwards placed as stars at the back of Taurus where they form a cluster resembling a bunch of grapes. This is why they are sometimes called **botrus**= 'a bunch of grapes.'

In the second story they are the virgin companions of Artemis. They were pursued for five years by the hunter Orion. Finally Zeus heeded their cries of distress and he turned them into doves, (*peleia*= 'ring-dove') placing both them and their pursuer in the stars. Some ancient coins had doves stamped on them, with the body of the doves often shown on the coins as a bunch of grapes. In the night sky only six of the seven stars are visible. Some call the seventh missing star Sterope and say she became invisible or hid with shame because she had intercourse with a mortal man. Others call the missing star Electra and make her disappear from the choir of her sisters because her grief at the destruction of the house of Dardanus overwhelmed her. Dardanus was her son with Zeus, the mythical ancestor of the Trojans.

Other versions made them the seven doves that carried ambrosia to the infant Zeus. In Arcadia there is a fabled place where it is said Rhea gave birth to Zeus. Traditions, according to **Pausanias**, tell us of a country called Cretea in Arcadia where Zeus was educated. According to some accounts it was on Mount Parrhasia in Arcadia where Zeus was born, but there are other sites. In the time of **Pausanias** the grotto of Rhea was still there, sheltered with dense bushes. No beast or woman would approach it, save those women who enacted the sacred rituals. Only the women sacred to the mother of the god were permitted to enter the grotto. The Apidanians call it the primeval childbed of Rhea. This Zeus is sometimes called the Arcadian Zeus - *Zeus Lycaeus*.

When you study the different local traditions of Zeus, it is not unreasonable to assume there are more than one. There were at least three divinities who, in their respective countries were supreme. In time these became united in the minds of the people into one great national hero. There is the above, the Arcadian Zeus. The Dodonaean Zeus possessed the most ancient tree oracle at Dodona. Then there was the Cretan Zeus: it was this Zeus that Rhea hid from Cronos and entrusted his safety to the Curetes, the nymphs and his nurse Amalthea. Crete was called the island or nurse of Zeus and possessed an ancient worship. The National Hellenic Olympian Zeus had his temple at Olympia in Elis on the Peloponnese. Zeus the father, the king of the gods, was worshipped throughout Greece and her colonies as the supreme deity.

The Curetes are found in Cretan mythology, and were demigods armed with weapons of bronze, to whom the new-born child Zeus was committed by his mother Rhea for protection against the wiles of Cronos. The Curetes drowned the cries of the child by striking their spears against their shields. They gave their name to the priests of the Cretan goddess Rhea and of the Idaean Zeus, who performed noisy war dances at the festivals of those deities.

In Italy the Pleiades rise in the heavens at the beginning of May and set at the beginning of November, thus the constellation was called *Vergiliae*, possibly from *virga*= 'a sprout, twig, as rising in Spring.' The Bible has the lines 'Cans't thou bind the sweet influences of the Pleiades, or loose the bands of Orion.' This quotation is found in Job.38:31 in the King James edition. The Breeches Bible (1579) has a marginal note for the Pleiades explaining, 'which starres arise when the sunne is in Taurus that is the spring time and bring flowers.' The Hebrew word so rendered is kimah, 'a heap' or 'cluster' and generally thought correctly translated; in Amos.5:8, it is rendered as 'seven stars,' with the same meaning. The Sicilians call them the Seven Dovelets. It is said the Rabbis named them

Sukkoth Rnoth, lit. 'The Booth or Tents of the Daughters or Maidens.'

The quest for this information concerning Pan's family connections with Hermes and Arcadia started from one line in a book that simply said the Spanish call the Pleiades the *Seven Little Nanny Goats*. An explanation was sought for the term and to see if 'goats' had any connection with Pan, and the reader has what we found. On his aerial trip on the wooden horse called *Clavileno Aligero*, 'wooden peg,' because of the wooden pin it had in its forehead, Don Quixote and Sancho Panza visited *Las Siete Cabrillas* - the 'Seven Little Goats.' As you can see, one thread is often enough to lead you to so many different, but interesting places; I fear I cannot let them lie and pass on the other side of the street, I never could, I doubt if I ever will.

Eratosthenes tells us Pan is the son of the goat Aix and foster-brother of Zeus, whom Pan helped in his conflict against the Titans. This is found in **Eratosthenes'** *Catasterisms*, in which he is referring to an older author called **Epimenides**. The passage explains the mythical origin of the constellation of Capricorn. **Epimenides**, an epic poet of Crete and one of the seven wise men of Greece, also tells us Pan was with Zeus on Ida when he made war against the Titans.

Now let us turn to the writings of **Nonnus**, a great poet who was a native of Panopolis in Egypt. He is the author of an enormous epic poem that has come down to us as the *Dionysiaca*, consisting of forty-eight books. As the subject of the poem is a pagan divinity, many have assumed it was written before his conversion to Christianity. After his conversion this naturally made the Christians put it abroad that it was written to ridicule the theology of Paganism. It is usually thought these arguments do not hold water for it does not explain why a Christian should not have amused himself by writing on Pagan subjects. Most do not seem to hold the work in high esteem from a literary point of view. We find the words 'bombastic, unconnected and inflated' used in criticism, although the writer is said to display 'considerable learning and fluency of narration.'

Coming back to Pan helping Zeus in his battle with the Titans: in **Nonnus**, Zeus tells Athena to go to the aid of the army of Dionysus/ Bacchus. Zeus speaks respectfully of Pan and the debt he obviously feels he owes him and this shows that Pan is in close contact with Zeus:

'The god of countrymen, himself the lord of the shepherd's pipes, Pan needs your aegis cape. He who once helped me in the defence of my inviolable sceptre and fought against the Titans, he once was mountain-ranging shepherd of the goat Amalthea my nurse, who gave me milk. Save him, for he in the aftertime shall help the Athenian battle, he shall slay the Medes and save shaken Marathon.' *Dionysiaca*. Book 27.

Pan discovered the sea water conch that he used in the manner of a trumpet to make the noise that panicked the Titans and put them to flight. When Zeus gained power, he placed *Aegipan* among the stars, with the goat his mother. *Aegipan* is often given as another name for Pan because he had goat's feet. The word is sometimes applied to Faunus, Silvanus and the sign of the zodiac, Capricorn. It is often given to those rural deities whose shape took on that of the goat, or had goat's feet.

Some legends of Pan are connected with Crete, where Pan is treated as the son of the monstrous Aix - the She-Goat. Aix is said to be the solar goat whose visage was too bright to look upon. She so terrified the Titans that they kept her hidden in a cave. Aix is equated with Amalthea, the nurse of Zeus. The Greeks have two words for goat, *tragos* and *aix*. The word aix is common in place names. 'Catasterism' is from the Greek, *katasterismos* from *kata*= 'down,' *asterismos*= 'a collection of stars, a constellation'; *aster*= 'a star.' *Capricornus*, a sign of the zodiac that is as a goat, was supposed by the ancients to be the goat Amalthea that fed Zeus with her milk. Some maintain it is Pan, who changed himself into a goat when frightened at the approach of Typhon. It is from this incident that Pan is called *Pan Agoceros*, for Zeus made him a constellation. When the sun enters this sign, it is the winter solstice or the longest night of the year. Of course this is the sign of Capricorn in the West, usually called 'the Goat' but, more correctly 'the Sea-Goat or Goat-fish' because it is a goat to the waist down and then a fish's tail.

This is because Pan slipped on a river bank and his legs went into the water which transformed the lower part, appropriately, into a fish's tail with scales. It also illustrates the height and depth to which this sign can attain. The natives under the sway of this constellation can rise to the highest peak of ambition, represented by a solitary goat perched on a mountain peak. I think it was a Capricorn who coined the phrase, 'it's lonely at the top.' Yet they also sink to the lowest place that can be reached on earth, the fish going down in the deepest and murkiest waters on the planet where it cannot be seen - chronic depression. Capricorn contains both extremes and any swing from one to the other is often violent and happens without warning.

Among other sources, **Epimenides** gives Pan's parents as Zeus and the Arcadian nymph Kallisto. **Aristippus** made Pan the offspring of Zeus and Ybis or Oneis. **Theocritus** says Pan 'was a child of Heaven and Earth.' Again Zeus comes into the equation with the nymph Thymbris or Hybris, the instructor of Apollo in divination. Some say his mother was Penelope while Ulysses was away at the Trojan war and he was the offspring of all her suitors who came to the palace. From this he received the name 'Pan' that, as written earlier, signifies 'all, everything' or, if this story has any credence - everyone. The arrival of Pan at Olympus delighted and charmed 'all' the gods. Pan was thought in the end to be the god of the cosmic whole or *all*.

The Greek and Egyptian systems of religion had begun to intermingle and combine, long before Pan was honoured at Athens, after the Battle of Marathon in 490 B.C. The goat-formed god of Mendes in Egypt was regarded as identical with the horned and goat-footed deity of the Arcadian herdsmen. Pan was elevated with unqualified dignity by the priests and philosophers, becoming a symbol of the universe, for his name signified *all*. As he dwelt in the woods he had the epithet Lord of the Hyle - *hyle*= 'wood, a wood, a forest or woodland.'

Some believe the idea of totality of Pan was grafted on to the traditional image of Pan under Egyptian influence. The Goat-God who originated in Egypt for Chnoum-Mendes was identified with Pan at a very early date.

Finally some writers maintain he is a very ancient god, this son of Cronos and Rhea. **Wm. Smith** writes: 'from his being a grandson, or great grandson, of Cronos he is called *Pan Kronios*= Cronos or Saturn (**Euripides**, *Rhes*. 36). I have written 'finally' but I think that is foolish, for there is very little that is final about Pan. With all these possible progenitors how is the writer best to serve the reader? Where does the writer stand regarding the matter, may be a better way of putting it. These questions are easily resolved for me personally. Regarding the first, the writer will give whatever information he has found concerning the various legends and myths and the parents from the myth in question. Regarding the latter, I have long thought that Pan is far older than he is given credit for and not fully understood even today. Personally I think Pan is the oldest god, or one of them, but this statement is based partly on knowledge and partly on instinct, guided by the heart.

We are seeking to know how the people of the past regarded Pan. We do this to try to gain a better understanding of Pan from our present, distant position. I regard Pan as a very old god, as **Stephen McKenna's** title of his novel *The Oldest God*. Therefore, I incline at least to the parentage of Cronos and Rhea. I sometimes think Pan may even have been with the Egyptian's earlier, in one form or another, perhaps even before he was with Greece. However, I can understand how the Greeks claimed Pan as their own and made him so special. This is feeling *not fact*, but sometimes feelings are all you have to work with.

Material about Pan is scattered abroad and it takes much work to gather the information about him. It is there, but it is so fragmented that even this work belies the amount of time it has taken to bring what is presented here together. It is a work of love, though I hope it is a work of love that informs. The time and labour involved in collecting the information and adding the personal views counts for naught, it is regarded as being a small service, given willingly, to the god Pan.

Whoever his parents were in the Greek legends, his mother brought forth a son who at his birth was as unusual as he was wondrous to see. He was perfectly formed and covered with long, unkempt hair, horns on his head and the feet of a goat, 'a noisy, merry-laughing child.' His mother gave birth to a child of this description in the Hermes myth and this form is the one by which he is known and loved. Evidence suggests this may not be his original form. He is sometimes to be found in human form, apart from the goat's horns and little tail, though the half goat, half-human form is virtually a trade mark now. I think if Pan appeared in any other form he would have to prove who he was. It is a tragedy this form has been so perverted by the Church for its own ends, to a point of destroying its use by the original owner. Recent events have done the same for that excellent solar symbol, the swastika, and **Wagner's** beautiful music in some quarters: not because they are evil of themselves, but because they were *adopted by evil.*

The people responsible were very thorough in their work, which makes invoking or loving Pan tantamount to raising their monstrous invention - the Devil. It was quite impossible to destroy all the pagan customs, and the fact very few of them could be destroyed, as the church quickly found out. So 'the Maid' tried to turn them to her own account by wrapping them in different packaging and presenting them as her own. She obviously did not bargain for the Pandora equation in people's psyche. There are those who are not satisfied or do not accept the appearances of things: the ones who have an all-consuming curiosity and have to lift a corner to see what lies beneath the presentation, no matter what they let loose or lose in the process. These people have been thorns in her side and a disquiet to her rest for centuries - the *hairesiachos.* The *heresiarch* or *heretic* is ever with us, the one who always has to know, interfering with the comfortable *status quo,* forever asking awkward questions.

When Pan's mother or the nymph Sinoe who, according to Wm. Smith, 'was an Arcadian nymph who brought up the god Pan, who derived from her the epithet Pan Sinoeis (Pausanius viii.30:2),' saw the babe the sight of him was too much for them. They fled leaving the babe with none to nurse him. 'Luck-bringing Hermes picked him up with boundless joy in his heart, very glad in his heart was the god.' Hermes wrapped the child in the warm skins of mountain hares and carried him to Olympus and set the babe before Zeus. The mountain hare is a symbol of Pan on some ancient coins.

The deathless gods were absolutely delighted with the sight and sound of him, especially Bacchus who gave him the name Pan. The gods were gratified with him for Pan reflected them all. Pan is regarded as a gift to the Divine and Hermes is the mercurial in Pan's makeup. Bacchus is said to have appeared as a goat. The choral odes sung in his honour were called *tragodiai* - goat songs. Often a goat was the symbolic prize offered at these occasions.

It should be observed that it was the human stock in the story who rejected him and fled. They were the ones who deserted him. His first connection with the human race was total rejection. When he needed them most, they were not there. Pan may love us but I am not so sure he always trusts us. The gods accepted and loved Pan with great joy and he was ever welcome at Olympus. The ancients represented him and an abundance of shaggy hair. The Gnostics saw represented in the shaggy hair of Pan a mystic allusion to solar rays.

PAN

The fane that bears Dictynna's name,
So thick with reek of altar flame,
Enshrines me, hoofed and horned Pan,
Alike the foe and friend of man.
A goat skin doublet, with shaggy hair,
Protects me from the nipping air;
I wield a cudgel carved of oak,
Dented deep with many a stroke;
I, when the wintry storm winds rave,
Deep lurking in the dusky cave,
With restless, watchful eyes survey
The sombre wood and hillside grey.
Unknown Ancient Author.

Servius tells us, 'Pan is a rustic god formed in similitude of nature and so he is called Pan, i.e. All: for he has horns like the rays of the sun and the horns of the moon: his face is ruddy, in imitation of the aether: he has a spotted fawn-skin on his breast, in likeness of the stars: his lower parts are shaggy, on account of the trees, shrubs, and wild beasts: he has goat's feet, to denote the stability of the earth: he has a pipe of seven reeds, on account of the harmony of the heavens, in which there are seven sounds: he has a crook, that is a curved staff, on account of the year, which runs back on itself, because he is god of all nature. It is fabled by the poets that he struggled with Love (= *Eros*) and was conquered by him because, as we read, love conquers all - *omnia vincit amor.*' Pan struggled with Eros all his life.

Many consider his goat's feet were like trees, firmly planted on the earth itself, for the earth is his place and he is 'planted' here. His hairy legs and feet represented the inferior parts of the earth, those of the woods and plants. Some write the star on his breast suggests the firmament. Others say on his back he often wore a spotted lynx pelt that was symbolic of the stars in the firmament, as above. God or St. Peter, in some early old English representations, is shown conspicuously spotted just as Pan was shown with a lynx or spotted cloak about himself. Pan is often found in the background of things, but sometimes he has to be looked for. Pan is like the countryside, ever around us: just like his music is, always there for those with ears to hear. He is the constant mediator between the gods and men. In this he is like one of his suggested sires, Aethyr, which naturally envelops all things, for Pan is the grace, blessing and joy of all things natural. 'Pan represents the positive magnetism of the earth uprushing in its return to the All-Father...bringing down the godhead into manhood in the hope of taking manhood up into the godhead.' **Dion Fortune**.

The Homeric Hymns have already been cited above, but he tells us Pan is the Lord of the Hills and Dales. Sometimes he ranges along the tops of the mountains, at times he pursues the game in the valleys. He roams through the woods, floats along the streams or drives his sheep into a cave and there he plays on his reeds. His music 'is not excelled by that of the bird, who among the leaves of flower-full spring laments, pouring forth her moan, a sweet-sounding lay.'

Pan delighted in sweet song and would dance with the nymphs, his feet moving rapidly as he joined in their dance.

FOREST MUSIC

Silent stand the forest and the wooded height,
Silent are the streamlets dripping down the rock,
Hushed the busy murmur of the noonday bright,
Hushed the mingled bleating of the wandering flock.

> Pan himself makes music on the pipe he loves,
> See his soft lips gliding o'er the close-ranked reeds!
> Nymphs that range the mountains,
> Nymphs that haunt the groves,
> Weave the dance around him in the grassy meads.
> **Plato** (*doubtful*): 4th century B.C.

In later times Pan's care was extended far beyond the realms of the herds, animals and hunting. He became the guardian of the bees and the giver of success in fishing and fowling.

Pan was called 'goat-footed,' 'noise loving,' 'dance loving,' as well as 'Bright-locked,' 'cave-dwelling' and 'sea-roaming.' Though a matter of controversy, Pan is often connected with *Apollo Nomios*, as his name is said to be a contraction of 'Paean or Paon' - the Pasturer - the former is also an epithet of Apollo. Some commentators think Pan is its Arcadian form. A paean is a religious or festive hymn, a hymn of triumph, originally in honour of Apollo, but also of other deities.

To some this connection with solar fire makes Pan a solar deity, the nether Apollo. It may be coincidence that when Apollo is at his height at noon Pan sleeps and woe betide those who disturb him. A torch race was instituted to honour him at Athens after Marathon which was usually given to those gods connected with the sacred fire. Opinions regarding Pan being a solar deity have been put forward defending his right to the sacred fire. Nothing conclusive has come from them; people appear divided on this point and there is only disagreement (see the section on the Orphic mysteries).

Hermes has perhaps, in Pan, his dark, chthonic side when the mind has its deep dark thoughts - the shadow of the mind. It could be Pan who brings to the mind (= Hermes) its sudden unpredictability (= *panic*) at times, a disturbing presence - like father, like son. However, although Pan may be thought by some as negative, this must not be taken as necessarily detrimental to us. Pan comes to our aid on many levels and he helps those that he loves by creating panic and confusion among their enemies who, like us, often do not see him. I have long thought with the toast 'confusion to our enemies,' many are unwittingly invoking Pan.

When the sun is at its highest - at noon - the shadows seem to disappear, the 'shadows' grow longer as darkness gains strength. Just as our shadow is at its least under a light directly above our heads, it disappears around our feet. The Master of the Animals has, from ancient times been represented as a horned deity. There is little difficulty is associating Pan with these deities, especially with our own Cernunnos.

Hermes, it is thought, would have association with Lugh.

There is another common factor that binds most of these horned deities: their rejection at birth by the human stock, the kingdom into which they are born. A higher kingdom than the human kingdom has no trouble in accepting them - the High Gods. A lower kingdom than the human kingdom not only accepts them but, for the most, accepts them as their ruler in some form - the animal kingdom. In this equation certain factors in the birth of Merlin comply. He was said to have been born of no father. There was the same disquiet at his appearance at birth among the women. His hairy pelt was such as 'they had never seen on another child.' Merlin was thought a wild man of the woods, where he spent a lot of time with the animals and he may have preferred them to Arthur's court. Merlin, no less than Pan, was half man, half beast, a medicine man or shaman today. These deities seem to represent the primordial state of unmanifest creation (= chaos), before Creation (= ordered) as we conceive it had taken place.

As others have commented, there is an element of the Trickster in their make-up and mythos - which is a form of Hermes as his myth shows. Many consider these rural deities to represent the carnal and archaic nature (= goat or animal) and the human and civilized (= upper human half usually) that has to be mastered (= controlled or subdued). There is some merit in this concept of these bi-form gods, but does it apply to Pan?

We know from old writers there was an earlier form of Pan that was not so conveniently divided, across the waist, into animal for the lower half (= the sex drive and the base animal desires), and human for the upper half (= the higher spiritual aspirations free of the lower), which the usual form is. This earlier form was held to be predominantly human in form, with small horns on the head, small pointed ears and a small goat's tail, an attractive concept. The later figure, so despised by the Early Church, was only reviled when the founders of the new religion decided he was the one to destroy. Prior to this Pan was greatly revered, so they must have greatly feared him.

Prior to their efforts even his bi-form appearance bore no stigma or fear, only great love and respect it would seem. So this necessity that is felt to subdue the animal nature to breaking point obviously had no credence until, theoretically, A.D.33 or the time of the Crucifixion. To many it does not have any credence even now.

In the Orphic hymns we find Pan described as 'Zeus, the mover of all things, the Pervader of Sky and Sea.' Pan was not only a god of the hills and a deity of the woods and fields, but also a sea-vagabond, for **Sophocles** has him wandering the seas.

'I shivered with love, in my joy I took wing. Io, Io, Pan, Pan! O Pan, Pan! Who wanders the sea, from snow-covered Kyllene, your rocky peak, appear, O lord of the dances of the gods, so that you may be with me and draw me into the spontaneous dance of Mysia and Knossos.

Pan's connection with the sea, in one instance, is thought to be shown by the fact that the syrinx is replaced by the conch when he terrifies his enemies. The god lends his traits to Capricorn (= *Aigokeros*) the goat with the fish's tail, the sign usually called Capricorn the Goat, more correctly known as the Sea-Goat or Goat-fish. Beside his more obvious epithets, Pan is called god of the rocky coasts and of the sea, the god of fishermen.

Pan is sometimes shown in a deferential position regarding the other gods. There are those who regard him as a minor or inferior divinity. This, in the writer's opinion, is patently foolish. It could be based, in part, on the already mentioned fact that Pan never chose to live on Olympus, nor was he one of the twelve Great Gods. Yet this did not seem to make the Olympian Gods respect him any less, and he was consulted and his services called upon. It is not the Olympian Gods who make him assume this position, but the artists and writers of the day. He chose to stay here with us. The earth was his charge and he did not desert it or us. This is his place and somewhere there is a connection that has not fallen into place. It is suggested here and there, but the threads are too tenuous to support most theories regarding why he stayed here.

Pan, like so many gods, is called one of the *semones,* the Latin name for some supernatural beings. They appear to have been like the Lares, a kind of Genii, demigods or guardian deities of the state who were regarded as inferior because they did not belong to the number of the twelve Great Gods. Included in the semones are Janus, Pan, Priapus, Vertumnus, etc., who received divine honours. The meaning of this word implies that they were inferior or lesser than the superior Gods but superior to men. I do not think it was intended to carry the derogatory inference that inferior has today. This is perhaps put better by a very old Latin dictionary as *Semo,omis*= 'a god of lower rank, such as Priapus, Vertumnus &c. were: also Janus so called.' (1693). **Seyffert** (1891) tells us 'the word has often been connected with *se*= to sow, (cp. *se-men*) and thus mean 'sowers'.' See the final chapter of the work.

This, however, seems to bring Pan closer to mankind. It is often through Pan that a divinity or groups of divinities communicate with us. In this he is as mobile as the herald and messenger Hermes, for Pan is a mediating god. Those hoofed feet are swift in their purpose and the goat is always thought to be sure-footed; for the terrain it inhabits, it has to be.

The celebrated Greek rhetorician **Hermogenes** writes; 'Then surely Pan, who is the declarer of all things, and the perpetual mover of all things is rightly called the goatherd. He being the two-formed son of Hermes, smooth in his upper part, and rough and goat-like in his lower regions. As the son of Hermes he is speech, or the brother of speech, and that brother should be like brother is no marvel.'

In one hymn we find, 'The whole earth and the sea are stirred by your grace; you are the prop of all, O Pan, Ah Pan.' The god Pan, to use the phrase in its origin form, is neither fish, nor flesh nor good red herring; in other words he is often very difficult to place. You think you have mastered the problem only to find that something about him upsets your plan of things and he is elsewhere. Pan always appears peripheral because he represents the difference the ancients felt between the religion of the city and the countryside, the *paganus*= 'of or belonging to a village, country, rustic' or 'a countryman, peasant, villager or rustic.' It is, of course, from this that we get the word *pagan*.

Pagans today are usually thought to be people who, while they accept that god exists, cannot countenance the form in which it is presented by official dogmas. This of course automatically makes them 'pagans' to those of the rejected tenet. I believe it was the Christians who first gave the Pagans their name, which became current around the fourth century. However, it does seem to have remained only in colloquial use, and it does not appear to have entered the Bible. The overall meaning of the word, as used by the Early Christians, is thought to be that pagans were those who 'had not enlisted through baptism as soldiers of Christ against the powers of Satan.'

Despite the disparity that appears on the surface of Paganism at times, there is definitely a common core. It is local and individual practices that seem dissimilar to the casual observer. The prime tenet in the broadest of brushstrokes is to honour the gods and to try to avert misfortune and evil for the individual and their clan. To give thanks to the god(s) for what is thought to be given from them. To offer gifts that solicit the gods 'to give to the givers,' or 'a gift for a gift' as the *Edda* tells us. My teacher always used to say that 'nothing for nothing was the Occult Law.'

There are no heretics in Paganism. Some would say this is because they are all heretics in the first place, which is a very jaundiced and autocratic view. Pagans do not bandy the word heretic about because the word to them does not mean a false doctrine: it is thought of more as another School of Thought. They do not follow orthodoxy but seem to prefer heterodoxy, and not simply to be contentious. It is more an agreement to disagree, the right to disagree and the space to do so. Some may consider this a weakness yet Paganism is still kicking in one form or another, despite hell, high water and an occasional Inquisition. So it must have something to recommend it because I cannot accept that they are all deluded people. There was, after all, dissent and fighting with bloodshed to spare in the now established religions during their early power struggles, before the winners took the reins and drove the cart for everyone else.

Christianity took hold faster in the cities than in the rural areas and those who lived in the latter were living in the paganus and so they were pagans, just as the heathens (= A.Saxon. *haethen*, from *haeth*; Dut. *heiden* from *heide*; Ger, *heiden*, from *heide*; all 'heath,' etc.) were dwellers on or of the heath. Pressure was exerted on them sometimes by the simple expedient of forbidding them to enter the city or sell their produce, unless they became baptised Christians. So I am sure they did! Being a Christian for a day posed no particular dilemma for them. Having sold their produce I am certain they went back to where they came from, to what they were, and carried on as if nothing had happened. They saw no problem in dealing with 'the God of Bargains' to make a living. Their gods understood and accepted this, even if the new one didn't.

It does not seem that Pan took part in a battle or was ever portrayed armed. He was always watching from a distance, remote from the actual fighting, using his excellent eyesight to see where advantage could best be taken. I am sure he took swift forays into the melee and, having gained his purpose, was back watching for the next opportunity to help those with whom he was allied. He is often represented as the *aposkopos*= 'a lookout.'

The locations of his cult, caves and sanctuaries, were far away from roads in places of difficult access. Pan was honoured as much or more by city folk who came to those places, as by the farmers and herdsmen who lived there. Pan's cave on the Acropolis served as a model for the caves dispersed around the countryside outside the city, the latter shrines being set up or created by individuals. Pan's landscape included the uncultivated land where the goatherds moved, this was at a distance from cultivated land, goats and cultivation do not mix very well. Cultivated land was of very little use to the hunters, who kept their distance from the fields. This marginal land between the two, the wild and the uncultivated, was an ambiguous land. When people crossed it and went beyond it they were, in the past, entering unknown territory for which civic life might not have prepared them. 'Out there' was the unexpected, the uncontrolled, the natural and, should they come face to face with it, they would be thrown upon their inner resources which, if meagre, could be dangerous or fatal. Pan had a intense antagonism for the civic, and the goats, which made up the main flocks of Pan were, like him, ambivalent. Goats were animals who were on the borderline between the wild and the domestic, in ancient Greece there were both wild and domesticated flocks.

Now we bring in the meeting of Pan and Pheidippides. Pheidippides was a herald, the bearer of news. Hermes was a herald as was the Roman Mercury, and is a patron of running and runners. When the Persians landed at Marathon, the Athenians sent their herald to ask for help from Sparta. Athens and Sparta were known as the 'Two Eyes of Greece.' This help was urgent and the message Pheidippides, a long distance runner, received from the Lacedaemonians was not the best of news. It was not that the Spartans were unwilling or refusing to help: they were quite willing, but they said that certain religious restrictions prevented them from starting out before the full moon. The time of this answer was the ninth of Boedromion (September-October) and the required full moon would not be until around the sixteenth, some seven days later. This was not good news for the Athenians because the Persians were already encamped near Athens.

It takes little imagination to know how Pheidippides felt on the journey back, especially when he did not have the necessary encouragement to spur him on and keep him going. It was on the third day of his return journey, when he was crossing the eastern part of Arcadia, that he met Pan. *Herodotus* tells us that Pheidippides gave the following report to the Athenians. He said he was on Mount Parthenion above Tegea when Pan presented himself and stopped him by calling his name aloud, so it was obvious Pan knew him. Pan asked him why the Athenians paid no attention to him. He told Pheidippides he had already been helpful in many ways to them and would continue to be so in the future if they would but do him honour. Pheidippides said Pan promised he would come and fight for the Athenians at the battle at Marathon in 490 B.C. In the battle the Athenians found things going well for them and believed what Pan had told their *hermerodromos* (= 'one who runs all day, a courier').

The Athenians believed Pan was the cause of the panic that helped them to rout the Persians by putting them to flight. Again, there is no proof that Pan fought in the battle or took part physically in it. It is generally conceded that Pan prevented the further spilling of Athenian blood by scattering the Persian forces in panic. In a sense Pan was said to have brought the peace of Aphrodite, in whose company he is often found. Not that the Persians would agree, for obviously they wanted to win. It was the Athenians who gained Aphrodite's peace. Panic in an army does not always take place while the army is fighting in the field. With Pan it more often than not took place during the night hours while the army was resting: when among the tired soldiers every sound and fear was magnified, especially when the imagination was allowed to run riot. **Suidas** tells us 'The terrors of Pan - something which occurs in military encampments; horses and men are suddenly thrown into agitation for no apparent reason; so called because these groundless terrors are attributed to Pan.' The god Pan was always considered the initiator of all kinds of dreams and visions, 'the instigator of sudden terror.'

The Athenians showed their gratitude to the god by dedicating a grotto to Pan, on the Acropolis at Athens. The choice of this cave was perfect for placing Pan within the city, something he was not always happy about, it was a place he visited rarely. It was wild and uncultivated, it had the desired sacred spring or water trough, and there were niches for votive offerings at its entrance. A perpetual fire was kept to honour Pan, which is a frequent feature of his worship. It was a perfect cave well suited to the wild God of Nature. Looking out from the cave you would have a grand picture of Athens, ordered, civilized and comfortable. The cave was everything the Greeks respected and feared in their gods, wild, uncultivated and uncertain. Here they could, within the precincts of their beautiful city, make contact with the sometimes wild and instinctive God of Nature. The basis of the belief was surely the recognition that the panic state exists in man, call it, the god taking possession. In the building and siting of temples in Greece, however ordered or rational the society, there is a conflict between the ordered, rational geometry of the site and the building, and the almost universal link to the natural phenomena, the emotive force behind the beliefs they enshrine.

The Cave of Pan is along Peripatos and it looks out over the Panathenaic Way that was built specifically for the Great Panathenaia. This was the greatest and most splendid of all the festivals held in honour of Athene, the patron goddess of the city. The chief object carried in the procession, to the temple of the deity, was the peplus of the goddess. The peplus was a crocus-coloured garment for the goddess, and it was woven by two young maidens, chosen from the distinguished families of Athens, by the king archon. The earlier approaches proved too narrow for the thousands of participants attending the festival; today the Way winds up to the *Propylaia* (= a temple-like porch leading into a temple enclosure), passing by the temple of Athena Nike. The Cave of Pan was once venerated as a shrine of Zeus Olympios before it was given to Pan. You can still make out clearly where the offerings were attached to the walls. Yet again we have this connection of Pan with Zeus, with something belonging to Zeus given over to Pan or shared with him.

The cave is on the north-west slope of the Acropolis, at the edge of an area roughly defined by the *Clepsydra* and the sanctuary of Agraulos, from where she threw herself down to save her country. A story tells us that Agraulos threw herself down from the citadel during a war to save her country. It was accordingly to her precincts the young men of Athens received their armour, shields and spears, and took their oath to defend their country. It is interesting to note that the Cave of Agraulos is a little further to the East, from the Cave of Pan. This cave is connected with the House of Arrephoroi, above, by a secret passage, which was rediscovered in 1937. The clepsydra was the most important source of water in the stronghold and was in use in the Neolithic period. Twenty-two small wells connect to a water source. In 500 B.C. a fountain house was built and the water led into a basin. A clepsydra was also a water clock or an earthen vessel filled with a certain measure of water. The best kind of water-clock was attributed to Plato. Such water clocks were used in the Athenian law courts to mark the time allotted to the speakers.

The siting of this cave for Pan is worth noting. It is not believed to have been an arbitrary choice, but was carefully thought out. When the Athenians chose a sacred site for Pan within their city, they did not, it seems, choose at random. They looked for a cave that would best serve this specific purpose and deity, I cannot believe that this cave was an arbitrary choice. Pan is lodged neither in the city proper nor within the sacred enclosure of the Acropolis, but on the wild, uncultivated side of a sacred hill. Nothing could be more apt for this God of Nature and all that is Natural.

Even in the heart of the city and on its most sacred centre, a wild locale was found for Pan. It is a solitary place: not an easy place to arrive at, compared to the paved and ornate splendour that had been built above. It is hidden and out of sight. At his birth Pan was deserted by the human stock, abandoned to the wild just as this cave was. To the Athenians this was the consummate place to do honour to this wild god of Nature. It also shows how well the Athenians understood this god. Some gods would have been enraged not to have had a prominent temple built to them on high. No doubt they would have exacted some form of revenge on those they thought had been disrespectful to their dignity and rank. I do not think Pan felt his dignity and rank had been offended, but rather well served; it was probably the only place where he could feel really comfortable in the city.

Pan, like his Italian counterpart Faunus, possessed mantic powers and was a god of healing. According to ancient tradition and legend Pan, like Asclepius, healed the sick through dreams, though also in the waking state. *Ephialtes*= 'The disease commonly called the Night-mare; or the Hag, which they think rides upon the party so troubled.' (1693). It must be remembered that Pan, like Faunus, Silvanus and Inuus, could bring nightmares and illness as well as pleasant dreams and those that cure. However, it must never be forgotten that what the gods give - they can remove.

To the Greeks Ephialtes was the name given to a spectre who accounted for a nightmare that was thought to have resulted from indigestion. Sometimes it was not distinguished from *Epiales*= 'the cold shivering fit that preceded an attack of fever.' Ephialtes was sometimes figured as a long eared owl. Owls were regarded as evil omens and an embodiment of the spirits of the dead which appear by night to suck the blood of the living. This superstition still survives in some areas of Greece today. At one time, in Rome, an owl seen abroad during daylight hours was caught if possible, burned and its ashes publicly scattered in the Tiber. An old Scottish superstition says 'to see an owl in the sunlight is bad fortune for the beholder.' **Artemidorus** commenting on the Pan connection with Ephialtes tells us, 'Ephialtes has been frequently taken for Pan, yet shows some differences; oppressive and heavy, he is the same in nightmare and terrors. However, whatever he answers is truth. He grants favours to those with whom he closely associates, and he prophesies when he does not act as nightmare. When he wishes them well he cures them, but he never approaches the dying.' Pan-Ephialtes, we should mention the late assimilation of Pan with the demon Ephialtes - 'who settles on people's chest and squeezes them when they are between sleeping and waking.' *Pan-Ephialtes* appears on the imperial coinage of Bithynia (= Nicea) under the name *Epopheles* (= useful, beneficial).

It has long been thought that dreams and visions can intermingle. However, nightmares can be so vivid that at times they are often confused for reality, even by those who are highly experienced in such matters. How much more so for those who experienced 'incubation' dreams in the holy sanctuary of the god, for within those precincts the god was thought to live. After all, the purpose for undertaking this form of treatment is the hope that the god will personally intercede and cure the affliction, or give the method of curing. It is little wonder such dreams can at times reach a fever pitch where the dreamers assume they are awake and have direct contact with the god themselves. At the seats of worship of Asclepius, a cure was often effected by the dreams of the patients who were required to sleep in the sacred building, in which there stood, as may be expected, a statue of Sleep or Dreaming.

The healing sanctuary of *Pan Luterios* - 'Pan the Deliverer' - was at Troezen, and from time immemorial had bestowed prophetic dreams and indicated cures for pestilence. *Luterios*= 'loosing, releasing, delivering or setting free from.' Troezen was a son of Pelops and the founder of the town of Troezen (or Troezene), in Argolis. The sanctuary was founded and built in grateful thanks to Pan, for the town's deliverance from an epidemic. The town officials had the remedies to counteract the epidemic given to them in dreams by Pan.

Incubation, a translation of the Greek *egkoimesis* denotes the practice of sleeping, or at least passing the night, in a shrine or other sacred place. The Latin is *incubo*= 'to lie down or pass the night in a temple for the cure of disease or communications from the deity.' The object was to attempt to receive divine revelation or divine aid. In a more specific sense, most commonly denoted by the word because of the Greek use of the rite, the aid in question is currently held to be the cure of disease. Naturally, the subject of incubation is connected with those of communion with the Deity, disease, dreams, omens, etc.

In a state of sleep, when the soul is released from the trammels of the body, it is particularly subjected to Divine visitations and may receive revelations from Divine beings. The Bible is awash with examples but perhaps the theory of incubation could not be better expressed than by the words found in Job:33.15-18.

> In a dream, in a vision of the night,
> When deep sleep falleth upon men,
> In slumberings upon the bed;
> Then he (god) openeth the ears of men,
> And sealeth their instruction,
> That he may withdraw man for his purpose,
> And hide, pride from man,
> He keepeth back his soul from the pit,
> And his life from perishing by the sword.

See also Genesis:28.12; 37.5; 47.36; 1 Kings:3.5-15., et al. Incubation was practised at sacred stones, as with the pre-Islamic priests who slept near the oracular stone of al-Jalsad and under sacred trees. Alexander the Great slumbered under the Plane tree at Smyrna, a celebrated seaport in Asia Minor, whose inhabitants 'believe that Homer was born among them.' Incubation was a common practice in ancient Egypt. It is thought the practice still exists in some Greek churches and in other countries. It also has connection with some of the saints in the Middle Ages.

The actual form and mode the Ritual of Incubation took are sketchy.

Medical men attached themselves to the shrines of the healing gods, co-operating with the god, though not superseding, the revelations given by the god in visions. There were kindred practices used in Ireland in Druid times in the *tarbfess*. When the kings of Ireland could not find a king for Ulster because they were united against that nation, they resorted to the ritual of the tarbfess. 'Tis thus this tarbfess was done. A white bull was slain and a man ate to saity of its flesh and its broth. A slumber fell on him from this saity, and the *os firindi* (= a certain charm) was sung over him by four druids. The sort of man who should be made king there was seen by him in vision, from his form and from his description and the sort of work he did. The man awoke from his sleep and his dream was told to the kings.' This is similar to the Irish *imbas forosnai* in which incantations were pronounced over the palms by him who sought the revelation. After which he placed his palms to his cheeks and fell asleep, during which he was guarded against all interruptions. The future was revealed as above.

The general method of the Greek incubation might have been as follows. On arrival at the shrine the patient was probably instructed by the priest or priests. The rites and sacrifices performed were thought to bring the patient to a thoroughly responsive frame of mind. A successful incubation was when, while the patient slept within the shrine of the god, they had been visited by the deity with an actual cure or counsel. Faunus as a sender of prophetic dreams has been written about **Virgil** (*Aen.* VII), likewise **Ovid** (*Fast.* IV). Regarding Faunus, first a sheep was sacrificed and the pilgrim was to lie upon the skin to sleep. The was a 'coronation of beech leaves,' abstinence and chastity was observed, and the removal of finger rings was necessary. In many early races a sparse diet or fasting was considered the chief means for securing prophetic dreams and vision.

The one healed was required to make payment of a fee, non-payment being punished by recurrence of the disease. Votive offerings were sometimes given, in some cases they were demanded by the god. It is thought the votive offerings and fees were instigated when the shrines became comparatively elaborate and costly to upkeep. Records show a boy offering the god ten dice for the cure and that he was cured without charge, as it often was for the poor.

It need not be thought that Ritual of Incubation is now a matter of history, to be read only in pages such as these. An altar erected to Pan, even a temporary one that is dismantled if circumstances will not allow a permanent structure, would be a worthwhile effort and worth anyone's time. Practised in the true spirit of the religious Ceremony of Incubation, for healing, attempting to contact the Great God of Nature and gaining counsel can be still be managed.

A goatskin placed before the altar should prove no problem. This form of rug can be bought in most good carpet stores, I have one and they are not that expensive. It is used for lying on and my own thoughts are, let as much of your skin make contact with the goatskin. Alternatively you can sit and meditate on it, whatever method you chose to follow I regard as a move in the right direction. Excessive noise and impertinent insistence should not be directed to Pan around 12 noon (1 p.m. when British Summer Time operates in this country), this time is best avoided for about one hour. This does not rule out the midday sleep when, *if he desires it*, he will come to you. Always used the correct *solar time* when attempting contacts of this nature, not *clock time* which might be in advance of the sun for daylight saving. Pan sleeps at 12 noon and your attentions might not be welcome, if they are not he can let you know this in no uncertain manner. Be respectful at all times by simply remembering who you are addressing and dealing with. At other times use the hours of Saturn on Saturday, or the hours of Saturn in the remainder. Alternative hours that can be used for Pan, for obvious reasons, are those of Hermes/Mercury on Wednesday or the hours of Hermes/Mercury in the other days. These are guidelines to help you to get started. Consult the **Table of Planetary Hours** at the end of the work and the explanation of its use, if you want to experiment with this system. It is really quite simple but sometimes appears more complicated than it is.

If you want to use an incense this is fine, but use a woody type of incense, they are best, pine, yew or cypress are excellent. I give below a formula for making an *Incense of Pan*, anything you make for yourself is best. It is best because *you know what has gone into it,* with bought incense you only know the main ingredient(s) on the label, god knows at times what else has been put in.

The Incense of Pan is taken from an earlier work. '*Incense, Its Ritual, Significance, Use And Preparation,*' a new edition of this earlier work is in course of preparation, for publication in the near future. Proportions were not given for all recipes as experimentation was encouraged, to formulate the incense to personal taste. The *Incense of the Gnomes* (= earth), the *Incense of the Undines* (= water), the *Incense of the Sylphs* (= air) and the *Incense of the Salamanders* (= fire) are included in the work, but I quote only the incense referring to Pan.

INCENSE OF PAN

'Pan, quite rightly, has many incenses created in his name. His incense is often called 'of lust and seduction.' It has to be 'very earthy, seductive and primitive,' what the old fire and brimstone evangelist would call, 'of the flesh.' I for one never heard, nor believed the cry 'Pan is dead!'

'The ingredients given below will produce an excellent incense for Pan. The ingredients in parenthesis may be added or used as an alternative, this will allow more choice when making up a compound to suit you own personal taste.

Ingredients

Patchouli Essence/Leaves
(Scammony)
Benzoin (Storax)
Pine - Pine is essential
Vervain (Musk)
Olive Oil (Yew)
Civet (Myrrh)
Wormwood (Mandrake pref. male)
Church incense as a base (= Frankincense).

'You can, if you wish, add a touch of oil of pine or oil of cloves, even both. I add a little heavy red wine to this, either in the mixing or to the incense before using. To the foregoing I would now add: 'Not too much wine or it will not burn, you want smoke not steam. Remember wine was offered to Pan but not to the nymphs, Athenian custom prohibited the offering of wine to the nymphs. If you are going to use this incense for Pan and the nymphs, then omit the wine; if its use is *for Pan alone*, then it is optional.' In the original book it was written: 'the best day for mixing this incense is a Thursday, in the hours of Jupiter, under a waxing Moon. Do not use the Full Moon.' Thirteen years later, I would change these times as follows. 'Mix this incense on a Saturday in the hours of Saturn, at the time of the New Moon or while the Moon is waxing. Do not use the Full Moon. If you seek an alternative time, then use a Wednesday in the hours of Hermes/Mercury,' but this is an alternative time; Saturday and Saturn is best for this. In the light of later experience these new times and days are better for this incense. Again, use the Table of Planetary Hours at the back of the book.

Incubation in its full meaning is far too widespread to be traced to any single locality for its origin. It is an expression of a religious conviction for a considerable part of the human race. These consultations, searching for an appropriate course to take for problems had developed the kind of incubation that, because of its prominence in Greece, has gained a natural, though not wholly deserved, prominence in the common parlance of comparative religion.

A Greek inscription of the 2nd century A.D. tells us that Pan reveals himself in dreams to people during their midday sleep, telling the story of the shepherd **Hyginus** who was cured by Pan. He was not cured by a dream, despite sleeping but in the middle of the day. The shepherd was afflicted with a serious physical complaint and around midday he lay down and rested with his flock. While still awake he believed Pan-Ephialtes, the god of shepherds and hunters, appeared in a very vivid vision and he was healed. **Hyginus** attests that at the time of the appearance of the god, his animals were in a state of panic and terror, which is an attribute of Pan. 'For you have appeared to all my sheep, not as a dream vision but in the middle of the day.' He offered an oblation to god for his cure. One of Pan's appelatives is Paian, only applied to him in the Orphic hymn, which refers to him as 'a helper and saviour, rescuing from illness.' Pausanias tells us that in the Asklepieion at Sicyon the porch was flanked by figures of Pan and Artemis.

Pan is frequently brought into connection with Artemis - 'uninjured, healing, vigorous' - as she also - 'grants health and strength to others.' She cured and alleviated the suffering of mortals. She was the goddess of the flocks and the chase, and the protectress of young suckling animals. Artemis ranged over forests and mountains. The Arcadian Artemis was the goddess of the nymphs and was worshipped as such. Her bows and arrows were made by Hephaestus and Pan provided her with her dogs. Her chariot was drawn by four stags with golden antlers. The temples of Artemis were near lakes, rivers and sacred wells. Artremis has many epithets which connect her with the river gods and so it is we find fish sacred to her. Her Arcadian epithets all show her as representing some part or power of Nature, which must ally her with Pan in many ways.

With the nymphs and Cephissus, Pan represented the hygiene of Nature at the altar of Oropos. The ritual for this shrine had a strong parallel with that of Faunus. Amphiaraos presided over the sanctuary of Oropos, and the high regard in which this dream-shrine was held is shown by its being consulted by Croesus and Mardonius. There was a fixed fee. The visitor, after a period of fasting 'to receive the oracle with a clear soul,' would sleep on the skin of a sacrificed animal, in preparation for the intimation of the god. Amphiaraos performed his miracles not during incubation, as at Epidaurus, but through dream-oracles that were naturally submitted to a dream reader for judgement. An important part of the treatment was the bathing, with separate compartments for men and women.

To the south side of the altar was the fountain of Amphiaraos that was used for therapeutic purposes. The great altar contained five divisions and contained everything connected with healing in the Attic religion which was brought into relationship with Amphiaraos. The third and central division belonged to the god himself, his son Amphilochos, Hermes and Hestia. The first division was for Zeus, Apollo and Herakles, with the second for heroes and heroines. The fourth division had the Athenian Asklepieion of Panakeia-Iaso-Hygieia with Athena Paionia. The fifth and final division of the altar was dedicated to Pan and the nymphs with Achelous and Cephissus (= eponymous river divinities).

It is usually thought that Pan was never given a constructed building. In this he was like the god Terminus, for the roofs of his temples were always open to the heavens as it was for the palladium (Gr. *palladion)*, an 'image of Pallas-Athene.' The Palladium was an old carved image in the citadel of Troy, on which the prosperity of the city depended. It is said to have been three cubits in height, with feet placed close together, an upraised spear in its right hand, and in its left either a distaff and spindle or shield. Athene was said to have made it as an image of Pallas, daughter of Triton, whom she had slain unawares, while playing at wrestling. Legends differ in their account of the manner of its coming to Troy.

According to one of them, Pallas gave it as a dowry to Chryse, the bride of Dardanus, and he brought it to Dardania, whence Ilus carried it to Troy; according to another, Zeus caused it to fall down to Ilus from heaven. Since Troy could not be conquered so long as it possessed the sacred treasure, Diomedes stole it with the help of Odysseus and brought it to Argos. However, according to the Attic story, it was Demophoon of Athens who deprived Diomedes of it. Following some accounts there were two Paladia and the one carried off by Aeneas and taken to Italy and preserved in the temple of Vesta, was the genuine one.

Wm Smith thinks 'the twofold Palladium, which was probably a mere invention to account for its existence in more than one place' as 'several towns both in Greece and Italy claimed the honour of possessing the ancient Trojan Palladium.' **Lempriere** tells us that statues of similar size and shape were placed near to the original to deceive sacrilegious persons who attempted to steal it.

Figures reminding us of the description of the Trojan Palladium are frequently seen in ancient works of art. This stone, as 'a thing hurled from heaven,' was not to be hidden from the sky. So it was that the *thunder-stone* of Terminus was usually placed under a hole in the roof of the temple, and this would account for the opening in the roof of the temple at Troy.

Caves were Pan's main place of worship, which was of an ancient form, sometimes with an altar being constructed as needed of rough hewn stones - *bombos*. Pan was honoured with an annual sacrifice - *thusia*= 'sacrifices, or the victim itself' - and torch procession. There are very few references to the *lampadedromia*= 'a torch race,' in honour of Pan. The epheboi ran in a relay race and lit their torches at the altar. Prometheus and Hephaestus had a common altar in the garden of the gymnasium of the Academy. It is known that the torch race of the Panathenaea began at this altar.

The epheboi lit their torches from the flames on the altar and carried them to the Acropolis and to the sanctuary of Athena. The ephiboi is the Athenian name for youths who have attained sixteen and over. When a boy reached this age it was the occasion for a festival. His long hair was cut and the locks dedicated to Apollo. He then offered wine to Prometheus and served for two years in gymnastic exercises. After being tested for fitness the name of the ephebe was entered in the list of their tribe and he was presented to the people, armed with spear and shield.

The winner carried the fire of the gods to the altar of the civic goddess. It is possible all the torch races began at the altar in the Academy, including the annual race held in honour of Pan. The race for Pan finished at Pan's altar, in his cave on the side of the Acropolis and not on the summit where the temples were. It is thought the time of Pan's torch race was when the sun was in the constellation of Capricornus the Goat. In this early period in Greece the race was held during the Attic month of Gamelion (January-February), see full table of the Attic months, at the end of the last chapter.

The *Lampadedromia*- torch bearing or race - was a game assumed to be common through Greece. Although we know most about the torch races from Athens, we hear of it at Corinth, Pergamon and Zerynthus. At Athens there was a race to Prometheus at the *Prometheia*, another to Athena at the *Panathenaea*. A torch race was given for Hephaestos at the Hephaeseia. The was one to Pan and another to the Thracian Artemis or Bendis, with torch races for Hermes and Theseus; they were even held in the festival of the dead.

Bendis was a Thracian divinity in whom the moon was worshipped. The poet **Catinus** called her *dilogchos*= 'with two spears; double-pointed, two-fold' - either because she had to perform two duties as she was invested with two powers, one towards heaven and another towards the earth; or she had two lances or two lights. One of these lights was her own, while the other was derived from the sun. In Greece she was sometimes identified with Persephone or Hecate, but more commonly with Artemis.

The **Bendideia** was celebrated annually on the twentieth of Thargelion (May-June). This festival resembled in its character those celebrated in honour of Dionysus. Though **Plato**, in whose time the worship of Bendis was popular, only mentions feasting and a solemn procession of Athenians and Thracians at Pyraeus, there was a torch race on horseback during the evening.

The Greeks themselves explained the torch race as a commemoration of the gift of fire by Prometheus (**Hyginus**, *Astron* ii), but it is thought the primary motive must have been something more than this. The torch is specially associated with Demeter. According to the **Homeric Hymn**, the goddess, after the rape of Persephone, rushed frantically in search of her daughter with lighted torches in her hands. The torch was an attribute of various Greek deities besides Demeter. Persephone has the same emblem as her mother. The torch is regularly associated with Hecate and Artemis, sometimes with the Maenads, perhaps because they were nocturnal creatures and many of their festivals were nocturnal. Ares sometimes carried a torch, an appropriate emblem for the god of war.

One of the fundamental features of the torch race ritual seems to lie in the transference of fire from one altar to another at the greatest possible speed. It is conceivable, therefore, that the underlying idea was the need of carrying fire from a pure source to take the place of a polluted fire. At Athens all the fires were quenched before the race began, at least in the *Promethea*, and were rekindled from the new fire; it should not be necessary to point out the similarity of this with the Celtic fire festivals. A belief in the pollution of fire is shown in the Argive custom of extinguishing fire after a death, and renewing it from another source. Similarly the fires at Plataea were defiled by the presence of barbarians, and new fire was brought from the sacred hearth of Delphi.

The action of carrying a lit torch from the Cerameicus to the Acropolis was a symbol of the benefit conferred by the Titan Prometheus when he carried the stolen, sacred fire from the habitation of the gods to earth and bestowed it on mankind. However, the gratitude to the giver of fire and light soon passed back to the Olympian Gods who presided over its use. Hephaestus taught men to apply it to melting and moulding metal. Athena too, might well have adopted a torch race, being the patron of the ornamental arts, handicrafts and metal working for which fire was obviously used; but it was more probable that she claimed the torch race as the supreme head of the city. As regards the festival of Pan, we know that the race was instituted after the battle of Marathon. Once established, the race became popular and was attached to other festivals, though some think it was done without religious significance, which I cannot believe.

Rider, competing in a torch race on horseback. Taken from a woodcut of a silver coin of Tantium

The torch race was thought to be about half a mile and was usually run on foot, though horses had been used in the time of **Socrates**. The preparation for these races was a principal branch of the gymnasiarchia. It was the *gymnasiarchus* (= 'the master of a gymnasium') who had to provide the *lampas* = a torch, a lantern, a lamp. This was a candlestick with a shield set at the bottom of the socket to catch any hot material and protect the hand. The woodcut illustration is taken from a coin in Mionnet, see illustration.

Leiturgia (= in Athens a liturgy - 'service performed for the public') is a term applied at Athens to either an ordinary or extraordinary service, which the State imposed on its wealthier citizens in accordance with a regular rotation. One of the ordinary services given to citizens whose property was within a certain valuation was the *Gymnasiarchia*, which imposed the obligation of training, in the Gymnasia, the competitors for the gymnastic contests, supplying them with proper diet while they were in training, and providing at the games themselves for the required arrangements and decoration of the arena of the contest. The most expensive type of this form of service was the *lampadedromia* or *torch race*, as the scene of the race had to be illuminated.

Regarding the torch race there are two conflicting accounts. In the first the *lampas* was carried from point to point by a chain of runners who passed it on to the next one, in the manner of a relay race. The art consisted in passing on the lit torch without extinguishing it. Those who did lost their share of the honour. The second account seems to show that it was a race run by many people all starting from the same point. This latter account implies competition, but if the torch was passed from one runner to the other, where is the competition, who were the torchbearers competing against? The runner who let the torch go out was the loser, but who then was the winner?

Wm. Young offers the hypothesis that there were several chains of runners, each of which had to carry the torch a given distance. This would answer the question and both conditions would be fulfilled. A torch would be handed along the chain that would answer the first condition, successive delivery. The chain in which the torch travelled quickest to reach its destination would answer the second, this being a race among competitors, with one team the winner.

In later times the same honour was paid to all gods who were in any way connected with fire. The god Pan had a perpetual fire in his grotto under the Acropolis, as he had at Olympia. Pan was called by the Greeks *Phanos* = 'bright, light, a lamp, lantern or torch' and by the Romans *Lucidus* = 'containing light, full of light, clear, bright, shining.' It is

The gymnasiarch provided the torch which, as
shown in the above illustration, was in the form of
a candlestick with a shield set at the bottom of the
socket to both shelter the flame and protect the
hand of the runner. This detail was taken from a
woodcut of an ancient coin.

noteworthy, in view of these epithets of Pan, that the most frequent dedications found in his caves were terracotta lamps. This suggests that the association of Pan with the principle of light and the sacred fire was well understood and accepted. *Pan Phanos* is close to *Phanes*, the Orphic God of Light with whom Pan has direct connection. More will be said of this later.

As written earlier, Pheidippides obviously knew who Pan was, as he reported to whom he had spoken without asking for the name or being told it. Pheidippides brought to the city a message from the god himself. It is further suggested that Pheidippides knew that Pan had connections with heralds. The god Hermes who, according to Athenian tradition was the father of Pan, was a herald. The herald's staff (Gr. *kerykeion*. Lat. *caduceus*) was an attribute of Hermes. Ceryx is the Greek name for herald. In the Homeric age the keryx is the official servant of the king, who manages his household, attends at his meals, assists in the sacrifices, summons the assemblies and maintains order and tranquillity in them. He acted as an ambassador to the enemy. As a herald his person, in ancient times and later, was inviolate. These are only a few of the extensive duties of the herald, he had a great deal to do in the service of the State. All of which was in keeping with the character of the god Hermes/Mercury, the messenger of the gods.

In some stories of Greek mythology Ceryx is a son of Hermes, the herald of the gods, and Agraulos the daughter of Cecrops or, according to another story, the son of Eumolpus. The standard version is that Eumolpus was the father Ceryx and it was from these two, the two hereditary clans of Eleusis claimed descent. The *Eumolipdae* were the priesthood, descended from Eumolpus. The *Kerykes* were the heralds, claiming descent from Ceryx and claiming Hermes as head of their family. Mythology regards Eumolpus as the founder of the Eleusinian mysteries, and as the first priest of Demeter and Dionysus; the goddess herself taught him, Triptolemus, Diocles, and Celeus, the sacred rites, and he is therefore sometimes described as having himself invented the cultivation of the vine and of fruit trees in general.

A bronze caduceus decorated with two heads of Pan has been found on the Acropolis. It is said to be dated from the period between the two Persian wars and this would make it contemporary with Pheidippides. The caduceus was the staff or mace carried by heralds and ambassadors in time of war. This name is also given to the staff with which Hermes or Mercury is usually represented. *Mercury Caducifer* (= bearing a herald's staff) was an epithet of Mercurius, though the early staffs were not depicted with the snakes; these were a later addition.

Various explanations have been given for these two serpents around the wand. Some thought the entwined snakes of the caduceus represented Jupiter's amorous dalliance with Rhea. Others say it was because Mercury placed his wand between two serpents that were fighting and they entwined themselves around it in peace. Sometimes Prudence is thought to be represented by the serpents with the wings for Diligence. These two assets are desirable in the pursuit of commerce that Mercury patronized. The caduceus was given to Mercury by Apollo, in return for his lyre.

The caduceus was an olive branch with stemma. Stemma= 'anything to crown it with, a wreath, garland or chaplet, wool being chiefly used especially when hung upon an ancestral image.' The word stemma eventually came to mean the wool itself. The original caduceus was said to be an enchanter's wand, a symbol of power that produced wealth and prosperity. It was also an emblem of influence over the living and the dead. The Psychopompos - *the guider of the soul* - was another name for Hermes who, with his caduceus, conducted the souls of the dead to the Infernal Regions; as Oneicopompus he oversees the world of dreams.

It has to be remembered that a symbol contains within it a wealth of ideas that can be drawn on. A sign for the most means just what it says: road signs mean what they say, or there would be little point in putting them up if they meant different things to different people. A trade mark is a sign which means exactly what it says because its purpose is to represent a product or a company. Consequently their copyright is registered and jealously guarded with dire consequences invoked against those who abuse those rights. You understand a sign, but you *meditate on a symbol* in the hope it will yield greater understanding and knowledge. Even in early times the caduceus was regarded as a herald's staff and a symbol of peaceful intercourse.

In one of its original forms it was thought to consist of three shoots of hazel. One formed the handle, while the other two intertwined at the top in a knot. It was this form that was later adapted into the one with the snakes which is now so widely used.

From caduceus the word *Caduceatores* was formed, which signified a person sent under a flag of truce, to treat for peace. The person of the Caduceator was considered sacrosanct, as were all heralds by civilized people in civilized lands. Shakespeare knew well the duties of the herald. In *Henry V*, Henry asks the French herald 'What is thy name? I know thy quality.' Henry is told his name is 'Mountjoy.' Henry tells him 'Thou dost thy office fairly.' Later he tells him 'Herald, save thou thy labour; come no more for ransom, gentle herald; they shall have none, I swear, but these my joints...' Finally, true to the family of the Kerykes and the head of their family, Hermes/Mercury, it is the herald Mountjoy who brings Henry the news of the outcome of Agincourt - 'The day is yours.'

The caduceus was not used by the Romans. They used instead *verbena*= boughs or branches of laurel, olive or myrtle. The sacred boughs were borne by the fetiales and priests suing for protection. *Fetiales*= Roman college of priests, who sanctioned treaties when concluded or demanded satisfaction from the enemy before a formal declaration of war.

Lucian, a witty Greek writer, but of Syrian parentage, gives an imaginary conversation between Pan and his father Hermes. In his *Bis Accusatus* - 'Double Accusation' - the author **Lucian** is arraigned by Rhetoric and Dialogue. He makes Pan express some resentment at his treatment from the Athenians. He writes that Pan thinks they do not honour him as he thinks he deserves, considering the barbaric army he sent packing from their front door. Pan says they come up two or three times during the year and sacrifice an uncastrated goat to him, which gives off an awful stink. After the people have performed the sacrifice they have a feast on the meat that he has to watch and then they honour him with plain clapping of hands. However, he does say he finds their laughter and pageant entertaining.

Who givest all

Alcimenes, an ancient man,
Though poor and humble ne'er forgot
To offer little gifts to Pan.
Spring water in an earthen pot

A fig, an apple, nothing more -
And standing made his lowly prayer.
'Thou giv'st me from thy plenteous store
All that my trees and seedlings bear.

So take this water from the spring,
The fruits that thou hast made to thrive;
Take not too close a reckoning,
But give me more than I can give.'
Ancient Author Unknown.

This cave on the Acropolis is in keeping with the manner in which Pan is often placed in groups or represented in art. Pan is often where he can see without being seen and sometimes higher than the rest, perhaps a ledge. It bears repetition that frequently you have to look for him. He could be very prominent as his myths show and he certainly was not afraid to take the centre of the stage, but primarily he is a peripheral god found on the edge of things. He is frequently found in places that are neither one thing or the other. Pan seems to prefer the boundaries between the wild and the civilized, the point of merging between cities and the rural areas. The same point can be reached in your personal affairs or thinking. A point is reached where you can lose your bearings because you are between what you know and what you don't. Then, because of the lonliness, due to loss of contact and without any seeming cause, you panic, because of losing your sheet anchor.

I sometimes think panic comes because this state has the likeness of a little death. When all the boundaries are out of sight we have no markers for our life so we quickly lose our bearings and drift, like sailors when the coastline cannot be seen, and clouds and fog blot out the stars and the compass is broken. Those who are seasoned mariners run the ship by instinct, but not everyone has this special type of instinct. We all have instinct inborn but often that is not enough, not if it has not been trained or exercised. If it has not been honed by experience into a reliable lodestone it simply runs wild and panics as a consequence. Good judgement is the result of experience gained, but experience is taught by bad judgement, thank god for youth when you can play the giddy goat and, for the most, get away with as it is almost expected of you. At times like these it is sometimes best to retreat or withdraw until a more suitable time.

At times like this there is a sense of *not belonging*. You know where you have come from but not where you are going. You do not know what lies between these two states and this, like the unknown, often leads to panic. This is why I have suggested a 'likeness to a little death.' It is a time of uncertainty on that dangerous periphery where lost or found seems to hinge on the turn of a card and your wits could desert you. When you are between certainty and uncertainty, the enthusiasm of Pan, which can take you now, can be overpowering. It is thought by some to be akin to madness or irrationality. To be without disquiet or trepidation, to be fearless, invincible and not to panic may appear a desirable state of affairs, but loss of contact with instinct is to lose Pan. In this case Pan would find no cause to appear in a life that is without emergencies or the need for self-preservation. He abhors a static life, homeostasis, for he needs something he can attend to show the natural wisdom of Nature or to throw you on your own devices.

Where you find panic, there you will find Pan. This is probably why many people advocate not trying to summon up the god, thinking you have to be very strong to do so and handle it, unless of course, the god comes unbidden and of his own accord. However, this panic must not automatically be presumed for all. To the average, ordinary Greek going about their daily business the appearance of Pan would be the cause of panic. Panic would ensue when a frolicsome Pan, Silvanus, Faunus or the other woodland spirits deliberately appeared to the lonely traveller in mountain and woodland. It was intended. There need not necessarily be this result to the person seeking to make contact with Pan. Such a person is seeking the life force and asking it to flow through them and them through it. In making contact with Pan they would have found what they were seeking - Life!

Of course this will challenge the vanity and ego of some who will want to show they are among the few who can call up Pan and handle him, as opposed to the many who can't! Thinking you can 'handle' Pan is very insecure ground to start with. Today so many people want something I think the Ancients would not have understood. They want to be comfortable with their gods. They belong to what I call the 'Hi there!' generation, those who stick your name on you, like a parcel, as soon as you enter the room. I do not think the Ancients would have understood this idea of being too comfortable or too friendly with the gods. I do not think they would accept this as the purpose of either religion or the gods. This is the reason for quoting *The Wind in the Willows* again, at the end of this chapter. I believe **Kenneth Graham** got it right: a balanced attitude and response to Pan, his kith and kin. In the tale Ratty and Mole are present when Pan comes among the animals. Ratty is asked by Mole if he is afraid of Pan. Ratty, filled with 'unutterable love' for the god says, of course he is not...and yet! It is this 'and yet' which makes the perfect balance. In other words, I think 'Ratty' and Graham got it right.

Sophocles has Pan, in one of his choral odes, as the 'Author and Director of the Dances of the Gods.' The Gnostics represented Pan as seated in the centre of the zodiac playing his syrinx or pipes, as did the Orphics.

The Gnostic writers wrote 'the Father of All is moreover denominated "piper" because that which is born is harmonious Spirit (or Breath).' Music was important to the Arcadians and, from a very early age, young boys were trained to sing hymns and paeans to celebrate the gods and heroes. They would compete yearly, accompanied by professional flute players, in a contest specially for them. This was separate from the men's contest, for whom it was usual all their lives to supply their own music rather than hire professional musicians.

Most people, when thinking of Pan, tend to place him immediately in his beloved Arcadia and regard him as an exclusively Greek invention. Pan is an Arcadian for the Greeks and all the ancient sources call him an Arcadian. I could not imagine Pan being anywhere else personally. Arcadia was called 'the land of Pan' - Pania. The Goat-God was its lord and it was usual to link him with the soil of his fatherland. The myths represent him as born of the earth - an autochthon. Autochthon (pl. *Autochthones*) = 'sprung from the land itself,' *autos*= 'self' and *chthon*= 'the earth, the ground.' 'One of the aborigines of a country, a man, animal or plant belonging to the race that seems to have inhabited it before all other races of a similar kind.'

Pan is an Arcadian, whoever his parents prove to be. Pan is firmly located in a real and familiar landscape, to which you can go even now. This is unique and all the ancient sources call him an Arcadian. No matter where his cult is practised, at Athens, Thebes, Egypt, etc., Pan remains firmly linked with Arcadia and nowhere else; wherever Pan is, there is Arcadia. However, never forget, Arcadia is both a psychic and a physical location. As the Phaedrus prayer of Plato at the beginning of this section tells us, it is 'out there' and 'in here.' We could derive great benefit from making the two - one.

There was an official meeting with the god and the Athenians that established Pan's cult in Athens. This was through the mediation of a herald and took place near Tegea; therefore, his epithet *Pan Tegaeus* derives from the worship he received there. The Boeotians referred to him as the *Lord of Arcadia*. The Arcadians themselves honoured him and styled him the sovereign of Arcadia, saying he was among the greatest of the gods. Pan and his powers were equated with this region of the country.

Arcadia is a mountainous country: it was hard to reach and strange deities were sometimes worshipped there. Sacred mountains of Pan are Mount Lycaeum, where he was born, and also Mounts Maenalus and Lampea. It was a pastoral economy, the home of huntsmen and the protectors of game, sheep and goats. Hunting was not just a matter of sport here. It had a *Master of the Animals* and he takes his place with those other deities, like Artemis, who are connected with animals and hunting. When Artemis visited the Goat-God at his home she found him butchering a lynx so that his fertile bitches could dine. Pan gave Artemis 'two half black dogs, three of them with spotted ears and one spotted all over.' These, it was said, could even pull down lions by clutching their throats and drag them back to the camp still alive. In addition he gave 'seven bitches of Cynosuria, swifter than the wind' to pursue deer and the unblinking hare.

This incident is given by **Callimachus** as occurring just after the birth of Artemis: she meets Pan and he presents hunting hounds to the future huntress. In Arcadia more than anywhere, Pan is the lord of the mountains. Some say Pan does not live in a cave and his premises are called, by the few authors who describe it, a kalia. This term has more to do with Pan as a herdsman. *Kalia* means a wooden hut, often made of boughs, that shelters the shepherds; as opposed to the sheepfold that protects the flock against wild beasts. It also means a barn, a granary, a bird's nest, or a wooden shrine (for a statue).

Old writers tell of a natural place on Mount Lycaeum that was sacred to Pan, a place where no wolf dared to enter. Goats and sheep might enter and seek sanctuary, as may any animal that was pursued by a predator. This strengthens the old belief that claims Pan is the *Divine Master* of the animal kingdom, both the domesticated and wild. This place was proof against the wolf and it is assumed the same against the hunter. The descriptions given of this sanctuary have caused some authorities to suggest that this was the famous *abaton* of Mount Lycaeum. No hunter would enter the abaton to pursue any quarry that had taken refuge there. The penalty for doing so was exile or death.

The abaton- *the forbidden place* - on Mount Lycaeum ('wolf mountain') was there for Pausanias on his visit. *Abatos*= 'untrodden, inaccessible*; of a river - *not fordable*; of holy places - *not to be trodden, inviolate*: hence *pure, chaste.*' It was not unlike the temenos of a temple, the sacred precinct where sanctuary could be sought. Again, any law-abiding hunter would not enter the abaton after any quarry that had taken refuge there. No person was allowed to enter the abaton. Plutarch tells us that even if the entry was voluntary the penalty was death by stoning. It was not only sacred to Zeus *Lycaeum* but also to *Pan Lycaeum*.

Pausanias tells us that those who did enter would die within one year, though he does not say what form the death would take. The hunter might have stayed outside the holy place and watched his quarry, but this was often thought difficult as 'no living thing within the abaton casts a shadow.' In other areas, for some reason, this lack of shadow only occurred when the sun was in the Crab, but in the abaton it was all year.

The Crab is the zodiac sign of Cancer with the fourth house as its natural house. In the astrological chart this sign and house are the natural sign of the mother, birth and one of the most protective, all-embracing and enclosing areas of the chart. It is at the base of the chart: today we use the term the home base for without a home we drift because we have no anchor. This area rules three of the most secretive areas of human life -

home, womb and tomb. These are three places that enclose the human body. The womb protects you at birth, the home while living and the tomb at death.

Stretching the analogy a little farther, in these three places you metaphorically 'cast no shadow.' Even when you are in your home people do not really know if you are there or not, for you have withdrawn from the light of public gaze. As above, you 'cast no shadow.' You are not abroad or on public display. You are not out 'in the light.' A phrase for this is that you are 'in the privacy of the home' and what is private should not be seen.

Plutarch, in his *Roman Questions*, tells why men of patrician birth wore on their shoes images of the moon. He said it was a token of the belief the moon was inhabited and, after our death, our souls shall again have the moon at their feet. This practice was always the mark of the most ancient families. Similarly the Arcadians, who were descended from Evander, were called *Proselenoi* - 'born before the moon.' All of this was according to **Castor**.

Mount Lycaeum (Gr. *Lykaion*) is important to both Zeus and Pan and bears out in some measure the connection between the two gods. Zeus bears the epithet *Zeus Lycaeus* and Zeus had a sanctuary there. There was an altar of heaped up earth and before it were two columns with gilt eagles on top of them, which were looking to the East. The festivals were thought to take place every nine years when the priests alone entered the mysterious precinct to offer unknown sacrifice. This festival is said to have been begun by the mythical king of Arcadia, Lycaon. He established the oldest town, Lycosura, on the Mount and sacrificed a child to Zeus on its highest peak, and on this account he was changed into a wolf. There are other legends regarding the impiety of Lycaon and his sons that was punished by Zeus. I am sure many have pondered these events and wondered if we have in them the basis of the later werewolf stories.

The man who performed the sacrifice at the Lycaea was chosen by lot and afterwards he was compelled to flee and wandered about for nine years. Like Lycaon, this was in the shape of a wolf, people believed. In the tenth year he was allowed to return and regain his human form, that is, the taint of the blood sacrifice was removed. There were athletic contests and the festival to the god.

Pan was very active on this mountain and he played a large part in the traditions of it I am sure, despite information being sparse. This sanctuary was surrounded by a sacred grove and there was a stadium there, near the temple. The Arcadians gathered at the stadium for the games that were called *Lycaea* (Gr. *Lukaia.*) These were games that were intended to honour Zeus Lycaeum but very little is known of the festival. It is thought that once it called for the blood of a human sacrifice on the altar of Zeus. **Plutarch** writes that the celebrations there resembled that of the Roman Lupercalia, which seems reasonable; see the next chapter.

The god Pan had a sanctuary built to him on Lycaeum, next to and adjoining that of Zeus. It is known from inscriptions found there that Pan's priest enjoyed equal prestige with that of the priest of Zeus. The two priests alternated in giving their names to the festival year. Unless there was a very good reason precious few have been permitted to equal Zeus on such terms. Zeus permitted very few to go before him. A similar feature is found on the coins of the Arcadian League. Pan Lycaeum has the reverse of the coins while the obverse has the image of Zeus Lycaeum.

In one of his poems Orpheus tells us that 'All things are full of Zeus,' in him is seen the earth, water, fire, day and night. He seems to be describing the entire universe, the head sparkling with a golden crown, the heavens flashing with the rays of the myriad of stars. His eyes represent the sun and moon, the expansive chest for the element of air, the wide shoulders, made salient by the extent of his wings, which gave swiftness to the winds and the rapidity of God when acting. If we did not know this was by Orpheus, we could be forgiven for thinking it was the ancient Greeks describing Pan and the Zeus called Pan - the whole or all - because he represents the universe, demonstrated by the symbolism used.

We are told that the horns represented the rays of the sun, the moon and the stars; the ruddy complexion, an attribute often found in nature gods, meant the aetherial fire; the masculine elements were represented by the beard; the spotted skin symbolized the sphere of the fixed stars and the staff with its crook turned to the rear, portrayed the power held over the things that he owns and the years that ever return to him. The syrinx - or heptaulus - with its seven pipes in his left hand expressed the celestial harmony of the seven planets of old, which are displayed in their motion. The lower limbs are hairy, rough and end in goat's feet for the rugged earth upon which they are planted, amid the herbs, plants, vegetation and trees. The goat's feet symbolize fecundity through which the life of the universe was preserved, both physically and spiritually. The Egyptians and Greeks sometimes show Pan or Zeus Lycaeus as a male goat, to represent continued preservation and creation.

A hieroglyph, representing Pan Lycaeus and Zeus Lycaeus, from the *Oedipus Aegypticus* of **Athanasius Kircher** (1601-1680) is shown on the opposite page, using the given key to the diagram, it is self-explanatory.

Pan/Zeus holds in his left hand his syrinx, and in the centre of his

Hieroglyphic representation of Pan/Zeus Lycaeus.

A: Ruddy face, the power of aetherial fire or, heat in the Universe. B: The power of the celestial rays on those things under the moon. C: Masculine elements. D: Power of the year, its return, and of all revolutions. E: All things are maintained by its virility. F: Power of the Firmament, the sphere of the fixed stars. G: (feminine) The earth abounding with plants, seeds and trees. H: (feminine) Fountain of water and liquids by irrigation fertilizing the earth. I: The fields, crops and other matters of vegetation. K: Harmony of the seven planets. L: Unequal and rough mountains of different heights. M: Power and fecundity. N: The cubical, or six-sided solid foundation. O: Power, energy and velocity of the winds and their rapidity of action palm is the earth. From his syrinx come the seven planets of the ancient world. He stands on the cube of the physical world in which he is firmly rooted, and on his body are the attributes which make up the earth and the universe.

Let us look a little closer into some current stories of Pan's birth that place him so close to Zeus and see what facts we have to account for this. We are told that Aeschylus, the earliest of the three great tragic poets of Greece, believed in two gods called Pan. Poor Aeschylus... it was predicted by an oracle that on a certain day he would die by the fall of a house or a 'blow from heaven.' On the appointed day he went to sit in a field, with nothing around him for miles but an eagle carrying a tortoise in its beak thought his bald pate was a rock on which to drop its prey and break the shell. Thus it was in 456 B.C. that Aeschylus died instantly in his sixty-ninth year. The manner of his death is well attested. Yes, I know 'the historicity of this story is extremely dubious!' However, one thing modern journalism should have taught us and they, in turn, are probably following a long well-established tradition. If the myth is better than the facts - print the myth! Man cannot live by facts alone.

These two Pans of **Aeschylus** could be explained in part much in the manner of Mars, depending on which aspect of Mars you were invoking. Were you invoking his help as a great God of Nature to help you with your agriculture or husbandry, or as the God of War to help you win a battle or litigation? In the latter aspect he would be girded as for war and stern, in the former without arms and gentle. It comes down to the direction you approached him and from what you wanted from him. Similarly someone can be described by one as stern and forbidding, while another will say they were kind and gentle. This will amaze another person, who may not have seen this side of that person's nature.

The first of these two Pans was born of Zeus and the nymph Kallisto. This birth would make him *didumaon* (= twin-brother) of Arcas. Let us briefly fill out this character in the plot. Arcas is the ancestor and eponymous hero of the Arcadians, from whom the country and the inhabitants get their name. He was a companion of Artemis. According to Pausanias, Arcas succeeded Nyctimus in the government of Arcadia, which had been called Pelasgia up to that time. Nyctimus was the only son of Lycaon who was saved by Gaia (sometimes Ge) from the anger of Zeus in the above story. Arcas taught his people the arts of making bread and weaving. He was married to the nymph Erato, by whom he had three sons Apheidas, Azan and Elatus, among which he divided his kingdom. He had one illegitimate son called Autolaus whose mother is unknown. Arcas' wife Erato was a prophet and priestess of Pan.

Once when Arcas was out in the chase, he pursued his mother, who had been transformed into a she-bear, as far as the sanctuary of the Lycaean Zeus, which no mortal was allowed to enter. Several Arcadians followed him to kill her. Zeus in memory of his love for her snatched her out of their hands and placed her in the stars, with her son to watch over her. These stars never set and **Homer** describes them as the only ones that have no share in the bath of the ocean. Tethys, the wife of Oceanus, did not wish to offend Hera, the wife of Zeus, so she refused to receive Hera's former rival into the waters.

The second Pan was born to Cronos and Aix was his mother, which made him a contemporary of Zeus. **Epimenides** describes Pan sometimes as the twin of Arcas, with Zeus and Kallisto their parents and sometimes as the illegitimate child of the monstrous Aix or she-goat who was gradually, it seems, assimilated with Amalthea, the goat that nurtured Zeus in his childhood. This makes Pan *Suntrophos*= foster-brother of the future ruler of the Olympian Gods. It is this latter Pan who is thought to be the source of 'panic' for he is the one who helped Zeus in his battle against the Titans, as mentioned by **Nonnus**.

Thus the second Pan has his mother cited by **Epimenides**, while **Aeschylus** only gives his father. One aspect of Arcadian genealogy tells us Pan is the child of Cronos, while another tradition has him the child Oinoe and Aethyr. **Pausanias** tells us that Oinoe was the name the people of Tegea gave to the nurse of Zeus. Pan is even given as the son of Uranus and Gaia, which makes him a very old god - perhaps the oldest god. The Arcadian myths generally seem to point to Pan being the half-brother or foster-brother to Zeus; but there is also the story of his being twin to Arcas, his Arcadian ancestor, which brings us back to the sacred Mount Lycaeum, where we find a joint temple, games, alternating festivals and the coins of the Arcadian League. I wrote earlier that the roots of Pan's birth are far from easy to find.

From early antiquity the Arcadians were called *proselenoi* - 'those who precede the moon.' **Ovid** said the Arcadians were 'older than Jupiter and the moon' and **Statius** said they were 'prior to the moon and stars.' **Aristotle** tells us the Arcadians took possession of their country before the rising moon. This is usually taken to mean they were there when the moon rose for the first time and one of Pan's conquests was Selene, the moon.

The Arcadians existed before the moon, living in the mountains on acorns. In an age before the deluge, they were called Apidanean Arcadians. This makes you wonder if they were refugees from somewhere else. At this early period Atlantis springs to mind though I have found nothing to support the idea, so an idea it must remain. The acorn of old was thought to be as far from Demeter's gift of grain as was an uncultured existence from a civilized one. The Arcadians were not the only ones to recognize the nutritive properties of the fruit of the oak. Generally it was poverty that forced people to live off them. In the West, beech mast (= beech nuts) were eaten by people and animals in time of great need. Beech mast is thought by some to be quite tasty, if it was not for the laborious shelling, extracting and picking out the good nuts. If the nuts were larger, it has been suggested they may even prove popular as a food. I have not tried them.

Pan is a god of all Nature: this is often overlooked and he is frequently thought of only as the 'master of the animals' or the wild or domesticated flocks. Because of this he does not seem to have had the same following as Ceres or Demeter did. In Europe there are many field spirits or Harvest Dolls connected with the harvest and one of these is the Habergeiss - *the Oat Goat*. Some believe it is from this particular spirit that we may get the term 'to sow your wild oats,' which would be in keeping with the nature of a goat. With the harvest the field spirit flees ahead of the reapers, leaping from one swath to another. It is empowered in the last sheaf and he who cuts this has captured the field or corn spirit. This sheaf is moulded and dressed into a shape in keeping with the inhabiting spirit and this is presented to the owner of the field who keeps it carefully until the next spring planting. We have, for example, the Corn or Harvest Mother, the Grandmother, the Rye or Old Barley Woman, the Kornwolf, the Hag, etc.

I do not claim the Oat Goat is directly derived from Pan but I feel that he appears somewhere in the line of its history. Goats, with their eating habits, cast iron stomachs and a farmer's yield are not the best combination for any harvest, yet here we have a *goat corn spirit*. Of course the goat has long been regarded as the most fertile of animals and 'fertility' as such, whether of animal stock or the corn yield, would be considered highly desirable. It is in eastern Europe, especially Prussia, where the last sheaf is made into a puppet that is topped with goat's horns. The reapers work at speed to keep ahead of 'the goat' who butts any laggards. Children were discouraged from playing or going into the cornfields by the threat 'the Oat Goat will get them.'

In some areas a live goat was turned loose in the field and when the reaping was over it was caught, killed and roasted as the main dish of the Harvest Supper. The skin of the goat was worn by the farmer while threshing. However, if any reaper had a bad back, it was given to them because the powers of the Oat Goat could cure any ills caused by himself during the reaping. This is in keeping with the skins of sacrificed animals when used in healing temples, which were often slept upon, in the Ceremony of Incubation, while asking the gods to grant a cure. Pan is a healing god, as is also Faunus.

In old Bohemia a mummer was dressed in straw with goat's horns on their head. This Oat Goat was taken from house to house during Shrovetide celebrations and it had a counterpart called the *Fastnachtsbar* (= the Fastnacht Bear or Shrovetide Bear) The latter was a man or boy clothed in straw, sometimes donning a bear's mask or clad in skins, who was led from house to house. The Fastnacht Bear danced in front of the houses or entered them and danced with the women, for which he was given food and money. Sometimes the women would pluck bits of straw from the Fastnachtsbar to put in the poultry nests, this was done to secure a bountiful supply of eggs. All the fertility of the Fastnachtsbar was attached to the Oat Goat and most of the symbolism of these particular corn spirits would not be amiss with Pan.

It has been suggested that oak oracles were introduced into Greece by the Achaeans who originally consulted the beeches as the Franks had. Discovering no beeches in Greece the Achaeans transferred their allegiance to the oak with edible acorns because that was the nearest equivalent. To this they gave the name - *phegos*, which is the same word as - *fagus*, which is Latin for beech tree. Roasted phegoi turn up as a delicacy. Originally all men lived on acorns but the Arcadians stayed faithful to this custom, which was abandoned by the other Greeks when they received the gifts of Demeter.

Acorns are widely held to have been the first of man's food. The Romans thought the oaks were the first mothers of men. Legend tells how the Roman goddess of agriculture, Ceres, replaced the acorns with corn. To acknowledge the debt due to the acorn, some part of the oak was worn in honour of Ceres by the reapers as they harvested the corn. Farmers regarded Ceres as the source from which all food came and so would keep her rites faithfully, fearing the failure of the crops.

The fact that the Arcadians ate acorns must not be taken to mean it was their staple diet. It was said 'they eat what they can get.' The Arcadians were frugal eaters. They thought eating to excess a vice and heartily disapproved of it. Their meals were communal affairs, bringing together all who went about the business of the family. Fathers, sons, slaves or free, all came to the table drinking wine from a common bowl. Their food and drink consumption was modest, even at the time of festivals. According to **Aristotle**, Arcadian wine was so dry that it frequently coagulated in the bottle, from where it had to be scraped out.

The Arcadians claimed to be the oldest inhabitants of the Peloponnese. **Pausanias** gives us a genealogy that makes Lycoan founder in Arcadia of the world's first city - Lykosoura. He was a son of Pelasgos, who was born of the earth, for the Arcadians, like Pan, were autochthonous - 'earth born.' They remain integral with the earth from which they were born. The Arcadians were regarded as fierce fighters, at least by the oracle at Delphi. **Herodotus** tells us that when the Spartans believed they were superior to the Arcadians they consulted the Delphic Oracle regarding the subjugation of Arcadia. In part the Pythia told them. 'You ask me for Arcadia? It is a great thing you ask me; I will not give it to you. There are in Arcadia many acorn-eating men who will stand in your way.' She said they could 'dance on Tegea' so they left Arcadia alone. They did 'dance on Tegea where feet strike noisily.' The trouble was it was their feet in the chains they had brought to enslave the Tegeans. They lost!

The Athenians and Greeks generally set up caves, grottoes and natural sanctuaries, some symbolical, at a distance from the urban centres. Pan joined the other pastoral gods who were thought to be the natural inhabitants of such places. It did not take long for them to be called the grottoes of Pan and the nymphs as his worship became more important. The image of the cave stayed with Pan throughout antiquity. No buildings were constructed for this creature of the wild. We remind the reader, even when he was honoured on the Acropolis in Athens, it was a cleft in a rock that became his sanctuary: not unlike the caves and clefts into which the shepherd and his flock of goats would huddle in protection from a sudden storm, taking temporary refuge from unpredictable nature.

Near Marathon, the grotto at Oinoe was sacred to the Arcadian god from the beginning of the fifth century. Its stalagmites were thought to resemble the goats of Pan's divine flock. It was already deserted at the time of Pausanias but it was still famous. When the Medes attacked Delphi, the people hid in the Corycian cave, which was sacred to the cult of Pan, Dionysus and the nymphs. By doing this they placed themselves under divine protection. There also is the cave of Melissani on Cephallenia, sacred to Pan and the nymphs.

Before the fifth century B.C. his cult did not travel much beyond the Peloponnese. Only after Pan's introduction into Athens, after Marathon, do we find an increased attention in Attica and later into Boeotia. The cult rapidly diffused over nearly the whole of the Greek world. Pan impressed himself very rapidly on the Hellenic consciousness. This image of the goat-footed god with his sweet smile was very beguiling: at once animal and goatherd, a musician whose music could charm and disturb to a point of possession in many, a dancer of the gods. **Pindar** calls Pan 'a most accomplished dancer. Pan and the nymphs danced at the birth of the poet **Pindar**, while bees placed the honey of inspiration in the infant's mouth. Bees appear to have been considered by the Greeks as emblems of purity, and as a symbol of the nymphs, who are sometimes called *Mellissae*, as were priestesses in general, especially those of Demeter, Persephone and the Delphic Oracle. *Melitodas* - 'sweet as honey' - occurs as a Euphemistic epithet of Persephone. Mellona, also called Mellonia, the rural goddess of bees and honey, worshipped by the Romans, she was believed to protect the honey, but is otherwise unknown. Pan was also regarded as the guardian of the bees.

The Guardian of the Hive

I left the vales of Thessaly,
Peristratus hath need of me;
And here my rustic rounds I make
To guard his hives for friendship's sake.

If thou art bent on thievish gain,
Know that I smite, nor smite in vain;
Nor think to fly; no mortal man
Can stride as swingingly as Pan.
Nicias: 3rd century B.C.

Pan's activity primarily was with the reproduction of animals, a god who protected the herds, the animals and the shepherd. He tended his flocks far from mankind in the high, lonely mountain places that were his realms and in which were found most of his sanctuaries. Early representations of him distinguish him from a goat only by the fact that he is on his hind legs and often found dancing with a maenad or nymph. Authorities tell us there was a steady evolution from an almost pure animal to a more human form of Pan, especially with regard to the torso. Once the god had left the confinement of Arcadia and the Peloponnese to become universally known his iconography was adjusted to comply with the existing iconographic canon. If the reader wishes to see some powerful, but more primitive statuary of Pan (one in particular), the basement of the British Museum is worth a visit.

With the subject of this work famous among the horned-gods, it may prove useful to take a brief look at these fascinating deities. Horns play an important part in the religious symbolism of cults and in magic. They go back to a comparatively primitive stage of thought and, therefore, the symbolism is still buried deep within us all. Horns were observed by early man, particularly their use by those animals possessing them. In many religions of antiquity and later, deities are often shown wearing the horns of an animal on their head, or this characteristic is shown in their myths. A very lengthy list could be compiled of this aspect of ritual and religious worship. The Egyptian deities are frequently shown with these potent symbols. In Greece we have the mystical Dionysus born of Zeus and Persephone as Zagreus, a horned infant.

Another symbol of Dionysus was the bull; he was sometimes called 'horned' or 'bull-horned.' Pan and the Satyrs show traces of their goat origins as does Faunus, Silvanus, the Fauns, etc. Pan was said to have pyramidal horns that tapered from the earth to heaven. This idea of horns representing light is sometimes shown in art. Moses is found in art with two horns on his head instead of two shafts of light or fire coming from his forehead.

Many divinities may have been represented with horns because of Egyptian influence. Io, often equated with Isis, is changed into a cow by Hera and Hera herself is sometimes identified with the cow; both goddesses had horns. We have selected those examples that are connected with the area of Pan but a word regarding Cernunnos would not be out of place. He was a god of the Gauls, a horned god of the underworld. It has been suggested that his name may come from *cerna*= 'horn, the horned.' Groups of nameless gods, some with stag's horns have an affinity with him.

Myth and art retained some part of the animal, the pelt, head, hoofs, and especially the horns. The horns, however, were retained for the powerful gods. The most obvious use of horns in nature noted by our ancestors was their use as a destructive and defensive force. Humans and other animals were butted, tossed, ripped and gored by them. This was a period in history when man was using horns as both weapons and tools.

Thus horn, or the horned animals, became a symbol of natural strength. In early myth and legend it was common to find gods and heroes compared to powerful, strong horned animals. Often the horn is figuratively used as a symbol of strength. The Hebrews would raise the horn of an individual or a tribe to denote pride or victory. Breaking this horn signified their defeat. God is called the 'horn of salvation' 2.Sam.22:3 for he raises his people. The tribe of Joseph is said to have horns like those of a unicorn in Deut.33:17, see also Ezk.34:21. A Concordance and a Bible will enlarge this study for the reader. Roman and Greek usage was very much in similar vein.

In **Plutarch's** *Roman Questions*, there is the tale of Antro Curiatius who was a Sabine. He was told by a soothsayer that the one who made sacrifice to Diana on the Aventine of the large and beautiful heifer he owned, would get for his country the Italian empire. Naturally he went to Rome for this sole purpose but King Servius had been forewarned of his arrival and the importance of the intended sacrifice. The King told him that before he could approach the altar he had to bathe in the Tiber and while Antro was doing this, Servius offered up the sacrifice to Diana in his stead. It was because of this sacrifice that the horns of a bull are hung on the doors of Diana's temple on the Aventine, while stags' horns are placed on the doors of all the other temples of Diana.

It must not be taken, however, that horns were always used in a negative sense. Horns had the power to exercise potent protection. The power to avert evil has survived in the use of horseshoes. When these horns were nailed upon buildings, their purpose was to guard the building and those within against ill fortune. Because it was essential that the horns should be erect this shows the horseshoe should be erect or the protection and luck will run out and it will be ineffective. Take care when identifying this symbol as it can be difficult. Sometimes animal horns can be confused with the 'horns' of the moon. I sometimes think this may have given some deities the power inherent in an animal's horns, when they were meant to have the power of the moon.

The horn of the unicorn was often taken to symbolise the 'Sword or Word of God,' it being a spiritual beast, often called the 'powerful one.' In some illustrations horned animals are often shown in an attitude of preparing to attack or butting. The act of butting in illustrations did not always mean physical attack or defence, but a metaphorical attack or defence by use of the intellect. We could still be using a remnant of this symbolism in the metaphors of today. We either ram or say that someone is ramming their argument home. Similarly we often rebut someone's opinions or say someone is rebutting all arguments. Of those we think either fearless or foolish, like the goat or ram we still say they go in head first or butting. This is a trait of those born under Aries, which rules the head and skull, of which horns were natural extensions: they have a tendency to go in headlong, headstrong, headfirst and the Devil take the hindmost.

Mythic animal gods often destroyed demoniac forces by means of their horns. Most woodland spirits have horns, in particular the semi-divine deities. Horns are frequently part of the regalia of the chief. Wearing horned helmets may have derived from the earlier custom of wearing a head-dress composed of the head of an animal with the horns remaining. Perhaps animal skins adorned with horns were impracticable for battle, making the helmet with horns more practical. It must have given the frightening appearance of an animal about to charge, more so if the opponent's horns were bigger than yours. It was a signal that I am sure was clearly understood by the enemy of the day for, as in the animal kingdom, it declared quite clearly who was claiming to be the headman and cock of the walk.

Many nations wore horns on their helmets including Anglo-Saxon warriors. Mimetic dances regarding future ventures were acted out for victory in battle, a successful outcome to a proposed hunt or a prosperous outcome of an enterprise. Today we would call this visualization, not unlike the ceremony of wassailing the fruit orchards to ensure a good crop next year. In Great Britain, Gaul, Germany, etc., horned dancers would take to the streets, often in quite riotous dance. These dances and mimes are likely to have had some connection with the early animal cults of the Celts. The human representative of the corn spirit in animal form often wore goat or cow horns.

As written, horns placed over doors or dwellings, like horseshoes, sought protection for the house and its occupants. The Romans did this and placed them in temples, such as those of Diana. It was not unknown in England. At Horn Church, Essex, the horns fastened over the east part of the church were said to be made of lead. The tassels that are sometimes found on the corners of Christian altars suggest the horns of the Hebrew altars. These horns were often sprinkled with blood at the consecration of priests and the sin-offering, which was often the sacrifice of the scapegoat. Some commentators think the sacrifice was tethered to them in readiness for the slaughter. The altar was a sanctuary for the criminal and it was customary to take hold of the horns to gain safety.

There was an altar within the temple of Apollo at Delos that was celebrated because it was built completely from the horns of stags and achieved without any form of adhesive. This altar was known as the Ceraton and it was said to be the work of the god who presided over the temple. The Ceraton commanded regard from worshippers and was claimed to be a wonder of the world. The altar was still in existence during the time of Plutarch. On his victorious return from Crete Theseus visited Delos and offered sacrifices on the Ceraton.

The cornucopia or Horn of Plenty needs little comment in this short diversion: this horn, Amalthea's Horn, was the horn of the goat who fostered Zeus in his infancy. The cornucopia with its overflowing fruits is an emblem of the gods of plenty and those gods who aided the fertility of nature, animals and people alike. In this aspect it became symbolic of fruitfulness because it belonged to animals associated with fertility - the bull and the prolific goat. The horn was a universal symbol used among primitive and civilized people alike.

There seems to be a connection between the horn and sleep, dreams and healing, as there is with plenty and fertility. The God of Sleep has a horn from which he drops slumber upon the eyes of those he lulls to rest. Pan and Faunus are horned gods and, like other healing gods, give remedies and healing in sleep, either within their sanctuaries or while the sufferer is sleeping elsewhere. With Pan this was held particularly effective during *the midday sleep.*

Called back

Pan, kindly, sire, the leafy forest's king,
Lord of the Nymphs who pour the woodland spring,
Master and chief of minstrelsy divine,
This doth thy servant offer at thy shrine.

Fevered I lay, my spirit well-nigh fled,
My weeping children gathered round my bed;
It was no dream, no vision of the night,
But thou thyself, in all thy sovereign might
Made visible, didst grant the gracious boon;
These eyes beheld thee; 'twas the hour of noon.
An unknown, ancient author.

The gods mentioned above, especially Hermes (one of the most prominent sires of Pan), have authority over the dream gods and send one, or sometimes another, to mankind. On some occasions they create dream figures themselves, or appear in person under different shapes in the chamber of the dreamer. The spirits of the departed, as long as they are not in the kingdom of Hades, have the power of appearing to the sleeper in dreams. A god of dreams was honoured, especially at the seats of the dream oracles and the health resorts of Asclepius according to **Homer**. Deceptive dreams come through the Gate of Ivory while true dreams come through the Gate of Horn. Further entries regarding Sleep, Dreams and Death will be found in the final chapter, on the Semones.

The aegis is the 'storm cloud and thunder cloud of Zeus.' This was a shield forged by Hephaestus, blazing brightly and fringed with tassels of gold. In its centre was the awe-inspiring Gorgon's head. When Zeus shakes the aegis, it gives forth thunder and lightning with horror and perdition falling upon those against whom it is raised. The aegis was not only borne by Zeus - *the Aegis-bearer* - but also by his daughter Pallas-

Athene and occasionally by Apollo. Athene took the aegis to help the army of Bacchus and Pan, at the command of Zeus.

As the same word means *a goatskin* it was explained in later times as the skin of the goat that had suckled Zeus. At the bidding of an oracle he drew it over his thunder shield during the contest with the Giants and fastened on it the Gorgon's head. When the aegis became a standing attribute of Athene it was represented as a skin either shaggy or scaly, with a fringe of snakes and the Gorgon's head in the middle. In use the aegis either served the goddess as a breastplate, was hung behind her to screen the back and shoulders or, was fastened to the left arm.

Gods, supernatural beings and their guests are mythically shown drinking from horns. However, horns also held anointing oils, medicines and fetish materials, including the materials used in spells and incantations. For many reasons it was easy for the horn to become the magical property of gods, fairies, elves, heroes, etc. Fairy tales and myth are rife with robberies of drinking horns because the stolen horn was a veritable cornucopia, with the blessings it could give.

The horn was used as a musical instrument, sometimes sweet in its call, at others the rallying call of both the gods and men. It has entered fairy tales, such as *Jack the Giant Killer*. It was the golden horn on a silver chain that, when blown, brought down the enchanted castle of the giant. This horn is not unlike the one used by Heimdal in Northern mythology. He is the watchman of the gods and he is stationed by the Rainbow Bridge into Asgard. Here he keeps his eternal vigil against the machinations and attacks of the Giants.

The drinking horn is, to this writer, an ideal combination of male and female in almost perfect balance. In the minds of most people the horn is wrongly ascribed only to the male and is usually thought of as aggressive. Would you like to face a horn bearing female, say a she-goat who is protecting her young kids? I would not! The drinking vessel, held point down not unlike a stemmed glass, is female and a vessel that receives and sustains, which is why we drink from it. The sustenance is poured into it and it holds it ready for consumption. If a person or clan did not want to drink with another in these earlier times, perhaps because of a recent or ancient enmity, they would turn the horn up and erect, in obvious symbolism. This was much the same signal then as today when, in the vernacular, a middle erect finger is displayed.

The horn can thus no longer receive in friendship or social intercourse. It is a defensive and obvious stance of refusal to participate with that person or clan, 'telling them what they can do.' Even today there are few people who will drink with those they dislike or mistrust. Drinking with another or a group is a particularly intimate human relationship still, which is why purely social drinking today so often leads to trouble, showing it does not possess this exclusiveness or special intimacy.

Any *intimate* group that exceeds twelve, you and eleven others, can lead to trouble or loss of that intimacy. Eleven is the maximum number of intimates a person can handle with success before a 'Judas' enters the intimate circle and brings it down with some form of treachery. Psychologists are now pronouncing something that astrology has known for years. Christ had his intimate circle, himself and twelve others; one defected, the thirteenth. I have very little interest in sport but most teams seem wisely to keep below this number for a winning combination and, in the intimate areas of my personal affairs, so do I.

When we or others are under the influence of wine and relaxed we may say more than we normally would - In Vino Veritas. This is why we choose our drinking partners very carefully - or should. When an enmity is healed quite often the first thing we do is to drink on it. We have a drink with the person to celebrate the renewal and sealing of the friendship and the healing of enmity because it does have a special meaning. The horn is turned again, one hundred and eighty degrees so it is the opposite of what it was. It is ready to receive, contain and enjoin.

In vino veritas

Attic flagon, from thy lip
Let the potent vintage drip;
Every draught the seal and sign
Of the mysteries divine.
Sage of wisdom, hold thy peace!
Bard of truth, thy prating cease!
Thee we worship, Thee we greet,
Love most sorrowful, most sweet.
Posidippus: 3rd century BC.

It is not unlike the old bond of friendship with salt and bread. We have the male exterior (= erect) containing the female interior (= containing), an excellent, all-embracing symbol of the male and female divinities and ourselves. Now we must close this short diversion into the interesting symbolism of horns and the horned deities before it becomes overlong.

The spread of Pan's cult and its almost instantaneous popularity caused a problem. Suddenly Pan had to be accounted for. Where was he from? Who were his parents? His birth was known in at least twenty different versions and suddenly it seemed that everyone wanted to claim him as their own, I would too. The problem of his origins is not unlike seeking Osiris after the malevolence of Set, but to this writer (with due respect to the insuperable task of Isis and Nephthys), the parts seemed even harder to find and assemble. This uncertainty, which appeared quite early, became more bewildering as time went on. If there was any agreement, according to **Herodotus**, it was in seeing him as a very young god who was born after the Trojan War. The story upon which most seemed to settle was that Pan was the child of Hermes and Penelope and many of his legends revolve around these parents. Most authorities agree that between the time of his true origins and Pan's welcome in Athens in 490 B.C., there is a hiatus in which there is an almost complete lack of mythology.

Pan was worshipped in Egypt, being regarded as a very old god in that land. According to **Herodotus**, the Egyptians regarded Pan as 'exceedingly ancient' and belonging to those whom they call the 'eight gods.' At Khemennu, Thoth was regarded as the head of a 'Company of Eight.' These were four pairs of divinities, or divine powers; binary powers of male and female, active and passive, positive and negative, etc. This is thought to be the oldest example of the Gnostic Ogdoad. Khemennu is said to mean 'City of the Eight (gods).' The work, *Thrice Great Hermes* by **G.R.S. Mead** will enlarge on this quite extensive subject for the reader should they wish to pursue it, space is the enemy here, and this time it would be a considerable diversion from the subject, even for me.

Herodotus tells us of Pan: 'Not that they think he is, in fact, like that - on the contrary they do not believe he differs in form from the rest of the gods...' Those Egyptians who are Mendesians consider Pan to be one of the eight gods who existed before the twelve and Pan is represented in Egypt by painters and sculptors just as he is in Greece, with the face and legs of a goat. We can read this as meaning the ancients had two modes of representing Pan, the original and the form now known to all. The former was perhaps where the artists sought to soften the idea of the god of shepherds. Some early representations of Pan were of a young man hardened by the toil of country life. There are short small horns on the forehead to characterize him and often the short goat's tail. He bears a crook and his syrinx. Sometimes he is naked, at other times he his clad in the light cloak called a chlamys. *Chlamys*= a broad woollen upper garment worn in Greece, sometimes purple, and inwrought with gold; a Grecian military cloak; a state mantle. It consisted of an oblong piece of woollen cloth thrown over the left shoulder, the open ends being fastened with clasps on the right shoulder. The chlamys was worn by the ephiboi or by military officers and it was commonly used for travelling or hunting.

Other examples seem to suggest the original form of Pan may not be that of an animal. This may suggest that the divine power of procreative nature had become grossly anthropomorphized. Pan, according to the Egyptians, was one of the eight gods who ranked before the other twelve gods, whom the Romans called *Consentes*. This could make him older than the twelve gods compared with whom he is now termed semones - or inferior and lesser in rank, though higher than the human race among which he lived.

More attention should be given to this land when thinking of Pan. We should not isolate him completely in Greece. It is true Greece has done more for him than Egypt that we know of, but keep the connection with Egypt in mind when dealing with Pan. The fact that the Greeks could associate some gods of Egypt with him may point to the fact that a prototype of some kind already existed there.

Consentes is the name the Romans gave to the twelve superior gods or Dii Consentes (*Dii majorum gentium*). The word *consentes* signifies - the name given to those who consented to the deliberations of Jupiter's council - *consentiens*= 'agreeing, according, harmonious.' They are twelve in number and their names are briefly given by **Ennius**, who put them into two hexameter lines, quoted under the name of *consentes* by **Varro**:

Juno, Vesta, Minerva, Ceres, Diana, Venus, Mars, Mercurius, Jove, Neptune, Vulcanus, Apollo.

Pan seems to have spent part of his day in comparative idleness, playing his pipes. It is said 'he delights in high-pitched' songs. He expended much energy in his favourite pastime of waylaying or deceiving the neighbourhood nymphs, with varying degrees of success. Pan's activity in this area is over stressed at times; it is not as great or as successful as people think. There seems to have been much effort with variable or poor results. It is the method of his detractors to present Pan solely as a lecherous deity whose thoughts did not rise much, if at all, above his waist. This may have appealed to Early Christianity which seemed to suppress anything that was natural as unnatural and to castigate Pan in particular.

Pan's sexual exploits are a frequently recorded activity. They seem to have occupied the time of the writers in the past, as now, more than they ever did him. These commentators at times gave the impression that Pan only functioned from the waist down. This could reflect their own thoughts and preoccupation rather than Pan's. It is true it was Pan's proud boast that he had coupled with all Bacchus' Maenads, but when listening to the boasting of the young bucks of today, are things any different? In this was Zeus any better? The main difference between Pan and Zeus, it would seem, is that when Zeus indulged himself in this sort of thing, and with Zeus it was tantamount to overindulgence, he was a 'gay Lothario.' When Pan had his little forays, which were small change by comparison, he was a lecherous little goat despite sex being one of his sacred and main functions on earth, with rituals performed to encourage him in this particular aspect. This thoroughly healthy aspect of his life has tended to overshadow his other commendable attributes and gifts, which are as boundless then as now. However, the old adage runs as true then as now. 'Give a dog a bad name and hang him' - yet history has more examples of the fidelity of dogs than people!

Lonely shepherds have undoubtedly practised two pursuits they share with Pan, masturbation (= *onanism*) and possibly bestiality. It is a frequent suggestion that Pan invented both. **Dio Chrysostomus** passes on the tradition that masturbation was taught to Pan by Hermes, his father. Astrologically, Mercury/Hermes has rule over the hands and its activities. Hermes watched his son wander day and night upon the mountain because of his love of Echo and, because Pan was unable to secure her, 'he had pity on his distress.' Let us examine the first of these pursuits and then the second.

As commentators point out, masturbation is often discovered spontaneously by animals, small infants and children in the normal evolution of growing up. Masturbation is, historically and anthropologically, a very widespread practice. It is a solitary sexual act and often it becomes a secret one later in life. Very few people after leaving childhood will admit to it. If it is carried into adulthood it seems to carry the stigma of being unclean or childlike, something that is not indulged in by mature and responsible folk, yet it can remain from infancy to senility, and in ancient time's, masturbation was regarded as a way of 'enacting Pan.'

It is well known that one of the methods used in Mediterranean countries to ward off the evil eye or 'overlooking' was manipulating the genitals or making sexual or genital signs. The panic caused by the evil eye was averted by propitiating the god who conceived the panic and masturbation - Pan. The form of sexuality that averts the fear and panic of Pan is not coitus, connection with another, but masturbation.

Even today in some areas around these shores, it is not advisable to stare fixedly at children for too long, nor touch them, particularly in rural areas if you do not know the parents well. Garlic in Greece protected against the evil eye. Gestures used by people, like 'horns' (= *mano cornuto*) or the 'fig' (=*fico*), both have a sexual or fertility connotation, and turn the evil eye from the maker of the sign. In ancient Greece and Italy, as with many other places since then, spitting was a powerful antidote. Averting the evil eye from a happy event which could be blighted by the envy of evil people is thought to be the origin of the bridal veil. **Aristotle** called the hand 'the tool of tools' and a powerful charm against all evil. The 'fig' is made by closing the hand lightly as if making a fist, and placing the thumb between the first and second fingers, making it protrude, the sexuality of this sign is obvious. To make the 'Devil's Horns' you bring the two centre fingers of the hand down to touch the thumb, this leaves the index and little finger raised like a pair of 'horns,' done well this makes an interesting shadow display.

Little wonder the church has been after Pan's blood all these years. In the past in the eyes of the people this act belonged to a god; therefore it had divine sanction, it was acceptable and a natural act. I have often wondered why the church put this sin at the feet of Onan and not Pan when they had evidence of his overt involvement with the act. Of course Onan was a man, while Pan is a god and this act mimicked the god and it was thought to be a way of summoning him. However, I do sometimes have sympathy with the Church because it has to deal with edicts set in place long ago and, even if it wants to, it seems unable to extricate itself from them. Sometimes you wonder if they were really set there by god in the first place, or put there by the zealots with their jaundiced outlook of life. I feel it is sometimes a case of what god sanctioned men punished.

In Judaeo-Christian culture, in which most of us in the West started our lives, masturbation is tantamount to a life and death issue. Look at the things the Catholic Church permits you to do in its latest list at the time of writing. For example, you can watch public hangings, take part in an insurrection and many other things, but the natural act of masturbation is still a cardinal sin. The act may relieve anxiety and at times even prove therapeutic, but it usually creates a far greater guilt to put in its place. It is attributed, with its strong religious overtones and stigma, in part to Onan. For Onan was struck dead by god for practising, it is thought, that which took his name, onanism (= *masturbation*). A rather drastic punishment for what is really a small and relatively harmless sin, and to call it an overreaction seems somewhat inadequate.

The matter is dealt with in Genesis 38:4-10. It tells of a Canaanite woman who bore three sons and she named the second son Onan. The elder brother Er, took a wife, but Er 'was wicked in the sight of the Lord, and the Lord slew him.' Onan's father told him to go and marry his brother's wife 'and raise up seed to thy brother.' Onan knew the 'seed' of sleeping with his brother's wife would not be his. When he went unto his brother's wife he spilled it upon the ground, because he did not want to give the seed to his brother. 'And the thing which he did displeased the Lord; wherefore he slew him also.' This seems to be a somewhat unlucky family.

The God of Israel regarded the matter as a sin 'against God' that warranted death, while with Pan it was regarded as 'enacting the god.' In some older dictionaries we have two definitions of the word. Onanism [From Onan (Gen.xxxviii.9), suffix-ism] Self-pollution (= a sin, Judaeo-Christian), masturbation (= a natural act, Pagan). Naturally the parentheses are mine. It is just as well the 'One God' desisted from his anger regarding this matter. Nonetheless, it would have solved the population explosion long ago because the population explosion simply would not have happened, not with people dropping dead like flies in the winter everywhere! It is a fact that when the writer is presented with a revised or a new dictionary of the English language, masturbation is one of the first words checked. This word tells me if the revision claimed has been undertaken or if large sections have been copied (without much checking) from an earlier, Bowdlerised edition, where masturbation is regarded as 'self-abuse.'

When the proofs were read by the dedicatee she suggested there might be another interpretation of this occurrence regarding Onan, with which I agreed. We pass the results of the discussion to the reader for consideration. She thought the event could have been misinterpreted or there could be another interpretation for the following reasons.

Onan was commanded by his father to sleep with and marry his late brother's wife. His father wanted him to 'raise seed to thy brother.' Onan was expected to step into the shoes of a dead man as a surrogate father and this was not uncommon at the time. Although married to her, he would not have the children in his own right let alone marry the woman of his choice. He knew 'that the seed would not be his.' It was intended that he should provide children for his dead brother and this statement shows he must have felt great alienation regarding what he was being asked to do. When he did go 'unto his brother's wife' we cannot believe he went there to masturbate in front of her. He obeyed his father, but we believe the resentment of what he was being made to do was so great he withdrew before impregnation took place. Onan did not give his seed to the woman because he 'spilled it upon the ground.'

Coitus interruptus rather than masturbation? We do not feel we can use the word onanism as in the past for the sake of euphemism. Now we entertain doubts regarding the safety of the word in the context of its usual interpretation. Neither can we understand why it moved God to such serious retribution, unless Onan was thought to be disobeying God's decree to 'go forth and multiply.' The Jerusalem Bible tells: us that what he did was offensive to Yahwah. Onan had failed in his duty to family and nation by putting his own considerations first, but this still seems somewhat drastic.

The second pursuit said to have been entertained by Pan was that of bestiality. This may have been more a *natural instinct* than a *perversion*. Pan was the divine fertilizer of the flocks - *the Lusty One*. Fertilization of the flocks was a matter of great concern to the people of the day. It was equally of concern that Pan performed this divine function, indeed it was encouraged and solicited. We must remember that some legends regarding the origins of Pan say he sprang from a goat (= animal) and a goatherd (= human). This legend was current for both Silvanus and Pan. **Probus**, writing on **Virgil**, tells us that the shepherd Crathis fathered the goat-shaped Silvanus from a goat, while **Aelian** gives the same origins for Pan's birth. Pan was 'the divine fertilizer of the flocks,' not only was this function natural to him, it was required and sought from him. This appears to make the charge of bestiality somewhat superfluous.

We still use the term 'animal' today regarding those people who have a sex life of which we do not approve. Many regard the so-called animal appetites as a part of human nature that should be subdued and controlled at all costs. It is strange that anything of which humanity disapproves is nearly always relegated to the animal kingdom. The natural kingdom condemned by the 'higher' human kingdom that sometimes 'acts completely out of character' from what is expected of it, in other words, unnaturally. As if that gets rid of the matter, by saying that is where it belongs so it can't possibly have anything to do with us. After all, we have long evolved from that 'lower state.' If you believe that - you can knit fog.

Pan is the 'fertilizer of goats and flocks' in his animal half, highly erotic and wild at times in his human half. There is little doubt his animal half influenced the human half. It must have been a strong power to contest against and, given the sexual potency of the goat, perhaps impossible. Perhaps this is why he did not appear to have too much success in this sphere of human activity. Affectionate people still call their children 'kids' though I am sure this will be thought derogatory today and frowned upon, especially by those who have nothing better to do with their time than trying to mould the world in their own image. For obvious reasons it is not disliked by the writer, nor his mother, who called him just that - 'our kid!'

In closing this section I must, however, cite a recent court case in which a farm labourer has been prosecuted, being observed having sex with a pig on the farm where he worked. There are also the highly distressing incidents of late regarding horses that have brought me almost to the brink of despair regarding God's presumed finest creation. These items are mentioned to suggest that we do not get on our moral high-horse because we feel secure in the belief the intervening centuries have distanced us from these obviously quite primitive savage people and their gods. Neither are they included to defend the past from the present; it is simply a statement of recorded fact. In the former incident the man was rightly prosecuted and I personally feel the greater sympathy for the pig. Such reports make me wonder if we have the right to throw stones, particularly as so many glass houses are being built today for future history to judge.

There is a ceremony that seems, on the surface, rather disrespectful towards Pan: no god could be treated this way unless it was an accepted ritual having a valid purpose. Pan did not, in keeping with other gods, always receive what I deem the best of treatment from his worshippers, as we can gather from Theocritus:

> And if thou do so, Pan beloved, may ne'er
> The Arcadian boys thy shoulders and thy sides
> Pelt with their squills when little meat is had;
> Seize thee when all thy skin is torn with nails,
> And in hot nettles may thou lie to rest.

Theocritus tells us this was the Arcadians' way of treating Pan when they returned from unsuccessful hunting. Nettles were sometimes used by shepherds on the udders of goats when they would not mate and refused to accept the male. The Samoyeds of Russia meted out similar treatment to their gods. They would smear their gods with fat when the hunt was successful and pelt it with dung when it was not. I think the Samoyeds must have had very understanding gods. I would not like to incur Pan's wrath, nor by disrespect would I want to, but things are not as they appear with Pan.

The abundance or scarcity of meat, whether from hunting or the domestic herds, involved Pan and his blessing of fertility. Hunters returning from the hunt would give honour to Pan when the catch was good. When the catch was poor, they would scourge a statue of Pan with squills, a ritual act performed by most of the hunters. In Arcadia it is thought the scourging of Pan's statue was enacted to rouse Pan into productiveness as a fertilizing power, on which the well-being of the Arcadian populace depended. The ritual of the squill was performed to induce Pan to grant his blessings of increased flocks, game and hunting and prevent the decrease in livestock. It was a ritual of stimulation because it was not done to chastise the god. With some examples of Pan's anger, I for one would not have taken the chance.

The ritual of the squills was performed to drive away scarcity and famine, for Pan is both hunter and shepherd. The fertility of wild animals and the domestic flock was the province of the goat-footed god. The landscape in which the huntsmen plied their skills was his: the mountains, hills, plains, rivers and marshes. Apart from the nymphs and maenads the territory of Pan, for both hunter and shepherd, was almost exclusively male. He has the epithet *Pan Aktios*= 'of or inhabiting a seashore.' He is the god of river banks and the ocean promontories where the goats went to get salt and fresh water. Thus, he was also given the deference and sacrifice of the fishermen. **Pindar** mentions Pan as the god of fishermen.

Squills contain an irritant poison and were used as a purge and diuretic before taking part in a ritual act. Thus the squill came to symbolise the removal of evil influences: a catharsis. In a different ceremony to that of Pan, the pharmakos, when ritually struck with squills, became a benevolent power due to the purging. *Pharmakos*= one who is sacrificed as a purification for others, a scapegoat. Though Pan is struck with squills he is not to be equated directly with the *pharmakos*, who was human, not divine. There is a similarity in the intent that was to avert a catastrophe, or danger in some form, from the populace. Regarding Pan, the ritual was to prevent infertility in animals and give protection from famine that, in an agricultural community, could have had the most dire consequences.

It was not performed as disrespect to the god or as a punishment in any way. I have always seen it was similar to the way a kitten kneads its mother's stomach to induce the flow of milk; sharp squills and sharp claws bear a resemblance and produce similar results -sustenance. Similarly in the mythology of the vampire, sharp stakes keep away evil which threatens life. Even an adult cat will knead you with its claws when it's lying on your stomach and you're half asleep: it is inborn and triggered by comfort and the desire to feed. The ritual was enacted for stimulation, purification and the exorcism of evil influences. Pan is a high god and not a human being, despite his human half, which makes some consider him otherwise. The pharmakos is a human being and he was often a worthless criminal. We are told 'that worthless fellows were reserved for this fate, an arrant rascal, a polluted wretch,' or in the Latin, *homo* (= a human being, a man) *nullus* (= of no account or moment, insignificant, trifling).

The pharmakos was either slain or he was burdened with the sins of the people upon his shoulders or he was driven from the land. We have comparable ceremonies in Europe. Our pharmakos could be said to be equivalent to the Green George or similar figures. In some areas these figures were often subjected to various indignities, which included beating and ducking in rivers, ponds or lakes to induce the fertile rain. After the person representing the Green George had left the effigy, it was sometimes ritually burnt.

The pharmakos of the West is found in the Bible, as the Scapegoat, the goat in Leviticus, selected by lot to be taken into the wilderness on the Day of Atonement. To cover the subject of propitiation (= *ilaumos*) reconciliation or atonement (= *katallage*) and (sometimes) cleansing (= *kaphariosmos*), with all the terms connected with it, would require a separate treatise, not a few paragraphs. However, a few paragraphs are all we have so we must do the best we can.

We have *Ilaumos*= 'to appease, propitiate, reconcile to oneself or the gods.' *Katallage*= 'exchange, profit made from exchange, a change from enmity to friendship.' *Kaphariosmos*= 'cleansing, purification.' Two goats were brought to the tabernacle on the Day of Atonement and the high priest cast lots, for one goat was 'for the Lord' and the other 'was for Azazel.'

In the Book of Enoch, Azazel is conceived as being chained in the wilderness into which the scapegoat was led. The Jerusalem Targum on Leviticus says that 'the goat was sent to die in a hard and rough place in the wilderness of jagged rocks,' known as *Beth Chaduda.*

The goat on which the first lot was drawn was sacrificed and the other became the scapegoat. The high priest, by confession, transferred his own sins and the sins of the people to the goat which was then taken out into the wilderness. We have three suggestions as to what happened next.

In one we find that the scapegoat was taken into the wilderness and set free according to the Scriptures - 'and to let him go into the wilderness' Lev.16:10. The goat was, in reality, the 'escape goat' or 'scapegoat perhaps, with the comma being dropped. In later times the goat was thought to be slain by throwing it over a cliff. This was the fate of the Greek scapegoat who was often a volunteer. He was bedecked with flowers, led around the city, taken outside the walls and stoned to death.

The third suggestion implies the Greek and Latin for *Azazel* was

Azazel, with the Scapegoat.

wrongly interpreted as 'the scapegoat' when it was in fact a demon, a satyr who lived out in the desert. Of course the word satyr is already mentioned in the Bible, as will be shown in the next chapter. In the Feast of the Atonement it is the satyr who is sent the goat with the sins of Israel on its head. Some writers point out that in 1530 the word scapegoat was employed by **Tyndale** as a translation of the Hebrew word Azazel. In the Vulgate this is translated as *caper emissarius*: *caper=* 'he-goat, goat' and *emissarius=* 'scout, emissary, spy.' I find the latter somewhat interesting, seeing that the caper emissarius was being sent out to a goat-like satyr in the desert with the sins of a nation on its head. This would in effect mean the satyr was receiving the goat emissary from the High Priest of Israel and, with that combination, the possibilities could be endless.

The Vine and the Goat

What though thou crop my branches to the root,
Yet will I bear one cluster more of fruit;
One cluster more, that shall for wine suffice
To make libation at thy sacrifice.
Evenus: 1st century A.D.

The ancient conception of the scapegoat is somewhat like the sin-eater, someone who takes upon themselves the sins of the dead by eating some bread or something else that has been placed on the breast of the dead, with some money being passed across the corpse. In the Scottish Isles the sin-eater was always a stranger to the dead person, often a passer-by. This was to prevent anyone with a grudge against the dead from taking their sins and flinging them into the sea, whence they could arise as demons to torment the poor soul. There must have a recognized method for doing this as it was greatly feared, but how it was done is not given that I can find, it is only written about.

Tramps were sometimes given a 'free meal' not knowing the burden that had been placed on their shoulders for 'they took upon themselves all the Sinnes of the Defunct, and freed them from walking after they were dead.' Wayfarers would oft be circumspect of a house where a death had recently taken place, nor accept a solitary meal in a house where there was an unburied body. The funeral feast was quite safe, 'as all present partake of the same food.' One scapegoat was of course the Christ, who took the sins of the world on his shoulders before death.

The idea of the scapegoat once survived in many European seasonal festivals, especially in Germany. At Easter or Whitsuntide a man or a woman was dressed up to represent Winter or Death. After a day of carnival they were chased from the village or district and then they were burnt in effigy, so people even 'chased out Death.' The theology of the sea had its scapegoat like that of the land. In classical times a young man was thrown into the sea with the prayer 'Be thou our offscouring'; a ceremony by which the people were supposed to rid themselves of the evils by which they were beset, not unlike Jonah in the Bible. Within living memory Orkney and Shetland fishermen hesitated before they rescued a comrade who had fallen overboard. The sea god had claimed his victim and they thought it might go ill with them if they interfered, for to rescue the victim could cause another to be taken in his stead. Such beliefs were obviously not confined only to these islands.

It must be stressed again that Pan is not solely a lecherous god, and though such an opinion may have suited the church, it is not accepted by all. Pan is a release from all that is unnatural and imposed restraints. I do not regard behaving with civilized moderation a restraint, but merely acting decently; you can act decently even when you are wrong. He has connection with the sign of the zodiac Capricorn and this is ruled by Saturn(us). The great feast of Saturnus was the Saturnalia when these restraints were abolished or overturned for a time and the normal behaviour expected throughout the year was abandoned. Greater detail regarding this feast will be found in the next chapter in the section on the deity Saturnus.

The Early Church Fathers, it has to be admitted, were a rather joyless lot, thinking that the flesh could be mortified and broken until it can no longer respond to the call of Pan. If the spirit was broken in the process so much the better, it was for the greater good of the sufferer. I find it strange that these people would lovingly train a thoroughbred horse while taking great care not to break its spirit, for to do that would be treating the prize horse, in effect, as if it were an animal.

An early rule of thumb for the congregation seems simple, though as history shows it did not always apply to the members of the ruling body. If the congregation or adherents of the faith enjoy it, ban it! Little wonder Pan was so loved by the Victorians, with the freedom he offered from restraint, at least in private if not public. Pan is equally the favourite Greek figure of poets. Those people who like compiling statistics tell us that Pan, in literature, outnumbers the other worthies of the Greek and Roman pantheon by some two to one. I take my cue from the writers of the past who tell us that the literature and art of the nineteenth century was particularly devoted to Pan. It bears repeating that at his birth he was rejected by the human elements who fled and deserted him. The babe was then wrapped in a warm animal skins by Hermes and taken to the High Gods of Olympus. When Pan was thrust into the physical world, his first warmth was an animal skin, not human warmth. The first love and kindness he received was from the high gods, so it is little wonder he views human contact askance and with distrust at times. The Olympian Gods delighted in him and accepted him with joy, no more so than by Bacchus. These great gods were the All - or Pan.

Of course the Goat-God Pan was not averse to the pleasures of sex. However, anyone who thinks sex is the sum total of Pan has missed the point, if they ever had it to miss first. They are more likely to be confusing their own aims and thoughts with his. Hermes asks his son, in one of **Lucian's** dialogues, if he is married yet. Pan tells him he is not because 'I belong to Eros' and he tells his father he could not 'be bound to one woman.' Yet Pan did have many associations with the opposite sex. Women who had been acquainted with many men in succession were known as 'Pan girls.'

Pan's exploits with his own sex are well known enough and male homosexual practices were said 'to honour Pan.' Some art displays, in particular those on kraters. give obvious examples of his exploits and forays with his own sex. *Krater*= 'a mixing vessel, a bowl, in which the wine was mixed with water from which the cups were filled.' Let us summarise his amours, some of which have already been mentioned. He captivated the goddess of the moon, Selene, under the form of a white ram. He was fortunate with the nymph Echo by whom he had a daughter Iambe. With another of the nymphs, perhaps the most famous as the affair produced the Pan or Pastoral pipes, he was not so lucky: of course this was Syrinx. Another was the nymph Pitys who was also beloved of Boreas; from her death Pan took the fir tree as his special plant. There is also his son Crotus by Eupheme, the nurse of the Muses. While roaming in his forests he fell in love with Echo, with whom he became the father of Iynx.

Some say Iynx was Peitho - 'the personification of persuasion.' This name also appears as a epithet of other divinities, such as Aphrodite in whose train she would appear. At Athens statues of Peitho and Aphrodite Pandemos sometimes stood close together, and a statue of Peitho stood in the temple of Aphrodite at Megara. It is thought the two divinities must be perceived as closely connected or that one, perhaps, is an attribute of the other. After all, who knows what love (=Aphrodite) will yield, when coaxed with gentle and eloquent persuasion (= Peitho)?

Iynx attempted to charm Zeus to make him fall in love with her, or she used her magical means to try to make Zeus fall in love with Io. Some commentators say Pan's daughter Iynx was a witch. This did not escape the eye of Hera (very little did), who metamorphosed her into a bird called the Iynx or Wryneck. Alternatively, Iynx and her sisters entered a music contest with the Muses and, for their presumption, arrived at the same result. This bird is the symbol of passionate and restive love. Aphrodite gave one to Jason who by turning it around and pronouncing certain magical words given to him, excited the love of Medea, a famous mythical sorceress. That Jason 'turned it around' seems to suggest this was a magical charm involving a wheel.

The Iynx or Wryneck (= *Iynx torquilla*) is a small bird that is a regular summer visitant to Northern Europe and Britain, so something connected with Pan gets here. It generally arrives before the cuckoo and in England it is known as the cuckoo's leader or the cuckoo's mate. Its general colouration resembles the nightjar which, like the owl, is considered a bird of ill omen because of their nocturnal habits and strange cry. In England the nightjar is called the Lychfowl, Corpsefowl, Fern-owl, etc. Its Latin name is *caprimulgus europepaeus*= 'a milker of goats, a goatherd or some such sorry fellow, a bird like Gull that in the night it sucketh goats, and mortifieth their Udder. An unlucky Bird, a Scritchowl.' (1693) This is an ancient and widespread belief regarding the goatsucker or goat-owl that existed in the time of Aristotle. The belief is that by sucking the goat's udder it made the goats go blind.

Among the Greeks the Iynx had importance in ritual as well as mythology. The wryneck is one of Aphrodite's attributes as well as Pan's. It is claimed Aphrodite created a love charm for Jason, by fastening a wryneck to a four-spoked wheel. The association of the wryneck with the wheel may have come from the circular motion of its neck and its arrival from abroad when the sun was rising higher in the heavens. The circular motion and the rising sun were thought to have magical import. The wheel has always had magical significance, representing as it does the path of the sun, moon and stars. From these ideas the bird became involved with more intricate ideas, of the sun and moon, of fire and fecundity, witchcraft and love, the gods and goddesses. Adonis is represented on a Greek vase holding out a wryneck to Aphrodite while on another vase Cupid revolves a wheel in front of Adonis, while a female figure holds a wryneck.

This form of love charm was pulled by a cord and, it was claimed, the spinning and whistling of the wheel was an infallible charm to draw the beloved to you. They are also described as oracular Wheels of Fortune operated by a rope according to **Robert Graves** in the **White Goddess,** called *iynges* - lit. *wrynecks.* He tells us one decorated the temple of Apollo and they were used by the Babylonians, Egyptians and the Druids.

One famous Druid of Kerry - Mogh Ruith - received his name *Magus Rotarum* ('the wizard of the wheels') from the wheels he used in his magical judgements.

The wryneck has the habit of feigning death when taken or when found on its nest. The name wryneck is derived from the bird's habit of writhing its head in various directions with a serpentine motion. When the wryneck senses danger the body is kept still while the neck lengthens, which it twists slowly in the manner of a snake. The head feathers stand erect and it half closes its eyes and this feigning usually has the desired effect on both man and beast.

Aristotle describes the bird and old writers say it had a cry that they compared to a traverse flute - *the plagiaulos=* 'the cross flute, German flute'; *plagios=* 'placed sideways, slanting.' Tradition has it this instrument was invented by Pan, though its invention is given to others also. A late fifth century gem in the Ashmolean Museum in Oxford shows Pan with a bird on his right arm that it would appear he is feeding. It has a very long neck so it is not unreasonable to assume it is a Iynx or Wryneck, one of Pan's symbols. A quotation from the **St. James's Gazette** of the 9th March 1887 may be of interest.

That curious bird the wryneck, so dear to the classical scholar from its associations with witchcraft in Theocritus and Virgil, is the first to arrive; and certainly the weird manner in which its head seems to turn every way, as if on a pivot, while mouselike it crawls up and round an old well, goes far to account for its reputation as an uncanny bird.'

Aphrodite Pandemos or Aphrodite Epitragia was often shown astride a goat as a symbol of wantonness. *Epitragia=* 'on the goat.' *Pandemos=* 'common to the people.' Pandemos describes Aphrodite as the goddess of low sensual pleasures - Venus *vulgivaga* or *popularis*. This epithet was exactly the opposite of her name as Venus (Aphrodite) *Urania* - the heavenly Aphrodite. Aphrodite Pandemos is represented in Elis, a nome of the Peloponnese adjoining Arcadia, riding on a ram. The worship of Aphrodite Pandemos was practised in Megalopolis in Arcadia, where a festival in her honour was held, the sacrifice being white goats. Pandemos also occurs as a epithet of Eros.

Let us look at Pan's other daughter. Iambe is a Thracian maid who met the goddess Demeter when she was drowning in her grief for the loss of her daughter Persephone. When Demeter entered the house of Celeus at Eleusis, it was the jests of Iambe that forced her to smile and laugh and restored her appetite. Epic poetry awakens admiration for heroes while

Iambic poetry is in direct contrast. The latter form uses irony, sarcasm and satire to hold up the faults and weakness of human nature to scrutiny, mockery, and even contempt.

This form of poetry confined itself to the simple, unadorned language of every day and made use of the pliant iambic metre that lent itself readily to such language. From the middle of the first century onwards lampoons in Iambic verse became common with the Romans. It was a popular poetic form to clothe the raillery that was a part of the rustic feasts of Demeter. The custom, style and application of the word iambus to verses of this kind, is traced to Iambe.

It was the redeeming laughter of Iambe that ended Demeter's mourning and made her responsive again to life, as laughter does for us all. I have also read that it was Pan who made her laugh. However, with the Iambic poetry and the *pannuchis* used in the Eleusinian mysteries of Demeter who initiated the mysteries personally, I think Iambe may have the better case than her father. *Pannuchis*= the rude language commemorating Iambe's rustic humour that made Demeter laugh, and used in the Eleusinia and Thesmophoria, sacred to Demeter. A more detailed explanation is given later when these festivals are discussed.

The testimony of **Pindar** and **Aeschylos**, initiated in the rites, say they were intended to animate profound feelings of piety and the cheerful hope of a better life in future. This is exactly the service given by Iambe to Demeter in her deepest grief, when all hope appeared to have vanished. Of course, with Iambe being Pan's daughter, it is still in the family.

The mistress Metaneira offers the goddess her own seat which she declines, but she accepts the one prepared by Iambe. She declines the wine offered by Metaneira but is persuaded by Iambe to take the restoring kukeon. *Kukeon*= 'a mixture, a mixed drink, a refreshing draught, usually compounded of barley meal, grated cheese and wine.' The kukeon given to Demeter by Iambe is usually said to consist of flour and water. Some even think this drink was devised by Iambe. The goddess Demeter undertakes the position of nurse to the queen's children in the royal palace, where she will nurse Demophoon.

In the above legend some say it was Pan who found Demeter outside the Phigalian cave were she had taken refuge in her grief and he told the gods where she was. Demeter went into mourning for her lost daughter in Pan's wild and natural country. She did not go to her ornate temples. When she decided in her grief she would no longer co-operate with the earth regarding fertility she found a deep, dark cave in Pan's territory. It was an uncultivated, wild and natural land that had never known the ploughshare. This was virgin land that had, unlike her, never produced a cultivated crop. She had been 'ploughed' and was no longer 'uncultivated' land. She had reaped the harvest of the 'ploughing' in her daughter. Now that 'harvest' was gone and it had been gathered and taken away by another, yet unknown. She returned to a natural, wild state and, like the land of the Goat-God, she did not want to be touched, cultivated or even render any produce.

I have long been of the opinion, although my thoughts on the matter are not complete yet, that Pan may be responsible for, or is likely to have some connection with depression and melancholia. This is something that I feel is shown with Demeter, so let us start collating those facts that have suggested this conclusion. Starting with astrology, we have Pan connected with the *Aegipan* or Capricorn. This is a sign that is ruled by Saturn, who as Cronos is the oldest suggested sire of Pan. Cronos and Saturn are often associated by the Greeks, and although their attributes differ in some aspects, they are both very ancient gods. An attribute of this planet and sign is depression, despair and melancholia.

Saturn often denotes pessimism and defeat when the burden of responsibility or loss becomes greater than a person can bear. This is very much the situation of Demeter: she cannot find her daughter and all her searching is in vain, so her existence seems pointless. It is to Pan's land she goes in this state. She had civilized, cultured temples and buildings to which she could withdraw but there would be in contact with people, including the gods, and they would know where she was. She chooses the wild uncultivated caves ruled by Aegipan the Goat and the lonely, wild mountains of the solitary climber. She goes to a place that is between, a place apart which is neither one thing nor the other. Somewhere that gives her a sense of not belonging with no feelings of obligation. Somewhere which has the minimum of comfort, people or possessions to hold her there.

Dressed in black that is a colour of Saturn, she is spotted by Pan, the Goat-god who tells the gods where she can be found. Someone who is in the grip of depression withdraws and does not encourage contact with others so it is to Pan's surroundings she goes to experience her sorrow and loss. Eventually when she decides to accept the children of the queen to her care as their nurse, she encounters Iambe who is the child of Aegipan and fully conversant with her father's nature. It is understanding, down-to-earth Iambe who uses laughter because it is one of the things Pan loves. It is recorded that it is 'Iambe's redeeming laughter' which brings her out of her melancholy. Pan says he likes the sound of laughter when being honoured. Further, laughter is one of the elements of his ritual and 'one of the gifts proper to bring to Pan.'

Until I took up the study of Pan one astrological rulership of Capricorn used to puzzle me. Why did this sign and its ruler have under its sway clowns of all things? It seemed to be an odd connection. I know people have always said that 'comedy is a very serious art' and I agree with that. It is a fact that if you can get a native of Capricorn to laugh, they stop taking themselves so seriously and start pulling themselves out of their depression. Laughter is probably the greatest healing force for good, immaterial of what sign you are born under. However, despite a keen sense of humour Capricorn is less prone to use it than others. I have had plenty of experience with my teacher, Madeline Montalban, who was born under the Sign of the Goat. We both withdrew and went into our caves now and then, though not a native of Capricorn, I have a very powerful Saturn influencing my life and its affairs. When she 'went into her cave,' I would get a telephone call saying 'Leo, come and get me out.' I was one of the few in the School who would 'go in' after her, it all depended on how deep in she had gone. Being alike in many ways and with a similar sense of humour, not unlike Iambe's in some ways, sometimes we would both decide to stay in the 'cave' and 'let them all get on with it for a while.' Now I would give a nod to Iambe and remember her father, Pan.

Clowns switch character from pathos to laughter, from 'acting the giddy goat' to serious and gloomy, not unlike the highs and lows of *cyclothymia.* Briefly, cyclothymia is a personality characteristic typified by marked changes of mood. People under its control may change, for no obvious reason, from being 'high,' cheerful, energetic, productive and sociable, then down to a 'low' being gloomy, listless, unproductive and withdrawn. These swings of mood might last days, weeks or months. Cyclothymia resembles manic-depressive illness in some respects but the mood swings are much less severe and can be better handled, once they are recognized.

Iambe with her broad rustic humour broke the grip of melancholy and enabled Demeter to function again, although in a limited way. She encouraged her to take an interest in her surroundings and the care of others, especially the children. Demeter is the 'goddess of fair children.' For this service Iambe was honoured in the Sacred Mysteries held in the name of Demeter so that this precious gift and its use would never be forgotten.

These are some reasons that make me connect those moods, ranging from cyclothymia to manic depression, with Pan. I feel there is some connection. Even if he is not the direct cause, he accepts the results and seems to have a hand in the healing of it. Pan is a healing god and perhaps he has more to do with the results than the cause. It was to his country that Demeter fled for safety to mourn her great loss. There she obtained peace and gathered her thoughts, rested to regain her strength and obtained the assistance that eventually gave her relief.

Pan could be withdrawn, retiring and very testy if caught wrong-footed and at the wrong time: his wrath is recorded as terrible to behold. I would be the first to admit these thoughts are not complete yet, but they are sufficiently so for me to try to develop them by continuing the study.

When Demeter finds out where her daughter is, she delivers her terms to Zeus for her return. Only if Zeus agrees to them will she assist the renewal of the harvest so that the people of the earth may be saved from starvation. First she is relieved by Iambe so that she can function in a limited way, then she obtains justice or as much as she can obtain at the hands of Zeus. Justice is under the rulership of Aegipan or Capricornus as is limitation and the practical acceptance of what is offered. This is especially true when it is seen that more will be forthcoming in the future, so it is practical to make do with less at first. I am sure it was a native of Capricorn who said 'half a loaf is better than none!'

Pan joins with Gaia and Hermes Enagonios in two festivals of Attica that were sacred to Demeter: the *Eleusinia* and the *Thesmophoria*. The Eleusinia is a festival of the Mysteries. Originally they were only celebrated at Eleusis at Attica and given in honour of Demeter and Persephone. All the ancients who mention the Eleusinian mysteries are in universal agreement that they were the holiest and most venerated of all the Mysteries celebrated in Greece. The festival and the mysteries are the subject of many works available to the reader. In part of the Eleusinian mysteries the pilgrims arrive by torchlight, and they drink kukeon. The women leave the men to keep vigil under the aegis of the *dadouchos*= 'a torchbearer.' At the festival of Eleusinian Demeter the torch represents her searching for her daughter Persephone (or Ceres seeking Proserpina in the Latin version).

The *pannuchis* was the rude language commemorating the intervention of Iambe with her rustic humour. The Eleusinian myth tells us the pannuchis is a festival celebrating the effects of good humour and the healing effects of laughter. Laughter acts upon the divinity, keeps her present, well disposed and dissuades her from leaving and neglecting her functions. *Pannuchis*= 'a night festival, vigil, a watching, keeping awake all night.' Lat. *pervigilium*, 'especially, a religious watching, etc.'

The *Thesmophoria* is another great festival and mystery celebrated to honour Demeter as the foundress of agriculture and the civic rite of marriage. It was found in various parts of Greece. In Attica it was only celebrated by married women of genuine Attic birth and a blameless reputation, though sometimes the ceremonies were performed by maidens. The Attic Thesmophoria was held during Pyanepsion (October-November), from the ninth to the thirteenth. On the last day Demeter was invoked under the name of 'the goddess of fair children.' Now that Demeter has solved her main problems, made her peace with the gods and will give assistance to the earth once more, it is time to leave her and Iambe, and return to her father.

In the heat of the noonday Pan seeks a shady grove or grotto in which to sleep. Noon was generally regarded as a good time to be quiet and at this time no shepherd blew his pipe. If he was disturbed, it was his custom to frighten anyone who did so with a fearful shout from where he was sleeping. This 'fearful shout' made the hair bristle on the head, filled men with great fear or sent them horrible dreams and nightmares. A goatherd in **Theocritus** tells us,

It is not fit, shepherd, not fit at noon for us to play the syrinx. We fear Pan. His hunt is over now; he's tired and rests. Then he is touchy, and the bitter bile is sitting in his nose.'

The same goatherd advises us that to disturb Pan at this time is to flout divine law. Pan looks with favour upon those who sleep at noon and respect his slumber. At this time it was thought best not to engage in any activity or mystery connected with the god. Pan is the god of noise and movement. Noon is typically silent and motionless, it is a time when you and your shadow are one. When the sun is low, sometimes your shadow leads you, at other times it follows you; with the sun high over your head it is gathered around your feet, it goes with you - you and your shadow are one. It is the still point of the day. To wake him at this hour, when he should be asleep, would be to invite him to make a commotion. To rudely awaken him at noon can rouse him to his greatest anger and our greatest danger, for it is then he may possess or dispossess us of our wits.

In his anger Pan has been known to transform the protector of the flock, the shepherd, into his own worst enemy, the wolf. **Valerius Flaccus** tells us that the shepherds were careful not to offend or arouse the anger of Pan so he would spare their herds from madness. As the Corycian cave on Mount Parnassus is already dedicated to Pan, the nymph Corycia and the nymphs it is a secure place of refuge for the shepherds and their flocks.

Pan looks with favour upon those who respect his slumber. Simply put, do not attract his attention or disturb him at midday. In the dusk of the evening or when he returns from the chase, he sits at the mouth of his cave and surveys his kingdom, most of which is settling down for the night. Only the nocturnal creatures are beginning to stir.

He sits in front of his grotto and plays his plaintive tune on his pipes of the reeds of the river, the syrinx or Pan pipes. For the sake of completeness we mention that Marsyas is sometimes given as the inventor of the syrinx or flute, as is Hermes. However, another tale says Hermes picked up the syrinx where Pan had carelessly left it. Claiming it as his own he sold it to his brother Apollo. This is completely in keeping with Hermes or Mercury who gave birth to Autolycus who, in Greek mythology, is 'the prince of thieves.' In astrology Mercury rules the hands and a thief must have nimble hands to serve a nimble brain if he is to succeed in plying his craft of theft and outwitting others. Shakespeare, showing his grasp of astrological lore with his engaging rogue Autolycus, has him say: 'My father named me Autolycus; who, being, as I am, littered under Mercury, was likewise a snapper-up of unconsidered trifles.' Mercury picks up all kinds of information and chitchat, he has to be the first to know and the first to tell. He is not called the 'news-vendor' of the zodiac for nothing, so finding 'a herald' under the rule of the planet Mercury would be most appropriate.

Sometimes the syrinx is called *Pandean Pipes*. This may prove to be an early form of a compound wind instrument, possibly the precursor of the organ, the *fistula* of the Romans and probably the *ugab* of the Hebrews. Lat. *fistula* - 'a pipe, tube, a water pipe (usually the metal lead); a reed pipe, a shepherd's pipe, said to have been invented by Pan.' Daphnis was taught to play his pipes by Pan who also tutored the Phrygian flute player, Olympus. He formed his pipes from the reeds into which a nymph name Syrinx was changed while fleeing from his love along the banks of the river Ladon in Arcadia. She was the daughter of the god of the river Ladon.

He almost caught Syrinx and it was his intention to 'offer her violence.' At her request, she was transformed into the reeds that bear her name to the Greeks. Pan, not knowing which of the reeds was his love, cut or broke some in frustration, at the place where he saw her last. It is thought that with that sigh of frustration of love or lust the reeds made a gentle strain of music beneath his breath. He bound the graduated reeds with wax and made them into the instrument called the Syrinx or Pan pipes and in playing his pipes at least he possessed her symbolically.

The Greek syrinx is either made up of a row of parallel reeds of varying length, or sometimes all the same length, fastened with beeswax, and the whole was braced with metal or wood. Pitch was decided by plugs of beeswax or the segments of each reed were cut to length for the pitch of that note, to which fine tuning could be applied. Though beeswax binds the reeds the epithet *kerodetos* (= 'bound with horn') is applied to the syrinx by **Euripides.**

The sound of the syrinx is invariably described as a liquid sound by most writers of the time. Pindar compared the sound with liquid honey, saying that Pan 'sprinkles his own sort of honey.' The pastoral music is seductive and enthralling which comes from the divine lips of the musician of the gods. It can be shrill and disturbing when required for it is not only made for seduction and love.

Pan Pipes

Pan, my belov'd, sit near me; to the reeds
Grown musical, thy wreathed lips be set;
And hark, how Echo in the sunny meads
Remembers what thou wouldst not quite forget.

Cometas*: 10th century A.D.

Pan appears constantly in the grip of restlessness and when he is restless he communicates this to all, human and animal alike. Pan playing his syrinx to the flocks brought an abundance of thick white milk and the propitious birth of twins to the goats or the flocks. The blessing of twins in the flocks was always attributed to Pan. Blessings from Hermes were called *hermaion*= 'a gift of Hermes,' good luck, an unexpected find on the road, a windfall.

With his pipes Pan and the shepherds led their flocks first to the cool districts, the summer mountains, then down to the warm districts, the winter plains.

"This is the way", laughed the great god Pan
(Laughed while he sat by the river),
"The only way since the gods began
To make sweet music, they could succeed."
Then, dropping his mouth to a hole in the reed,
He blew in power by the river.

A Musical Instrument: E.B. Browning.

It could be of advantage to stay a little while longer with his instrument. Panpipes have a very widespread distribution throughout the world and are found wherever there are rural or pastoral communities. It is a simple instrument to make, well within the capabilities of most people even if unrefined in construction, and using the materials found to hand. My first panpipes were made from alder bound by a blue cord; they were crude, but they worked and were more in tune than I hoped for, primarily they were symbolic. The Panpipe is found in most areas of Asia and it has crossed the oceans to South America but for the most, it still takes its name from Pan and Syrinx. They can be found in China where they contain male and female tonal sequences. The Chinese developed instruments with twelve to sixteen reeds. Symbolically the Chinese linked them with Spring, bamboo, mountains and the East, the direction of light and the rising sun.

Male and female pipes are often found in Asia and South America and sometimes they were placed on the same instrument, as with placing two fans together, and played by one player. It was more usual, however, to have a set of two pipes, one male and one female, which divided the melody between them, each set of pipes possessing half the notes required to play the melody. To play the music required two players because, as already said, each player could only play half the melody on their instrument. In some areas the male pipes had five reeds with the female six. When the pipes were separate instruments they were often connected by a long cord and in many places they were considered to be 'man and wife.' Many panpipe players in South America preserved the segregation of the male and female instruments but how the notes were allotted as 'male' and 'female,' I do not know. In the case of the six-pipe female and five-pipe male it may be simply that the female takes the odd notes (1,3,5,7,9,11) and the male takes the even notes (2,4,6,8,10), this making up the eleven notes of the two pipes combined, but this is pure speculation. Panpipes were known in South America long before the Europeans came there, being common in Peru.

The undisputed masters of the Panpipes in Europe were considered to be the Rumanian Gypsies who achieved a exceptional virtuosity to almost orchestral standards. Sometimes the pipes were tuned by dropping peas into certain reeds to sharpen or flatten the note. In South America this was often achieved by using sand or water.

The panpipe was, in early days in England, the customary instrument for Punch and Judy shows, while in Italy the children made *fischietli*= 'whistles.' The panpipes and flutes had significance in love. The flute is a solitary instrument and has long been thought to have the power to attract certain animals and to represent some aspects of Nature. It has long been the chosen instrument of the shepherds and goatherds because of the power that could be exerted over the herds with its plaintive music. The flute is included with the panpipes because Pan is said to be the inventor of both. Greek *aulos*= pipe, Latin *tibia*= shin bone. The double flute was often found, especially in theatrical performances, funerals, sacrifices and festival processions. The two flutes were played simultaneously with either one or two mouthpieces. The right hand (= *tibia dextra*) played the bass flute and the left hand (= *tibia sinistra*) played the treble. This instrument had as many notes as the syrinx.

As well as the flute being used as an accompaniment to funerals and dancing, it was used for animals, the harvest and love dances. The fertility aspect may have come from the flute's use in love dances because its phallic form gave it procreative significance. Going back to the panpipes mentioned above which had the spread wings of the male and female grouping, these were thought to be the wings of the Phoenix with the connotations of resurrection. Authorities have noted the similarity of pitch, scales, and methods of binding and they have come to the conclusion that the American panpipes are taken from a general European or Asiatic ancestry.

Having touched upon South America concerning the panpipes, there is some interesting information in *The Lost Language of Symbolism* by **Harold Bayley**. He writes that Pan and his consort Maya were worshipped in Central America. When the Spaniards came to the town of Panuca or Panca, they found wonderful temples containing images of Pan. If this were true the people would have been thought of as Devil worshippers and treated accordingly by the ambassadors of his Catholic Majesty, as would both the buildings and any images. He says this information is from **Brasseur's** introduction to **Landa's** *Relacion*, a work I do not know. He says that the words 'Pan' and 'Maya' have entered the Mayan vocabulary. 'Maia being the same as Maya, the name of the peninsular.'

He further tells us that 'Pan combined with Maya forms the name of the ancient capital Mayapan.' This work is in print for those who would like to check the details and it does have many other interesting aspects, although he does write that the Chinese 'for mountain or hill is 'pan' when actually it is 'shan,' I cannot find 'pan.'

As written earlier, Pan's liaison with the nymph Echo gave him Iynx. It was Echo who prevented Hera from surprising her husband while he dallied with the nymphs for company. This she did by continually chattering to her. Hera became wise to this ploy and punished Echo by making it impossible for her to speak first or to be silent when anyone else was speaking. Echo came to an unlucky end because of her love of Narcissus and pined away through unrequited love until only her voice was left. In Greece there were certain porticoes called *Porticoes of Echo* because of the echo that was heard there. There was one stoa at Hermione with a threefold echo and one at Olympia with a sevenfold echo, **Pausanias** tells us.

In part of the ritual to Pan we have the clapping of hands - *krotus* - and this was done to give him honour. Therefore, it is no surprise to find Pan being called *philokrotos*= 'loving noise or din' and *polykrotos*= 'ringing loud or clearly' in **Homer**. The nurse of the Muses, Eupheme, bore Pan a son called Crotus. The Muses protected his infancy. Like his father he spent all his life in the labours of the chase and paying due honour to his patrons. At the request of his mother and the Muses, Zeus placed Crotus in the stars. He became the 'bowman of the zodiac,' known as Sagittarius, because he had been a skilled archer. His sign of Sagittarius is naturally next to the one associated with his father Pan, Capricorn, which is in the highest position in the natural chart.

Pan had greater success with the nymph Pitys, who preferred him to her former suitor Boreas, the bitter North Wind. The anger of Boreas at her rejection of him was so great that he cast the nymph against the rocks and crushed her limbs. In pity Gaia transformed her into a fir tree, so Pan took a branch of the pine as a garland to adorn his head and those who serve or invoke him should do likewise: not necessarily a garland on the head, but they at least to hold, have or wear a sprig of fir.

He had greater success with the seduction of Selene, the moon goddess. Pan disguised himself and his dark fur as a dazzling white ewe by throwing a skin around him, or he took the form of a white ram and drew her into the depths of a wood in Arcadia. It is said he persuaded her to ride on his back and seduced her. Pan or Faunus, with whom the Romans identified Pan, also paid his addresses to Omphale the queen of Lydia. See the next chapter for the well known story of how Pan (or Faunus) was received by the one he thought was Omphale.

We have already mentioned the sudden terror - panic - which attacks the wanderer without reasonable cause, especially in the solitude of forest and mountain, attributed to Pan. Panic brings disorder, when people are in the grip of imagination, but there is a stress on without reasonable cause: they are usually groundless fears. What has no cause is ascribed to Pan. As said earlier, when you say 'I don't know what came over me,' Pan 'came over you.' Let me reiterate: do not think this gives you a convenient scapegoat for your life and the actions you take. Pan has been bearing that burden for far too many centuries. It bears repetition and I make no apologies for doing so: *you are, have been and always will be, responsible for your life and the actions you take.* How you use Pan is your responsibility, not his. What he gives is natural, very much as breathing, eating and drinking. However, what you choose to breathe, eat and drink is your responsibility, not his.

It is said that Pan had a magnificent voice and it was his sudden shout, in the long war between the gods and the Titans, which finally caused the precipitous retreat of the Titans. We have already mentioned the battle of Marathon. The panic of Pan can also be experienced by whole armies, as it was with the Gauls under Brennus, whose army fell into Pan's confusion at Delphi after their defeat there. **Pausanias** tells us they rested where darkness overtook them and during the night they were seized by panic and terror. Imagination is at its most vivid when we are connected to it instinctively.

The first disturbance came at dusk and at first it affected only a few. These were driven out of their minds because they thought they heard the onset of an enemy attack. They heard the hooves of the horses coming toward them. It did not take long for this panic to sweep through the entire camp. They took up their arms and, not recognising their own language, the features of their companions or the shape of their shields, they slew each other. They were so out of their minds that everyone thought the others were Greek. Not only did they seem to be speaking Greek but appeared to be in Greek armour. This was a mutual and bloody massacre on a vast scale.

It seems that Pan invented panic as a weapon while in the army of Dionysus in India. It is not to be regarded though as only a trick of the god, which would be patently foolish. I am sure Pan had the power of trickery in his armoury: if I have it in mine why not him? Pan had the power to instil fear and panic in a person or people. Sometimes one of the signs he has entered your affairs is that you are coping with the unexpected or some disorder, all emanating from an unknown and unseen source. Pan is the unknown something that interferes with the normal running of things. He is an unseen presence perhaps, but one that is strongly felt nonetheless. Often Pan is felt more than seen, although he does appear when the need or love is great.

At the defeat and capture of Zeus that spread dismay among the gods, Pan and Hermes went in secret to the cave where Zeus was a helpless prisoner. Pan gave another shout that frightened and panicked the monster Delphyne guarding Zeus, who had been disabled by Typhon, so Hermes could free him.

Pan taught the art of prophecy to Apollo though it is more accurately said that Apollo wheedled the art of prophecy out of Pan. When Apollo finally took over the oracles the nymph Erato remained

Pan's prophetess and did not pass into the service of Apollo.

His epithet 'the physician of the gods' also passed to Apollo and his son Asclepius. **Horace** wrote of the protection and blessing the gods had afforded him and the gifts they had bestowed upon him. He was especially warm in his affection when writing of Pan who 'had come there often, though he himself had never been face to face with the god.' Like the similar figures of Silenus and the Satyrs, Pan was brought into connection with Dionysus, in whose train he proved himself useful on his Indian expedition by means of the terror he inspired. Dionysus is even said to have gone to Iberia and, on leaving, he entrusted Pan with the government of the country, **Plutarch** tells us.

As a god of nature, Pan was a companion of Cybele and, due to his amorous nature, he is associated with Aphrodite. There is a beautiful set of figures (c.100 B.C.) in the Athens National Museum (the votive offering of a Syrian merchant, found at Delos in 1904). This shows Pan surprising Aphrodite at her toilet. Pan is being playfully restrained by a laughing Eros who is grasping one of the horns on his head while in flight above them. Remember Pan was always fighting Eros. Pan is being threatened with a slap from Aphrodite's raised slipper for his temerity as he tries to embrace her, but it does not seem to be too serious a rebuke. Pan's worship was well established in Arcadia where, not unnaturally, it had its largest following and greatest success, but it was not confined there.

In Egypt he was worshipped with great solemnity and we read that his statues represented him as a goat, not because this is how he really was. When the gods fled to Egypt he arrived in the town of Mendes (see the next chapter under Min). The word *mendes*, we are told, can also signify a goat and there was a sacred goat kept with great ceremony and sanctity there - the Goat of Mendes. Its death was always the cause of great ritual and solemnity and, like Apis/Serapis at Memphis, the sacred bull of Egypt and a symbol of fertility, its death was universally mourned. The *Goat of Mendes* is a favourite of writers and films of the horror genre, symbolic of Satan or the Devil.

Pan's cult was confined to the country for he never lived in Olympus with the other great gods. He was worshipped with the nymphs in caves and grottoes which is the sign of very ancient worship. His image was sometimes set up under trees where his worshippers brought it simple offerings of milk, honey, must, rams or lambs. The first fruits were often dedicated to the gods, while to Pan and the nymphs came the hunters and breeders. In one book of **Homer** alone, **Hastings** tells us, Pan receives thirty-four more dedications than any other deity.

Not infrequently the offerings to Pan, as to the nymphs, consisted of cheese, milk, honey or cakes set around the altar. As mentioned earlier, the *thusia* offered to Pan differed in one essential point from the ritual proper to the nymphs. The Goat-God received libations of wine. Athenian custom prohibited the offering of wine to the nymphs. It is true that some reliefs do show a libation to the nymphs but usually Pan is present. It must always be remembered that the nymphs are as divine as he is. **Theocritus** calls the nymphs 'dread divinities.' Madness menaces those who see the reflection of a nymph while bent over a spring.

Tradition forbids that one approach this god in silence, says **Menander.** An inscription tells us that the gifts most proper to present to Pan are laughter and good humour. Some elements of his ritual may well prove: *Euphrosune*= good humour, glad, light-hearted. *Krotos*= the sound of striking, the sound of clapping, generally, a loud rattling or noise. *Gelos*= laughter, humorous, facetious. There exists a Greek deity called *Gelasinus*, the god of laughter, from *gelao*= 'to laugh.' Pan loved dancing and perhaps he would like to see a sprig of the pine tree being worn. Pan is credited with inventing the open-air *danse champetre*= the rustic/rural dance. *Numphai phiai, phile Pan* - 'Dear nymphs, dear Pan' - is an invocation for use. Pan's deceptions produced numbness, sleepiness, forgetfulness of danger and ensnaring and the syrinx shares this bewitching power. Pan helps those he loves by creating disorder and confusion among their enemies, etc. The animal sacrifice to Pan is generally an uncut (= uncastrated) goat or sheep, but note the following beautiful words:

My Dog

To Pan and the Dryads here
I dedicate my hunting spear,
My dog, the bag that holds my store;
I am too poor to offer more!

Nay, but my dog I cannot spare!
He must return my crusts to share,
My daily rambles to attend,
My little comrade and my friend.
Macedonius: 6th century A.D.

The Grotto or Cave of Ephesus contained a statue of Diana to which was attached a reed given by Pan. Another version tells us that Pan said when he invented the syrinx he hid away in a cave that he consecrated to Artemis. He forbade any woman who was not a virgin to enter the cave, and so when the people of that district near Ephesus were uncertain about the virginity of a maiden, she underwent the judgement of the syrinx.

The maiden was sent by public decree to the grotto. She entered the grotto in proper dress and the doors closed behind her. If she proved a virgin the pipes of Pan were heard as sweet music floating on the air. After a time the doors opened of their own accord and the virgin emerged with a chaplet of pine foliage on her head. If she lied about her virginity then the pipes were silent and a low moan was heard or, alternatively, if the pipes gave forth a hideous noise then all was not well and the deception was discovered. The people then went away and the women was left inside. After three days the virgin priestess of the place returned. She found the woman had disappeared and the Syrinx lying on the floor. At the desire of Glaucon of Lesbos, Corinna put the grotto to the test and 'was never seen again by the eye of man.' It has been suggested it was Pan who did the testing, which is a task I think he would have liked.

The Greeks proclaimed that he Egyptian god Amon-Ra was the same as Pan. They called Amon-Ra's sacred city Panopolis - the City of Pan or Min - saying it was inhabited by 'pans and satyrs.' Some of the things sacred to Pan are mountains, caves, old oaks, the hare, blasted trees, pine trees and the tortoise. His attributes are the syrinx, the shepherds crook 'which like the year turned back on itself,' a garland of pine or fir leaves or twigs of the tree. The fancy of later times is reported to have invented as Pan's companions, younger Pans or Panisci. These Panisci were a species of forest imp who were fabled to torment mankind with all sorts of apparitions, nightmares and evil dreams.

Plutarch, writing to Klea of the mysteries of Isis and Osiris, tells her that the Pans and Satyrs at Chemmis (= Panopolis) were the first to sense the passion of Osiris. They gave voice about what was being done which caused 'sudden disturbances and emotions of crowds' which to this day are called 'panics'. In upper Egypt the Greek colonists fancied they could see the familiar and comforting image of the Goat-God in the enigmatic figure of Min of Coptos, lord of the roads in the eastern desert.

Pan, like all the gods, could be invoked to grant inspiration, or as **Plutarch** calls it 'enthusiasm.' He cites the inspiration of divination by Apollo and the Bacchic frenzy of Dionysus, to which he couples the orgiastic ecstasies of Cybele and Pan. There is the warlike frenzy of Ares and what he calls 'the fiercest and most fiery of all - the frenzy of love.'

The power of Pan often surfaces during sleep, when the censor of our actions is not present. Goats are often seen in the dream state by those who are under the sway of the god. The Romans took note of this fact and identified the Greek god with a kind of incubus, Inuus, and thus we have Pan-Inuus. Inuus was originally an independent pastoral divinity. He was identified with Faunus and Silvanus, the other Latin correspondence to Pan. Such a spirit was commonly called an incubus, from Lat. *incubo*= to lie upon. These incubi were described as lascivious spirits that appeared only at night. They were credited with the power of producing supernatural births by actual intercourse with women. The men had their version called succubi who acted in similar fashion towards them.

This belief was held by the Jews: 'for a wicked spirit loveth her, but as soon as a man tries to approach her, he kills him.' Tobit.6:14. It is referred to by **St. Augustine**, 'The story is often repeated by people who have experienced it and by some who have heard it from eye-witnesses whose truthfulness is above doubt, that the Silvans and Pans, whom the people also call incubos, always carry on shamelessly with women, desire them and perform intercourse with them.' *De Civitate Dei* (= 'City of God').

Heraclitus tells us of the pans and satyrs: 'They are born in the mountains and not used to woman, if they meet a women they have intercourse with her. In great numbers they are wont to frighten the women into panic and terror.' In the Middle Ages this was accepted by theologians and lawyers and scores of women were burnt for the crime, when perhaps some of the reasons should have been sought more on the physical plane. Some Church fathers held that the incubi were the demon lovers of women. These incubi were able to foster children that were considered a demonic enactment of the Virgin Birth. However, if it had the blessing of the church it would appear to be fine, as it must have been at the shrines of St. Giles in Normandy and St. Rene in Anjou. Here it was acceptable for women to lie at night with the *saints* (ithyphallic) images in the hope of conceiving children. Same play and script - different scenery and director.

Pathologically the incubus was a sensation of an oppressive weight on the epigastrium (Gr. *epigastrios*= the belly or stomach) during sleep and of an incapability of moving or speaking - a nightmare. The male version was the succubus, from the Lat. *succuba*= a strumpet; *succubo*= to lie under; *sub*= 'under' and *cubo*= 'to lie.' This was thought of as a demon who was believed to have the power of assuming the shape of a woman to consort sexually with men. To complete the picture there is the Lamia. In later times the *Lamia* were conceived as handsome ghostly women who by voluptuous artifice attracted young men, to enjoy their fresh, youthful and pure blood. They were thus, in ancient times, what the vampire is to modern legend. In an earlier nightmare form they were fabulous monsters, evil spirits having the semblance of a serpent with the head, or at least the mouth, of a beautiful woman that they assumed for securing the love of young men.

Faunus as good spirit of the forest, plains and fields, gave fruitfulness to the cattle and was therefore identified with Inuus, who was also a rural deity, a good spirit of the fields, forests and pastures. There was a place named Castrum Inui in Latium, with another near Caere in Etruria. From Greece the worship of Pan was transferred to the Romans. They called him *Inuus* because he taught them to breed cattle and *Lupercus*, because he taught them to employ dogs for protecting the herds, wild and domesticated, against wolves.

The Old Shepherd

Daphnis, I that piped so rarely,
I that guarded well the fold,
'Tis my trembling hand that fails me;
I am weary, I am old.
Here my well-worn crook I offer unto Pan the shepherd's friend;
Know ye, I am old and weary;
of my toil I make an end!
Yet I still can pipe it rarely,
still my voice is clear and strong,
Very tremulous in body,
nothing tremulous in song.
Only let no envious goatherd tell the
wolves upon the hill
That my ancient strength is wasted,
lest they do me grievous ill.
Macedonius: 6th century A.D.

Now let us discuss Pan in the Orphic mysteries. The Orphic mystic societies were important to private religion. In particular they brought a Thraco-Phrygian tradition and influence into Greece. Although we are going to discuss Orphism, paradoxically, there is really no such thing as Orphism in the sense that Orpheus created a religion or desired one in his name. Nor did any particular prophet or sect have exclusive use of his name. There is Orpheus the legendary singer of whom many stories were told. There is Orphic literature, a body of poems created in different places and, for the most part, having nothing in common save that

Orpheus was claimed to be their author. Not very long ago it was taken for granted that these poems collectively represented the teachings of a people called The Orphics, who claimed him as their founder, and the great religious movement called Orphism was established and written about.

The best know stories of Orpheus tell us that he sang so beautifully with his lyre. Not only were the creatures of the wild tamed so that they came and stood entranced around him. Rivers stayed in their courses and mountains, rocks and trees sidled closer the better to hear him. 'Above his head there hovered birds innumerable, and fishes leapt clean from their blue water because of his sweet music.' **Simonides**. Legend says that Orpheus took part in the famous expedition of Jason and the Argonauts to gain the Golden Fleece, where his music becalmed the raging sea, it also stilled the clashing rocks which would have destroyed the ship. His most famous exploit was his descent into Hades to recover his wife, the nymph Eurydice, after she had been fatally bitten by a snake. The condition of her release, his beautiful music had gained her freedom, was that he should not look back at her during their passage through the realm of the dead. In his impatience he did look back and saw his wife and she was compelled to return while he left without her. Orpheus is one of the few who went to the land of the dead and returned to tell the tale. Several accounts of his death are given.

Originally Orphism was associated with Dionysus and later with a Phrygian divinity called Sabazius, commonly described as a son or Rhea or Cyble. His orgiastic worship was very closely connected with that of the Phygian Mother of the Gods, Rhea-Cybele, and of Attis. Later he was identified with the mystic Dionysus, who is sometimes called *Dionysus Sabazius*. Sabazius is also called a son of Zeus by Persephone and was said to have been reared by the nymph Nyssa; the philosophical speculations of others make him a son of Cabeirus, Dionysus or Cronos. He was torn into seven pieces by the Titans.

The connection of Sabazius with the Phrygian mother of the gods accounts for the fact he was identified, to a certain extent, with Zeus himself. Zeus is often mentioned as Zeus Sabazius. His worship and festivals were introduced into Athens in the 5th century B.C., though in the time of Demosthenes it was not considered reputable to take part in them. In later times it was widely spread in Rome and Italy, especially in the latter days of paganism. His festival, the *Sabazia*, was celebrated at night by both sexes with purification, initiation and immoralities. Serpents were sacred to him and took a prominent part in the processions. Sabazius was represented with horns because it is said he was the first to yoke oxen to the plough for agriculture. Like many of the oriental deities, he represented the flourishing of nature, which sinks in death, always to rise again. As an emblem of the yearly renovation of nature, the symbol specially appropriated to him was the snake. Accordingly, at the celebration of his mysteries, a golden snake was passed under the clothes and drawn over the bosom of the initiated. In the *Characters* of **Theophrastus**, when the superstitious man 'sees a serpent in his house, if it be the red snake, he will invoke Sabazius.'

We are not here attempting to undertake a critical study of the cult of Orphism as a whole and the private sects that grew up under its shadow. Extensive commentaries on this particular philosophy are extant, and easily obtained and so are beyond the brief of this work, because they are readily available. We are interested in Orphism primarily where it has contact with Pan. Dionysus (like Pan) was originally a great nature god powerful over vegetation, especially the vine. By the sixth century B.C., as well as being a lord of life on earth, Dionysus was a nether divinity. He was a lord of the world of souls with whom the dead votary entered privileged communion. His rites were mystical, nightly celebrations that were frequently marked by orgiastic self-abandonment in which the votary became at one with the divinity of the god. Women played a prominent part in the rituals. There were some savage forms of animal sacrifice in which blood and flesh were regarded as an incarnation of the deity.

Pan was with Dionysus in his expeditions to India. Dionysus did not meet a kind reception or open acceptance in many places and the deity frequently had to fight battles. However, Dionysus, with his host of pans, satyrs and Bacchic women, conquered his enemies. He taught them the cultivation of the vine and other fruits, the worship of the gods and himself, and gave them civilization. **Polyaenus** styles Pan as 'Dionysus's General.' Dionysus is said to have gone to Iberia and on leaving he entrusted the government of the country to Pan. Pan is called the Godfather of Spain in some works, the name Spain being thought to be a contracted form of the far older *Hispania.*

One of the lasts feats of Dionysus bears repeating because of the repetitive symbols used regarding him and Orphism. He hired a ship belonging to Tyrrhenian pirates to take him from Icaria to Naxos. The ship, however, passed by Naxos and steered towards Asia, the intention being to sell him there as a slave. The god saw through this plan and changed the masts and oars of the vessel into serpents and himself into a lion.

He filled the vessel with ivy (= the plant of Dionysus) and the sound of flutes (= the instrument of Pan). The sailors were seized with madness and leapt overboard where they were turned into dolphins. The symbolism of interest is that the oars and masts became serpents, while the god became a lion. These are frequent symbols used concerning the Cosmic Egg of the Orphics and connected with Dionysus and Pan.

The cult brought with it the name of Orpheus. Crete and Egypt are thought to have contributed to Orphic doctrine and ritual. One of our earliest authorities for these matters is **Plato's** *Republic*, in which he speaks contemptuously of the itinerant ritualist who uses the name of Orpheus to hawk his wares. These itinerant magicians knocked on the doors of the rich, like travelling missionaries, promising absolution, happiness in the world to come and ritual initiation. The name may have changed but I think they are still with us in another form. The 'purified' were guaranteed they would feast with the gods for ever, while 'the rest lie in the mud.' **Theophrastaus** notes it as 'a mark of the superstitious man that he takes his family every month to the "Orpheus-ministers" who no doubt charged him a suitable fee for securing his salvation.'

This was quite unknown elsewhere in Greek religion, this missionary spirit that preached to all and sundry the Orphic message or propaganda. Dionysus is the one god who, if a Greek god had gained the upperhand in European religions, might have won the day with his Orphic literature. In these mystic brotherhoods can be discerned the germs of high religion and conceptions that have played a great part in the religious history of Europe. Now let us turn to that part of the Orphic mysteries that concerns Pan.

This brings us directly to *Phanes*, a mystic divinity in the Orphic system. Phanes is also called Zeus, Dionysus, Helios, Eros, Ericapaeus, Metis, Protogonus and 'Pan, the universal god who encompasses heaven and earth.' This god is said to have been born from the Mystic or Cosmic Egg and to have been the father of all gods and the creator of men. The primal egg is often used as a symbol of the Cosmos, according to **Clement of Rome**, especially when the Cosmos was in its original and abstract state of conception. It represents an innermost state of existence, concentrated like an egg, before its process of hatching and evolving. Orpheus declares that Chaos first existed, eternal, vast and uncreated. It was neither dark nor light, nor moist, nor dry; nor hot, nor cold, but all things intermingled. During eternity, its outer parts became denser. The sides and ends were made and it assumed the form of a gigantic egg. Let us enlarge upon this god who is also called Pan.

Time - *Chronos* - is portrayed as a winged serpent that has the heads of a bull and a lion, 'with the face of a god between them.' Taking the above line let us lapse briefly into astrology which this symbolism seems to suggest. We have four symbols here and I believe they are the symbols of four very powerful astrological signs, the signs that fix and establish matters and people alike. The early seasons were threefold, consisting of the lion, the goat and the serpent. This tripartite year consisted of the lion for spring, the goat for summer and the serpent for winter. These signs also fix the fourfold year that followed with the addition of the 'man' (= Aquarius) or a cherub.

We have a serpent around the Orphic egg that consists of a bull - Taurus, a lion - Leo, with 'the face of a god between them' which is part of the human figure of the Water Carrier - Aquarius. The final fixed sign is Scorpio, represented by the usual scorpion today, but its early sign was sometimes an eagle so that its highest aspect it should live up to this symbolism. The scorpion, usually found skulking under rocks ready to sting without warning, was its lowest. One symbol is soaring in the element of air, while the other is hiding under the element of earth. A far older sign for Scorpio was the serpent, and Scorpio is said to hold 'the serpent stars.' This fourfold scheme gives us the composite serpent of the Orphics, which contains the head of a bull, a lion and the face of a god between them represented in the zodiac by the fixed signs. Enlarging a little on the sign of the Water Carrier. It is said that Christ heralded the new age of Aquarius, and this may be hinted at in the Biblical stories. His disciples asked Jesus where will they go to prepare to eat the Passover? He sent into the city two of his disciples and told them, (abridged): 'Go ye into the city, and there shall meet you a man bearing a pitcher of water: follow him...wherever he shall go in...the goodman of the house...will shew you a large upper room furnished and prepared: there make ready for us.' Mark 14:12-16.

Each quarter or season of the year contains three signs of the zodiac. The first sign is called a *cardinal* or *outgoing* sign, a time of greatest activity and initiation of the particular season, whether for growth and establishment (= spring and summer) or decay or death (= autumn and winter). The second sign of the group of three is a *fixed* or *foundation* sign, which fixes or establishes the activity started by the cardinal sign. The third sign of the group is the mutable sign which *mutates* or *changes* the season in readiness for the initiation of the next season in the succession. Four sequences or quarters of the year that *initiate, fix* and *mutate*, as they do within spring, summer, autumn and winter, and so the seasons pass. The cycle of Nature is of death and decay, fertilization, gestation and rebirth.

We have already discussed Pan's association with the Pleiades. In this legend of his birth Maia, the most beautiful of them, was the mother of his father Hermes. This naturally made her Pan's grandmother. They all had connections by birth with his land of Arcadia. The constellation known as the Pleiades or the Weeping Sisters are in the sign of the Bull - Taurus. Anyone with planet(s) in their chart around twenty-nine degrees of Taurus will often find they will likewise have something to 'weep about' in their lives. Incidentally, at twenty-four degrees of Taurus we have *Caput Algol*, the head of Medusa of the serpent locks, whose head was lost. It was placed on the goatskin Aegis of Zeus. Medusa lost her head as can anyone with planet(s) here.

This is the first of our diversions into astrology. Now let us return to our story again. Ageless Chronos symbolized as a serpent with the heads of a bull, and a lion with the face of a god between, produces a shining egg in the bosom of the darkness. Heaven and earth were one form. In ancient mythology the serpent is often found as an emblem of the Wisdom of God. With a pair of wings it becomes a seraph, coiled in a circle holding its tail, representing time without end - eternity.

The serpent has also been made a symbol, par excellence, of sin in the Christian church, despite Christ's injunction, when he sent the apostles forth, 'be ye as wise as serpents, and as harmless as doves.' Matthew 10:16. He obviously did not hold the serpent in the same abhorrence as the religion that bears his name or the people who came afterwards, claiming to be speaking in his name. Now we come to our second short astrological diversion.

I wonder if this could take us back to Orpheus/Dionysus/Pan and the Orphic mysteries. The Pleiades are known in Sicily as - *Sette Palommielle* - the Seven Dovelets which, as we have mentioned above, are in the zodiacal sign of Taurus. The accursed serpent of old is in the opposite sign of Scorpio. In modern Christianity the dove is representative of peace and the serpent of temptation and evil incarnate, but here peace (= *the dove*) and wisdom (= *the serpent*) are reflected in each other and there is great attraction in opposites. It seems here that Christ is telling us to reconcile the opposites. Recurring symbols catch my eye, particularly when you read how some writers couple Dionysus and Christ, and some imply they are aspects of the same incarnation.

This Cosmic Egg contained the male and female nature, and within it were many seeds. It is sometimes depicted as having four winds blowing around it. In some reliefs these winds are represented by four outside figures. From this Egg a splendid creature hatched, an incorporeal and biform god that had golden wings on his shoulders. He had various animal heads about him: for example, bull's heads on his flanks. On his head were a huge changing snake and horns.

All the gods and cosmic forces are contained within this god. He is of both sexes. He has two faces, one in the front and one behind. He had male sexual parts in the front and female behind. The Cosmic Serpent is still around the Egg, despite it having broken into two halves across its equator to release the god. The serpent (= *Wisdom*) connects these two halves and takes the superior position, it should be noted. The serpent connects and holds the upper half above the god (= *heaven*), to the lower half below him (= *earth*). Within the two halves of the Cosmic Egg is contained the figure of the new god - *Phanes*.

From the lower hemisphere flames shoot upwards with the god standing within them, for from them he is born. A luminous being, Phanes the Radiant was also 'polymorphic, a beast-mystery god.' His face reveals the features of Helios, he bears golden wings, but he is of the moon, and the glittering heavens are shown by the zodiac that surrounds him. He is 'lightning,' which is represented by the thunderbolt he holds in his right-hand and the sceptre on which his left is resting; this symbolism identifies him as Zeus. In Orphic theology he is celebrated as *Protogonos* - '*first born*' - and Zeus the 'marshaller of all things and the whole cosmos,' whence he is called Pan.

His feet end in cloven hoofs, showing he is also Pan with the goat's feet and twofold in form or a 'biform god.' The upper half is human and smooth while the lower half is rough and goat-like. He is half man and half beast, of whom **Plato** writes that he is called, *aipolos*, because he is forever revolving the cosmos. In this figure we appear to have the Zeus and Pan of **Eratothenes** who tells us Pan is the foster-brother of Zeus, which makes Pan equal to Zeus and older than Hermes, the most popular candidate for being his father. The Hermes legend produces the most myths about Pan.

When the creation of the world was complete the deity Phanes soared over it as Zeus. He rose in the summit of heaven as Helios, the god of the Sun, where he illuminated the world. As Dionysus/Pan, he maintained the rotation of the starry sphere. Phanes/Zeus/Pan/Dionysus/Helios is the life of the world, its Aeon, the life span of this world that will endure as long as Aeon (= Chronos) does. He is the great cosmic year because he orders the years into seasons, months and days by the movements of the stars, and this takes place in and through him.

This perhaps would explain (in part) why some commentators regard Pan as a solar and a fire deity, which others deny. We have said often here that the earth is his place. Pan did not leave the earth to dwell in Olympus despite being welcome there. Pan is so intimately bound up

Pan the Piper, set in the centre of the Zodiac.
Drawn from a woodcut of an ancient gem.

with this planet which is a planet of *earth* created from *fire*, which contains *water* and holds *air*, hence life and a unique planet. This strong association with fire and earth may be the reason Pan is found included with those deities specifically connected with the sacred element of fire. Pan was given a torch race and cave with a perpetual fire on the Acropolis, after the battle of Marathon; he also had a perpetual fire at Olympia which was fed from the altar of Zeus. It should be noted these two examples were not the only sites where a perpetual fire was kept burning on Pan's behalf.

In many reliefs and representations Phanes appears in the centre of the zodiac. There are also many representations of Pan in the centre of the zodiac. On one cut stone Pan has the addition of seven chariots of the gods around him, as the symbols of the seven planets. To be surrounded by the zodiac is to represent the sun in its path with the seven planets of old in their orbits, see the illustration. Mythical and mystery thinkers of the past often placed both gods and cosmic forces within each other. They did not always regard them as existing separately as is sometimes done today. All are really manifestations of a single god and a single cosmos that some say is Phanes himself, with all the powers that he both discharges and encompasses.

G.R.S. Mead in his *Orpheus* writes, referring to the rites of Phanes, 'The Triple god born from the Egg was called Phanes, also Metis and Ericapaeus, the three being aspects of one Power.' Later he explains. 'Of the three aspects Phanes is said to be the 'father,' Ericapaeus the 'power,' and Metis the 'intellect' in Platonic terms...Phanes is also called Love (= *Eros*)...also the Limit or Boundary; also Intelligible Light.'

Let us take a brief look at some names of this new god Phanes: the Light-giver, Life-giver, Power, Counsel and Manifestor. Light becomes the Light of Reason, the Light of Life, and - for he is also Eros - the Light of Love. Ericapaeus is one aspect of his trinity - a symbol of Action. Metis is the third trinity aspect, given as the symbol of Divine Wisdom. Thus we have the Higher Self manifesting as the Divine Aspects - Will (= *Phanes*), Wisdom (= *Metis*) and Action (= *Ericapaeus*), the ubiquitous trinity of practically every religious philosophy.

The Godhead is symbolised in three aspects as the Three Witnesses on Earth, agreeing to lift up the human soul. It is said that the 'first born Love' (= *Eros*) of the Highest is the force that attracts life upwards. Regarding the origin of the world the Greeks, for the most, appeared satisfied with **Hesiod's** explanation of the beginning of the world. Out of the shapeless mass or *Chaos* was first born the spirit of love *Eros* or *Cupid* and the 'broad chested' *Gaia*, followed by *Erebos* who was 'darkness' and then *Nyx*, who was 'night.'

Orpheus was said to have heard the three names Phanes, Metis and Ericapaeus in a prophetic dream. Orpheus said these divine powers are one power, one might and One god. Eros (= *Love*) was regarded as a fundamental cause in the formation of the world, in as much as he was the uniting power of love, which brings order and harmony to the conflicting elements of which Chaos consists.

Proclus on **Plato** tells us: 'The theologian Orpheus taught there were three Ages of Man.' The first or Golden Age was ruled by Phanes. Mighty Cronos is the ruler of the second or Silver Age. The third is called Titanic. The ruler of it is Zeus, and it is called Titanic because the men of that age were created by him from the remains of the Titans. The idea of Orpheus is that these three periods comprise every stage in the history of the world.

Finally we come to Pan. **Plato**, writing of Pan in the Orphic mysteries, said Pan was called - *aei polon* - because he is forever revolving the cosmos, and *aipolos*. Because Pan is twofold in nature, smooth above but below rough and goat-like, he is the mediator between heaven and earth. He goes to heaven (= Olympus) and he is welcome there, but he always returns to here (= Earth) to be with us, and he never deserts us. Now it is time to close the section on Pan, Orpheus and Orphics and pick up the main threads of his story once more.

Pan symbolizes the sympathetic system of natural man, through which the desires and the feelings are increased and brought into relation with the objective mind. In the myth of Hermes, Pan is the product of mind and speech that has been brought forth. He is desire - *the goat's legs* - and he delights all the gods. He is the perfect instrument through which Dionysus can evolve the lower nature that keeps us earthbound. Pan can be the saviour of the soul.

Pan corresponds to Orpheus, because both co-ordinate through the harmony and order of their music. This is borne out in part by the pastoral shepherd who plays music, often the flute which Pan plays, to his flocks to make them secure, calm and to tame them. The lower qualities of human nature are often symbolically represented by flocks or herds of animals, whether domesticated or wild. In this metaphorical herd are those qualities which we have domesticated and those which are still wild in us. For when we hear the Pipes of Pan and the herd runs instinctively, it is hard for the domesticated members not to run with the wild.

They are symbols of appetites, desires and passions, the disciplined and the undisciplined. It is usually the undisciplined that escape from us to play havoc. Like anything natural they decline to be fettered and will escape if they are able. They are the ones that make us act out of the character we assume and approve of, *the persona*, and reveal instead the character we perhaps disapprove of, because it does not comply with what we or others think we should be. It cracks the mask, the part we elect or have to play, perhaps it shows us what we are.

Remember, Pan is on the border of things: he is the watcher, the *aposkopos* - the 'lookout.' Like Silvanus, he is on the edge of civilization and the beginning of the wild wood that he rules and prefers. This may account for the fascination cats have for some of us because they never quite belong to us. They stay because they want to, they go if they don't and they play the game better than we do; they've had centuries more practice, once being gods. Pan is everything that is natural no matter how much we may disapprove of its existence.

The symbolism of the goat alone could run into many thousands of words I am sure. Bacchus is said to have appeared as a goat and the choral odes sung in his honour were called *tragodiai* - goat songs. A goat was the symbolic prize given on these celebrations. As previously mentioned, the Greeks have two terms for goat - *tragos* - and - *aix*.

Goats are often used as a symbol of the lower qualities of human nature. However, the white He-Goat was used to represent the Higher Self within the Lower Nature - white symbolising perfection. The zodiac sign Capricorn, in its positive aspect, is often shown by a white He-Goat who has the aspiration to climb the mountain. It climbs to the realms of the gods, who dwell in the peaks, away from the valleys where the mass of the people live.

Mountains are sometimes used symbolically of the lower aspects of life and the lower nature of humanity, which should be transmuted into the higher nature. Teachers urge us, again, to ascend the mountain of our mass to the higher realms or higher nature. Obviously a mountain peak is a symbol of the higher planes and nature as with, for example, Mount Olympus which is the summit or perfection where the gods themselves live. These high gods may come down to earth, but they go back. Pan goes up but does not stay on high, he comes back to his kingdom. Pan is styled the *President of the Mountains*. With variations the same symbolism applies to ladders, stairways, steps, the act of climbing, etc.

As said, the goat is the solitary climber who leaves the flock in the valley below and takes this lonely path. This is the true child of Aegipan (= Capricorn) who, like the ibex, climbs to the peak and, planting its four hoofs on it, surveys all. It also dares anyone to try to take the position to which it has aspired. Capricorn is ambition and success. All these traits are inherent astrologically in the planet Saturn, the sign Capricorn and the tenth house, which is the highest house in the chart. It is therefore the highest, physically, that you can climb. Once you have reached the highest on the physical plane there is only heaven and your god above you, so you genuflect or go down on your knees - which are ruled by Capricorn and Saturn. Those people born under Capricorn often turn to religion late in life.

To this sign belongs 'To Gehenna or the Throne - He travels fastest who travels alone' for Capricorn folk are often solitary people by nature. This is one of the secrets of the card called The Magician, in the Tarot. The Magician stands before the altar with its symbols, his empty left hand pointing downwards to the earth (= Gehenna), and the Wand of the Will in his right, points upwards to the heavens (= the Throne), the card is saying 'choose!' The Magician or Occultist quickly learns they often have to go alone, and sometimes without, on their journey if they are to travel 'fastest.' *Gehenna* is Hebrew = 'Hell', (Gr. *geena*), the place of eternal torment.' It refers to the Valley of Hinnom west of Jerusalem, where sacrifices were made, and it was famous for its abominable religious practices. It was changed into a public refuse dump, a permanent place of burning where the fire does not go out. In this valley the corpses of the worst malefactors were burnt so it is used as a name for hellfire or hell. Gehenna became symbolic of an accursed place of eternal punishment *par excellence.*

If you are to achieve success in your ascent (= Saturn) you will need the surety of the goat's feet to prevent you from stumbling and falling (= Saturn). As you walk your rock-strewn (obstacles= Saturn) and narrow way (= Saturn) the path of ambition is narrow and steep (= Saturn). Only those who are most resolved will even attempt it (= Saturn), I think this has made the point. At least you will need these attributes until you reach where Pan will reveal his human half. Then, if he offers you his hand and if you are wise enough to accept it, he will lift you up and hold you, safe and secure in strong arms, calling you 'My Beloved Child.'

My own thoughts have long been predated by others including **Madame Blavatsky** who writes of the god that 'Pan was at one time Absolute Nature, the One and Great All; but when history catches a first glimpse of him, Pan has already tumbled down into a godling of the fields, a rural god; history will not recognise him, while theology makes him the Devil.' Pan was to the Greek psyche, more than any other deity, the personification of instinct. A lot of midnight oil has been burned about instinct. To some instinct is archaic, a mechanical response to life now long outdated, something that cannot evolve. To others it is a primordial intelligence that knows more about life than we ever will. To this I would add that Pan is the positive magnetism of the earth, who with his grace and blessing gives unalloyed joy to all things natural. How sad to find all that remains of this 'lover of merry noise' is the monstrous, false imagery of the cloven hoof and horns of the Christian Devil. There was a habit once, in rural Britain, of 'speaking the Devil fair,' and calling him 'the good man.' He being a survival of the genial Pan, exemplifies the tendency to compromise.

I mostly leave things like Tarot cards alone. I do not feel the need to 'bring them up-to-date,' or 'into the twentieth century,' often a retrograde step, which is often done in the cause of some espoused 'ism.' Quite often it isn't always the changes I disagree with, but the reasons for them. Now, as in the past, reforming zeal overexcites the ill-informed whose zealousness inflates their lack of discrimination, which it seems they must share, why should they be the only ones to suffer? This they do by inflicting it on everyone else whether it is willed or no. There has been a fever raging the past few years of almost epidemic proportions, which I hope has begun to run its course by now, to bring things up-to-date and 'into the twentieth century.' Speaking for myself, I feel that these cards have been serving people for many long years and I see no need for inflicting my vanities upon them. I accept the Tarot cards were new once and I am not against change, *but not change for the sake of it*, which most of this is as far as I am concerned. However, I do admit throwing one card out a long time ago from my private pack, *the negative Devil*. Now he is *the positive Pan* and I do not worship the Devil because of this. Nevertheless people have been sent to the Inquisition, for the 'good of their souls' of course, for less than a card. The Inquisition in its old form may not be with us today, but that doesn't mean the 'Inquisition' is dead by any means, nor has persecution ceased. True, it may not be fire, rack or strappado. Castigation, persecution, being called to account for your thoughts and actions with the threat of losing your job have not disappeared for thinking, reading, saying or subscribing to, the wrong things. Any of which could call for you to be 're-educated.' The spirit of persecution has not yet died out in the land. It takes very little to excite the fanatics who would again raise the cry of 'Crucify! Crucify!' The actors, scenery and times may have changed, but the play is very much the same as it has always been.

Pan gave these early zealots the god sent imagery of horns, cloven hoof, and the rank smelling, erotic lower half of a goat - their opinion; yet nothing smells nicer or more wholesome than clean, healthy animals - my opinion. We are told that the lower, earthy animal half debased the upper, divine and human half with that foul distraction of the Devil, sex. From early times the goat has been depicted as the constant companion of sin, lust and lechery. Yet, concerning this foul distraction of sex, a goat was often set under the seats, in church stalls, etc., as a sign of abhorrence and dishonour, especially for those ecclesiastics who were bound by the law of continence. The law of continence is a law of moderation and self-restraint, especially regarding the sexual appetites. In the indulgence of sexual enjoyment due moderation had to be exercised and, more often than not, complete abstinence was expected or demanded.

The customary and long accepted process of creating the Devil for the new religion, from a chief god of the old canon was begun. This was achieved in part by stressing the animal form, the sex and lechery, all the undesirable traits that are assumed to describe the wholesome and natural, Pan. The Early Christians naively thought by creating the Devil to explain away the evil that exists in the world, which of course was nothing to do with them or their God, for a new religion destined to replace all others had to be perfect with no blemish. Their God was responsible only for Good and he could not be held responsible for having included Evil in his creation, his created world and the creatures that were to inhabit it; if there was Evil in the created world it must have been brought in from the outside.

If there was a Power for Evil that God had not created, and it was leading the righteous astray and upsetting God's plans, then this power could exist in its own right and could challenge God. If God is 'all' there really is then he must be so: then nothing can exist outside the 'all' or it cannot be 'the All.' I sometimes think that when the Devil was created they did not know what to do with Satan. 'And the great dragon was cast out, that old serpent, called the Devil, and Satan, which...' Revelations. 12:9. This example, to me, could imply two separate entities, the Devil, *and* Satan, or two names for one entity - the Devil *or* Satan. Sometimes I get the feeling Satan is added in any list of the Devil just in case or for good measure.

It was in making evil a separate entity, something outside the Christian religion that had to be vanquished and destroyed, that Christianity dissents from most other religious philosophies. Yet in the Lord's Prayer it is God to whom we address ourselves, not the Devil, when we pray that God will not: 'lead us not into temptation.' What is more this appears to be correct, for in Isaiah. 45:5-7, the Lord tells us: 'I am the Lord, and there in none else. I form the light, and create the darkness: I make peace, *and create evil*: I the Lord do all these things.' (my italics).

The early Primitive Church identified sin with Nature and all that is natural. The God of Nature, Pan, was identified with the eternal tempter against which the flesh must be mortified without mercy. It was even worse for the female Nature Spirits. The venom of the early Church was especially virulent *against the female aspects of Nature*, the nymphs, dryads, etc., who were transformed into witches and hags. To listen to, let alone follow a natural impulse, was to heed the whispering of the Goat-footed and Horned Devil. However, the Devil is as good an explanation as any other for the existence of evil. This late into the work it may seem foolish to ask where did we in the West get this cloven-hoofed Devil, the clever creation that has kept most under such tight control these long centuries.

Finding the major god of a new religion fighting the old gods for 'the throne' is not a new idea, these 'wars in heaven' have been fought many times before; Zeus had to do it and in his challenge he was ably assisted by Pan. Perhaps this is why the One God tells us at the very beginning: 'Thou shalt have no other gods before me.' At least he does have the courtesy to acknowledge there are other gods before him, and some have obviously not been vanquished. Neither will he permit their worship with dire punishment for doing so; or is he being honest, is his achieving the status of the One God something he aspires to? When any of the old gods demanded such absolute obedience they were called tyrants. Evil, as the Devil, was something the early Christians thought they could preach out of existence. They thought they could lay the sins of the world on its back for good measure and, like the scapegoat, he could take them with him when he went, as he must; so they could start with a clean slate. It didn't work! For this it was Pan who was made to suffer. Many philosophies, religious or otherwise, represent Evil as the shadow of Good, or Good perverted from its natural course. You can rarely have light without shadow, and to rid yourself of a shadow, you have to get rid of the light, but then you are left in darkness, at least before you had a choice, you could see where you where going.

In a minor Greek myth, given by **Ennius** in his translation of the *Sacred History* of **Evemerus**, and preserved by the Christian Father **Lactantius**, we are told of the young Jupiter being led to a high mountain by Pan. The mountain is called the Pillar of Heaven, the young Jupiter ascends the mountain with Pan showing him the way and at the peak he contemplated the distant lands. On the mountain, Jupiter sets up an altar to Coelus or Uranus (= heaven), and on the altar he made his first sacrifice, it was here he looked up to the Heavens as we now call it, etc.' *Divine Institutes*: **Lactantius**. Any representation of this scene would show a young god standing with a Demon by an altar, on a high mountain top. To Christian eyes this could only mean that the Devil was asking to be worshipped in return for the kingdoms of the earth, to which he was pointing. To a Pagan, however, Pan, as the Lord or President of the Mountains, was in his natural place and what would be more natural than his being there with 'young' Jupiter. This tale appears to put Pan as older than Jupiter, but does the story sound familiar?

'Then was Jesus led up of the spirit into the wilderness to be tempted by the devil...Again, the devil taketh him up into an exceeding high mountain, and sheweth him all the kingdoms of the world, and the glory of them; and saith unto him, All these things will I give thee, if thou will fall down and worship me. Then saith Jesus unto him, Get thee behind me Satan: for it is written, Thou shalt worship the Lord thy God, and he only shalt thou serve. Then the devil leaveth him...' Matthew.4:1-11. The early Christian Fathers spent much time manipulating the Pagan gods into demons and devils for their own purposes. They seemed to have little other thought but to ridicule the old mythologies, but failed to recognize the quality of their own.

From time immemorial Pan was projected as the Devil by Jews and Christians alike. Even to the Pagans he was called the 'terror striker' because he possessed a fearful side, which his enemies could exploit and develop with ease into any image they wanted, by stressing this facet of his nature. It must not be forgotten that the sign Capricorn, the sign of Pan: 'leads the sun from the lower places (*ab infernis partibus*) to the highest'; just as the nature of the goat goes always: 'from low places to the highest rocks.' *Saturnalia*, i, 21: **Macrobius**. We find, in ancient Arcadian myth, that the Sun - Uz - was called 'the Goat,' because the Sun was the Climber, the High One, *par excellence*. Eventually the word *uz* came to signify a goat. The sign of Capricorn, the Goat or Goat-Fish, marked the beginning of the Sun's upward climb in the heavens. Therefore, was Pan showing the young Jove his course in the heavens when he took him to the 'high mountain,' for 'he led the Sun on high.' When the Sun enters the sign of Capricorn (= Winter Solstice) it starts the climb to its highest position, when the Sun reaches Cancer (= Summer Solstice) it starts its decline in the Northern Hemisphere, to return to its nadir.

It has been suggested that Mount Atlas may be 'the Pillar of Heaven' - the 'mountain of the world' - Atlas bears the pillars of heaven and earth. Atlas was the father of the Pleiades and, as already mentioned, the Pleiades are called 'the seven little nanny goats.' Atlas, 'who knew the depths of the whole sea,' is connected by family with Pan in one legend, and Pan's sign of Capricorn ends in a fishes tail. Pan can sometimes be found carrying a shell or conch in his hand. It was Atlas, in one account, who 'first taught men to regard the heaven as a sphere.' **Diodorus Siculus**. iii, 60.

A primary pairing of the gods, in their connection with Pan, or the Goat-Gods suggests itself. Zeus with Pan (= the Greek Goat-God); Mithra and Silvanus (= the Roman Goat-God, a variant of Pan); Apollo and Marsyas (= a satyr or Goat-God, a Phrygian variant of Pan); Dionysus and Silenus (the oldest of the Satyrs, and goat-like, sometimes Pan is given as his father); Jesus and the Devil (= represented as a goat-man, usually Pan). All, but the last, seem natural pairings, while the latter appears a distorted or unnatural one. In the former they are usually teachers or guides. Silenus, in late art has become a comic figure, but in his highest form he is the 'worthy teacher and guide' to the young Dionysus, 'arousing in him the highest aspirations,' and to him Dionysus 'owed much of his success and his fame.' Diodorus Siculus iv, 4. Though Marsyas, having lost his music contest to Apollo, was flayed alive for his presumption and from him the river Marsyas sprang. The fauns, satyrs and dryads all wept at his fate, and some think their tears formed the river named after him. His statue was generally erected in independent cities to show the intimacy between Bacchus and Marsyas, as symbols of liberty, and at the entrance of the Roman forum where business was transacted.

Now let us turn our attention to Satan, meaning - *an adversary* - the chief spirit of evil, now the Devil. The Hebrew word indicates any adversary, but when used as a title or proper name, it usually has the article prefixed - *the adversary*. The latter title can be found in the Bible, the Book of Job being the main example. We meet the word 'Satan' more than thirty times in the New Testament, where it has become interchangeable with *diabolus=* 'the devil,' a word meaning primarily - 'slanderer' or 'accuser.' There is little room for doubting that the Scriptures recognize the distinct personality of Satan, so naturally this means that others deny his personal existence all together. Some maintain that the Jews themselves entertained no such opinion until the Babylonian captivity when, it is alleged, they borrowed the notion from Persian mythology. We are advised there is nothing to intimate that Satan was ever regarded by the ancient Jews as the first cause and eternal principle from which all forms of evil, moral and physical, emanated.

It is strange that we find so few direct and positive statements regarding Satan in the Old Testament. The Apocryphal books seem to agree with the canonical in recognizing Satan as the tempter of man. As already observed, Satan is most frequently called 'the Devil' in the New Testament. He is the constant enemy of God, of Christ, of the Divine Kingdom, of the followers of Christ, and of all truth; full of falsehood and all malice, and exciting and seducing evil in every possible way - I don't think I have left anything out. I do not think the reality of Satan's temptation can be questioned by those who accept the New Testament. In this part of the work we only need sufficient facts for the discussion in hand, the subject is enormous, and we have only scratched the paint work. We have taken most of our examples from Hebrew and Christian literature, and the Cabala - a system of Jewish theosophy; the latter is dealt with in more detail in Chapter Two.

The entire universe is balanced upon two opposing forces which produce the equilibrium and harmony of ALL and so sustain it; these opposing forces are in physics, religions, philosophy, intellect, everywhere, save in the Deity who is entire. The ancient Greeks represented these forces by Eros= desire or love, and its opposition Anteros (*antero*= 'to speak against, to gainsay') or Aversion. There is, obviously, a connection between Eros and Anteros which should be noted, for they were, initially, opposites; the latter is usually thought of as 'love returned.' Originally Anteros was opposed to Eros and fought against him. This conflict was conceived as the rivalry existing between two lovers, and Anteros accordingly punished those who did not return the love of others: so that he was the *avenging* Eros.

We read, in Cabalistic literature, regarding these opposing forces: 'There is not any life without motion, no motion without inspiration, no inspiration without struggle, no struggle without opposition, oppositions are everywhere essential, but the Divine Power conciliates every opposition.' *Sepher Khozari*: **Yehudah ha-Levi**. The Cabala does not recognize in Good and Evil, two independent, autonomic, opposing powers. It asserts that Evil springs out of Good, and only originated from a diversion of the latter. Evil exists 'for God's own wise purposes,' and by sufferance of the Absolute One. This has often made me contemplate the results of either side winning the Eternal Battle outright, or one side gaining the upperhand by being much the stronger, here, on the physical level. I think the whole edifice would seriously deteriorate, perhaps even disintegrate or become unstable. Like cutting the rope of a straining team of tug 'o war, both sides would collapse, with neither side appearing to win. However, Chaos would really rule, because the teams are unconnected, disorganized and in disarray. They will remain so until the rope (= the tension) was repaired (= the status quo reinstated) and the combatants competing again (= two organized sides pulling against each other), with the balance restored.

Now it may seem that we have wandered from our purpose but my intention is to expand a little more the reasons why we find the existence or creation of an individual Devil, who was to take the form of Pan as his own. As already mentioned, devils as such have long existed in most lands, and this subject could almost make another book. We already had, for the most, an officially sanctioned 'Satan - the adversary' - who appeared to be doing a good job. Witness the response of the Archangel Michael, when he disputed with Satan, over the body of Moses. Michael says of Satan he, 'durst not bring against him a railing accusation, but said, the Lord rebuke thee.' Jude.8-10. Why, when Michael was an Archangel, did he 'durst not' something? What or who prevented him? It seems even the Talmud was influenced to comment on this problem: 'Satan appeared one day to a man who cursed him daily, and said to him; Why doest thou this? Consider that God himself would not curse me, but merely said "The Lord rebuke thee, Satan."' *Kiddusheem*: **Treat.**

When the Lord was praising Job, he asked Satan 'hast thou considered him?' He told Satan that Job was 'a perfect and upright man,' but Satan told the Lord that was because of the blessings and protection he had bestowed on Job. Satan said, 'But put forth thine hand now, and touch all that he hath, and he will curse thee to thy face.' At this point in the story Satan is not tempting Job but the Lord and, what is more, the Lord takes up the challenge. 'And the Lord said unto Satan, Behold, all that he hath is in thy power; only upon himself put not forth thine hand.' So Satan went forth from the presence of the Lord.' Job.1:11. In this the Lord lays down the rules of the game. I am sure there are further examples to be found, but these examples, to me, point to a special relationship or understanding existing between God and Satan. Not unlike Zeus and Pan in some respects, some consider Pan the foster-brother of Zeus and equal to him in many ways, but Pan was definitely not 'the Devil' for Zeus. The records show that both Zeus and the One God were quite capable of administering their own particular vengeance when upset or disobeyed.

Cities are usually the first to pick up the latest trends, no less then than today. When the cities were satisfactorily converted to Christianity, which meant the majority would happily report the lapses and misdemeanours of the minority. Only that unknown quantity the countryside, or *paganus* and its people, pagans and heathens all, had been left untouched. Who or what was 'the Devil' out there, who was 'the adversary,' that had to be fought, there among the unsophisticated and uneducated? Who was it that had to be taken on and triumphed over, in the name of the One God and for his greater glory?

Walking through the country to the villages these emaciated zealots of the aesthetic, pale Galilean found that people were reluctant to give up their friendly and robust gods who were so full of life. The Nature gods who were ever present around them, always there and in all that they saw, ate, drank and did. Denial or rejection of the Nature Gods would get them in return, a tortured, broken and emaciated God of Denial. Everywhere these priests found life and yet more life. Fertility of fields, animals and people was evident and rampant. Who was this god who permitted such uncontrolled, undesirable, passionate, obviously debauched behaviour and pleasure?

They sought him and they found him, in carved figures, votary offerings, icons and artwork, on pottery, kraters and the like. A creature half-goat, half-man with horns on his head, the lower half a goat with hoofs and a small tail behind. It was playing music and dancing and was worshipped as - Pan, 'the All.' What was more, this creature had the audacity to use the epithet reserved for their god - the All. It was standing erect, like god's own supreme creation, mocking them, with cloven hoofs no less. The rest, as the cliché runs, is history.

I must, however, congratulate Pan's enemies because they have done their work well. By giving this praise, I hope to show that even I am prepared to give the Devil his due. However, I find the idea proffered naive, narrow, and one-sided because it does not allow any middle ground or healthy wholeness within with which to work: all things and all people must be either good or evil, black or white with no shades of grey between. I sometimes love those grey areas because I feel comfortable in them as they are not sterile, in any sense of the word.

Such an idea demands that you accept one side of an argument, at the expense of the other, and we all know that an opposing idea is not always *completely wrong*. It often has some degree of merit, no matter how begrudgingly we admit it, even if it is only to ourselves. This attitude of choose your side for you can't have both, is an either/or idea rather than an either/and one. The latter idea permits a more flexible approach to life and its problems and I believe it makes them a little easier to accept or solve.

The either/and idea, is complementary and at times infinitely more acceptable because its parameters have greater flexibility: not unlike people and life itself. Sometimes life is like a tightrope that people have to negotiate to keep their balance and get through the day. The either/or idea only knows one side or the other. Everything and everyone must be one thing or the other, black and white, right and wrong, when sometimes what it right in one set of circumstances, is wrong in another. This is often presented as being decisive, knowing what you're doing and entertaining no doubts whatsoever, which is fine in theory, but life is not like that. Sometimes, most of the movement is marking time because all you are doing is moving from one side to the other and getting nowhere fast. Although there is movement in your life, *you do not move forward*, only from side to side to the other, yes or no, black or white, this or that, sometimes dealing with the same old problems repeatedly which never seem to be resolved. You constantly fall into Scylla while avoiding Charybdis and vice versa, with much the same results.

The either/and idea is not unlike the slack wire at the circus. To get to the other side you have constantly to adjust your position to retain your balance or you will fall. First you have to move to one side and then the other. By the time you have reached the other side at least you will understand something of flexibility, balance and that there are two sides in most things and not just one point of view - yours. I am sure there is a point of evolution where all these arguments and the duality of life here will disappear because they will no longer be valid and will seem trivial. However, not yet or here I feel, and if you want to deal with Pan, I suggest you remain flexible as much as you can - either/or - which is the reason for these arguments being presented.

Let me close this part by offering to the reader imagery that I still use for this in the hope it might help some. If you were to ask someone to divide a circle into two equal halves they would, as most of us would, put a line straight across the centre, not unlike an equator. The trouble with that arrangement is that there is a clearly defined boundary between the two halves and they have little or no contact with each other, because neither will cross the border of the other. As the Chinese book the **I Ching** tells us, 'heaven and earth are out of communion and all things are benumbed.' *Hexagram 12* from this work, further tells us then when what is above has no relation to what is below, confusion and disorder prevail on earth. This is the 'either/or' idea.

Now we come to that brilliantly conceived circle of the Yin and Yang of the Chinese, with brief explanation, and what a masterstroke of design it is.

The dividing line, between the two halves, is curved like an 's' - a sigmoid - in the white half is a circle of black, and in the black half is a circle of white. Each half contains the 'germ' or 'seed' of its opposite. Part of the feminine or earth is in the masculine or heaven half of the circle, and vice versa. What is more, each half is equally divided as in the first example given above, but there all similarity ends. If you draw a straight line on this symbol, across its centre to 'divide the circle,' it is impossible to avoid including some of the opposite side, no matter how you turn the line on its central axis - this is the 'either/and' idea.

Try to stop regarding Pan as if he were equally divided by a straight line across the waist, the animal, instinctive and earthy, below, the human, intellectual and spiritual above - this is an either/or idea, one thing

The Chinese Circle of Yin and Yang.

A brief explanation of this symbol might be in order, having introduced it in the text. Although the symbol is very well known, I think it would be wrong to assume that everyone will know the symbols inherent within it. In China, the masculine principle - **Yang** - was expressed by a white circle and represents heaven. The feminine principle - **Yin** - was represented by a black square and represents earth. The white circle stands for energy and the celestial influences, and the black square for the earthy or telluric forces. The shared response implied within this dualism is represented by the famous symbol of the **Ying-Yang** circle, where they are divided into two equal sections by a *sigmoid* (= Greek - 'sigma,' curved like a letter 's'). The white section - **Yang** - has a black spot set within it, and the black section - **Yin** - a white spot. These two spots teach there is something of the feminine in the masculine, and some masculine in the feminine. The sigmoid line is often used as a symbol of movement and communication in art and, like the swastika, signifies rotation, imparting a dynamic character to this dual symbol. The two sections appear to be swirling around each other on a central axis. The laws of polarity fascinated the minds of Chinese philosophers as much as those in the West and, possibly, for a greater time. All creation consisted of two kinds of energy, one is active and positive and the other, passive and negative. In the year, for example, there is a given amount of energy that can be drawn upon, in varying proportions, from the six parts of **Yang** - the *bright and active* period of the year, spring and summer, and the six parts of **Yin** - the *dark and passive* period of the year, autumn and winter.

or the other. You cannot cut him in half so there is no contact between the two halves, for 'confusion and disorder prevail on earth.' *Hexagram 12.*

Imagine the Yin and Yang circle diagram superimposed upon the image of Pan, with the white half uppermost in the human half, and the black half on the animal part of the figure. Place the boundary between the two halves across Pan's waist. The dark circle near the head suggests the necessity of setting instinct (= the ancient, instinctive, animal half, the black section) on a level with intellect (= the spiritual, intellectual, human half, white section). If instinct is denied by the intellect, or if intellect has, like the circle of Yin and Yang, no seed of instinct within it, then I think instinct will make its presence felt one way or another; in the extreme, perhaps a 'road to Damascus.' The white circle placed on the lower, animal half suggests the gods natural and joyful procreation being in harmony with, and having the blessing of, the spiritual laws above. The division across the waist blends the mixture of both sides rather than separating them. For any line drawn straight across the waist will contain some of the opposite attributes. The 'tail' of the black half sweeps upwards to the head, while the 'tail' of the white half sweeps downward to the hoofs, the circle is complete.

Now visualize the circle rotating in front of the figure. Slowly at first, do not go too fast to start. You will find a natural 'speed' to settle on if this works for you. The rotation merges the two halves so that 'their influences meet and are in harmony, so that all living things bloom and prosper...Heaven and earth unite.' (Hexagram 11). By rotating the circle of Yin and Yang you are not seeing Pan as a human with a goat half, or an animal with a human half. Pan is a blending of human and animal. You are merging the two halves by motion and energy, which is life, into one, because you are no longer looking at Pan as a duality, but unity. Pan is no longer divided, but complete. Not unlike the way, in my first science lessons, I painted the seven colours of the spectrum on a wheel and then rotated it quickly. When the colour proportions and the rate of spin were correct, the seven colours blended into white.

These are some of the ways I have thought of Pan, approached him, and dealt with him. Although this is personal to me, it is given because it might help some and encourage others to formulate their own method of contact in the way they draw near and seek Pan. Remember, it bears repeating often, the things you do for yourself always have more power built into them. However, this does not mean you cannot adapt and build upon what others have done, we all need some help at times. By all means take what is given, but make it you're own, by stamping it with your individuality as soon as you can. Naturally, the foregoing pertains mostly to those who are working alone. If you are working in a School, the question will not arise as you should be given any necessary instructions. Remember the warning of **Francis Bacon**:

Animus ad amplitudinem Mysteriorum pro modulo suo dilatetur; non Mysteria ad angustias animi.' (*Let the mind, as far as it can, be open to the fullness of the mysteries; let not the mysteries be constrained to fit the narrower confines of the mind*).

To end this short essay on Pan let us look at his reported death! Believing, as I mostly do, that there is little new under the sun, I can't believe **Mark Twain** was the first to say 'the report of my death was an exaggeration.' This was in a cable sent from London to the Associated Press, on the 2nd June 1897. I am sure Pan had a good laugh at the report of his 'death' and I am sure he found it equally 'exaggerated.' Pan is not the only powerful god who did not live amid the Olympian twelve. By their exalted standards he is assumed by many to be quite a humble fellow. He is regarded by some as a minor god, which is a serious mistake by my reckoning. As I have repeatedly stated, this is one of my 'either/or' preoccupation's that has little or no middle ground, in this I play the zealot for Pan, though trying to convince and not enforcing.

Pan was quite content to live in his beloved Arcadia with the rural peoples. It is precisely this that made him accessible, then as now, to lesser mortals such as ourselves. Hades and Hecate, for example, knew their presence in Olympus didn't exactly set bells of joy ringing. Pan, at least, was always welcome in Olympus. As history shows, most of the gods that predate Christianity were frequently reported as personally accessible to mortals one way or another.

It was the later One God who left earth and became inaccessible in some unapproachable, unknown realm. He is accessible only through his priesthood, and this is called the true religion! The early gods remained on earth and were approachable: not only could they be prayed to, sometimes they could be confronted. Greek priests, like Christian priests, interpreted the will of Zeus at Dodona to those who asked his blessing or advice, and to him the people prayed, but this is called a false religion!

Pan has the unique position of being the only god to 'die' in our time. In the reign of Emperor Tiberius, the news of Pan's death came to a mariner, a pilot named Thamus (Tammuz in some accounts). Thamus was bound for Italy and was becalmed just off the island of Paxos. Suddenly across the still waters he heard a mysterious voice call to him from the shore of the island three times, 'Thamus!' Naturally he answered his name and the voice said, 'When you reach Palodes, proclaim that the great god Pan is dead!' This Thamus did when the vessel drifted towards land later. The pilot gave out the news as told to do so, 'the Great god Pan is dead.'

The news was greeted from the shore with groans, lamentation and great weeping. When he arrived in Italy, he was summoned by the Emperor himself who called in the great scholars to interpret the event. Most of the scholars decided the Pan named was not the Pan, God of Nature, but a demon of the same name. At the time of the message it is said two curious coincidences occurred. The first is that all the oracles in the land suddenly became silent. This is strange if most of them were in the hands of Apollo, yet they were silenced at the reported death of Pan. The oracles were not silenced, but *the Oracle was* - and the oracle was Pan! It was not Pan who died, but the effective and creative voice of Nature that had been silenced.

The second proved stranger. Traditionally, Christianity was said to have been born in Judea when Christ was crucified, on the exact day and at the exact hour of the given message that Pan was dead. Two Shepherds died, for both were the Shepherds of their Flocks: one of the past and the present, while the other had yet to come into his own when this event was supposed to have taken place, for Christianity was not yet born. The church has always eschewed legend, but tacitly permitted this one, along with the others it needed. As with other Christian legends it turned a blind eye to this one and permitted it to flourish, perhaps they even started it, fully realizing its value to a young, vulnerable religion.

All reputable religions had a sustaining archive of myth and legend that made their antiquity respectable. So a little incorporation was felt a desirable asset to give the new religion a respectable stock of myth and legend of its own. Photographs of the fourth century mosaic in the *Basilica Theodoriana, Aquileia* shows The Good Shepherd. It is a shepherd carrying a sheep around his neck in the manner of the day. He is holding the feet of the animal with his left hand but in his extended right hand he is holding panpipes.

Early Christians found it difficult to portray the figure of Christ as he was both human and divine, and this is one of the reasons he is infrequently portrayed in the art of the catacombs. He does appear as a child in the arms of his mother or being baptised in the Jordan by John. Most of the pictures in the Roman catacombs seem to represent his presence or work, for example, as the parable of the good shepherd finding his lost sheep, etc. To these one scene from pagan myth was common, Orpheus and his lyre, usually taming the beasts with his music, as if Orpheus was a pagan prophet of the coming of Christ and it could be taken as an indication of Christian interest in the poems and oracles ascribed to Orpheus. It has been suggested this may have been because Orpheus used charm and gentleness instead of guile and force and he, like Christ and a few others, was one of the handful who had been to the land of the dead and returned. In the *Catacomb of Domitilla*, Rome, Orpheus is depicted 'charming the beasts,' with a goat prominent among the animals, but his customary lyre has been replaced with panpipes.

Matthew 25:32 tells us 'And he shall separate the nations one from the other as the shepherd separateth the sheep from the goats; and he shall set the sheep on his right hand, but the goats to the left.' Here I believe we are being told in unsophisticated symbolism that the animal of the new shepherd (= *Christ*) is the sheep (= *Christians*) which is diametrically opposed to the animal of the old shepherd (= *Pan*), the goats (= *Pagans*).

'But suppose we leave souls out of account for the moment, and think only of spiritual qualities. I admit that these can only exist in the experience of the souls, but it is these which constitute the sheep and the goats, and not the souls. Souls can be freed from them or acquire them as the case may be, can accept them or reject them as time goes on, but there is no necessary eternal association of a soul with any quality. Once we see this the parable becomes luminous. You could draw a dividing line between the sheep and goats with absolute clearness. The sheep are the good things in our nature, the Christ-like qualities in our character and experience; the goats are the opposite.' **R.J. Campbell** - Sermon, *The Eternal Fire.*

This sermon was published in the *Christian Commonwealth* on the 18th of June, 1913. It is thought to contain (probably) the first published reference to the important idea of *soul-qualities* being meant in scripture, instead of souls, in many cases. The sheep (= Christ) are set on the right hand, while the goats (= Pan) will go to the left hand, perhaps with all that is implied by going 'to the left.' Goats were often used as a symbol of the lower qualities, though in my view why lower than sheep I can't imagine; sheep follow without question while goats seem to have a mind of their own. We read, 'Mine anger was kindled against the shepherds, and I will punish the goats.' Zech.10:3.

Now, I have nothing against sheep but I have always regarded them as particularly stupid animals that do not seem to have a will of their own, only a herd instinct; and that is why, in my early churchgoing days, I objected to being regarded and spoken to as a member of 'the flock,' particularly as I got older. This implied to me that I was being blindly led to where it was thought I should go, by a shepherd carrying a crook, who was to me by now the wrong shepherd and pedum (= shepherds crook; a sheep hook), without my having any say in the matter regarding my spiritual welfare. It was explained that it was the special flock of the Good Shepherd; with confidence of youth I claimed my soul as my own. I did not take the Left-hand Path, as I think Matthew would have had it, but I did become a goat, which to me was not the same thing. I also became goat-like and solitary, because I went to church for quite some time on my own, when the flock which I did not wish to join and shepherd were not there, so there was nothing between God and me. I still go now and then, using whenever possible, a highly symbolic church in London which is, internally, a circle surrounded by twelve strong columns, six columns on either side of the aisle. To the above sin should now be added a lack of humility and great pride, but with the Angel(s) that had fallen for the same sin, I felt I would be in decent company.

Naturally the Early Christians took great comfort from Pan's death in the belief, mistaken as it proved, that it marked the moment of decline and the death of the Pagan era. The Early Christians claim this happened, although Christianity as we know it wasn't born at the precise time of Christ's death. Modern Christianity was hammered out much later by Paul. I have written about this often in the past and I am not the only one to think this. The Christianity of today is more a religion *about Christ*, than *of Christ*. It makes me wonder if the originator of it all would recognize what was being done in his name all these years later, or at any time in the last two thousand years. I have my doubts.

The above coincidences have always seemed a little strange and a little too convenient for some writers. Some think what the sailor actually heard was a ritual lamentation in honour of Adonis. **Graves** has suggested that the Egyptian sailor misunderstood the cry. What he heard, giving a wrong report, was a ritual lament in honour of Tammuz - '*Thamus Pan-megas Tethnece!*' - which he gives as 'The all-great Tammuz is dead!' **Graves** believed that because the name of the god (= Tammuz) and the sailor's name (= Thamus) sounded alike, the sailor thought he was being personally addressed. The Egyptian mistook what he heard for 'Thamus, the Great Pan is dead!'

Plutarch believed it and published it in his work, *On the Decay of the Oracles*. About a century later, when **Pausanias** the Greek traveller and geographer made his tour of Greece he reported that the altars of Pan, his sacred caves, the shrines and sacred mountains were still very much in use. They were frequented by the people and generally doing very well. As late as the 4th century **Iamblichus** still refers to those who were 'seized by Pan.'

Sanctuaries, caves and sites are frequently mentioned, particularly in Arcadia, as at Heraea, on the Nomian hill near Lycosura, and on Mount Parthenius. There was an ancient oracle at Troezen, at which the nymph Erato had been his priestess. There was the well of Eresumus, between Argos and Tegea, one at Sicyon and another at Oropus at Athens, near Marathon. Another well was on the island of Psyttaleia. There is the most famous and sacred shrine of the Corycian Cave near Parnassus and another at Homala in Thessaly. Another shrine was at Megalopolis, near Acacesium, where a perpetual fire was kept burning in his temple, as it was at Olympia, the flame being taken from the altar of Zeus.

Even when Christianity considered itself an established religion, pilgrims were still drawn to him and frequented his established shrines, in Arcadia, Attica and elsewhere. Pan's shrines and altars were being visited by some visitors while travelling in Greece as late as 1989. It was a major reason for their going there.

So is the above report true? Is Pan dead? If you believe the report then he is dead - or to you he is and so is a part of you. Pan, despite the unnecessary and spiteful stress laid upon his sexual exploits at the expense of all else, is a very subtle and haunting presence, which pervades this planet still. He can still be found in the right places or invited to come to a suitable space prepared for him. Of course you have to want to find him.

Many people think any ritual or work invoking Pan is a fraught process, not for the fainthearted; and this could be true. I think Pan is not a god for idle experimentation, neither for example would Cernunnos or Herne be. The Horned Gods could be very difficult to handle if they decided to take you at your word, especially if they can see the matter has no gravity and is little more than an entertainment. They could answer just to see what you would do with what you now have. Many people today, more than in the past I feel, find it a diversion from ennui to involve themselves and their friends with bookish ritual and melodrama from the material available today without sufficient preparation, but then fools always find bigger fools to admire them but 'the only impossible thing is a fool.' **D.H. Lawrence**. Would they pour molten metal into a plastic container while lying underneath it? Most would rightly say that would be stupid, for the plastic would melt because it could not contain the molten metal. It is unsuitable as a container - but what is the difference between the *unsuitable* and the *untutored*? Their ritual, literally *an invitation*, could be taken up by some shape-changer seeking a channel to use, which channel they tend to forget is themselves, to the material plane. They are then faced with a guest of unknown qualities and temperament that they have invited in. They do not know how to ask the guest to depart or have sufficient authority to control it while it is there and, what is more, the door is still ajar with the possibility of other 'guests' coming in to put their feet under the table and join the party. If everything was flooded with water, for example, would it occur to them to consider calling on *Charbiel* the angel who was 'appointed to draw together and dry up all the waters of the earth?' It was Charbiel, in tradition, who drew up and dried up the waters after the Flood in Genesis.

Thank goodness most of these attempts do not work and many are delivered from harm by stupidity which saves them from their folly. **Schiller** said: 'Against stupidity the very gods themselves contend in vain.' Perhaps we should take a lesson from Semele.

Semele was beloved of Zeus. His wife Hera was jealous of the affair and determined to end it. To this end she borrowed the girdle of the goddess Ate, the personification of error and mischief who had caused such jealousy and sedition among the gods that Zeus banished her from heaven forever. She came to earth, because Zeus hurled her here, where she spent her time inciting mankind to all manner of wickedness and sowing the seeds of perpetual dissent among them. She is the same as the goddess Discord of the Latins. The girdle of Ate made its wearer an adept in wickedness, deceit and perfidy. Hera appeared to Semele in the guise of the aged Beroe, who was formerly her nurse.

The false Beroe induced her to demand from Zeus that he appear in the same splendour and majesty as that in which he appeared to Hera or she would withhold her favours. Zeus having promised Semele he would grant her every request appeared as God of Thunder and she was consumed by the fire of the lightning. Semele was pregnant at the time and Zeus saved her six-month developed child by hiding him in his thigh, until the appointed time of birth - this was Dionysus. Some say the child was protected from the fire by a shield of ivy that was his particular plant. Regarding this compare the legends of Acteon (= Artemis/Diana), Aglaurus (= Athene), Astrabacos (= Artemis Orthia), Teiresias (= the Gods or Athene) for other examples of impudence suitably rewarded.

Occultists in the past undertook stricter regimens regarding the preparation for ritual and study. Although I do not believe some of these could be undertaken today, which is why I have chosen an extreme case, however, I do think more could be done regarding discipline in this particular area, for much experimentation is attempted by what I call the 'instant coffee' generation, who expect it to be as easy as just adding water. The preparation, especially by those outside the discipline of a School are sparse for the most, if any preparation at all. The preparations undertaken, for example, in the *Abra-Merlin* system could be beyond the means of most practitioners and the conditions of life today, including myself. The practitioner goes as far as dividing his house into two and renting another house to 'accustom himself to the solitary life.' The operation was undertaken for 'Six Moons without omitting the slightest detail.' Christ himself went into the desert for forty days and nights and what he underwent there is not recorded.

Most of the prophets seeking spiritual guidance or contact in Biblical times seemed to prefer the desert and scorpions to human company and crowded towns. John the Baptist is another obvious example. These solitary excursions have taken place in most religious philosophies. Part of the process is that the god-form should enter the body and cleanse it of dross, thus purifying it. 'For he is like a refiner's fire.' Mal.3:2. It is here we come against the unknown factor that I would hesitate to define for myself, and would definitely not attempt to define it for another.

How much dross is present? If there is a small amount then refinement would take place without any real trouble and the results would be extremely advantageous, but what if the internal dross was greater than thought? Say, much to our chagrin and opinion of ourselves, as high as 95 percent? Spontaneous combustion? This strange fire burns from the inside out and hardly touches anything else around the person while happening without any seeming cause. This is a fact in all cultures and races no matter how it is described. If this is a possible cause then what is a *safe level* of dross that can stand the 'refiner's fire' and how do you assess it? Hera knew how much it was I am sure, which is why she chose this form of temptation, while Semele didn't. It's just a thought.

Pan, like Mars, had a hand in wars, so I suppose he could be called a god of war. He sent terror and panic not only to the single traveller through his kingdom, but to larger groups of people including armies, where he used his skills for the side he supported and they usually won, as we have already seen.

Valierius Flaccus tells us that the terror and panic that was fatal for the Doliones, was attributed directly to the shouts of terror and trumpet calls heard in the night. It runs 'Men's rest was disturbed, the god Pan drove the doubting city distraught. Pan, lord of the woodlands and of war, whom caverns shelter from the daylight hours. About midnight, in lonely places was seen the hairy flank and the rough leafage on his fierce brow.' **Flaccus** knew his Pan. For the most Pan never comes down to the cities of men, unless it is to confound them.

Pan did not, however, suffer the fate of Mars who is only thought of now as a god of war and strife, at the expense of his being a great god of Nature. This, as with Pan, does Ma(vo)rs a great disservice through ignorance. Pan has survived the passing of the centuries, the propaganda, the purges, Inquisitions and most of the things that have been thrown at him. He is a god of great love that he wants to give and receive - *a gift for a gift*. Yet he has one enemy walking abroad he cannot wholly cope with - indifference - who can? Neglect may wound Pan but it will not kill him; he will simply withdraw and bide his time until there is a change of climate and heart. He has somewhere to go, it's we who don't.

He's used to the waiting game, he's been playing longer than we have and he has more time than we. It is slowly sinking in that we are placed here on this planet with Nature and she has provided the place where we must live and work out our destiny. Change must come with the deity reinstated in the hearts and minds of people. When such thoughts and the desire for change appears in the hearts of people, it is the nymphs and Pan still working their subtle magic through us. I have not attempted to hide my bias regarding the main subject of the work, or where my loyalty and defence lie. Even I have to accept an either/or concept sometimes if I agree with it and it is valid, thus coming down decisively on one side. My defence of Pan is either/or, you are for him or against him, with some things you cannot compromise, they are too important; for me this is one of them. Without Pan's guiding spirit and help our present contract with Nature and Gaia, Mother Earth, is internecine. However, here is a gentleman who thinks as I do...

> 'Pan of the garden, the fold,
> Pan of the bird and beast,
> Kindly, he lives as of old,
> He isn't dead in the least!'
> *Pan Pipes*: **Patrick Chalmers**.

I would like to end the section on Pan with a final brief quotation from the chapter *The Piper at the Gates* from **Kenneth Graham's** *The Wind in the Willows*. After Mole had looked in the very eyes of the Friend and Helper, he turns to Ratty.

'Rat!' He found the breath to whisper, shaking, 'Are you afraid?'

'Afraid?' murmured the Rat, his eyes shining with unutterable love. 'Afraid! Of Him? O never, never! And yet - and yet - O, Mole, I am afraid!'

THE TREE OF PAN

A
Path Working.

THE TREE OF PAN

A Path Working.

This chapter on the god Pan is a pathworking, an exercise in visualization. There is a certain amount of evidence that the 'island' within this text does exist physically, but we do not have sufficient evidence to prove the case. There is an eighty per cent chance it exists on the material plane. However, as a man who complains that the Tree of Life is being hammered into shape to fit any scheme that takes someone's fancy of late, I cannot hoist myself by my own petard by pursuing a similar course, at least not until further substantiation of the facts agrees with the theory, assuming it ever will. I do not believe one swallow makes a summer. It's true I have more than one 'swallow' but I doubt if I have a flock; therefore, I have no summer.

We will use the Tree of Life and the Celtic Seven Chieftains of the High and Sacred Grove. We will use 'the stuff that dreams are made of' and, when our island is created, pull it down to the physical plane and try to make it our own according to our personal ability. The diagram we use exists and it has existed for many, many long years and when you start to think about it, the first stage of its physical existence begins. The Mona Lisa did not exist as we know it once in its history. This was when it was in the mind of Leonardo and perhaps in its most critical stage. It would have been lost for ever if he had not brought it out from the darkness and given it form.

He took what was in his mind, hidden in the darkness where it was born, and made it physical or concrete. He brought it out into the light. This bears out the premise that if you want to secure the future, do not leave it in the future; put it in the past and that will secure it. For example, if you take a future project that is still in your mind, write it down or explain it to others, whatever its value. It has been placed in the present when you write it down and explain it; this passes quickly into the past and *it is the past that secures the future*. The future is potential, the past is actual; leave something in the future and you could lose it - for ever. What you have put in the past is deposited there, like a granary in which you store your harvest.

The artists, writers, dramatists and composers, among others of the world, are the few who see and hear what many do not. These abilities are what make some of them a Leonardo da Vinci, **Mahler**, Milton or Shakespeare. When you give something form and substance, you are operating under the laws of Saturn. Leonardo used the Saturnian laws of form to make his creation concrete. Now we all can share in his creation, *La Giaconda*. Most of what we achieve starts in the darkness of the mind, hidden, out of sight. There is nothing special about this. It is quite natural and the way Nature works; we all possess this to some extent. We are not all Leonardos: nature throws up few of them, and we have to do the best we can with what we have.

Most seeds and ideas are planted in darkness. There in the fertile darkness these fragile abstractions gestate. When they are at the stage when they can face the light, they emerge and take their chance, as we all do. We gathered our strength in the darkness of our mother and when the vehicle of the body was ready, it emerged into the light for further development and growth. Seeds are similarly planted in the earth and are protected within the womb of the earth until they can face the light and develop. This is why darkness must not, as is often the case, be regarded as evil or negative.

People think because light is good that darkness must be automatically evil. Youth is good so we must fight old age tooth and nail; growing old must be regarded as a mortal enemy, something that must be defeated at all costs. Darkness of itself is not evil, but whatever or whoever avails themselves of the use of it often is. Under the cover of darkness we need greater honour and restraint in many things, much as we do when we are in a crowd, because a negative crowd is a mob.

When the terms dark, negative and passive are found in writing of this nature they must be regarded as intended, of equal status. Of course darkness can be evil but then so can light in its negative aspect. Light can be equally highly destructive, as in the negative sun of the atomic bomb, and even eternal sunshine, so beloved of the sun-seekers, would give the earth no rest and destroy more than it created. One cannot exist without the other at the physical level of existence. In the opening lines of **Wolfram von Eschenbach's** sublime and epic work *Parzival* we are told: 'A dauntless man's spirit is both black and white like the magpie's plumage. Both colours have a share in him, the colour of heaven and the colour of hell.'

At first our Tree will exist only in our thoughts. There it will be formatted and given a form that can be used for our purpose. Great benefit could be secured by calling this Tree into existence, so I will set down some suggestions as to the methods that were used for its creation.

A problem of this part of the work is that two groups of readers with different viewpoints may be interested in the present work. The first is the reader whose preferences are for myth, legend and folklore, but not necessarily for those matters that are generally termed 'occult and its literature.' To these people a visualization exercise that suggests an attempt to see the god Pan is of little or no interest. They may deem it not only impractical but little more than a flight of fancy of the writer, or any other who thinks it is possible by such methods.

The second group has similar interests to the first in myth, legend and folklore, with one difference. They accept or practise occult philosophy and because of this they will have little or no difficulty with what is being offered here. Visualization exercises, in one form or another, are normal practices of their lives; for others it is called positive thinking and that, to a certain point, is correct. When anyone, for example, runs through in their mind an interview they will attend for a position, considering and rehearsing their replies to possible questions that may be asked by the prospective employer, the manner in which they will present themselves, and foreseeing a positive result to support a positive attitude to give a good impression, this is visualization to many no matter what others may choose to call it. The practice of visualization is a very old one, the most obvious example being the mimetic dances of earlier races, enacting the hunting and kill of those animals necessary for the survival of family or clan. One member dressed as the prey sought that day, the rest as the hunters seeking a successful outcome.

What is being suggested here is an experiment or experience that is passed on for appraisal and use, even if the reader's present studies have not entered the area of study called Cabala. Cabala is a difficult subject to avoid in the Western Tradition. There are so many branches of study available they cannot all be undertaken. There is likely to be some awareness of this philosophical or magical system, perhaps some knowledge of its basic tenets. We often have to undertake an acquaintance with subjects associated with our main interest, the better to understand our interest, fellow travellers, writers and speakers.

Many comments in the following will be directed to the latter readers and those who want some very basic instruction to help them understand what is attempted. For those readers unable to follow or accept the teachings of occultism, no difficulty should be met if what follows is read simply in the spirit of a story that takes place in an unusual land, which it is. In view of my interests a colleague was surprised that

I quote the Bible frequently in writing and speaking. He told me he had read the Bible very little. He could remember some brief content from when he was a child. I suggested he should read the work again and he said he couldn't do that because he was an atheist and not a Christian. I asked him what did that have to do with the price of fish? Why should that prevent him from reading the Bible as literature? Why did he deprive himself of reading one of the greatest books written?

Christianity as such need not be considered when reading the Bible as literature, although it is irrefutably central to the Christian creed. This is not intended to upset those whose religious beliefs are bound up with this monumental work; at least I am advocating it should be read and not ignored. It is a work that has afforded me great pleasure and endless study. Of course the conclusions and interpretations I draw from it, I am sure, will not accord with the views of the orthodox or fundamentalist, but for the most part they do not lack respect and I am, no less than they, trying to seek the truth, they largely through faith; others largely through knowledge.

Heresy does not apply only to the heathen, it is also applied to dissenting Christians. We have the Christianity of the winners and some of us would like to know what the losers had to say. All that is required to be a heretic is to disagree with the majority, which is a comparatively easy task. It's when the majority agree that I get suspicious for 'The opinion of the majority is not the final proof of what is right.' **Schiller**. Later my companion told me how much he was enjoying the Bible as a book. He thought it sad that he had permitted his atheist prejudice to deprive him of such excellent literature. Now, why has this little anecdote has been included here for the reader?

We are not equating what follows here with the Bible. That would be 'vaulting ambition, which o'erleaps itself.' *Macbeth*. We merely suggest that those who do not hold the occult beliefs placed within the text could, as suggested above, simply read it as a tale of Pan. They must have some interest in Pan to be reading to this point in the text.

Those readers who are interested in works of Science Fiction and the Horror genre often have to learn strange names and titles. They accept them when they read of strange countries and sometimes even stranger people whose appearance does not accord with ours. These people frequently have powers not found on earth that, in the spirit of the story, they accept. This seems to present little difficulty as the vast quantities of books, films and videos of such subjects show. There is really very little difference to what follows. This adventure is given and is based upon a living, working hypothesis being used by the writer and thousands of people, even now as I write. It does not make any claims to being unique in any way, except to the writer because it was personal to him; that is why, at first, it was going to be omitted.

When the writer, for example, makes the suggestion to the reader that they should learn the paths of the Tree of Life 'by heart,' this suggestion would only be relevant to those interested in studying the subject of Cabala or intending to take their studies further.

Readers whose interests are in Pan, but do not encompass the philosophy of Cabala would obviously not learn them by heart, or at all. These readers would use the path numbers and Kingdoms of the diagram to know where a particular part of the story is taking place and where the 'traveller' in the tale is going to and where they have come from, not unlike someone using a map to find their way in an area that is unknown to them. These readers could, without prejudice, go to the section entitled 'path working' now and omit what follows.

However, even a cursory glance at what ensues would give a better understanding of this part of the work and the locations where it all takes place. It is a simplified outline of a complicated subject and it makes no pretence to be any more than that. Only those aspects that are relevant to the task in hand have been used, which was not easy, the subject of Cabala is both vast and powerful. The planets and the rulerships involved with the seven Kingdoms of the Tree are mentioned within the text. I feel sufficient content is given within the text to make extensive lists and lengthy explanations unnecessary here.

Those readers who have studied the works of folklore, myth and legend will have little difficulty with what follows. Those who are familiar with the subject matter, generally called the Occult, will see this uses the diagram known, in Western Tradition, as the Tree of Life. Though naturally this plan did not originally belong to Western Tradition, it has been adopted by it and made its own. This diagram is involved with a study called Kabala(h), Cabala(h) or Qabalah. This chapter will only take us into the shallow waters of this very specialist subject, for in parts the study is very deep. The study of the system we call Cabala is the study of not one, but perhaps many lifetimes. We will wade into its waters just far enough to enable us to pursue the subject matter of this chapter.

For those who do wish to undertake or extend their understanding and knowledge of Cabala there are many excellent books available. It is no exaggeration to write that the subject has produced virtually millions of words in print; to which (it seems) I am about to add a few thousand more. The reader's attention is drawn to the works of the late Dion Fortune, those of Gareth Knight, the late William Gray, Papus, Eliphas

Levi and the excellent works of Z'ev ben Shimon Halevi (Warren Kenton). As always, omission does not imply rejection or criticism; it is lack of space that is the enemy. I repeat, we will be using a diagram of the 'Tree of Life' and some very simple principles of Cabala.

When we have created our Island of Pan we will plant our 'Tree of Pan' on it and, hopefully, nurture it to growth. I must point out the idea of gathering related knowledge and assigning them to this diagram is *not original to this writer*. This unique diagram has been used in this fashion long before the present writer appeared on the scene and will be here and used similarly long after he has gone. Each writer uses their own variation of the basic scheme. It is to the credit of its creator(s) that it is still being used and adapted in so many ways so long after its original conception. At times it would appear to have been put through the mangle to make things agree with it. Old works and prints show the diagram of the 'Tree of Life' has undergone many changes. For example, the *Porta Lucis* of **Paulus Ricius** (Augsberg, 1516) gives the Sephirotic Tree that has only sixteen paths instead of today's twenty-two. Older diagrams, for example, show the Kingdoms as always, numbered one to ten but the paths numbered from one to twenty-two, instead of today's system of numbering the Kingdoms from one to ten and the paths from eleven to thirty-two, continuing the numbering after the Kingdoms. This makes path one of the old system become eleven, path two - twelve, path three - thirteen and so on. However, we use the later scheme with the paths numbered eleven to thirty-two that is the more prevalent, because it avoids any confusion between Kingdoms and paths.

We are told in the Cabalistic writings of the Zohar that the Source made a current that formed a vast basin called 'the Sea.' The basin divided into seven channels (= paths?) and the water from this sea goes into these seven channels. Should the Creator or Source elect to break these channels the waters would return to their Source, leaving only broken vessels (= Kingdoms?) that 'would remain dry and without water.' The Source, the 'current,' the 'sea' and the seven channels make ten in all. This may even suggest that at one time the tree only had seven paths. This, however, is pure speculation on the part of the writer and should be taken in this light.

We must first explain in simple terms certain fundamentals for the benefit of those who may not be familiar with the Tree diagram. A diagram of the 'Tree of Pan' has been placed at the end of the book which can be folded out while the text is being read. It will be seen that the Tree consists of ten circles in a set pattern. These circles are usually connected by double lines, making a secondary pattern, called 'the paths' or

The Sephirothic Tree from the Porta Lucis
of Paulus Ricius, Augsberg, 1516

'channels'. **Kircher,** writing on these paths says they are 'luminous roads by which holy men of God, through long usage and experience of divine things and long meditation upon them, can attain the hidden centres.'

These paths, like the circles, are numbered in a specific order. The numbers are necessary to show which path between the kingdoms is being used and the direction taken. Of course they are numbered as in the original diagram. The paths are not used here as in strict Cabalistic teaching, for the channels contain great detail that is omitted here. They will be used here somewhat as street names to identify which paths we are talking about and the Kingdoms they connect. However, if their order is memorized, this familiarity will stand you in good stead should you wish to take your Cabalistic studies beyond the scope of this work. One small matter must be mentioned before we proceed. The titles of the Kingdoms sometimes have different spellings, depending on which book you use and its age. I have standardized the spelling for the purpose of this work, to avoid confusion, but be prepared to see it a little different in other works.

You would know, for instance, that path 30 is the path between the ninth Kingdom of Yesod and the eighth Kingdom of Hod. You would know paths 23, 26, 27, 30 and 31 all lead to and from the eighth Kingdom of Hod. The 23rd path will take you to Geburah, the 26th to Tiphereth, the 27th to Netzach, the 30th to Yesod and the 31st to Malkuth. As said, the paths of the Tree can be used here in much the same way as you know how to get to a specific destination in your locality. Maps of your locality have streets that have names, not numbers; but learning to use the tree like a street map would be the right idea. Whatever context you intend to use it for, it would be advantageous to be completely at home with it. I cannot repeat this enough.

Each circle or Kingdom is called a Sephirah (pronounced= Seff-fi-rah) and collectively they are called Sephiroth (pronounced= Seff-fi-roth). They are sometimes called Spheres, Emanations or Kingdoms. Because of the nature of the pathworking and the way in which they are used in the text, we will use the latter title of Kingdoms. They each have a title as Cabalistic works show and this does suggest the nature of the Kingdom, so we give them below. These Sephiroth are numbered from the top downwards, from one to ten, and the order does not change.

The traditional titles for the individual Sephirah are as follows. No.1 - Kether - 'The Crown'; No.2 - Chokmah 'Wisdom'; No.3 - Binah - 'Understanding'; No.4 - Chesed 'Mercy'; No.5 - Geburah - 'Strength or Severity'; No.6 Tiphereth - 'Beauty'; No.7 - Netzach - 'Victory'; No.8 - Hod - 'Glory'; No.9 - Yesod - 'Foundation' and finally, No.10 - Malkuth

- 'Kingdom.' However, those readers who have already inspected the diagram will see there are eleven circles upon the Tree given. This is not a mistake so let us place this eleventh Kingdom in context.

Superimposed upon the Tree, near to the top, is a dotted circle which is placed at the base of the 1, 2 and 3 triangle. This sephirah or Kingdom is usually left unnumbered and its title is Daath or 'Knowledge' (prounced= Daarth). This Kingdom of Daath is mentioned in early Cabalistic writing but despite this it is thought to be a modern idea, 'modern' in contrast to the known age of the Tree. It is held to represent a hidden Kingdom or sephirah of the Tree. Early texts are unambiguous that there are 'ten Holy Sephiroth, not nine and not eleven, but ten.' Notwithstanding, this eleventh Kingdom makes and important appearance in what follows and, therefore, must be given in the text.

Some titles of Daath are 'the invisible sephirah', 'the 'Unrevealed Universal Mind' or 'the Upper or Empty Room.' I have always thought its position on the Tree a very perilous one, sitting, as it does, astride the Abyss. I have written that Daath sits 'astride the Abyss' even though the Kingdom of Daath is clearly shown below the Abyss on the given diagram. It has long been the writers view that the influence of this Kingdom extends well over the Abyss, hence the existence of the *Pons Periculosus*= 'the bridge perilous,' the *Pons Asinorum*= 'the asses bridge,' perhaps the *Pedica Asinorum*= 'the 'fool's stumbling block?' This 'bridge' is sometimes found spanning the Abyss, it does not always appear to everyone, this makes me wonder if it is tempting you - or testing you. This bridge is mentioned a little later in the text.

The writer has always associated the time of midnight with the Kingdom of Daath and considered it a time when this Kingdom may be at its most active and so, possibly, most accessible. King David was accustomed, without fail, to rise at this hour and give his praise; he knew this time influenced the earthly judgements of kings, upon which hung his rule. 'At midnight I will rise to give thanks unto thee because of thy righteous judgements.' Psalm.119:62. This Psalm is the one that has the twenty-two sections starting with Aleph and ending with Tau of the Hebrew alphabet. The twenty-two Hebrew letters are often placed on the twenty-two paths of the Tree of Life.

According to the **Zohar** or its commentaries, nightly at midnight, 'the Holy One' rises and goes with his entourage to the Garden of Eden to converse with the Righteous. 'Midnight' has been given as a title of the Holy One. The Accusing Angels are busy in the world below during the first three hours of the night but at midnight all accusation ceases, this being the time when God enters the Garden.

At midnight the time of dispassionate and veracious judgement begins everywhere. Midnight draws from the two sides of night, Judgement and Mercy, possibly the only time when it can for at midnight the night is balanced. I have assumed this is time being divided as at the *equinox=* equal day and night; the night beginning at six in the evening and ending at six the next morning when the day starts. This would make midnight the point of balance of the night.

The first part of the night being the period of Judgement or Severity(= Binah), the latter half takes it illumination from the side of Mercy (= Chesed). Expressing a personal, though difficult opinion to express. At midnight the writer conceives the Holy One as descending through the Kingdom of Kether, coming down path 13 the Holy One enters the Kingdom of Daath, for a short time, *on our side of the Abyss.* While the Holy One is in the Kingdom of Daath, seated in the Throne of the Pillar of Mildness; the Pillars of Judgement and Mercy are energized; these 'Three 'Pillars' are briefly explained below for those who are unfamiliar with them.

In today's timing, midnight is the border between one day and the next. It is a period of change, when time is neither one thing nor the other, a crack when time has not yet left night and not yet become day. Similarly Pan is found on land that is merging from the uncultivated (= the intuitive and sensual) to the cultivated (= the controlled and abstemious). In the Celtic calendar we have at least one such night, *Samhain* or *All Hallows* on the 1st of November. The Eve of Samhain was held to be a time, particularly at midnight, when the barrows of the fairies were opened and the veil between 'other worlds' and ours was at it weakest, a time when it was held that 'contact' could be made with least effort. It was the point upon which the year 'hinged,' when the boundaries between the world of nature and spirit were at their weakest, a time of divination and rune-casting around the night fires.

A little more information about the diagram is required before we can make a start. As with so many objects, affairs, situations, people and things we have to deal with on the physical plane, the Sephiroth are given over to the planetary rulership of the seven planets of old. These Seven Planets of the Ancients are the Sun, Moon, Mercury, Venus, Mars, Jupiter and Saturn.

Many modern writers place the later discovered planets of Uranus, Neptune and Pluto on the diagram, thus distributing one planet to each of the ten Sephiroth. We only deal with the seven planets of old astrology, not with these three new planets in this section, I am not against progress, as I have mentioned before, but I sometimes think that during the last few years it has produced nothing but changes for the sake of it. More runes than the ancients gave us and tarot cards created purely to promote a personal 'ism' rather than to advance knowledge upon what was previously given, the list is endless, which seems to indicate some people have too much time on their hands and too little to do with it. 'Remove not the ancient landmark, which thy fathers have set.' Proverbs 22:28. The main reason, however, for these later planets not being included is simple. They were not included at the time of the event recorded and given later, so they are not included because they are there now.

The Seven Chieftains of the High and Sacred Grove are seven ancient and sacred trees. These are the Birch, Willow, Holly, Hazel, Oak, Apple and Yew. They are found in Celtic mythology. These seven trees have the same planetary rulers as the seven planets of old and seven of the sephirah. Therefore, I feel they can be legitimately placed on these seven sephirah. It is now necessary to decide where these seven planets and their groves are to be placed on the diagram to enable us to construct our proposed 'Tree of Pan' in preparation for what is to follow.

The customary scheme, the one most widely used by Schools and Cabalistic Books, is to place the four elements of air, fire, earth and water within the tenth Kingdom of Malkuth. The Moon is set over the ninth Kingdom of Yesod, the planet Mercury rules the eighth Kingdom of Hod, Venus is in the seventh Kingdom of Netzach. The Sun is ruler of the sixth Kingdom of Tiphereth, Mars in the fifth Kingdom of Geburah, Jupiter in the fourth Kingdom of Chesed and Saturn across the Abyss, in the third Kingdom of Binah. The second Kingdom of Chokmah is give to the Zodiac and the first to the Primum Mobile that contained the other nine and produced them.

This scheme is given here to avoid confusion for those readers who may read or have read books that show these more usual placements on the diagram, the system as used by *The Golden Dawn*. Most students who are in a School or with a teacher are likely to use these placements on the Tree of Life. I will not be using this system of planetary placements for personal reasons and there is another system which has been proffered in the past. Occasionally I do 'plough a lonely furrow' and I shall do so here. This is not wilful perversity just 'to be different.' Nor am I being like Bunthorne, 'the meaning doesn't matter if its only idle chatter of a transcendental kind' for...

...everyone will say,
As you walk your mystic way,
'If this young man expresses himself in terms too deep for me,

Why, what a very singularly deep young man this
deep young man must be!'
Patience: **W.S. Gilbert**.

The reason for this change from the usually accepted placements,
however, cannot be gone into at this point as this is not a book on Cabala.
What follows is based upon a slightly changed scheme, so it has to stand
as the plan used in what was given. The system of Cabala used in this work
was not created or invented by the present writer, it was in existence long
before he was born It is simply the system he prefers and the system is
explained a little more, later.

The Sephiroth of the first Kingdom of Kether, the second Kingdom
of Chokmah and the third Kingdom of Binah are known collectively as
'the three Supernals'. They make 'the First Trinity' of the Tree of Life,
paths 11, 12 and 14. These three Supernals are separated from the
remaining seven Sephiroth below them by the Abyss, sometimes called
the Veil of the Abyss - 'which normal human consciousness cannot
cross.' It is said 'the roots of our existence' lie over the Abyss that is
'hidden from our eyes.' The Cabalist does not define God but worships
him in his manifestations of Thought, Wisdom and Intelligence, which
reflect in Love, Justice and Beauty, which correspond to divine power.

While with the subject of the Abyss. The thick line, representing the
Abyss on the Tree diagram supplied, is given to show the relative position
of the Abyss in relation to the Kingdoms. The contours of the Abyss on
the diagram are purely artistic and arbitrary, they are not meant to imply
an accurate description. A straight line would have served the purpose
equally as well, but some readers may have inferred from this that the
Abyss was also straight, which it is not.

First among the Three Supernals is Kether which is sometimes
represented as an 'Open Eye' and the Zohar has something to say about
the eyes. In ancient times Sleep and Death are closely associated. In
Greece and Italy they were regarded as twin brothers; see the last section
'Semones.' The **Zohar** tells us that every man has a foretaste of death
when he sleeps during the night because at this time the holy soul leaves
him and an unclean spirit rests on the body, making it unclean. When the
soul returns to the body it drives the pollution out but not from the hands;
therefore, no man should pass his hands over his eyes before he has
washed them. When he does so 'he becomes sanctified and is called holy.'
To perform this sanctification two vessels are required. One vessel is held
above the hands, and the water from this is poured over the hands and
caught in the vessel under the hands which is known as the vessel of

uncleanness; the lower vessel receives the water of contamination. The upper vessel is called - 'blessed' and the lower is 'cursed.' A jug and small basin kept solely for this purpose would be ideal. An adaptation for modern, everyday conditions could be, wash your hands under a running tap (= the upper 'blessed' vessel) with the water running into an unplugged basin (= the lower 'cursed' vessel) with the 'contaminated' water running away where it can do no harm to others, as recommended in the next paragraph. Once the hands are clean and the 'contaminated' water has gone, the ablutions can be performed with the basin plugged. The hands have now been ritually cleaned and the eyes can now be touched.

To be exemplary this ablution should be performed by one whose hands have already been washed clean of pollution. The water of contamination should not be emptied within the house. This is to prevent anyone becoming contaminated with it for it acts as a 'gathering-place for the elements of the unclean side, and so one may receive injury from the unclean water.' It must not stay in the house overnight and it should be religiously avoided since it is 'the water of curse.' It has to be thrown out where people do not pass, for it is liable to cause harm by the unclean spirit that clings to it. It can be poured down a slope into the earth. It must not be given to witches because by means of it they can do harm to people.

Now back to the three Supernals. The first three Kingdoms, with the mysterious Daath, collectively contain within them symbolism relating to the head region. This, in Archetypal Man, represents the highest level of consciousness. Therefore I find myself unable to place the mundane planet Saturn at this level across the Abyss as it is in the traditional scheme. If Saturn is placed in the traditional position over the Abyss it destroys the Trinity of the Three Supernals though to some he simply becomes part of it. I use the modified scheme given below. This is not adverse criticism of other works or systems. It is simply an alternative scheme that is better suited to this writer and his particular philosophy. It is also the reason why his Cabalistic work is, more often than not, solitary.

An alternative diagram that is sometimes called *The Sephirothic Tree of the Latter Day Qabbalists* can be found in **Kircher's** *Oedipus Aegypticus* and *The Qabalah* of **Papus** who gives it with the 'letters of Eliphas Levi - First Lesson.' It is often reproduced in textbooks of magic. This construction is said to be by the Latter-day Cabalists and it is claimed to be built with the benefit of hindsight and constructed upon the fruits and labours of those who had gone before - hence the term 'latter-day.' This scheme gave the same conclusions and planetary placements I had reached on my own with many hours of working late after being pointed in this general direction by the School to which I belonged for many years.

Therefore, not unnaturally, I agreed with it and I felt more comfortable with it when I discovered its existence later.

In this scheme the seven planets of old are placed beneath the Abyss; none of them are set over it on the other side. The First Trinity over the Abyss is retained intact, without any astrological rulership; the seven Kingdoms and their planets below the Abyss, all with astrological rulership. I think very few can cross the Abyss and have sight of these three highest Kingdoms. Let alone enter them.

I think it possible that Messengers and Teachers from these hidden, highest Kingdoms on the Tree cross the Abyss and come down to the seven Kingdoms below from time to time. They do so to adjust a course, avert a disaster, to right a grave injustice, or to give guidance where it is imperative. Perhaps at those times we say our Guardian Angels took a hand or 'came down and looked after us.'

Was it from over this Abyss that Moses crossed when he came down from 'on high' after receiving the Tablets of the Law and the Word of God? He came down from on high to the 'twelve tribes' waiting for him in the valley below. The twelve tribes who are equated with the twelve signs of the zodiac and ruled by the seven planets of old. There are several lists for these, they are arrived at according to the compiler. A list is given in **Barret's** *The Magus or Celestial Intelligencer*. (1801), for those who would like to have one to work with. I have not worked out a list for myself, which is why one is not given, according to my own reasoning, but I would have thought that the tribe of the Lion of Judah would have been Leo, not Asher, which it is according to the list given in **Barret**, now you see the problem.

Moses went up alone where none could follow, only he could enter the highest of the Kingdoms, because he had authority and permission. Some of his people could follow him so far, but then they reached the ring-of-pass-not imposed by Saturn, beyond which they could not go. 'The people cannot come up mount Sinai: for thou chargedst us, saying, Set bounds (= Saturn) about the mount and sanctify it (= Jupiter)...but let not the priests and the people break through to come up unto the Lord, lest he break forth upon them.' Exodus.19:23-24.

Saturn not only rules the skeleton which gives the body its form but its outer limits, the skin. Earthbound people can rarely exceed this limitation and thus they cannot leave the body and assume another vehicle. Those who are able to get past this limitation do so at times, and some can do so at will, with the aid of the planet of the metaphysical, the only planet who can break Saturn's hold and make him let go - Uranus, which is why I think he may well rule the Kingdom of Daath, see later.

People who study those matters which are generally termed, the Occult, Astrology, the Metaphysical, etc., (not Spiritualism, that is under the sway of Neptune), often have a prominent or strong Uranus in their birth chart and their lives, which is often why they do not follow usual paths; but these are other matters.

Lucky are those who are 'not forgetful to entertain strangers; for thereby some have entertained angels unaware.' Hebrews 13:2. To make the point clear, use the diagram included with the text. As mentioned before, unfold it so you can see the diagram while you read the text. This will be useful to those readers who have little or no knowledge of Cabala: I repeat, we use a very simple construction that is very easy to follow.

The seven Sephiroth or Kingdoms, separated from the first triad, are 'the seven primitive and dual gods who descend from their Celestial Abode and reign on Earth.' In what follows the planetary placements will be as follows. The fourth Kingdom - Chesed - is ruled by Jupiter, the fifth Kingdom - Geburah - is ruled by Saturn, the sixth Kingdom - Tiphereth - is still ruled by the Sun, the seventh Kingdom - Netzach - is ruled by Mars, the eighth Kingdom - Hod - is ruled by Venus. The ninth Kingdom - Yesod - is ruled by Mercury and the tenth and last Kingdom - Malkuth - is ruled by the Moon. Readers following the former system will have to temporarily adjust the scheme or suspend that teaching in what follows; it should not be too hard. Putting all this into two simple sentences, without the explanation, it would be this.

In the system operated by most Occult Schools and given in most literature, the seven planets are placed on Kingdoms three to nine with the Four Elements placed on the tenth Kingdom. In the system which follows, the seven planets are placed on Kingdoms four to ten, they are kept below the Abyss and *do not cross it*, and the Elements, already inherent in these planets and their Kingdoms, are not placed separately.

Despite wishing to keep this preamble as simple as possible, perhaps two other aspects could be mentioned before we go on and the first concerns the term Qliphoth (pronounced Cliff-foth), singular Qliphah (pronounced Cliff-far); even though it is not mentioned in what follows the term is often met with in works of this nature. These names are interpreted as 'harlots' or 'shells,' the distorted reflections of the holy Sephiroth. They are interpreted as the evil and adverse Sephiroth. They are not principles or factors of the Cosmic Scheme but are the shadow that light casts, the obverse side of the coin, and if you deal with magic you must deal with them. They cannot be avoided and will not conveniently go away simply by ignoring them.

A small lesson I used in the School was to present the junior school members with a coin of the realm, telling them that heads were good, and tails bad. The idea was they had to spin the coin and let it fall to the ground, if good (= heads) was uppermost they had to pick it up without disturbing the bad (= tails) on the other side, try to take one and not the other. If bad (= tails) was uppermost how did they get to the good (= heads) which was under the bad side. The idea behind this was to show that the two exist and both have to dealt with because they can rarely be separated; they are the two halves which make up the coin at this level of existence, both are 'the complements of a unity.' In the former if they took the good they had to accept the possibility of disturbing the obverse, the bad; in the latter, that it was sometimes necessary to go through the bad and accept it, to get to the good.

The German philosopher **Hegel**, held that something can only exist through its opposite, that the thing and its opposite must arise together, and both eternal, as the complements of a unity. Black is not black without white, nor white without black. Good is not good without evil and vice versa. Some Cabalistic works tell us that at the beginning of the life spark, death and dissolution contest its vitality and endeavour to destroy it. The entire existence of man in this world, is a ceaseless struggle to preserve that vitality. If Good ever succeeded in conquering Evil, I think there's a chance that the whole fabric of the world would collapse, because the tension had been destroyed; not unlike cutting the rope of a heaving tug o' war team, both teams would fall down and neither would win.

You cannot ignore or deal with evil by cutting it off and destroying it, as **Jung** said, not *against* it but *through* it. If you work against evil forces you set up a polarity with them and a link will be formed, even unintentionally sometimes. You may claim you are working in a positive way for a positive good and that could be so, but evil polarizes this with its negative mode. This positive and negative polarity completes the circuit because it is polarized; see the comments below on 'The Three Pillars.' What could not 'flow' before now can and usually does. This is why some teachers say this is one area you should avoid, particularly in the early stages of learning. If you stir up a hornets' nest you should know how to deal with it; if you can't deal with it, you are in trouble.

The second aspect is a pattern on the Tree that perhaps may be mentioned in what follows: these are 'The Three Pillars.' This configuration is simple to explain on the diagram of the Tree, as long as the reader understands that this is a very simple explanation of a complex subject. It really does no more than draw the reader's attention to them. The Tree possesses Three Pillars and they are often show diagramatically as such, with the relevant Sephiroth written upon them. A tall pillar lies in the centre with two smaller, but equal pillars on either side of it.

The Pillar of Mercy is on the right-hand side of the Tree diagram and is composed of the three Masculine, Light Sephiroth of Chokmah, Chesed and Netzach. The Pillar of Severity or Judgement is on the left-hand side of the Tree diagram and is composed of the three Dark, Feminine Sephiroth of Binah, Geburah and Hod. The Pillar of Mildness or Balance is in the centre of the Tree diagram and is composed of the four Sephiroth Kether, Tiphereth, Yesod and Malkuth. The outer pillars give the theme of polarity where the distinction of opposites is emphasized. Male and female, positive and negative, dark and light with the central, balanced pillar placed between them. I must now stop, returning to the subject of the work, Pan.

We are going to suggest a scheme that may be used for visualization. It must not be thought that this example is the only way in which this can be achieved. What is given here was given to me and, although it has proved successful for others, this does not guarantee it will be so for all. This is not offered as an excuse should it fail, but as a reality. Your doctor would like one pill for every illness, but he is painfully aware that he is dealing with people, not test tubes. In dealing with the visualization in this section, always remember you are limited only by your imagination. If you like the suggestion given and choose to use it, then you must at the earliest opportunity start to imprint it with your own personality and thoughts. Make it a part of you when you can.

No matter what matrix your visualization takes, the 'skeleton' upon which you will build your construction is the 'Tree of Life'. This is why we have laid great stress upon getting to understand the diagram as well as you know the area where you live. You must know where you are going and where you are, always. If you have lived in your area for some time and you were put down anywhere in it you would know roughly where you were and how to get back home. This is the familiarity you should seek with the diagram called the Tree of Life.

After reading this paragraph and before going any further, make a copy of the diagram for yourself. Perhaps it would be of advantage to make two diagrams of the Tree. Make one diagram small enough so that you can have it with you in your wallet or purse. In this way you can consult it at any convenient moment you have and you can have a large copy for when you are at home. The smaller one is for carrying around, not unlike the maps of the London Underground that are often printed in the backs of pocket diaries. There are usually large copies on the walls of the Underground.

Do not make any strained effort to learn it by heart. There are no prizes given for speed of learning; gradual assimilation is the object of the exercise. Take it at a speed that is natural to you and it will all be come familiar and second nature. *Do not 'Photostat' the diagram from the book*; you could, but far better to trace it or draw it out for yourself. Above all, do not worry if it does not look exactly like the printed diagram, though you should make every effort to make the drawing as accurate and to scale as you possibly can. Some Schools and teachers would insist it was accurate in every detail and scale - in a School I would agree. If doing this is too laborious or you cannot find or make the time, then candidly you should not be bothering at all; if you put nothing in, why be surprised that you get nothing out. People will always find time for what they want to do, which is why, for the most, the entertainment industry flourishes. Just draw the circles (use small coins) and join them as shown. Make it as artistic as your ability permits. *Remember, what you make for yourself has far greater power than something in which you had no hand. The effort you have put into it makes a link between your diagram and you.* I cannot stress this strongly enough. Now let us begin by creating the craft in which you will sail to find the Astral Sea - the Astrum Mare. It can be a craft of your own design or choosing, of any period in history or belonging to any race. It would be better if it is a ship you are already familiar with because you will know your way around it. Your craft can be manned or unmanned. Myths often have ships that are prepared for going to sea at one's command, either spoken or thought, by an invisible crew, not unlike the *Flying Dutchman.*

Remember you are not restricted by the same laws you know and work with in everyday life, the laws that govern the physical world. If you succeed in your venture you will not be in the physical world or using its laws. The laws of this world operate here, and if you are in the Astral World you operate with the laws there, which are just as real and valid there. If, when relating a dream, you said you were flying or crept through a keyhole as in a fairytale, you would not feel foolish telling someone these events. Most people accept in the world of dreams you can do that sort of thing and do not think it odd in the least. It will not cause you embarrassment to tell people of the experience because the experience is common to all. Even if it is not fully understood at least it is accepted that in the world of dreams strange things can and do happen.

The Astral Plane has it own Laws and they are the *status quo* when you are on that plane, and only experience there will teach you about them and how to use them. Very few can walk under water on the physical plane but in your imagination you can do anything. If you are going into a particular environment, you have to obey the laws of that environment to live, work and survive there. To disregard the rules usually brings you trouble. I think the point has been made.

Set 'sail' from the same place if you possibly can. It can be a location you are familiar with, a cove or harbour with which you have a strong mental impression or affinity, perhaps somewhere visited on holiday; it need not even be in this country. One of my 'harbours' is Tintagel, with another in Greece. Use the location as a physical 'anchor' point so that you have a definite starting and finishing point. Thus you will know where you are going from when you have come back to harbour. Choose a time and place, when you know you will not be interrupted for the time of your attempted 'journey.'

If possible, try to keep to the same time when you attempt your exercise, not unlike a timetable of sailing, which will prepare you (by anticipation) for the event. You know when you are going and will want to be off; this is desirable but not essential. The object of the visualization is an attempt to try to meet the god Pan. However, do not make the time around noon, for it is then Pan sleeps and when he is at his most testy. If you feel the use of incense may help then try to use pine or any 'woodland' incense. Set the sails and head away from your base, set your barque in the direction you want to go or let it go where it will. A compass on the ship is useful.

If an island appears on your sea, you can either land and explore, or pass it by according to your fancy or instinct. You may discover endless islands before you find the one you seek. It may be found quickly, take a long time or never. Sadly there are no guarantees. So often effort and worth is not always adequately rewarded. The secret is to keep searching until you find it for anything worth having, is worth looking for and working for. At least you have a skeleton map of this Treasure Island that will give you some idea whether you want to land on it or not.

The form the island may take has to be discovered but you do have a good idea what you are seeking and frequently that is more than most have. Concentrate on the basic design. The human race has a skeleton and it is that basic shape that gives us the ability to recognize ourselves as human, not simian or a spider.

Keep a log of the journey as any good captain would. Write down your results as quickly as you can when you come back to base. Memories fade quicker than we think and they can play strange tricks. Make sure you are honest in what you write. Even if you are mistaken in what you saw or do not understand it, at least it will be honestly written. If you do not do this you will only be fooling yourself, no one else. Record in your log what you have seen, where you think you have been.

For instance, was it a forest, a city, a town, village or a temple? Remember these details in case you want to try to retrace your steps and go there again; you need to know if you have been there before. Who did you speak to? Remember they do not have to be people. Animals and inanimate objects often take on a different life, often they can speak and move in these worlds. What did they tell you, if anything? Were they friendly or hostile, helpful or hindering, talkative or taciturn? What were your feelings towards them and the places you went?

Again I stress the need to be scrupulously honest in all this, record what is and not what you like it to be. If you keep the records private, for your teacher or an intimate few, you will have little need to write to impress others. If others are going to read them as general notes, we know they will judge. It is sometimes hard to avoid making subtle alterations to embroider or justify our work and skills. Do not be like **Gilbert's** Poo-Bah, (a favourite quotation), who said it was 'Merely corroborative detail, intended to give artistic verisimilitude to an otherwise bald and unconvincing narrative.' *The Mikado*. I repeat, the only person you fool will be you if you do. Keep a factual diary in which to record the date and conditions at the time of your attempt. Was the room warm or cold and what was your general mood at the time? Of course if you were upset or worried you should not be doing it.

You should always make a record of the phase of the Moon when the attempt was being made. The Moon, with Neptune, is held to rule clairvoyance. The influence of the Moon, for clairvoyance or any task requiring strong imagination, is often individually strongest when in the same phase as it was at the time of birth. Incidentally, women can often conceive at this time in their chart, so this can be the best individual period to try, unless Nature has physically forbidden the result. You should not attempt the visualization if you are depressed, feeling low or are worried. Use whatever methods you can to stimulate your imagination, preferably not by artificial means, unless under strictly controlled conditions with someone of proven and impeccable credentials - better not at all really. Read books that stimulate you, listen to music that puts you in the right frame of mind. The Tone Poems of **Sir Arnold Bax** are particularly apt. **Bax's** love of Ireland and its literature has misled many into believing him Irish born, but he was born in Streatham. For example, from his music there is the *November Woods*, *The Garden of Fand*, *The Tale the Pine-Trees Knew* and *Spring Fire*.

There is **Novak's** beautifully evocative work, *Pan*. **Granville**

Bantock's *Pagan Symphony* - 'Et ego in Arcadia vixi.' Again **Bantock's** highly sensitive *Celtic Symphony for string orchestra and six harps* and *The Witch of Atlas* with music written for Silenus, Faunus and Priapus in the Tone Poem. **John Ireland's** beautifully evocative *The Forgotten Rite*. *Myths for Piano and Violin* of **Symanowski** including *The Fountain of Orathusia, Narcissus* and the *Dyrads and Pan*. The orchestral settings of some Irish folk tale's of **Hamilton Harty**, as with *The Children of Lir*. **Debussy's** and **Sibelius's** *Pan and Psyche*, **Neilson's** *Pan and Syrinx*, **Rousel's** *Symphony No 1 - Le Poeme de la foret,* etc. **Cavalli's** *La Calisto*, with parts in the opera for Jove, Mercurio, Diana, Callisto, Silvanus and Pan. **Einojuhani Rautavaara's** highly original work of Nature, *Cantus Arcticus*. In **Purcell's** opera *King Arthur* we can find the 'Bright Nymphs of Britain' and

'For Folded Flocks, on Fruitful Plains,
The Shepherds and the Farmers' Gains
Fair Britain all the World outvies:
And Pan, as in Arcadia Reigns.'

Most of the above is music inspired by nymphs, satyrs, Silvanus, Pan, woodland glades and forests, etc. I readily admit this list is personal as it must be; it cannot be claimed that it will suit all, but it is suggested here as a starting point. To it I would have to add the music of **Wagner** and **Mahler**; a lot of my writing is done with these two composers and those above, especially **Mahler's** *Third Symphony* which he was going to call The *'Pan' Symphony*. Mahler claimed Pan came to him while he wrote it and 'he frequently panicked.' Mahler's wife Alma, many years later, wrote that when he was composing this symphony in a wooden hut by the lake away from the house he would often panic and run out of it. He would come rushing to the house and seek the company of his own kind to work; he said 'the eye of the Goat God was on him, Pan was there.' Mahler said that in the music of the first movement of the symphony Pan was summoning Nature forth from the Unmanifest - I believe him. In one of the rare occasions I step into the world of popular music I must mention a short piece called - *The Return of Pan*, by **The Waterboys**. The words are excellent, the spirit and heart of it are definitely in the right place and for the right reasons. Here I must stop or the list will overwhelm the work.

The purpose of the journey is simple. You are attempting to find or make contact with Pan, the Great God of Nature. To this end you are seeking an island that he could come to or where he could be found, because the conditions there would be right for him. Never forget the reason for creating this circumscribed area is more to limit you than him. You cannot limit him and nothing we create will contain him unless he wills it to be so; you can invite, you cannot order. It is you that has to do the preparing, just as you should when you invite a guest to your home to stay with you.

I am sure Pan can be found in the concrete and asphalt sprawl of a city, and that he has been found there, though I am sure under duress or a course of action he cannot avoid. In this exercise he is more likely to be found in the hills and mountains, the forests and caves. Pan is better found where there are less people than flora and fauna. In this exercise you are the creator and can create the ideal Arcadia in which to find him, a place where is he is as free to range as your imagination allows. Give him plenty of space. Find somewhere where he will not be lying on his back with his hoofs in the air, gasping for breath. You are initially in charge in this Arcadia and can create the ideal Arcadia to find him if he will come. The English, as a race, have been having a love affair with Pan all their lives. For long years they have tried to recreate an 'ideal Arcadia' in their gardens with their rolling lawns, statues, temples and follies, especially in the big estates, as mentioned earlier.

In this land you will be breathing 'new air that has never been breathed before' as that great lover of Pan, **D.H.Lawrence**, put it. A land that may not have received the imprint of a human foot at any level, for there are very few places in the material world that can lay claim to that. However, you must find the island first, then explore it to see if he is there and then attempt to seek out the God. In this mental hinterland, which borders your physical existence, there are many islands to which we all travel now and then. Remember, Pan is a peripheral god, so he is more likely to be found in areas that merge, places that are neither one thing nor the other: the lonely places where we can lose our bearings and panic. Sometimes it is simply a place for escaping a boring routine, job or people. We call them 'fantasies' but others say it's daydreaming and ask you 'where have you been, because you weren't here?'

This time, however, you are attempting to control and direct these energies into a more constructive path. You know why you are going and what you are attempting to do. You will know if you have found it like some *Shangri-La*, and you are going to try to find your way back. This is something you have to seek out for yourself and want to do. It's there if you want to reach it, it's always been there, but you must want to go. Roald Amundsen arrived at the South Pole on the 14th of December 1911 because he wanted to go there. I personally wouldn't go near the place for all the tea in China. As an example let us cite an 'Island of Pan' that has already be 'found and explored.' I want the reader to pay particular attention to these final sentences before beginning, *The Tree of Pan.*

I have tried to change what follows as little as possible even though, at times, this leaves in some repetition and awkward phrases; the reader will have to make some allowances for this because of the nature and manner of its writing, which was explained in the introduction. The log of the venture undertaken shows it came about in this way.

In the beginning...

Having set sail, an island appears on the horizon that at last looks promising; it has been one of many. At first it is a shapeless inhospitable place until closer approach shows that it is shrouded in mists. You do not know at the time that this is the island you are seeking, for you are writing this with the benefit of hindsight. It is very imposing and the cliffs tower above your craft, making it appear very small. Rocks at the base of precipitous and inhospitable cliffs offer no possibility of landing.

Heavy mists pour down like water from high peaks lost in mist and shrouded in cloud. Great waterfalls cascade down from an invisible source and crash upon the rocks below augmenting the mist and spray already swirling there. It appears a very uncongenial place that seems to offer only one message to the traveller - keep away!

You decide to steer a course that will take you down one side of this magnificent headland. You take the right-hand side, which puts the island on the left of your craft. As you travel parallel to the land you begin to wonder if it is an island. It could be a mighty headland of some great continent jutting out into the sea, but you will have to continue your course to find out.

As you go forward you become aware of a deep roar that grows slowly louder as you progress. You feel the pull of a strong current that causes you to give the order to take a passage away from the island coastline. The current is beginning to pull you towards the island but there is still is no place to land. As you sail down the coastline the current is getting stronger.

There will be a decisive moment where it will be impossible to get the ship free from its pull. Now you give the order to steer well out from the coast, the wheel turns with your order and you continue with your parallel line. Now you see the cause of this strong current. God, this is a terrible place. The headland appears to have been severed by an enormous ravine that cuts it off from the rest of the land. Into this fissure the sea is pouring as if trying to fill a bottomless pit with a deafening roar. Anything caught in this powerful current would never get free. It would disappear into this open maw, never to be seen again.

You continue your progress down the coast and the land starts to appear more hospitable. The coastline is gently falling in height giving the land the appearance of a wedge. From the sea you can see hills and mountains inland, so it is not flat. One remarkable feature now strikes you. The mists and clouds of the headland do not cross the deep ravine but stay on their own side of the land.

The current is safer now, there is no noticeable undertow and the sea appears quite calm compared to what has gone before. You now deem it safe to take your craft closer in to the shore, so you give the order. The coastline starts to bend around to the left. As your craft begins to sweep around it you see what is obviously the other end of the island, for an island it is. You can now see that the island is either inhabited or it has been in the past.

The First Kingdom...

Sailing around the end of the island you come upon the white walls of what may be quite a large harbour or town. The walls are like the island, wedge-shaped, and they diminish in height until you can see inside without any difficulty. At this end the island sweeps down to a beautiful beach and meets the sea in calmness and safety. The walls have a break in the centre that permits entrance and it is now you see that the harbour is a perfect crescent, not unlike a new moon. On either side of the entrance there is a glass lighthouse or beacon.

A beach within the harbour echoes the shape of the walls. This gives the harbour its crescent shape. It is filled with mirror-still water that reflects the light back as green, pale violet and light blue. At the ends of the crescent, where the lighthouses are, the water is at its deepest, though there is anchorage for ships of all sizes. You choose to go to the left where ships of similar size to your own are moored, the smaller craft being in the middle of the harbour.

There is a space and you go there to berth. You settle down and wait to see if your arrival has been noted, though it could hardly be missed, and what may happen because of it. Your mooring, though observed, does not seem to have caused that much of a stir. The people in the harbour area do not seem unduly worried by your appearance; perhaps the harbour is a busy one and boats arrive and berth frequently. There are many ships and boats here of all shapes and sizes. Some of the ships are berthed and others are going about their business. Perhaps another ship more or less does not matter.

Feeling a little more confident you leave your ship, walk to the end of the harbour and climb the steps to the base of a lighthouse. It seems to be made of crystal with a framework of silver. Both lighthouses are lit by enormous candles of white wax whose lustre is not unlike mother-of-pearl. The flames of the 'candles' within the lighthouses are even and steady, and the candles do not appear to have diminished any for being lit. You leave the lighthouse and go into the harbour area towards the town, where you notice there are more women than men.

The atmosphere is predominantly feminine though in no way hostile to the male, for there are men here. It is very relaxing and has a feeling of comfort and security about it. Some men are talking and sitting with the women in groups. Some are obviously from the ships in the harbour. Many women are discussing business, or talking sociably, while others are teaching or telling stories to groups of children. These are matronly and pleasant in appearance, in white dresses with silver belts and fillets in their hair studded with pearls and white stones. Younger women in similar attire go about their affairs; many are obviously pregnant and others are nurturing babes.

Lakes, rivers, cascades and rapids of water abound. There are pools in which fish, turtles and aquatic life swim and crabs scuttle about their business. Clumps of water lilies grow in the river and the lakes and ponds whose edges are overhung with willows. These trees trail their branches in the flowing or still water for both are found here, rich with watercress.

White fountains decorated with silver and pearl adornments are scattered throughout the area with silver taps and cups for drinking the clear water. Geese and ducks are either flying, asleep on the river banks or preening themselves. They seem to have no fear and are tame and indifferent to your approach. Melons and pumpkins grow in patches, as do white poppies, lilies, night-scented flowers and white irises.

The symbolism shows the strong lunar connections. If on your map this is Malkuth, the tenth Kingdom of the Moon, there will be a Sacred Grove of Willows somewhere, besides the willows already seen. Your map shows there are three paths out of this Kingdom. The 31st path takes you to the eighth Kingdom of Hod, Venus and the Sacred Grove of Apples. The 32nd path goes to the ninth Kingdom of Yesod, Mercury and the Sacred Grove of the Hazels. Finally, the 29th path should take you to the seventh Kingdom of Netzach, Mars and the Sacred Grove of Holly.

These three paths will lead you into the heart of the island. To get there you must make for the other side of this kingdom. This means keeping the harbour you have left behind you. Should you find these three paths this would confirm that the scheme of the island is based on the Cabalistic Tree of Life and its Kingdoms. The island could be the right one for your purpose.

There is a central river, obviously the main one, emptying into the middle of the harbour so you choose to follow that through the city into the land. Gradually the buildings begin to thin out which shows you may be coming to the city's outer limits; in time they get less and finally stop. The countryside is pleasant, the river gradually narrows and you keep going in that direction. The land begins to rise gently and now the river falls over steps of natural white rock. It has begun to wind and, although continuing in the same general direction it does not hold a straight channel.

The countryside is pleasant enough and you feel no threat, but there is a hint of desolation and great loneliness. You turn with the river that takes you through a grove of willows. At the top of a mound there is a wall extending to the left and right, and there is a large entrance in it, with a large tower on either side. The river and path go through this gate. You can see them winding gently over the hills to the distant horizon, a land that is in twilight lit by moonlight only.

To the right of the gate you see a large dog, while to the left sits an equally large wolf. One thing you have not noticed though, because it has happened imperceptibly, is that it is now twilight on this side of the gate. Faint stars are visible in the dusk above your head. There is a magnificent full moon, occasionally crossed by clouds that cast a shadow over the landscape. Everything is seen clearly by the soft glow of the moon that is over the land. It is to the moon that the dog and the wolf raise their heads at intervals and bay. You begin to wonder what is real and what is not. You decide to rest and watch, drinking the water and eating the fruit you have with you, while you take stock.

Awaking with a start, you realize you have been sleeping. This does not particularly worry you for the moon rules the hours of sleep and dreams and you were dreaming but not vividly. You remember the gates in the dream, but were they of horn or ivory? You can't remember the dreams. Perhaps you are dreaming now but the wolf and the dog are still there guarding the gate and your passage. You are reminded of the 18th card of the tarot. You wonder if the towers are pylons and the path takes you through the Land of Emania. Is this path the moon-path in the sky that takes you to the Kingdom of Mania, the Queen of the Shades, where the dead are taken?

You see a few people passing through the gate and some coming back to your side of it. They seem to go through on the right, the side of the dog, and come out on your left, the side of the wolf, and you decide to do the same. You wait a time thinking to go through with others but, as if to test your strength of purpose, none come: you have to go through on your own. Summoning up your courage, you go towards the gate. You cross a ford the river to the right-hand side. The dog turns its head at your approach and watches you with brown eyes. You walk slowly so as not to cause any alarm by sudden movement. It still watches.

You look to see what the wolf is doing. It is watching you with red eyes like fire. The dog is still watching you as you are now getting close. Its eyes have a strange depth, as if someone else is watching you through its eyes, already knowing who you are and why you are here. It rises and walks towards you and, being uncertain, you stop and do nothing. The dog smells you and looks up into your eyes; you gain courage and instinctively say 'I seek him whom we both would serve.'

It licks your hand as if in tacit consent, turns and walks back to lie down, head down but still watching. Again you look across to the wolf and it watches you, through half-closed eyes head on paws, but it seems to have lost all interest in you. Feeling confidence with this acceptance you walk through the gateway but you know it is following every move you make as you pass through.

Once through the great gate you turn and look back at the animals. Their interest lies elsewhere. Both are watching the approach path and you appear to be of no further interest: perhaps once through the gate, you aren't. You walk up the path that rises gently and finally you reach the top. Some white marble steps go down before you and the river has now been enclosed in banks of white marble. At regular intervals the river is crossed by white bridges. Between each bridge on both banks a beautiful willow tree is characteristically trailing its lowest branches in the water.

At the end of this approach is an enormous circular building with magnificent white columns supporting it. The river runs through a large portico in the centre. You go up the steps and pass through this central entrance which tells you that the building is not circular: what you saw was a crescent-shaped facade. Entering this courtyard, for that is what it is, you come to three impressive fountains. The centre fountain is circular with two crescent fountains on either side. All are made of iridescent nacre. The fountains look like the moon at new, full and last quarter.

This courtyard is circular with five columns to your left like a crescent. There is a break in the circle opposite for a portico, with five columns to the right. In the fountains there are fish and oysters that are open to reveal pearls worth a king's ransom in your world and representing a life of ease. What if you were to stop the journey now and try to take them? Is it a test and would you be permitted to take them? By failing would it be a case of losing the traditional pearl of even greater price? Admiring the pearls but leaving them, you pass on to try to find Pan. The journey is but started and you cannot believe he will be found that easily. You do not believe he will be found here.

Crossing the courtyard, you go through the portico opposite. You find a straight walk flanked by mother-of-pearl columns. The walk, like the courtyard, is open to the sky. Ahead are two closed doors made of silver, studded with pearls, moonstones and crystal. An excitement fills you and your whole body tingles. Your stomach feels tight, which you feel is right, for the moon is held to rule the stomach.

You approach the doors and look at them for a time. They join perfectly and are almost seamless, with only the huge hinges and a line down the centre to suggest where they open. After a while you call upon the goddess Isis to help you, more in instinct than knowledge. You step back to look at the building, trying to work out your next move and how to get in, when slowly and silently the doors begin to open. You stand well back as they swing open effortlessly on their hinges. When they are fully open and no one comes out, you decide to go in. Crossing the threshold, you hope some clue to Pan will be found here, though you feel he is not present. It is never that easy. Entering the Sanctuary slowly you look within.

You find yourself standing on the edge of a very large circular chamber. The dome of the building is undoubtedly made of crystal which fills the chamber with soft, pure moonlight. This light is reflected internally by the white material of the building itself. The crystal dome is supported by ten immense pillars, also of crystal. These pillars gently glow, as if there was a light set in the base, but you know the light is inherent in the material itself.

There are five pillars to your left and five to your right. Opposite the silver doors you came through is a huge veiled alcove. Behind these crystal pillars, on either side of the veiled alcove, are ten grottoes in which are growing the archetypes of all the willow trees ever grown. These ten trees epitomize great age and wisdom. They have a feeling of stillness and timelessness about them.

Surely this is the Sacred Grove of Willows growing in the lunar Kingdom of Malkuth. Does this set a pattern for the sacred groves in the remaining Kingdoms of the Sephiroth? You wonder, will you find nine hazels in the Sacred Grove of Mercury's Kingdom in Yesod? Will there also be eight apple trees in the Sacred Grove of Venus, in the eighth Kingdom of Hod?

The only way to find out if this is true is to try to go there. While you stand within the temple contemplating, you do not notice the silver doors closing silently and effortlessly behind you. You know your way back has now been effectively blocked, but you do not feel threatened by this. Now you have to find out what it is you have to do to carry on with your journey and you know that part of the answer lies here.

In the centre of the circle marked on the floor, almost imperceptible at first, a beam of soft light appears. You cross to stand in it and find it shines through the largest crystal, which is set in the centre of the dome. You can see the new moon in the old moon's arms. The beam fills with beautiful moths fluttering in the light. They are larger than usual and the largest flutters down and lands on the veil of the alcove, opposite the silver doors. You look at it and it turns into a small point of swirling light that grows in luminosity. until it finally fills the alcove with a vibrant light that casts no shadow.

You are standing in the centre of the chamber, under the dome. There is a circle in the centre in which you are standing. Instinct again takes over and you call upon the goddess to help you in your quest: you seek the great god Pan who was known to Selene. The alcove pulsates with light, the veil is torn asunder and first you see Isis. You hear no words but you know she is telling you that although the veil is torn asunder, no man shall know her.

Then, like the Empress of the Tarot, you see Venus, full of stomach and fertile, and at her side is a cornucopia, a stream flows behind her with field of gently waving corn. She is followed by Aphrodite with a he-goat lying at her side, with the hare and a swan. Doves sit or fly in the apple trees and rose bushes are in full bloom. She is quickly replaced by the chaste Diana, slender and beautiful, her hunting hounds at her feet, her bow fully drawn with an arrow ready for flight.

Now Isis appears again as the mother of Horus, weeping for the murdered Osiris with her young son. Then Mary appears as the Magna Mater, proud with her Son at the Temple, next as the Mater Dolorosa, grieving, holding the broken body of her dead Son in her arms. Now comes, Selene, covered in a long robe that falls to her feet, at which lays a dazzling white ram, whose eyes are intent on watching you and you cannot take your eyes from it. Above her a crescent moon sheds a mild light. So many aspects of the goddess are shown to you, some unknown to you and far too many to remember. It seems the moon goddess is presenting herself in all the aspects by which she has ever been known.

The dark side of the goddess is represented by Hecate, Mania, Melania, Bendis and all the other dark goddesses, too many and too quick to remember, some quite unknown: all in an ever-changing kaleidoscope that causes your mind to reel and you finally believe your brain will burst. The white light within the alcove intensifies to a level that overpowers the images presented. The light gets stronger. Putting your hands over your eyes does not completely block it out because you can still see it. You now feel yourself drawn by an unknown force towards the light. You resist the temptation to enter it for you are certain it will surely destroy you, but it is too powerful to resist. Slowly you enter the light and you know it is all around you, but can you stand the sheer power of it? Then, suddenly, the light goes out.

Unsure, you stand for quite some time with your hands covering your eyes. You know there is firm ground beneath your feet and a light breeze is passing around your body. You slowly take your hands from your face and open your eyes, not sure what you will find. When your eyes become accustomed to the light, you discover you are standing on a vast plain where three paths meet. You remember that Hecate rules the meeting of roads and is a triple goddess. Far, far away to the left you hear the howling and whining of dogs. In Ancient Greece when Hecate hovered at the cross-roads, foretelling death or misfortune for someone, the dogs were aware of her presence and gave warning by their call. Their call is answered immediately by the plaintive notes of pipes that come from your left, at which they fall silent.

You feel no alarm. In the centre of the roads you see dishes containing offerings of food. Lights appear, flitting in the darkness, like the will-o'-the-wisp. You wonder if this was why the dark goddesses were revealed last in the Sanctuary. Looking back to find the High and Sacred Grove of the Willows you see the Sanctuary is far behind you and quite small in the distance. You seem to have come through the tenth lunar Kingdom of Malkuth and your are now standing before the triple junction that you were trying to find when you entered the tenth Kingdom, the entrance to the island.

The exit from the Kingdom was through the Sanctuary. You also realize that without getting through the gateway you could still be in the Kingdom of Malkuth and no farther for it. Is this the limit of the tenth Kingdom of Malkuth or are you already out of it? Taking a deep breath you make for open country and you are on your own, not knowing what there is to face.

The three paths before you are confirmed on your map. There is one path going off diagonally to the left, and according to your map this is the 31st path. This path will lead to the eighth Kingdom of Hod ruled by Venus and the Sacred Grove of Apples. The path leading off diagonally to the right is the 29th path. That will lead you to the seventh Kingdom of Netzach ruled by Mars and the Sacred Grove of Holly. The path straight in front of you is the 32nd path that will take you to the ninth Kingdom of Yesod ruled by Mercury and the Sacred Grove of Hazel.

Three options: one path of love and peace, one of defence and protection and the other of knowledge and communication. You do not feel particularly threatened by the island. What you want is information and knowledge about it. If you choose the ninth Kingdom next, followed by the eighth, you will be following the inverse path of the lightning flash, which brought our species down so quickly from the 'lightning struck tower.' It was so unexpected, the sky was blue and cloudless at the time and so we did not suspect that anything was amiss.

The path of the serpent wisdom is so long and tortuous by comparison: particularly to the impatient of the species who, troubled by a divine homesickness, want to go home. You decide on the 32nd and central path which will take you to the ninth Kingdom of Yesod. The journey on this path is uneventful and the land is pleasant enough with little of real interest. A river meanders along the side of the path and gives some company with its chatter. First the path is on this side and then the other, causing you to cross a variety of small bridges and fords.

The land does not seem inhabited and you do not meet anyone on the journey, but the bridges show that someone had been here at sometime in the past. In the increasing light you start to see solitary trees, small copses and at times there is the reflection of water. Although it has not taxed you, the ground has been gently rising.

The Second Kingdom...

Finally you reach what you assume is the top. From there you overlook an enclosed area looking like a city that is surrounded by hazel trees, in various stages of growth. The descent is not steep and the path itself now becomes lined with hazel trees, hanging heavy with sustaining fruit. Remembering you have not eaten for some time (although you do not feel hungry), you take some to eat. The whole atmosphere of this Kingdom is markedly different from the last one.

The place bustles with life and activity: people appear so busy, talking, discussing, reading sheaves of notes and the printed page and comparing the places they are discussing. Then you are struck by one important difference. Most of them are young people - youths and maidens. This place has all the appearance of an ancient seat of learning. Occasionally you see some inhabitants that leave you uncertain as their features and manner are almost hermaphroditic.

Watching a group of young people, you cannot decide whether they are males or females. Then, when you remember the ruler of this Kingdom, it comes as no surprise. Mercury rules youth and the young and he also rules another important facet of the human race. Looking for confirmation you find it as you notice that many of those who are present are twins.

Many buildings here are places of barter, exchange, selling and trading. There are rooms obviously set aside for learning and languages. Some appear to be recording and checking in many different scripts and there are many books, volume upon volume. None of this would be out of place for this Kingdom and its ruler, for the older people you see are obviously teachers. Around the buildings are pigeon lofts, which you thought were dovecotes, but it is the wrong Kingdom for those. These are messenger pigeons for many have messages attached to their legs, though not all. The birds are going off in all directions with others arriving, for all is activity.

Those who are not engaged in any particular activity are being entertained by jugglers, acrobats and magicians. On display there are feats of legerdemain performed by skilful hands, nimble fingers and a nimble brain behind them. The robes are bright yellow with variations down to subtle blends of browns and greens like autumn. Coming to what may be described as the city centre, your find an open area with nine sides and a hazel tree in each corner. At its centre you find the most unusual of fountains: it is made of agate set with yellow stones of every hue and size. The fountains are obviously not made for drinking because, from nine elaborate silver nozzles, pour what seems to be liquid silver.

You watch for some time because you find it fascinating, but you must find the Sacred Grove that you know exists here. You walk around the fountain to inspect it. Then you notice that its enormous size was hiding a straight avenue that is paved with slabs of agate, the colour of which makes the road appear yellow.

Walking down this avenue with buildings on either side you notice that the pace is not quite so frantic. It is obvious from the people here that it is dedicated to medicine, health and hygiene. There are places that seem to resemble schools or laboratories as you know them. The sight of people resting and sleeping gives the place a feeling of rest and calm. In the surrounding areas, at the sides of the avenue, you see some dogs, especially the swift greyhound, and some foxes.

You call a dog only to find your voice immediately mimicked behind you. Turning to find out who it is who mimics you so well, you find a bird looking at you quizzically from a small hazel tree. Repeating your call, as if mocking you, the bird flies away. The river is on both sides of the avenue and here it is very slow moving and filled with silver darting fish that move at an amazing speed. Now and then you see some beautiful salmon. At the end of the avenue you find some wide steps that take you up.

On either side of the steps there is a cataract down which the water is pouring. Salmon are leaping up the cataract to get to the top. Some salmon retreat to try again when they fail, leaping upwards repeatedly. You climb to the top and here you find a magnificent pool, clear and timeless, truly as you would expect to find the Fountain of the Sweet Land of Youth.

Around it are nine beautiful hazel trees whose boughs hang low and touch the water with the weight of their fruit. These venerable trees, like the Willows in the Kingdom of Malkuth, seem to have been here from the beginning of time. They must be the original trees from which the hazel trees on every level of existence have come. Such dignity and age do not manifest in a short time.

Standing at the edge of the pool, you look at the reflections on its surface. The serenity of its surface is broken only when one of the nuts fall into the water. It cuts through like a red arrow, leaving a stream of bubbles and ever widening ripples on the water's surface. A dark shadow darts from the depths, hidden from sight, and the nut is taken by a salmon; another spot appears on it skin.

You lie at the side of the pool and put your hand in the cool, clear waters. Some salmon come to your hand, lacking fear, for there is nothing to fear. You stroke the fish's back gently with your finger and then under its mouth. Suddenly the fish dart swiftly away and you wonder at the nature of your offence. Their place is taken by the largest salmon you have ever seen. You look deep into the eyes of this hoary salmon and feel you can see the knowledge of countless ages in them. After what seems eternity you ask, not sure if you will get an answer, 'Please, tell me if you know where is the one that I seek?'

A voice, gentle and clear, speaks, as if spoken in your head or heard with an inner ear.

'He is close, as he always is.'
'Will I meet him?'

'That will depend upon you and none else. Many seek him, some for the wrong reasons. A few do find him because he wants to be found. When Pan and the Nature spirits withdrew they did not withdraw from their charges on earth, only from the sight and ken of men. They were thought to exist no longer by later generations, being only fairy-tales told by the old to children to amuse them. They were effectively banished to the realms of legend and myth, sometimes dreamt of but seldom sought now. With no voice to speak for Nature she was abused and mismanaged. There was none to defend her for her voice of conscience was gone and heard no more by many, only by the few.

'Their world became a fairy-tale inhabited by gnomes, fairies and elves for children, for the children still believed, but it is the fate of men that they forget. They are not believed in, wanted or sought. They are forced to live in exile and appear indifferent though they are not. You can see the results for yourself when the human race is divorced from Nature. Many people no longer bother about Nature since she always provides, but the point may arrive where she cannot, or will not!

'We can replenish the places where the spirits used to be from the archetypes, but only if there is a place to replenish. However, this will happen only if it is acceptable and the place is capable of being replenished.'

'I believe this to be the case. Pan and his Kingdom is the reason for my quest. Will you tell me where I can find him?'

'I could, for he is close. Now and then a heart opens and seeks him. Some of you are like the 'salmon people.' You feel a divine homesickness that you do not fully understand. Some of you sense it, even if you do not understand it. You feel an inexplicable feeling of loss, but you do not know what it is you have lost. You know you do not 'belong there' but 'here' and you want to 'come home,' but where is home? Like the salmon you want to return to the distant spawning grounds that gave you birth. You are not quite sure where that is. Like the salmon, those below this pool, you leap the cataracts called 'life' with its troubled waters. Just as here, there are so many who fail and do not make it.

'Enough make the pool, but if ever a time comes that none arrive or none even bother making the journey, then the pool must withdraw also and perhaps the Kingdom will be lost, never to return, which does not bear thinking about. Many salmon die of their wounds in the attempt. At least they are trying to find and learn of the way. We are watching and it is noted. I promise you it is not always difficult. Many of them will die in the shallows of their own life, before their appointed time. Others die without ever having learnt how to live, so perhaps they were born not to know?'

'Will you show me the way I must take?'

'Unfair though it will seem to you, and it may even be so, even I cannot transcend or transgress the Law and I would do so at my own peril. The way you seek is there but you must find it for yourself. On many levels it is the case that what is attained with ease is seldom appreciated or valued. We are always watching and willing the seeker on to success. Until a certain point is reached, our help would be deemed interference from above and because of this we are often considered indifferent by the kingdom below, but we are not.'

The great salmon turns and brushes your hand gently with its tail; it feels a gentle caress. As you are resting on the bank with your fingers dangling in the water a sleep of well-being falls upon you like a soft warm cloak. You willingly succumb to it and fall into a dreamless sleep.

Awakening greatly refreshed, your hand is still dangling in the water of the salmon pool; or so you thought, but you are no longer there. You are lying on a grassy mound, with your fingers in a small pool. The Salmon King - the *Eo Feasa*- is gone and you are in open country again. The pool surrounded by the Sacred Grove of Hazels is gone. Desolation takes hold of you as you stand up to take your bearings. Behind you is the 32nd path that brought you to the ninth Kingdom of Yesod and the land of Mercury/Hermes.

Ahead of you is the 25th path that should take you to the sixth Kingdom of Tiphereth and the land of the Sun. There you should find the Sacred Grove of Birches. This 25th path should have a crossroads in its centre, where the 27th path crosses it, connecting as it does the Kingdoms of Hod and Netzach. To the left is the 30th path that will take you to the eighth Kingdom of Hod, the Kingdom of Venus and the Sacred Grove of Apples. To the right there is the 28th path that would take you to the Kingdom of Netzach, its ruler Mars and the Sacred Grove of Holly. You are at a triple path and a decision has to be made.

You remember Mercury is a planet of the mind. Did you create the Kingdom of Yesod or does it always exist, simply waiting to be called into being? Would it be the same for the others? The Kingdoms all seem very real to you. Would your description of the Kingdom and the events tally with those of the other travellers who have returned from this land? As always there are too many questions and too few answers: you even feel you have a few more questions than when you started but still not enough answers. Someone must have them. Someone must know.

You have some information about Pan and you told the *Eo feasa* it was love that brought you to him and Pan. From here you decide to go to the eighth Kingdom of Hod and Venus or Aphrodite. Venus is the astrological and mythical goddess of love, which is the gift you are trying to bring. You take the 30th path to the Kingdom of Hod because you have decided to take the Kingdoms in their order. This path is uneventful as most of the paths appear to have been so far. A gentle mist clings to the land on either side but nothing distracts you or hinders your travel. Gradually the land on either side of the path begins to take on a cultivated look, the work of human hands.

The Third Kingdom...

The odd tree is seen growing. Some may be seeds that have escaped from cultivation. Their fruit shows them to be pear, peach or apple trees. Rose bushes appear and they are dominated by the deep red variety. The air takes on a pleasant perfume that is as pleasing to the sense of smell as the land is to the eye. Rabbits scamper among the trees with doves flying or perching in their branches. The whole ambience of the place is of comfort and ease. Here, like a lotus-eater, you could be lulled by ease and resting that would hinder your progress to find him whom you seek.

Yet you know Pan is here too, for you know he prefers places less cultivated and more natural in their growth. Then you see that certain areas have been left wild. You feel this is an obvious and deliberate concession of leaving parts of Nature in her natural state. Perhaps they are for the use of the Elementals. Dwellings appear as do people to whom they belong. The dwellings are well designed and comfortable and here there are people of all ages. They are well dressed, acknowledge you as you pass, and appear both courteous and friendly.

Fields take on a more formal layout, the gardens are well kept and the orchards are well cultivated and tended. Occasionally there is an enclosed well encompassed with crab-apples and around these people are sitting, talking, resting and eating from baskets or small tables. With the experience of the previous Kingdoms you move towards what is obviously the centre. The buildings become more impressive as you progress and none are in a poor state.

You would say the buildings appear to give an outward show of considerable wealth, as you judge it. The largest buildings may be for communal use as they are spacious, well designed and have a symmetry of style. Tower matches tower, doors and windows correspond, and you feel if you closed the facade of some of them like the pages of a book, they would match exactly.

Now the doves are in ornamental dovecotes with myrtle trees close by. There are fountains as you have found in the other Kingdoms. In this one they are inlaid with jade, lapis lazuli, emeralds, sapphires and other stones of green or blue colour. The fountains are octagonal with eight ornamental spouts of copper pouring wine into copper basins that are shaped as large sea shells. You are certain, if previous patterns are anything to go by, that you will find a road that will lead you to the temple, the spiritual heart of the Kingdom. There you will find the trees of the sixth Chieftain of the High and Sacred Grove, which will be the Sacred Grove of Apples.

You rest on the benches near the central fountain and count the blue crystal cups around it, and naturally there are eight of them. Taking a cup you drink and eat the fruit from the copper bowls that have been placed around the perimeter of the fountain. You do not do this because you are hungry or thirsty for you are not, but you do like wine. The white wine is cool and refreshing and the fruit is good. You are not sure, but the wine may have been red when you sat, yet it is now white the wine you prefer. You watch the people going about their business and decide to move on. The pleasant surroundings could make you rest far longer than you intend.

As you rise, you notice the bowl from which you took your fruit does not seem to be diminished. You would swear the bowl and fruit were exactly as you had found them when you arrived there. Taking your bearings and keeping to the central path, which you assume is still the 30th path until it reaches the centre of the Kingdom, you keep going forward. This proves to be wise. As with previous Kingdoms, it leads to a wide spacious avenue of great beauty that should be the approach to the spiritual centre of the Kingdom. You join the people who are moving in that general direction.

They are of all ages, well dressed, the older people in rich brocades of pink, blue or turquoise; the young are not so formal. Always the clothes are well cut and occasionally lined or hemmed with luxurious fur. Many wear gloves that are beautifully ornate, with some highly decorated with small jewels. As the weather is so clement you take it that they are worn more for ornamentation than protection. It presents a beautiful scene of harmony, well-being and obvious prosperity.

The avenue is lined with fine apple trees and myrtle, with formal beds planted out, mainly with roses. You are sure this will lead you to the Sacred Grove of the Apples and the spiritual centre of the eighth Kingdom. You know if you find these trees they will be the finest of all, such as you have never seen before. When you come to the end of the avenue you find it ends in a high wall. There is one path going to the left and the other to the right. However, this time there is one slight difference.

There does not appear to be any visible entrance opposite the approach avenue, as in previous Kingdoms.

There is a sight that takes your breath away. Set in the wall is a sea shell that has been fashioned out of what must be the biggest piece of lapis lazuli you have ever seen. It is the height of the wall and its width is equal to its height. Set in the centre of this lapis lazuli shell is a magnificent carved seat, a throne you think, carved from one piece of deep green jade. The seat is approached by eight steps at the front. There is the same number of steps at both sides. On either side of the throne is a beautifully carved and sculptured apple tree. The trunks and branches are made from lapis lazuli, with jade and emeralds for the fruit.

You go down the left-hand path quite a way, but that only shows you the wall is circular. Nothing is found which even suggests the way in, if there is one. A similar journey to the right proves equally unproductive. You begin to wonder if you have approached it from the rear this time. However, the grand avenue of approach seems to belie this, for this is a major path of approach to the Kingdom.

Another alternative suggests itself to you. If it is a throne, perhaps this is not a temple, but a palace, though it's unusual to have a throne on the outside of a wall. Could this throne be where the ruler meets the people on ceremonial occasions? You noticed others resting on the banks of well kept grass. Deciding to sit on the bank under an apple tree, opposite the throne, you will watch for the time being. For a long time you watch the people coming and going, and many acknowledge your presence with a friendly nod and smile. None attempt to help you and none go near the seat.

You get a little drowsy in the pleasant and beguiling atmosphere and as this has helped in the past you do not resist. Next to your head the tree's branches are hanging low under the weight of their harvest. You take an apple and bite into it and you slip into a pleasant sleep. How long you have slept (if you have), you do not know, for it only seems a few seconds. When you open your eyes, as with the other occasions, you are no longer where you were, but where you are makes you feel a little uneasy.

Quickly taking your bearings you find they cause you a mixture of excitement and concern. You are sitting on the seat within the lapis lazuli shell, flanked by the jewelled apple trees. There is the reverberant sound of the jewelled 'fruit' moving in the breeze but is this a gentle solicitation or a tocsin? Are they proclaiming a benediction or sacrilege? Not wishing to give offence you feel a little apprehensive, but looking around you find you are the only one here. You still have the apple in your hand, taken from the tree on the opposite bank from where you are now. It has your tooth marks in it that show you did bite into it: with the apple's mythological and magical properties, did it get you here?

Though you feel you are tempting Fate you close your eyes, lowering your head, and you bite the apple again. Did you feel something? You know you are still seated within the jade shell. Taking a deep breath, you open your eyes. You can see the eight steps in front of the throne and those on either side. Just when you think nothing has happened, you raise your head and realize you are no longer seated outside the wall but obviously inside it.

Around the wall is a broad walk, which has alternate squares of a blue and green glass material, bordered with myrtle and apple trees. It obviously mirrors the path outside the wall. Standing in front of the throne, you see that from this path other paths lead towards the centre. You cannot see all the paths, but you hazard a reasonable guess that there will be eight. The paths are not unlike the spokes of a wheel that go to the centre, which you can see.

Walking down the path leading from the throne to the centre you make the guess that all the paths will end with a throne. At the end of the path there is a large mound that is ascended by eight steps. On the mound there is a large circular building that has the appearance of being cut out of pure blue ice, until you realize it could well be sapphire.

Because you are quite high up you can look at the paths coming to the temple. They are eight and there is a seat where they end at the wall, which is circular and unbroken. Around the temple is a covered walk whose roof is supported by eight columns of jade. The eight radiating paths from the thrones of the outer walk come up these eight steps and end at the base of the eight jade columns. A portico of lapis lazuli faces you when you reach the end of the path that came from the outer wall. You turn to look at the throne again, but it has gone. There are two large closed doors made of rosewood inlaid with sapphires, lapis lazuli and burnished copper. There are hinges but no handles or a keyhole.

Approaching them you feel that if you are welcome they will open and if you are not they will debar you and stay closed. You kneel in silence before them and within a short time you are relieved to see they open to admit you. The temple appears to follow the pattern of the previous buildings save that the altar is in the centre, under a dome constructed of pristine copper. The altar is made from an enormous cut emerald and the top is faced with a slab of sapphire. In the centre of the copper dome is another enormous emerald that seems to have a sapphire embedded in its centre. These two stones cast a light that merges into turquoise on the altar below.

Instinctively you bend the knee and head in respect. On the opposite side of the circular pile is a complementary set of doors that are closed. There are inlaid alcoves around the wall of the temple that house the Sacred Grove of Apples. These alcoves contain the eight sacred trees of the Kingdom of Hod.

Their fruits are as nothing you have seen on the earth plane and you feel that apples will never be the same again for you. Perhaps once they, or something very similar, may have grown on the Isle of Avalon? These trees must have supplied the apple that Paris gave in his judgement and those that filled the casket of Iduna; you feel they are only felicitous for the deities, not man. You walk around the left-hand side of the altar and face the opposite doors. You feel a tightening of the stomach and an excitement.

A hand is placed very gently on your right shoulder but you do not turn. Out of the corner of your left eye you see another hand holding a staff of jade topped by a large polished, but uncut sapphire set in copper. There is the edge of a blue robe edged in green, long tapering fingers and on the index finger a large emerald ring. You now turn slowly and face this venerable keeper of the Temple of Venus.

A gentle voice that allays any possible fear asks '
What or who do you seek?'
'I seek the great god of nature, Pan.'
'Why do you seek him and what do you take to him?'
'Love.'
'For this Kingdom that is enough. Each has within them part of the Chalice, but most let spiritual love atrophy for the sake of the physical and both should live. The Chalice becomes empty save for the dregs and love suffers through lack, just as it can through misuse. It was lack of love and the lack of faith it engenders which made these Kingdoms withdraw.'

He continues, 'Now and then someone awakens and undertakes the quest to try to find the hidden way; they attempt to make the journey and we are glad. We watch and do all we can, but sadly cannot always help until a certain point is reached. Unless the faith is strong an apple in the Kingdom falls; it withers and dies, and we know that someone has given up and we are sad. Every morning we watch to see if there is new fruit. We tend it carefully if there is, hoping it will come to fullness and ripen.'

'What if there is no new fruit?'

'Sadly the temple and Kingdom would fall into decay, for its purpose would be no more.'

'I have love enough for whom I seek. Is it enough?'

'It is. However, never let the Chalice run dry and always keep a little for yourself, for it is your right. Be gentle with yourself and do not be too harsh. Try not to spill this most precious of life's wine and use discrimination where you place it and to whom you give it. For you are less than halfway on your quest and with love we send you on your way and wish you success. Maintain your strength and courage and do not be discouraged; be like the salmon, ever on and upwards.'

The staff is slowly brought down in front of your face until the great sapphire is level with your eyes and you submit willingly. The sapphire begins gently glowing. It pulsates and the focus of your sight is diffused and loses it sharpness with the rhythmic pulse of its pure blue light. The light is strong and yet so gentle it does not even make you blink. It seems so all embracing that it holds you within its sphere. You hear what you think are doors closing gently behind you and the light and temple are gone.

This time you stand at five paths. One of these is the 30th path by which you arrived. On the extreme left is the 23rd path that leads to the fifth Kingdom, the Kingdom of Geburah, Saturn and the Sacred Grove of Yews. The next path to the right is the 26th path. This would lead you to the sixth Kingdom of Tiphereth, land of the Sun and the Sacred Grove of the Birch. The central path is the 27th path that leads to the seventh Kingdom of Netzach, the Kingdom of Mars and the Sacred Grove of Holly.

The next path to the right is the 30th path by which you came to this Kingdom from the Kingdom of Yesod. To your extreme left is the 31st path. This path would bypass the Kingdom of Yesod and take you directly back to the Kingdom of Malkuth and the harbour where your craft is moored. Have you had enough? Do you want to go back and leave the remainder of the journey for another day?

You know where the island is now and you can return. If you did so, then you could go direct to the Kingdom of Netzach using the 29th path from Malkuth. This path would be on the right from the Kingdom of Malkuth when you landed again. You could go direct and not pass through the Sacred Grove of the Willows. However, as you have decided to take the Kingdoms upwards, in the reverse order of the descent of the Lightning Flash, you take the 27th path.

On to the seventh Kingdom of Netzach you will go, the seat of Mars, where you will seek the Sacred Grove of Holly. Like most of the other paths taken the journey is uneventful. In many respects you are grateful for that, but for the first time you notice that the surrounding countryside is taking on a different appearance. The change starts roughly when you have crossed over the central crossroads where the 25th path crosses the path you are on. To turn left at the crossroads would take you to the sixth Kingdom of Tiphereth. Turning to the right would take you back to the Kingdom of Yesod. This confirms that you are where you think you are and you are going in the right direction.

The land starts to rise as with other parts of the island but this time more steeply than before and taking on a more severe aspect. There are rocky outcrops in the surrounding area, not seen or noticed in other areas. Surveying what lies ahead from one of these bluffs, you see the rocks grow more frequent and much larger. In the distance you get the impression that you are heading, for the first time, into quite high country. There is a small mountain range, small from this distance at least.

The journey is not tiring, but you are moving up at a steeper rate than the previous paths. The path rises to a little hillock and at the top, to one side, there are some rocks of unusual shape. Unusual in as much as they have a chair carved in one of them. Leaving the path you climb with little effort and seat yourself in this impressive chair and it is very comfortable. It is then you notice the unusual design of the place that was not obvious from the path.

It proves to be a circular outcrop of rock on a gentle downward slope. Only the carved chair is high enough to be seen from outside. None of the rocks are higher than the height of a small man. When you sit in the carved chair there is a series of seats lower down which are facing you. These seats make two concentric crescents in front of the higher seat. The outer crescent consists of twelve chairs carved in the inner face of the rock. Apart from the seats, the rock has been left in its natural state. The inner crescent consists of seven separate rocks with seats carved in their faces. Because the backs of these two crescents have been left natural, they look like an outcrop of rocks from the path.

Only the high seat is visible from the path because it faces it. If you had not seen the high seat nothing would be seen from the path. So you have one high throne facing a semicircle of seven, with another semicircle of twelve seats behind them. You think the plan may prove astrological. You think the twelve seats represent the twelve signs of the zodiac with the seven seats representing the seven planets of the Ancients. If this is so, who occupies the thirteenth seat? You do remember, however, that Pan has been placed in the centre of the zodiac belt by some authorities.

A path leads you into the stone circle and although not deeply etched, it shows you are not the first to be here or sit in the seat. When seated you face the direction from which you came, because of the greater height, you can see a roseate glow in the far distance. You know this is the Kingdom on Hod in the distance.

You are amazed how far you have come in what appears so short a time, but by whose time? Your watch stopped working the moment you set foot on the island. You turn to look behind the throne, for now you have decided that is what it is and you have already been using this term for some time now. There is the path you will eventually take. The land is undulating and the path winds its way through this landscape towards the distant mountain ridge. You are not cold, nor do you feel the immediate desire to go on. You want to stop and gather your thoughts, review what you have seen and what has happened so far on the journey.

First, the Kingdoms have appeared much as you would expect them to be according to the nature of the planetary rulership placed upon them by the system of Cabala you subscribe to. Each Kingdom groups within itself all that the planet rules. The Kingdom contains the symbols, signs, energy, plants, flowers, buildings, animals, birds, the people, etc., that you would have expected to find. You have seen some magical images and the mundane affairs of the Kingdom, mainly their virtues with little of the vices that also exists. There has been some reference to the pack known as Tarot, but less than you thought there would be. Does this mean that the Kingdoms appear to you according to the preconceived idea you have of them? You did an experiment in one Kingdom by trying to mentally alter the images you found there. If they had changed with your thought then they would probably have been the product of your thoughts, but they did not change in the way you wanted them to.

Does a person with a richer, more extensive vocabulary and repository of symbolism have a richer journey than someone who has not? Would they be given symbol overlaid with symbol, making multiple forms, because it would be known that they would be understood and even if they were not understood at the time, the symbols would be retained to be analysed later? It seems reasonable to assume that people are given what they would understand. There would be little point in undertaking the journey if you brought nothing back because it was not understood. You could have two people undertaking the same journey together, but anyone reading the accounts of the journeys later could be forgiven for thinking they had gone to different places.

I think it reasonable to say that the Powers do not appear in their original form. Remembering the fate of Semele when she asked to see Zeus in all his glory, you wonder if it could be borne if they did. I think they choose a form familiar and acceptable to the traveller according to their evolutionary state, birthplace, racial characteristics, traditions, teachings, etc. Perhaps there is some truth in the old saying that when Death comes, he comes 'as a friend,' because we would go with a friend.

They choose a form that is acceptable to the traveller and not one that will scare them to death. Therefore, can it be assumed that each traveller will see the form they are familiar with; which could be different to each according to the above precepts?

Great discrimination is obviously at work. There is little to be gained by scaring the traveller half or wholly out their wits, possibly destroying the mind and the vessel containing it as well. There would be little profit in such a contract for either party, with a hollow victory for the stronger. Your musing begins to falter and you see, in our terms, what could be taken for daybreak over the distant ridge. You do not really know how much time you have spent sitting on this throne of stone and you still have no idea to whom it belongs. On it there is, or was, some carving but this has long lost its detail; the only part that is showing is the head carved on the top. This you conclude is either a ram or a goat and that pleases you.

You feel refreshed and decide you have done enough reflection and now it's time for action and to move on with your quest. You rejoin the path again below the circle of seats and make off towards the ridge. In this direction you hope to find the Chieftain of the High and Sacred Grove of Holly. The appearance of the landscape begins to establish the approach of the Kingdom, as it did with the previous Kingdoms. It is slow, in much the same way that the characteristics of a country do not change immediately you cross its borders. It establishes itself slowly the deeper you travel into the realm.

The Fourth Kingdom...

The first signs are obvious. Small holly bushes break out among the rocks as do thistles, thorns, gorses, brambles and all those bushes and plants with spikes and spines. The first flower you find announces its presence by its acrid smell, pleasant to some: the geranium. The path winds its way through small ravines that at times blot out the countryside, though they are not large. Every time the path rises to another crest you expect to see a village or city, as with the other Kingdoms.

However, one thing is missing, this time. The outlying dwellings that came with the approach to the centres of the other Kingdoms are not here. After climbing many such crests, hills and ridges you finally arrive at the one that gives you your answer. Your path turns to the left and there below is a vast city, turreted and walled.

Its colour gives it the appearance of having been modelled in cast iron with the familiar red rust, though it hasn't. The roofs, balconies, doors, etc., are mostly in red of various shades. Most of its banners and flags have symbols of silver or a pewter colour, which are unfurled, it seems, over almost every building. Each building has a marker, not unlike a coat of arms, announcing family or clan. Despite the dull appearance of the city, a shining dark grey, it does not give the impression of gloom, being charged with great activity.

A deep chasm blocks the approach to the walled city. You had expected to see a drawbridge and portcullis protecting the main and only entrance from where you stand. From your high position you can see there is a point on your side where you think a causeway ought to be. There is a short projection into the chasm that ends abruptly, which is flanked by two towers. There is another short projection on the other side that leads to the porte-cochere, not the line of defence you expected. The path is cut through a small ravine that hides your view of the city and turns to the left and down.

The path becomes a staircase that widens as it descends to approach the towers which are much larger than you thought. They appear to be they appear unmanned. Upon inspection the towers do not seem to have any windows or entrance of any kind. For what seems an age you take stock of your situation, trying to see if there is any obvious way by which you can enter the city, knowing it is the sacred centre. You feel you are being watched, but this feeling has been with you from the moment you set foot on the island. Therefore, you do not make any move that could be construed as hostile or disrespectful. You look about to see if there is any means of crossing the chasm and gaining entrance, but there is none that you can see.

Perhaps there is another entrance from another direction, but the higher view showed you that the city is backed by gaunt mountains of rugged granite. This must be the only way in, but how? By now you have walked quite a way around the top of the chasm, looking at the unapproachable walls on the other side. Perhaps you should retrace your steps back to the high path, the better to view the situation. You arrive back at the towers to find they are connected by a bridge of solid granite that spans the chasm to the gates on the other side.

The gates of the city are now standing wide open. Nothing ought to surprise you, yet it does, though by now you feel you ought to have learnt to expect the unexpected. With confidence you cross the bridge, feeling its appearance means you are meant to go into the city to find that which you seek, or so you hope. Entering the gate, you pause to take your bearings on the approach to the city. Looking behind you, you see the bridge no longer exists and all is as it was when you saw it first. The great gates are slowly and silently closing behind you.

Many of the buildings are tall, as is usual in a place built on a small area and housing many people. The city is protected at the rear by high mountains. There are attractive squares and you find the people are attired in a mixture of styles that you know is an amalgam of one of your favourite periods of history. The men wear dress armour, light and decorative in style. As opposed to the heavy armour of conflict, it is court armour. In some squares men are engaged in arms practise with sword, mace, lance and shield and some are engaged in teaching the young these arts. These are exercises designed for fitness, agility and strength. Older men and their female companions watch, applaud and instruct; some take friendly wagers on the outcome of some matches.

Some fountains are set in the walls of the houses, accessible to all who pass with a lower basin for the animals. Some fountains have a deep red water gushing from them, and you realize the water is probably coloured by iron. Following the familiar pattern you make towards the centre of the city. Here you find a large and impressive seven sided area with a holly tree in each angle.

People are all over the square, for you think of it as a square despite its shape. There are many chariots with fine horses with both male and female riders. The main transport appears to be a heavy and ornate carriage pulled by two or four quite heavy horses. In the centre of this septilateral area are the familiar steps rising in seven sequences of seven that lead to an enormous temple that echoes the seven sides below. It is obviously a central meeting place with people sitting and standing on the steps, some alone, with others in groups.

You climb to the temple and from it you see that the city is based upon seven main avenues, radiating like the spokes of a wheel which is a familiar pattern seen in all the previous Kingdoms. The temple doors are bronze and inlaid with rubies, carbuncles, bloodstones and red stones you do not recognize. The doors stand wide open and you enter. The building is lined with marble veined with many shades of red. There are seven alcoves with granite pillars on either side in which are the seven Chieftains you seek: seven magnificent holly trees with berries in clusters like rubies.

At the back of the alcoves, behind the trees, are windows of pure red that are made from cut sheets of flawless ruby. The light of these windows shines through the trees, casting seven rays of red light on the central high altar. The altar, like the building, is seven sided and is under a bronze canopy that is held up by seven ruby pillars. It is draped with a brocade of the deepest red and a vibrant crimson. Opposite the door through which you entered is an ornate chair in the shape of a magnificent chariot. There is a smaller seat to your right, which puts it to the left of the ornate chair.

Although you already know the answer habit causes you to count the steps that ascend to the throne and it is of no surprise that they are seven. You look through the open door and see people outside getting on with their affairs. Despite the door being wide open the temple is deserted save for yourself. The temple is quiet within and, not knowing quite what to do, you decide to do nothing and quietly wait to see what happens. You do not feel that you should sit in this throne. You go to the small seat and sit on the bottom step, with your back to a ruby pillar.

You are not aware that you have slept but you did close your eyes to rest them and to contemplate your situation. The tranquillity of the temple, as with most of the others, has little difficulty in lulling your senses. It is possible you slept a while. You are beginning to learn the results of closing your eyes in these Kingdoms. You open your eyes with a start, stand up and then you become aware that the large throne is no longer empty. Seated in it is a man of mature years, his close cropped beard lining a firm chin, which he is resting on his left hand. You are not sure how long he has been quietly watching you.

He wears a light cuirass over a robe of deep red that reaches the floor and which is trimmed with gold. He rests his right hand on the hilt of a splendid curtana. Around his brow he wears a thick gold band with seven large spikes, each having a ruby at its base. You bow to him while stammering your apologies for your disrespect and lack of courtesy. He reminds you of the 'Emperor' of the traditional tarot pack, which makes you think you may be right in not wanting to alter established packs; or is he conforming with your views on the matter? Perhaps picking up your thoughts, he smiles paternally and asks 'How can this Kingdom be of help to you?'

'I seek, respected king, the great god Pan.'

'Are you prepared to meet him?'

'It is for that I have come.'

His voice has gentle reproach in it. 'That is not what I asked. Many have sought him out but not all were prepared. They come under the prime law of the physical plane duality - this or that, light or dark, good or evil. Your world has been thrown from one extreme to another by this law. This results in most of your teachers speaking of the 'golden mean.' They exhort you to find the balance between the extremes of life and your existence, which is apparently so hard to achieve.

'Very few do so, as is shown by the conditions prevalent in your world. Yet the physical plane could not become balanced, or have all awakened simultaneously; only a few at a time, otherwise there would be none to serve that plane and it would become void.'

You ask, 'Do other laws operate on the physical plane than those that seem to dominate us? This lurching from one excess and extravagance to another, calling it progress, action and choice, because that is what it is thought to be...'

'There are,' he replies, 'but you must first master the ones you have and make duality your servant and not your master. The conditions of your existence show the chaos this simple law can bring, though even it has been rather complicated. There would be little point in revealing other natural laws, which must be sought and found, until you have mastered what you already have.

'Most of your present philosophies strengthen their thrall and hold over you. They appear to set you free, but it is to a large extent only an appearance. Your philosophy operates almost exclusively on it. Your religious books give one law, giving for the most only two choices. The 'fruit' offers duality - a choice between good and evil. Most of your religious leaders reinforce this idea by the eternal fight between God and the Devil, which one or the other must win. This is an idea that is static and lacking in dynamism because it assumes that if something is deemed good its opposite must be evil, but Good and Bad are not absolute, only relative.'

'Something that is good is not as good as something higher on the scale, but it is better than something lower. Therefore, something can posses both good and bad, regulated by its position on a scale or the viewpoint from which it is judged. As you so often say when being criticized and justifying yourself, "It depends on the way you look at it!" This of course implies that there is more than one way of answering the charge; two at least, if not more.

'Wherever on the scale you start your judgement, this becomes the point from which to begin your assessment. This principle used with wisdom enables you transmute one mental state into another, not unlike transmuting lead into gold. This is all a part of the "Divine Paradox." The Great Hermes, when asked pertinent questions by the more advanced of his students, would press their lips tightly together by way of an answer, saying nothing. Possibly he was suggesting there was no answer to some questions - 'for the lips of wisdom are closed, save to the ears of understanding'. Perhaps he was simply saying there was no answer for them, for if they did not possess understanding, they were not sanctioned to have the knowledge.

'I ask again are you prepared? For what do you seek - God or the Devil?

'I come to find a slandered and maligned god, to defend him if I can, if he needs it. Though I do not think I can do much.'

He does not reply immediately, but looks at you for a long time. Finally he replies, 'Defence we understand, it is one of the pillars that sustain this Kingdom. Defence if honest, if it is from the heart, is commendable. Your "defence" may yet be put to the test to see if it is indeed strong enough to withstand the trial. Not necessarily from without, that is often the easiest form of defence to sustain, but from within.'

He continues, 'We will watch your progress with interest and add our encouragement to those of the other Kingdoms you have visited. We saw your still small light coming from the other Kingdoms. After each Kingdom your light was a little brighter and we shall add our portion, but take care, stronger lights than yours have been blown out. Never relax your vigilance, for the approach of those who carry a torch is seen from afar. There are few ways to hide a flame, sacred or otherwise and there are those who abhor light.'

As he speaks, he descends from his throne. He leaves the curtana and with his right hand he leads his consort from her throne. Engrossed in his every word you had not noticed that his lady had joined him. You start to give your apology but a hand is raised with an extended forefinger to smiling lips, showing it is not necessary.

They stand in majesty like the tarot Emperor and Empress. She places her right hand on your shoulder and a circle of contact is complete. He turns his gaze from her to you, your eyes meet and you see the wisdom you would expect from the ruler of this Kingdom. You feel a vitality pass through them to you that seems to stimulate your entire body. You close your eyes for a split second, realising too late this can be a fatal thing to do in these elusive Kingdoms at the wrong time. You are right. It was the wrong time, for the Kingdom is gone.

You are standing at a triple road again. As it was with the Kingdom of Hod, there are two other paths on either side making five paths in all. The path to the far right is the 21st that would lead to the fourth Kingdom of Chesed. Here you should find the Sacred Grove of Oak, in the land of Jupiter. The path on the far left is the one you would take should you want to leave the island.

This is the 29th path, the one that would take you back to the Kingdom of Malkuth and the harbour where your craft is moored. This is a mirror of the 31st path, from the Kingdom of Hod. The central path is the 27th path and was the one that brought you here from the Kingdom of Hod. To its left is the 28th path that would take you back to the Kingdom on Yesod. To the right of the centre is the 24th path and that is the one you seek.

The 24th path will take you to the centre of all the Kingdoms, in the lower part of the island. This is the path that takes you to the sixth Kingdom of Tiphereth, the land of Sol and the Chieftain of the Sacred Grove of the Birch. This is the next Kingdom in the order you have elected to follow in your ascent.

From where you entered the harbour it is obvious the island rises, like a wedge, to the enormous mist-shrouded headland you saw when you approached. The high part of the island is divided from the rest by the Abyss into which the seas were pouring with such danger. Whether you can cross this Abyss, whether you will want to try, you do not know. You feel the sure way is taking the Kingdoms in their natural order of ascent to see what happens when or if you ever get there. Put simply, crossing that bridge, though if there is one you doubt, when you get there.

It appears the paths rise in their approach to the Kingdoms and you divine that this is the form the island takes. If you are right, the Kingdom of Sol will rise high and as if to confirm your thoughts, the clouds in the centre of the island clear. There is a magnificent hill with the Sun behind it. You set your feet on the 24th path that you know will take you to the sixth Kingdom. Tiphereth is the Kingdom of the Sun, where you will find the Chieftain of the High and Sacred Grove of the Birches. The path away from the Kingdom of Netzach takes a downward slope until it levels out on what you think is the plane.

The holly trees of the previous Kingdom start to disappear. Between the Kingdoms the land takes on the usual neutral appearance, with nothing to note. The horizon shows a very large hill in the distance that rises in the centre of the land. Your map tells you this is the centre of the seven Kingdoms below the abyss and it should have eight paths leading to it and from it.

All the Kingdoms have a direct path to it save the Kingdom of Malkuth. This Kingdom has to go through the Kingdoms of Yesod, Hod or Netzach to get to the Kingdom of Tiphereth, its most direct approach being Yesod. You wonder why the important Kingdom of Malkuth is set apart in some respects as it is. You know there are commentators who consider Malkuth as 'a fallen kingdom' and if it was restored the Tree would in balance again.

The hill continues to rise above you as you approach it and you realize that distance made it look smaller than it is. Unlike the Kingdom of Netzach there are no crags and rock faces; the hill has small outcrops of rocks but these are not as forbidding as the last Kingdom. The path to it is broad, as if trodden down by many, many feet over a long period.

The Fifth Kingdom...

You are not surprised to see the birch trees that begin to line its edge, and dotted around the landscape. Then you notice they are not exclusively birches. There are small oaks here and there. Set in a patch of sand and water, you see an occasional palm, resembling a small oasis.

The path widens to a broad avenue. The birch trees appear equally spaced on either side which shows human planting rather than natural growth. The hill is spreading outwards to a considerable size that is beginning to blot out the rest of the landscape. Large buildings are built closer together as they and you approach the summit. Formal gardens appear, with beautifully designed parks, containing the ubiquitous fountains. These fountains are of pure white marble that have spouts of gold. Many of them are six sided but not all; now and then there is a circular one. In these gardens and parks there are many peacocks and peahens.

You reach the base of the hill and rising above you is a marble staircase to the summit. Your map tells you there will probably be eight stairways like this, because there are eight paths to this central Kingdom of Sol even though it is the sixth Kingdom. The dwellings become more sumptuous as you approach a great arch set in a golden wall, through which you enter the city. Inside the city the houses appear to give way to what you would describe as mansions; these in turn give way to pavilions and to palaces and all this confirms that you are going towards the centre of the Kingdom, perhaps of the entire island?

Statues of golden lions are on either side of most of the staircases and they are found as symbols on houses, flags and banners. There are many birches and oaks in which are perched many eagles. You find acacia, bay and laurel trees and the vine. There is a strong smell of olibanum in the air. An unknown bird sits in a large, untidy nest, and although it is only a guess you think it is the legendary Phoenix, or is it the Bennu, bird of Osiris? An emblem of resurrection in both cases, you feel you will only see one here.

The people who pass you are dressed in the most luxurious clothes of silk, brocade and furs of the highest quality. Ermine and sable are evident. Many have golden bands around their heads, with a sun-disc in the centre. The females have a solitary diamond, but the older people have a corona of gold made into various symbols that may well suggest rank or family. They are accompanied by various animals that all have one quality in common - high pedigree and breeding.

The roads around the city to the left and right obviously run parallel around the summit. They are connected from the centre by stairs, paths and roads that take you from one level to another and are filled with people. Gilt or golden coaches disappear under arches and stairs to appear again on the other side. Given the ruler of the Kingdom it does not surprise you to find you're using 'sunny' and 'golden' to describe the atmosphere of the place.

There are so many people no one seems to notice another. You do nothing to draw attention to yourself and carry on with the purpose in hand. You want to find the temple and Sacred Grove of the High Chieftain of the Birch. This will be the fifth Sacred Grove of the seven you seek. This only leaves two Sacred Groves to complete the hallowed number you hope will take you into the presence of Pan. Arriving at the top of the stairs you find a more magnificent paved walk made of white marble flecked with gold. It has a balustrade on the outside of the mound, the inner side leading to the grand temple.

Taking note of a large palace (its design and crest), you start walking around it to the left. Being a solar Kingdom, you decide that deosil is the correct way, going in the direction of the physical sun. The broad path is octagonal and not circular, which it seems. When you arrive back at the step that has the palace you used as marker, you know that you are back to the 24th path that brought you here.

You also now know there are eight paths leading to the city and eight stairways can bring you to this broad walk around the temple. However, when you face the temple with your back to the city, you count six stairways. These stairways have six golden steps with lions of gold on either side, top and bottom. The lower eight stairways have eight steps of white marble, likewise they have lions top and bottom.

You decide not to use the stairway on the 24th path, the path that brought you into the city, but to move to the next stairway deosil. This staircase (the next of the lower eight) will be on the 25th path and on the central column of the tree diagram. This central path, called the balanced path, is opposite one of the six staircases that take you to the temple.

There are three important Kingdoms to be found on these central paths, the 25th and the 32nd. The Kingdom of the Moon (= Kingdom of Malkuth) which is of the Element of Water. The Kingdom of Hermes/Mercury (= Kingdom of Yesod) with its Elements of Air and Earth and the Kingdom of the Sun (= Kingdom of Tiphereth) which is of the Element of Fire. These make up the four elements of your own Kingdom from where you came and these four elements are also said to be found in you; the central paths are the only paths which contain all four elements.

With the temple being under solar symbolism and rulership it is, as you expected, circular in construction. From the outside it has a high domed cupola of amber with gold supports. This is crowned with a short spire on which is set a large golden orb. Set in the circular wall are six large columns of amber with a gold top and pediment, between the columns are six large windows, consisting of the largest diamonds you have ever seen. Each one has countless facets, which will reflect the light inside the building.

There are two massive doors made of burnished gold. At the point of opening are two huge diamonds set in gold, not unlike door handles. Overawed by the pure metal shining at your feet you feel reluctant to tread on the gold. For a time you remain at the bottom step while waiting to decide what to do. You idly begin to examine the golden lion. Tracing the fine carving with your index finger from its diamond eyes, you move down the finely carved body to the diamond claws in its feet. You run your hand down the pedestal and along the bottom step until you find a pair of golden sandals that were not there before.

You raise your eyes and a white robe hemmed in gold appears, then a girdle of gold. Next there is a curved neckline trimmed in gold, then a golden chain with a sun-disc on which concentric circles are engraved around a circular cut diamond. Each carved orbit has a different precious stone set in it, resembling a map of the heavens. Finally you come to a white beard and a pair of eyes that seem amused at your close inspection of the lion. His hair, falling down either side to his shoulders, is kept in place with a broad golden circlet, on which are set six spires of gold.

This ancient appears as the archetype of all the guides, mentors and golden age leaders the world has ever seen, as represented by clairvoyants, sculptors and artists alike. Perhaps sensing your reluctance to tread upon the golden staircase he extends his right hand, showing that you should go up. In respect you silently suggest he should precede you, which he does while you follow at a respectful distance. He approaches the great doors and it does not surprise you that they swing open silently at his approach.

You stand on the threshold of the doors and as with all the other Kingdoms a wonderful sight is there for you to see. The amber columns are half outside the temple and half inside. They glow with an amber light that seems to be inside the columns. Between these columns are six alcoves. The centre is a large area with three alcoves on either side.

In this central area there is, hanging in the air with no visible support that you can see, a large crown of gold that is rotating very slowly. Behind the crown are three curtains of varying thickness. They are suspended, one in front of the other. You can see the three rods of gold that support them.

The first is the thinnest for it is like gossamer. Through this you can see the second curtain, which is just thin enough to show the third, thickest, curtain. This last curtain hides the gold of the back wall of the temple. In front of the large amber columns are the six Birches of the High and Sacred Grove, whose leaves shimmer with the sheen of burnished gold. As with all the previous temple trees they are the largest of their kind you have ever seen. The tree branches curve with the dome of the temple, and almost meet in the middle.

There is a low balustrade concentric with the outer wall of the temple. This separates the alcoves and their trees from the main floor area. Set in front of this balustrade are eight thrones though this is the sixth Kingdom of the seven. Do these thrones agree with the eight roads that lead to the temple, eight coming to six? Who comes down these eight roads to the sixth Kingdom to occupy the eight thrones? Your guide is looking intently into your eyes as you muse and you are sure that he knows every thought.

There are two thrones opposite the door where you stand which are raised on a dais. In front of these is a third throne set at floor level. Two thrones are set to the left side of the temple and two to the right, making seven. One throne is set behind you and faces all the others as you stand in the doorway, making eight in all. This seems to upset the plan of six a little that you had expected within the temple area, but eight paths brought you here

The floor is white marble inlaid with a golden sun which has eight rays that extend from the central altar to the edge of the small balustrade. Between these are eight smaller rays that do not quite reach the perimeter, giving the floor the appearance of a stylised sunburst. Your guide is no longer with you so you walk towards the altar in the centre where your eyes are drawn upwards.

Through a huge diamond, in the centre of the amber cupola, a white light flows to the floor below. This is reflected in a diamond of equal size. The lower diamond is supported on six gold legs which end in the claws of a lion. Each claw is holding a ball of amber. This ray of light is exceptionally intense and pure yet not blinding. It seems to have within it flecks of gold streaming down from above.

Suspended in the ray of light, but surprisingly casting no shadow nor seeming to interrupt the flow, is a large orb of gold. Around it spin other orbs of varying sizes. You realize you could be looking at a plan of our universe revolving around a central sun represented by the orb of gold. The Earth is an emerald with a silver Moon in an orbit around it.

Around the central orb and close to it is Mercury in a volatile silver. Venus is a sapphire, Mars a ruby, Jupiter a large amethyst with its satellites in stones unknown to you. In the outermost orbit is Saturn in shining lead or pewter with jet rings and satellites. The whole thing is slowly revolving. Though it is an extremely large model, it is obviously a miniature of the universe as you know it. It revolves within the altar light, casting no shadow, like an unsupported Orrery or eidouranion.

How long this display keeps you fascinated is impossible to tell. What sense of time do you have in these Kingdoms? To your surprise the central Sun, although appearing solid, begins to glow with a pulsating light. You turn to see what may have produced this effect, perhaps a reflection from somewhere else. You start when you see the throne of gold is now occupied by the grand man whom you saw outside.

He is now holding in one hand a sceptre of gold set with a great diamond, though he is still wearing his circlet of gold with the six golden spires. He smiles and shows with a hand, on which there is a heavy ring of gold set with a diamond, that you are to look to the altar again.

This time it is the Moon that glows with light and again you turn to the old man. The silver throne on his left is now occupied by a beautiful woman dressed in an identical robe to his except that the trimmings are all silver. In her right hand she has a sceptre with a large moonstone in it, in her left hand an orb that is a great pearl surmounted by a silver cross. On her finger is a silver ring mounted with another great pearl and her crown is silver with ten spires.

Sensing the rhythm you turn to the altar again and this time it is the precious stone representing Mercury that glows. You find a young man on the lower throne of silver. He wears identical robes with trimmings in bright yellow and a silver ring set with a large yellow agate. He sits between the Sun and Moon; you know that is what they represent.

His throne has the appearance of liquid silver and seems volatile to a point of instability. In his hand he holds a caduceus, on his head is a circlet of silver with nine spires that, like his throne, has the appearance of liquid silver. Again you turn to the altar where the sapphire representing Venus glows and you turn to see which of the thrones will be occupied. You know that it has to be the throne of jade, on the side of the Sun.

Seated there is a beautiful, mature woman with robes of light blue and green trimmed with a copper coloured material. She wears a copper ring set with a sapphire and emerald. Her sceptre is copper set with a sapphire and copper is her circlet with eight spires. Turning to the altar you look for Mars which you know will be next. As anticipated, the ruby glows and the iron throne is occupied next. He is a handsome, mature man in the same robes as the rest but they are of a vibrant blood red trimmed with a deep red. His bronze ring and sceptre have large rubies set in them, and set on his head is a circlet of pewter, with seven spires of bronze.

You turn in expectancy towards the altar again. The whole procedure has been carried out in complete silence. The only addition you notice is the heady perfume or incense that has accompanied the appearance of each of the great personages. You wait but nothing more happens. You walk around the altar to the empty throne standing by the doors through which you entered, but the altar remains inactive.

You look intently at the occupants of the five thrones, to try to divine what may happen next. It is then you notice a secondary pattern on the floor, over the golden sun rays, which you would swear was not there when you entered the temple.

You stand facing the central alcove that contains the suspended crown and Three Veils. Now an amber inlay on the floor comes out from the central alcove. This inlay starts somewhere behind the Three Veils. It comes down to the thrones of the Sun, Moon and Mercury and passes underneath them. It crosses next to your right, to the throne of Mars, then straight across to the throne of Venus. Then it crosses diagonally under the central altar, to the empty throne of amethyst, on your right.

You know this is the throne of Jupiter for on it lays a circlet of amethyst with four spires representing his Kingdom. The inlay then crosses to the left, to the throne of lead and pewter, on which is laying a circlet with five spires. This you know to be the throne of Saturn. Next it comes to the empty throne that is facing inwards opposite the thrones of the Sun, Moon and Mercury. Going under this throne it goes out of the door you came in.

It comes from behind the three veils in the alcove of the crown. It criss-crosses right and left connecting all the thrones, taking the path of the lightning flash often represented on the Tree of Life. Finally the inlay on the floor goes out of the temple to earth itself - perhaps to the Earth itself?

You remember your map. You know the Alcove of the Crown is in line with the 13th path that leads directly to the First Kingdom of Kether: The Crown, the Primal Glory 'to which none can attain,' which Kingdom is in front of the three veils that have been called the Three Veils of Negative Existence that hide from human eyes the beyond. Through which very few, if any, have passed from this side of the Abyss.

The Kingdom of the Crown is on the Pillar of Equilibrium which is the central path of the Island of Pan and the Tree of Life. You look to the thrones of the Sun and Moon who use their sceptres and point to the empty thrones on their respective sides. These two thrones belong to Jupiter and Saturn.

These Kingdoms have not yet been visited and you have not contacted them yet. The parts are incomplete because not all have given their consent to it. You now know these planets on the altar will not pulsate nor glow, neither will these rulers occupy their thrones.

So many unanswered questions go through your mind. Some of their number are missing so the quorum is not complete therefore it will not operate, perhaps cannot? The Kingdom of Tiphereth may prove the linking Kingdom or focal point of transition or transmutation. All the paths from the other Kingdoms merge into this Kingdom save one: the path from the Lunar Kingdom of Malkuth. The path of this Kingdom has to pass through the Kingdom of Yesod to arrive directly.

No words have been spoken throughout the proceedings in the temple, but there has been no lack of understanding. However, one mystery remains, the throne next to the door with its back to you. Who does it belong to and what is its place in the scheme of things? It proves to be made of emerald that, although very beautiful, seems lifeless. You stand in front of it to note that the pedestal upon which it is set seems crude compared to the polish and shape of the throne itself. It is a base of solid granite, a roughly hewn ashlar of rock. It gives the impression that the workman did not come back after taking a break in its construction and left it unfinished.

What planet, if any, does this belong to, for you already have the seven planets of the ancient world here? Who does it belong to and if it has a mystery, will it yield it? Then, like the lightning flash that has appeared on the floor, you understand the obvious. You go back to the Orrery of the planets and count. There are not seven orbs on it but eight. All the orbs have been accounted for in the eidouranion save one - the planet Earth! We always seem to leave our planet out of the equation, even in our astrology which is geocentric; the earth could be placed in the birth or any astrological chart if desired, its position being exactly opposite the sun.

In an unguarded moment you place your hands on the arms of the emerald throne which begins to vibrate. At first it is slight but it grows in power. Then a sudden surge of power that you think may destroy you for your desecration and impertinence goes through your body. You hear a voice, a voice you have never heard before, vibrating with power one word - Pan!

Who uttered the name? Was it you? You forget. The force is such that you are sent reeling from the emerald throne and backwards towards the altar. You stagger to your feet, pulling yourself up by using the stand, and the temple begins to vibrate. You wonder what you have done. The vibration increases and you look towards the doors as a possible route of escape before the whole edifice comes crashing down around your ears.

The doors that have been open throughout silently close, effectively blocking your escape. You look towards the king who befriended you for help, but all you can see are the sceptres of the Sun and Moon being slowly brought together. Like an eclipse, the diamond of the sun disappears behind the moonstone of the moon. The temple darkens until you find yourself in total blackness.

There is a silence that you judge lasts about a half hour and then gradually the darkness lifts. You do not attempt to move until your eyes grow accustomed to the light, as experience has taught you. When eventually you can see, you find yourself on a large rough granite rock. Like a spider you are in the centre of eight paths, but both temple and Kingdom are gone with nothing to show of their passing.

You have no idea of the actual size of the island. It appears enormous in as much that one Kingdom does not appear visible to the others, and the ones you have visited were big enough. It occurs to you that you have little idea regarding time or an awareness of it which would give you some idea of how far you may have travelled, as it would if you were on the earth plane.

Neither have you noticed, by physical standards, any particular fatigue involved in the quite extensive travelling. You are not using a physical vehicle on this plane. Everything is obviously under a different set of laws. Whoever comes here will have to get used them. Neither have you, so far on the journey, experienced any difficulty on the paths to the Kingdoms. Some travellers have reported great difficulties, delays and hindrances, unfriendly inhabitants and occasionally, adverse conditions.

Do we carry these conditions around inside and so with us? If that is the material available, is that what is used? Is this why reports are so variable? What are the rules regarding these factors and experiences? As always, here or on the earth planes, there are far more questions than ever there are answers. Yet it is still a not a bad thing to wish to know and have the questions to ask.

However, like most travellers in a strange land, as you acquaint yourself with an area, the less strange it appears. As you spend more time here you assimilate the laws and mores of this strange land and then, as with all civilized people, you accept and accord with them. Thus, you are less likely to make mistakes or give offence. The important keywords seem to be - respect and courtesy - which, after all, cost you nothing personally and could give you more in return for what is given, courtesy is the hallmark of Heaven.

Now you must gather your thoughts for the journey again and take your bearings, if you are to try to find the fifth Kingdom of Geburah, the land of Saturn and the High and Sacred Grove of the Yew. You know that you have been taking the reverse path of the lightning flash that descended from the first Holy Kingdom of Kether, from the first Kingdom to the tenth, in a sequential order. It is often represented on old diagrams of the Tree as a lightning flash because of the way it zigzags, from side to side, on the diagram. This symbol is often used to represent the fall from grace.

Old diagrams often depicted a serpent entwined around the Tree's branches (the paths) that touched the paths but not the Kingdoms, which is the 'brazen serpent.' The serpent crosses the paths in succession to give the order of their numbering. The serpent path is long and winding and, with the serpent often representing knowledge and wisdom, it showed to all that the climb to grace was long and arduous. You know now what is meant by this. You have not completed the ascent by any means for there is still a long way to go. Perhaps you should have been concentrating on the paths to the Kingdoms rather than the Kingdoms themselves, the Serpent Wisdom and not the Lightning Fall?

In some old diagrams the head of the Great Serpent rising out of Chaos goes to the Abyss, but does not pass it. You are equally certain you will not. However, it is a path those who have gone before you have taken. You have one problem now and that is, which direction are you facing?

There is a path straight ahead of you and there is another straight behind with no paths at right-angles to it. The paths radiate diagonally from this straight path which could show that the path ahead is the 13th path and the one behind you is the 25th path. If you are facing the wrong way you go back to the ninth Kingdom of Yesod and whichever you chose they both have a cross-roads about halfway down them. So you face the path you consider to be the 13th: you feel it is correct because there are two paths diagonally off to the left (22 and 17) and two to the right (15 and 20). If you turn and face in the opposite direction, there is only one path to your left (24) and one to your right (26) and this confirms your decision, for this must be path 25.

When you were in the temple and the eclipse occurred you were facing the Alcove of the Crown or Kether. Behind the Great Crown there were Three Veils hanging, of increasing density. These Three Veils may represent the veils that are said to hang behind the Kingdom of Kether or Crown. These Three Veils you feel are something of which you will never have knowledge. You wonder if the mists hanging over the top of the island, hiding it from view, could physically be a representation of the first of them. If so, you know you will never get anywhere near them, let alone understand them if you did. You drop your speculation about the island there and then, wisely deciding that your sole object is to go as far as you can, or as far as you are permitted to go, and to be satisfied with that.

Feeling you have not turned, you decide that you are at the beginning of the 13th path that would take you higher up the tree. If you are right about this island this direction will take you up. The land behind you appears to fall away, while that ahead appears rising. You count the third path to the left, which should be the 22nd path. This should lead you to the fifth Kingdom of Geburah, the Land of Saturn and the Sacred Grove of Yews.

The land continues to rise as you hoped it would and this confirms in your own mind that you have taken the right direction. The path is uneventful as most have been to this point. First there are rocky outcrops dotted over the landscape, but these are larger and more frequent than before. You also become aware that the mountains you are approaching are really mountains, vast and with far greater severity and starkness than those in the Kingdom of Netzach.

Now the land is dotted with evergreens; everywhere are to be seen splashes of dark green colour, leaves and needles. There are yews, pines, cypress and fir. At first there are single trees, then pairs of trees, copses, finally small forests. The path runs through ravines with young trees clinging to their sides in what seem insecure holds and growing high on the ridges. Occasionally you catch glimpses of long-horned cattle and many forms of the goat family. Often you think you see a particularly swift animal keeping a parallel course with your own: something that is sure-footed, but the distance it keeps (if it is really there), is too far for you to see what it is.

Small stones coming down from the ravines tell you there must be some animals on the ridges. The falls are light and do not threaten and they give you no cause for alarm. The path gets steeper though it does not cause you any real exertion yet. You take countless ravines and gorges in your stride and finally come to the most imposing ravine of them all. Above you the sky becomes a thin ribbon of blue but there is plenty of light by which to travel.

Sometimes the sides of the ravine open out like an enormous circle. In them are pastures with animals grazing on them that run at your approach, stopping when safe to watch your passing with curiosity. Down either side of some ravines pour cataracts of mountain water that runs into the valley, chattering over the rocks. You drink some water and it tastes as good as it looks, cold and fresh. Pine and fir trees hang precariously on rock ledges taking the moisture and adding a generous splash of green to the austere rocks. The ravine narrows as it comes to an end and you begin to think you have taken a dead-end path . You get through without any real difficulty and find that it opens out in a large cleft cut into the rock face.

The Sixth Kingdom...

You climb out through the cleft and when you get through, as seems usual with this island, a stunning sight meets your eyes. You have come out on the side of a very high rock face that sweeps round to the right and left, making an immense crater of rock. You are in a vast bowl which has a large plain in its centre; it is so vast the opposite side looks unreal by contrast. You see some very large openings breaking up this otherwise solid wall, and leaving nothing to chance you count the openings. Allowing for any that may be hidden by the mountain rising in the centre of the plain, your guess is right: there are five entrances including your opening.

More impressive than this natural amphitheatre is what you find rising in its centre. It is a massive mountain in which, it appears, the natural elements of this island have formed enormous towers and turrets of natural rock, giving the effect of a huge fortress. It towers above you, and with its summit in the clouds it cannot be seen fully from your vantage point. The summit looks an inhospitable place and from what you can see of it, it looks as if it is made from pure blue crystal, which you take to be ice for there is snow on the outside high up. It looks as if there are paths and natural bridges on the face of the mountain but they look small from where you are, so you could be mistaken. You begin to ponder how to get up there and down from here.

Taken in by the sight of the Kingdom you have failed to notice the steps beneath you that gradually widen as they get to the floor of the valley. They are well worn, dispelling any vanity you may have thinking you are the first to have found this place or use the stairway. You descend to the plain and take the path across it. The mountain towers so high above you its higher levels and summits are lost to sight.

The path meanders across the plain and soon you are faced with an uninviting sheer rock face. You wonder how you will manage to surmount this obstacle, which is greater than any you have met with so far anywhere on the island. However, without vanity, you feel that if you are meant to enter it will be so, thus there is no need to fret or despair. Looking back in the direction from which you have come establishes your bearings. When you turn back, you find yourself standing outside a vast entrance cut in the solid rock face, which the path now enters.

It has two goats cut in half-relief with lifelike detail; they face each other standing on their hind legs with their front hoofs touching, as if jumping over the arch of the entrance itself. Between their arched bodies is a wide tunnel that is lit with pewter torches held in malachite brackets. The paving within the tunnel, like the stairs that brought you down, shows the wear of countless feet before yours. You sense no danger and feel the entrance has appeared to admit you, so you enter. The tunnel is long and quite well lit as there are torches at regular intervals.

After a while the tunnel widens into quite a large chamber and then divides, one mouth to the going right and the other to the left. To your left there is an entrance to what you assume to be a room that is too dark to see into the room. As you stand deliberating which tunnel to take you think you hear a slight movement within. You call and politely ask the way to take. Your request is met with more movement. You peer into the place but cannot make out anything, so taking a torch from its bracket you cautiously look inside the cavern.

Many things have prepared you for the unexpected on this island but not for what meets your eyes as they become adjusted to the light the torch gives as the place is so large. In the middle of the chamber is the largest tortoise you have ever seen; the light reflects the shape of its huge shell and you gaze in wonderment. It may well have been in hibernation or just sleeping. It raises its head from its bed of pine leaves and opens its eyes to find the cause of the intrusion. Deeming that you are unimportant, it draws its head back into its shell and goes back to its rest.

Relieved at the lack of a hostile reception and grateful for being ignored you leave, put the torch back into its bracket and decide to take the left-hand tunnel. Cut into the sides of the rock are cells. They are similar to those you would expect to find in a monastery, bare and austere and not it seems, occupied recently. Your ascent carries on with very little change until you see a smaller gallery leading off to the left.

You decide to investigate this and after a while you are out on the face of the mountain. The path is not wide and carries you around the face of the mountain. You decide to follow it for a short time at least, to see where it will lead you. Turning to the right, you find a bridge you saw from below going across a crevice. This leads to another tunnel entering the mountain a little way ahead.

You would like to explore farther but for one thing. Standing on the bridge is a large mountain goat, like an ibex with two magnificent ridged horns curving back over its head. You look at him, he looks at you, then you look over the edge of the path, surprised at the height you have already ascended. He does not give you the impression of being dangerous, but he does give the impression he will not give his ground. You decide you didn't really want to go this way. Carefully retracing your steps, you leave it to him.

Rejoining the main tunnel again you start the journey upwards. The air has a fresh scent and does not have the smell of stagnant air trapped in rock and cavern. There is the smell of fresh pine forests. A slight draught in your face tells you the air is coming down from above. Remembering how far up the summit is you wonder just how long it will take to get you there.

The one thing you notice in this Kingdom is that you are more aware of the passing of time than at any period since you have come to this island. This, you conclude, is not surprising considering that Saturn is the planetary ruler and he is the Lord of Time among other things. You carry on for what seems an eternity and you find yet another gallery to the left, similar to the one you took lower down.

By now you must be at quite a high level inside the mountain. Having no idea of how high you are you decide to explore it hoping it will take you outside like the lower gallery. However, unlike the lower gallery a different sight meets your eyes when you go outside. Outside the mountain an impressive storm is raging with pouring rain driven by high winds. Thunder rolls and lightning illuminates the mountain face in a short but eerie light, which seems unnatural and makes everything look the same.

An electric blue light, of great brilliance, rips the sky apart which leaves what you have witnessed impressed on your sight long after total darkness has descended again. You know there is a wide ledge outside and you want to see if you can see how high you have climbed. With the next flash of lightning you go out on the ledge and into the storm. To your surprise, instead of being afraid, you are quite exhilarated by it.

You find the naked force of the elements impressive and stimulating. You lie back against the solid rock and let the wind and rain drive against your body. The area is brilliantly lit by the lightning that casts bewildering and moving shadows on the surrounding rocks. It makes some of them appear to have a life of their own and what is real or false difficult to know. It lights up the valley below and you are higher than you thought.

You cannot take yourself inside for quite a while, so great is the feeling. Only when you feel you cannot take any more do you go and stand inside the opening and watch the storm raging outside. Your action puzzles you a little but at the time it seemed a perfectly natural reaction.

You are about to come in when a bolt of lightning lights up everything as if it were daylight. You find you are gazing straight into the eyes of someone standing in the shadow of a large overhanging rock. It shakes your composure more than the storm, but you realize that whoever it is there is no danger; you are not being threatened but observed.

You wait for the next flash, not daring to move your eyes from where you saw the figure half behind the rock. The next flash quickly follows, almost as if to oblige, but there is no one there. The lightning is of sufficient length for you to explore the space, but there are only rock and shadows. Now you have to consider whether it was a trick of the light, so easy under such circumstances. Did you imagine shadows to be other than they were?

There is a small cell near the entrance. Sitting on a ledge you assume would serve as a bed if it was occupied, you watch as the lightning fills the cell with a blue light. The thunder rolls over the summit of the mountain. Occasionally you go to the outside entrance, more in hope than curiosity. You must have slept for when you wake the storm is no more, all is silence and what a silence it is.

You still feel a certain elation from the experience. It was as if you were standing naked before Nature and letting her pervade your being in a way she has never done before. On all levels you feel cleaner, as if you had been charged by the forces in which you stood. You stood against the rock, supported by the most substantial of the elements - earth. The element of water was driven against your body by the wind, the element of air and washed it clean. The sacred element of fire manifested in the lightning and thunder that charged the whole atmosphere with power.

You go out to the place where the figure was seen. The ground is soft but any evidence you were hoping to find has been washed away by the rain. You retrace your steps back to the tunnel and start your climb again. The tunnel is still wide and starts to curve towards the right a little. After a time it is joined by a tunnel of equal size and you wonder if this was the right-hand fork you could have taken at the entrance.

You muse on what you may have found on that side deciding that if you do come back this way, you will take the other side on the return journey. Going under a vast arch where the tunnels meet, you find yourself at the bottom of a large and impressive staircase cut into the rock. It rises straight in front of you and at the top there is a small circle of light. The stairs have torches set in the walls and, with your renewed vigour, you start your climb.

As you get closer to the top you stop and listen. You hear voices for the first time since entering this Kingdom. As you arrive at the last few steps you can see that you are going through another archway, similar to the one at the bottom of the stairs. Looking back and down you see the stairs disappearing and the archway is a small speck of light. You look through the archway and, for the first time since entering the Kingdom of Geburah, you see some of its inhabitants. The entrance has led you into an enormous cavern that is lit from a circular opening high in the roof.

Your archway, however, is not the only entrance: equally spaced from your entrance are four others making the expected five. You speculate that these entrances may be in line with the five entrances you saw around the high walled crater in the valley when you entered it. The walls of the cavern are lined with substantial dwellings. They are sober and utilitarian and cut into the face of the rock. They are tiered one above the other, making five tiers in all.

There is a large circular area in the middle that has at its centre a raised platform of rock on which there is an ornate seat. Like the island it is wedge-shaped; you feel it is somewhat like a model of the island. The platform slopes behind the throne as if it ascended from the rear, in much the same way that you are climbing the island. This slope joins the bottom of a very large set of stairs that reach about halfway up the cavern wall and then disappear through an ornate entrance. You assume this leads to the summit itself.

The throne is made from a solid piece of smoky quartz. It is inlaid with jet. On its back panel are carved two curved goat's horns that are made of coral. Two more coral horns make the armrests. The main light from the circular opening in the roof illuminates the throne with a soft light. You know without counting them the steps that rise to the throne will be five in number, but you count them just the same: they are five.

From this seat radiate five walks. They are set in the floor and are inlaid with a rich green malachite edged with lead or pewter. The paths end in the ubiquitous fountains that have been found in all the Kingdoms so far. Each fountain has five bowls on a single pedestal that goes through their centre. The largest bowl is at the bottom, with the bowls above it getting progressively smaller. Water gently overflows from the small top bowl to be caught in the larger bowls below. The bottom bowl empties into an ornamental pond where it drains away.

Around the front and sides of the central seat are long carved benches in five concentric semicircles, which are broken by five aisles. Everywhere the people, of both sexes, seem to be of mature or advanced age, but there is no feeling of senility here: only healthy advanced years and stability. Nothing seems to disturb the atmosphere of fellowship and sobriety. There is no haste, no unpremeditated or untoward actions. Quiet voices and gentle laughter can be heard at times so all is not solemnity, though now and then there is a gentle admonition to those younger.

All the faces are gentle, though one or two appear sterner in aspect, but you have already noticed not all are old. There are young people here and it was their attire that made them blend in. It is true the older people predominate as you would expect in this Kingdom, coming as it does under the aegis of Saturn. You make a closer but unobtrusive inspection and see people of all ages. The younger people are either in the company of the older as if they were being given instruction or advice, or talking among themselves with books and papers. Some are by themselves reading or just sitting in thought.

You have the impression they could be here from other Kingdoms and are here either to be taught or to be given counsel. It could even be simpler. They, like you, could be here from elsewhere to seek the advice and guidance not so readily available where they have come from.

The fifth Kingdom of Geburah is placed on the Pillar of Severity. Teaching, education, the acceptance of instruction and a regimen, requires varying degrees of discipline and the acceptance of responsibility. Responsibility need not be oppressive, which here it does not seem to be, but you feel you would not like to step out of line. If instruction is taken in a casual, lax manner the results similarly prove casual and lax. Merely having the desire to learn and undertake guidance is not always of itself enough. It has to be given a form, discipline and order that would be no problem for this Kingdom.

You appear not to be noticed though the older people, when passing, always smile in acknowledgement. Perhaps they believe you are here for a purpose that is already being attended to by some else. You wonder how you can get the guidance you seek without giving offence by appearing forward or rude. You walk around looking at the people, finally stopping in front of the central throne. Others are sitting on the lower steps and after a while they are beckoned by an older person It occurs to you that sitting on the steps could show you need help and advice.

You think this is the most contracted Kingdom you have visited so far. It appears to have so much concentrated in one space, even if a large one. It is not like the others visited, save the Kingdom of Netzach, which was not spread over an outside area. There is another major difference. You have not seen where the Sacred Grove of Yews may be found. In most of the other Kingdoms they were reasonable easy to find once you had been admitted. However, you think the large staircase behind the throne is important and may well have something to do with the sacred centre of the place. Although the stairs disappear into darkness, they are going up from here.

People come and go and it never appears to be your turn to be invited to speak to someone or for someone to speak to you. However, you do feel your presence is being watched and noted, but you cannot place who or where the attention is coming from. You begin to feel a little despondent, though prepared to wait as long as it takes. You look to your far left and see a man who is well advanced in years. He is sitting on the end of a bench, on a large fur skin. In front of him is a lectern holding a large bound book on which his hand is resting.

His hair is white and falling to his shoulders. Once more you feel he is what you imagine the personification of wisdom and understanding would be. You look at him for quite a while and he returns your gaze. The eyes are deep and dark brown. You feel in some strange way that you have looked into them before. It seems most natural to rise and go to him. Sitting on the edge of the goatskin, for that is what it proves to be, you look into his face.

You do not know how long you stay like this. Although nothing is being said, you know everything is being said without words. He is reading you as he would the open volume before him. Like the book, he is reading what is there, without passing judgement on what he sees. Though you think it superfluous, you decide you will speak to him, but you are sure he knows what you seek and will understand before you say anything. In a very quiet voice you ask, 'Father, can you help me to find him whom I seek?'

'Tell me, who is it that you seek?'

'The Great God of Nature, Pan.'

He rises slowly and he is taller than you expect and, with greater agility than you thought, he ascends the steps and sits in the throne. A silence falls upon the hall and without exception all turn towards the centre, and you know he is important to this Kingdom. He turns and gestures that you come to him. You falter and stop at the bottom step, but he smiles and motions again that you come to him.

Showing that you should kneel before him he takes a small pewter phial from his belt. Putting what is obviously an oil on his middle finger he places it in the centre of your forehead. He then takes your hand and raising you he leads you around to the rear of the throne. There is a path that slopes down to meet the staircase behind the throne. The Ancient points to the staircase, showing you should take it. You bow low to him and take your leave.

Arriving at the bottom of the stairs you stop and look up the staircase, which seems endless for you cannot see the top. You turn to give further farewell to the king. The hall is empty and it is as if the king and the people had never been. From the oil placed on your forehead there is the beautiful fragrance of pine, a smell of open forests and mountain air.

It makes you forget for a short time that you are enclosed in solid rock and it lulls your senses. You close your eyes the better to savour the moment but remembering this has sometimes caused you to lose what you have, you open them quickly. When you open them again, you are standing at the top of the stairs and now you are on the summit, which is higher than you thought.

The peak is a microcosm of the valley outside and the mountain itself. It is a crater like the valley below. The crater has five openings in its walls. Around the perimeter of the summit stand five tall spires of granite, giving it the appearance of a coronet. In front of these rock spires grow the five magnificent Yews of the High and Sacred Grove. It was on this summit you expected to find them. In the centre there is a smaller version of the mountain and the five steps that lead to a malachite throne, not unlike the throne you saw in the great hall below.

This temple is the first you have been in which is completely open to the elements; there is only the sky over your head. All the other temples were covered in some way but this one is reminiscent of a temple of Terminus who, like Saturnus, is a god of boundaries and limits. You walk around the summit deosil pausing only to place your left hand on the trunk of each tree, asking the dryad to grant a blessing on your quest. When you return to the top of the stairs, the malachite throne is no longer empty. Waiting for you is the patriarch who sat in the throne in the hall, but this time he is dressed differently. The king is dressed like the other rulers you found in the temple of the sixth Kingdom, Tiphereth.

His robe is the darkest green with trimmings of jet black. On his head is a circlet of pewter or lead with five spires. Perhaps it is the actual one that lay on the unoccupied throne of lead in that Kingdom. On his right hand, on the centre finger, he has a ring of pewter set with jet and malachite. In his other hand he holds a pewter sceptre with a circular mirror of obsidian that flashes with reflected light with every movement he makes.

You go to the foot of the throne and kneel. When you raise your eyes to meet his you find he has already extended his right hand to you again. Taking his hand you climb the steps of the throne, sitting at his side on the goatskin. He speaks to you in a voice pitched low and quiet.

'The one that you seek is near and he watches your progress with interest. Although no great tests have been presented to you, he is pleased that you do not seem to swerve from your purpose. Sadly all too few seek him today and this is a cause of great sadness to him, for he is a god of love. He was good to the people of the earth and still would be, but they grew away from him saying, they could live without him. Now his subjects have no voice to speak for them and his kingdom is often wantonly destroyed. Pan was turned into myth and fairy tale, something with which to frighten children, and yet it is the "children" who still believe. You do have to be a child to reach the Kingdom of the Gods. As with so many myths and legends, they become petrified by man's indifference and scorn. They were turned to stone. Look around you.'

'You mean . . .?'

'It is so,' he interrupts, 'however, all is not lost. When an understanding and loving heart seeks them out, this enables their Kingdoms to rise and live again, even if it is for a short time. Under their aegis even your Kingdom may flourish as before. This Kingdom rules form and crystallization among other things. Form is an aspect of death because it limits the freedom of gods and spirit alike. Even yours.

'Form brings order to the lower planes and the ability to function there. When the form is worn out and can no longer serve efficiently, then the form must disintegrate and die. So it is that life brings death as you know it, and then you leave by the door through which you came. We give the gods form and Pan has a form once loved and revered. His form has been so perverted he can no longer appear to those who are unprepared for him.

'He seeks love but would for the most part only find hate and fear in the majority. So the virtue that was love is now turned into its vice of hatred. Good law and respect can be pushed into law administered without temperance or mercy. Even the Kingdoms at this level of the Tree have their virtues and vices. These turn our powers into a duality that can both help and hinder, according to those who use them and how.

'Each Kingdom is dual, it is feminine to "receive" from the Kingdom that lies above and masculine to "send" to the Kingdom that lies beneath it. Both forces and powers are needed within it for at this level one cannot act properly without the other. Thus you have this duality within you, though it is greatly misunderstood and misused. If the wrong duality is in operation when a virtue is offered, it can well be distorted into a vice, misunderstood, misrepresented and misused.'

'Will I find him whom I seek? I seek him in love and would serve him in duty gladly.'

'We of this Kingdom understand duty for it is one of the pillars upon which this Kingdom rests. Look deep into the dark glass.'

He slowly brings his sceptre in front of your face. You look into the obsidian glass and at first you see nothing but your own reflection. Then you smell the odour that brought you here as it rises about you. It is the scent of fresh pine, of forest and glade washed clean after rain, of freshly turned earth. The leaves of the yews on the summit rustle, but you can feel no wind.

You start when you see in the glass the forests and glades. Goats leap from rock to rock and there are cattle in the pastures below. You see fleet, fleeing animals with one who is distant, alone and apart, swifter than all the rest. Then all is still and silent; for what seems eternity there is a silence so deep it can almost be felt.

A melody reaches your ear that is faint. It is like a distant call. You practically have to twitch your ears to hear the notes and the glass shows a lone peak on which you can make out a small figure. The notes rise high in the air and fall like gentle rain, the blessed gift of Jupiter Pluvius. It is a melody you have never heard before but some have got close to it. You hope you will never forget it. The old king leans over your shoulder and, like a gentle wind in your ear which dies as he speaks, he whispers, 'Listen my son...listen...listen.'

You concentrate and covet every note heard. The mirror is bringing the figure closer but it has its back half turned away from you so you cannot fully see the face. Finally the music stops and the figure slowly begins to raise its head. You can hardly stand the waiting and begin to feel panic because you fear you may lose him. Slowly the figure turns in your direction and the head is very close in the black glass.

You feel you will burst and with the growing agitation you start forward and call on Pan. A voice, too late, cries, 'No!' The mirror shatters into a thousand shards with a sound that must be how the Crack of Doom would sound. Instinctively you place your hands over your face in protection, knowing that when you take them away, your impulsive action will have cost you dear. Impulsive actions sometimes do; they do not always work. The Kingdom will more than likely be gone.

You open your eyes to see you are learning fast, even if it is too late. You are standing again at the junction of the paths. You take your bearings. To the right is the 23rd path that would take you back to the Kingdom of Hod, the land of Venus and the Sacred Grove of the Apple.

Next to your left is the diagonal 22nd path that brought you from the Solar Kingdom of Tiphereth. Straight ahead is the 19th path that will take you to the fourth Kingdom of Chesed ruled by Jupiter and the Sacred Grove of the Oak.

To your extreme left is the 18th path that could lead you to the third Kingdom of Binah and would take you to the limit of the island. It is also one the three highest Kingdoms on the island. You think if you even caught a glimpse of that Kingdom you would regard yourself as lucky and that would be enough.

Further, you also know in that direction is the vast Abyss which separates the end of the island from the part where you are moving, apparently, so freely. It bears repetition, the Abyss isolates the headland of the island from the rest; it crosses below the third Kingdom of Binah, passes over the top of the Kingdom of Daath and below the second Kingdom of Chokmah. This places the Kingdom of Daath on your side of the island and the Kingdoms of Binah and Chokmah over the Abyss.

It is a very uncertain path at this juncture of your travels. The fourth Kingdom is logically the next to take because, as the Kingdom of Tiphereth taught, you do not want to arrive short of anything you may need. One thing you do not want is more empty thrones or incomplete rituals.

It is the 19th path, leading to Jupiter's Kingdom of Chesed and the Sacred Grove of the Oak, which you must now take. The 19th path lies straight ahead, which should take you to the last of the Seven Kingdoms and the last of the Sacred Groves. You make your way across the island. Some way down your path it is crossed diagonally from the left by the 17th path. Your map tells you this is the one that connects the Kingdom of Binah and the Kingdom of Tiphereth, for those who can use it.

The terrain is losing its mountainous appearance and levelling out as you come to the second path, coming at right angles to yours. This crossroad is the 13th path that comes from the highest Kingdom, the first Kingdom of Kether or the Crown, to the Kingdom of Tiphereth. You wonder if the Kingdom of Kether can reach the Kingdom of Tiphereth through the Kingdom of Daath, or vice versa?

The Kingdom of Daath is sometimes represented on the Tree diagram but not as a physical Kingdom as with the others because its presence is a subject of dispute. You feel excited as this Kingdom has always fascinated you, being regarded as a mysterious channel from above, you think it is not so much a physical place as 'a presence.' The prospect of going up this 13th path to see what you will find is almost irresistible. The thirteenth card of the tarot should usually be left untitled.

'Death' is the traditional and mundane interpretation of the thirteenth card, often better thought of as 'transformation' which, if you successfully reached the end of the thirteenth path to the Kingdom of the Crown, would occur to you.

You pause a while then go a little way along the rise to see where it is leading. When you reach the crest you sit on the edge of the path a while looking in the direction that it takes. This path takes you on to the Abyss, the Kingdom of the Crown and the ever mystical Kingdom of Daath. This path is absolutely straight and does not seem to deviate an inch from its course. It is the straightest path you have seen on the island, even in the cities.

As you expected, ahead the ground rises again. You know if you walked to that crest there would be yet another crest on the path. You cannot see very far as the path is always rising. With this path you would go to the top of the island. The trouble with continuing along this path is that you would be going towards the Kingdom of Daath and be short of a Kingdom again. The quorum would be incomplete and instinct tells you that would be wrong. You notice that the sky above the land gets darker as it rises above the horizon. There is still a trace of light, which diminishes until it is a black curtain pricked with the light of many stars. The stars seem to shine with a purer light here because of the clear atmosphere.

Hanging high in the heavens over this path that leads to the most mysterious and secret part of the island, you are surprised to see a familiar constellation: seven stars brighter than all the others and in the familiar form we call 'the Plough.' You deliberate on the fact that they appear in a form familiar to you and wonder if this is so that you will recognize them. It seems the island is all things to all men, yet there are seven Kingdoms that are matched in the heavens by the seven stars.

The impulse to carry on to the next ridge is strong. You start to walk a little more up the path. You turn and look at the crossroad again. Again you go farther up the 13th path, stopping when you think you hear the faint baying of hounds. The trouble is that in the still air the sound seems from all directions at once. You slowly turn to try to get the focus of the sound and then you realize it is not on the land. It sounds all around you because the hounds are in the sky, a pack baying at the full moon that has appeared very large in the night sky.

Both moon and hounds lie to your right, towards the Kingdom of Chesed. You go back down the path, turn left, and start again along the 19th path, in the direction they are moving. Just as the hounds begin to cross the face of the moon, like clouds, they break up and are gone. Their call seems to die away in the moon.

You trouble yourself for a short while with the vexing question - dogs or clouds? You conclude it doesn't really matter for you are on the right path again. This is a better solution for you would have gone off without the seventh piece of the puzzle. Even so, you do not know for certain that you will find what you seek in the Kingdom of Chesed.

Your foray into the Kingdom of Tiphereth was unsuccessful because you lacked all the pieces of the puzzle that were necessary, which was accidental because you had not got the knowledge. This time you do not lack knowledge, so this present deviation would have been deliberate and foolish. It could abort all you had gained to this point. Your path is crossed diagonally from the left by the 15th path which leads back to the Kingdom of Tiphereth.

The land takes on a similar elevation as the other side. The mountains and rocks here are less jagged in appearance. They are covered with lush pastures and trees giving a less foreboding aspect. You see very few outcrops of rock compared with the previous Kingdom. When you do see some you get the impression it was a landscape gardener who put them there but then, what is Nature if not that? You see a single white horse racing across the grass plain. It stops and looks at you, smelling the air, then gallops off at a great pace behind the hill.

Your path takes you over this hill and when you reach the top, there he stands. He and other horses are in the low valley and he is obviously the leader. As in the other Kingdoms, young oaks and birches begin to dot the countryside. At first you see only one or two trees, then three and four, and finally small groves and forests.

The Seventh Kingdom...

You start meeting the inhabitants of this Kingdom quite soon. Unlike the previous Kingdom they seem to be living well out from the centre, to which you feel there is still a long way to go. They are all well dressed and live in substantial houses, the outlying houses of the settlement. The fields are filled with flowering and fruiting vines and with cereal crops. There are many wine presses, vats and everything for making wines and liqueurs; large barrels and small casks.

As with the other Kingdoms there appear to be no poor dwellings. The houses become more impressive and this suggests you are getting closer to the centre. Now there is a large square surrounded by the most impressive of these dwellings. The square is obviously a centre of commerce and a meeting place, as it was in the other Kingdoms. Around the square there are goldsmiths and silversmiths, eating and drinking houses set with tables. You would like to have something to eat and drink, but what do you use for exchange in this Kingdom?

As you stand and watch, a man sets food and wine on a table and beckons that you should come and dine. You show that you cannot pay by pulling out your pockets to show they are empty. This message serves well enough on the physical plane but he finds this amusing. Again he offers his hospitality then goes into the house smiling. You sit, eat and drink. The place appears a happy one, as the people show. Men and women sit at tables playing games of chance, which shows that the coin of the realm may be a heavy gold or silver coin. When you have had your fill, you go to the door, give thanks, take your leave and start on your path again.

The country is rising all the time in a gentle gradient and soon you see why. In the distance you see a large mountain rising. It has an impressive summit that shows through the clouds shrouding its peak, when they break. You now know by experience that this is where you must make for, as it is the centre of the Kingdom. It could hardly be missed as all paths lead to it. The communities become many and more lavish as you near the mountain. When you finally arrive at its lower slopes you are almost overwhelmed by the strong smell of lavender, purple and white lilac and cedar wood. The poppy is growing on all sides.

High up you see something very swift moving off and away from you into a thicket. You cross to the place to investigate but not even a twig has been broken, there is nothing to show that anything has passed through. Just when you think the whole thing was a figment of your imagination, you find a soft patch of earth on which is imprinted a single hoof. It could have been a small horse you saw, but you are not sure what it was. You are a little disappointed but you remember the old king's words, 'He is near....'

True, it could be the imprint of a goat's hoof and you elect to think it is the one whom you seek. In case you are being watched, you stand and raise your hand in a salutation, then resume the path, striking out with renewed vigour for the city you know will be on the mountain somewhere. You come through the forest quicker than you thought and your path suddenly joins an enormous staircase rising up, which the trees had been hiding. You start to climb and are amazed at the ease with which it is done, and you begin to wonder if the stairs themselves are moving.

Standing still there is nothing you see which confirms this, yet when you resume your climb again you would swear, they move. Perhaps they only move when you do, but as nothing surprises you about the island anymore, it doesn't really matter. If something is so, then just accept it, as no explanation is necessary. It's taking you up and that is where you want to be.

In what seems a ridiculously short time for the length of the stairway you are at the top, at the gates of the city itself, over whose archway there is an eagle that looks as if it was just about to land. It is made of gold with amethyst eyes. The city wall is high and straight on either side of the gate and you are sure it stands foursquare. Going through the gate you fine the architecture of the city is lavish and symmetrical in style. You feel nothing would be permitted to disturb the symmetry and order. Opulent buildings have their ornamentation picked out in gold. These buildings are matched only by those you saw in the Kingdom of Tiphereth. Considering the rulers of the two Kingdoms, you are not surprised.

Here, embroidered in gold thread, are flags and devices that are moving in a slight breeze. The inhabitants are well dressed with fine clothes and furs, well fed and seem prosperous. You turn with the city wall to your left and along the walk low walls on the right show well kept gardens with foursquare fountains in gold. The high walled gardens have decorative breaks in them so that you can look in, though some are private and have only closed gates, with grilles in them.

You walk around this busy street freely with the high wall always on your left, and off to the right are many interesting side streets. Although the city is large, the journey appears to take very little time. Each time the end of the high wall is reached, you have to turn to your right. Your circumambulation finally brings you back to the gate by which you came in. It confirms your original thought that the city is built foursquare.

It appears to be built around the customary summit in the centre. This, like the Kingdom of Geburah, is a large peak which though hidden in clouds and mist, dominates and overlooks the whole city. Your journey to the centre of the city is suddenly blocked by another huge wall like the perimeter wall. It towers over you and offers no view or suggestion of what may be on the other side. As you did with the outer wall you walk to your left and the ends of this wall turn right each time until you come back to where you started. Unlike the outer wall it has no gate or any kind of entrance. The wall encloses the summit and, like the Kingdom of Hod, it is unbroken; but there is no throne as there was in Hod.

By now of course, knowing some ways of the island, you know there is a way in somewhere, somehow or by someone. If you cannot find it then you must be invited to enter. Turning from the wall you look down the street that led you here, but it does not help. You do not see anything or anyone that could give you a clue to the problem. You turn back to the wall, hoping in your heart that it may have opened to admit you, as happened in other Kingdoms. It hasn't, but what you do find, as usual, takes your breath away.

Scattered on the ground, at the base of the wall, are uncut and cut diamonds and amethysts, some set in gold, among many other treasures. They were not there before and are a veritable king's ransom. You look around you to see if someone may have dropped them, but no one is near and those who are passing ignore you and the treasure. You stop someone and point to the treasure but they shake their head and hand, showing it does not belong to them or they are not interested. After you have done this twice, you give up.

You kneel and run your hands through the stones, picking a square amethyst that fills the palm of your hand. It throws out shafts of light and the effect is quite hypnotic. You feel yourself beginning to fall under its spell: you think what you could achieve with this one stone alone if you could take it back with you. You give a sigh of regret. You are seeking another treasure that, if found, could never be taken from you. It may prove the traditional 'pearl of great price,' as you thought in the Kingdom of Malkuth, and you put the stone down.

When you raise your eyes the wall has a large, impressive entrance and standing in it is a very tall, middle-aged man. He has a small, narrow coronet of gold on his head with four golden spires. In his hand he holds a gold staff with a large square amethyst set in it. This stone looks more than familiar to you but you dare not look down. His hands are slender and elegant, and on his index finger is a gold ring set with a square amethyst. He is dressed in robes which on earth would be called priestly. The robes are purple and rimmed with thin bands of sable.

Around his neck he wears a gold chain that has a golden oak hanging on it. It looks like a living tree. Gold sandals show beneath his long robe. You bow and think you have found the Ruler of the Kingdom. At this thought he smiles and shakes his head gently from side to side as if saying - 'not so!'

He extends his hand inwards, inviting you to enter. Remembering the precious stones at your feet you attempt to step over them. He smiles and looks down and when you do the same there is nothing there but dead leaves. Smiling, you enter the gateway and when you turn to look back, as you expected, the entrance is no more.

You are within the compound and straight in front of you are broad steps of marble, which rise to an entrance that seems to lead into the mountain itself. The priest, for such you call him, shows that you are to climb the stairs. When you reach the top you turn to see that he has not followed you but is still waiting at the bottom, watching you. He raises his hand and you return the greeting; then upon entering, you see the sight the mountain hid.

Inside a vast crater is an area of lush greenery. It is totally the opposite of the landscape you found in the crater of the previous Kingdom. Here are trees, lakes, fountains, rivers and waterfalls. The cliff walls rise sheer to an enormous height. The summit outside appeared damp with its clouds and mists. Inside the crater the whole place is genial and balmy, the ambience is almost tropical. You go back down the stairs, go outside and look up to confirm what you saw. The outside gives no hint of what is hidden inside the mountain. The peaks look forbidding, inhospitable and inaccessible, going back inside belies all this. You have to admit it is somewhat like **James Hilton's**, *Shangri-La*, in *Lost Horizon*, made into a the film that is well known to you.

Because the floor of the crater is lower, you have a high vantage point inside the mountain. You can go down into this beautiful area for there are paths leading down. The first thing you notice is the familiar pattern for the Kingdom, which is the fourth of the ten. Coming from four entrances, of which yours is one, there are four wide paths going across to the centre like a giant cross. They meet in the middle at four enormous staircases that lead up to a large promontory.

In the centre is a building of white marble flecked with gold, not unlike the temple in Tiphereth. Each staircase ends on the promontory at a large door, obviously one on each of the four sides. There are wide, paved and covered colonnades around the building. The pillars of the colonnade are marble with purple bases and crowns of carved amethyst. This gives the building an appearance not unlike the Greek Parthenon.

The central roof, resting on the inner walls, is made of four triangles of purple glass. it is a giant pyramid of glass held within a framework of gold, giving the temple the appearance of being a marble square topped by a purple, glass pyramid. This pyramid is surmounted by a magnificent golden eagle, like the one over the gateway to the city. This time the golden eagle appeats as if it is about to take off. Your journey across to the centre and the temple is slow for your eye is taken by a new delight at almost every step: nooks and crannies of flowers, glades of oak and cedar trees, so many natural bowers that beckon with quietude and rest.

You decide to rest in one and a white horse comes to you without fear and nuzzles your hand. You stroke its head on the side, move to its mane and to the top of its head, which reveals something you had not noticed. Nestling in its thick white mane you feel what you think is some damage to the little creature. When you part the hair, you find a small horn growing out of the centre of the forehead. You gently feel the little horn on its head and rest your head against that of the little unicorn.

It turns its head to look behind it and when you look you see what you know to be its mother. She stands tall, with an impressive head, in the centre of which is growing a white, twisting horn that would be some three to four feet long. She makes no move as you caress her baby, which eventually goes to her and, being small enough, stands between her front legs. You go over to them, feeling just a little uncertain for the first time in a Kingdom. She lowers her head and you raise your hand slowly to stroke it and look into the deep brown eyes. Again you feel you have seen them before. She turns and leaves the glade, stopping and giving a backward glance at you, before finally disappearing with her offspring.

You finally find yourself at the foot of the stairway that will take you to the white and gold temple. Realising how beguiling this vast garden has been, you want to see if it is here, you will find him who you seek. Your first move is around the broad covered walk that goes around the outside of the building. It shows that each of the four stairways ends in four identical doors. The large pyramid roof is supported by four of the largest columns you have seen. The doors of polished cedar with gold hinges and fittings stand wide open. You return to the stairway you came up and enter the square building by that door.

From each door is a broad path of gold set in the marble floor that, meeting in the centre of the floor, make an equilateral cross. They lead to a central dais of four steps, rising to a throne of gold. Supported on four columns of amethyst is a beautiful canopy of purple brocade, with a cloth of gold inside. Above this canopy but below the roof, suspended in the pyramid of purple glass, is a golden orb that is slowly turning without any means of visible support.

Among the four paths and doors is the High and Sacred Grove of the Oak. The trees are four in number and their leaves look like dark green enamel, with their cups and acorns like burnished gold. Despite their unearthly appearance they are real and these are the father and mother of all oaks. You walk around the temple and touch the trunks of the oaks. Then you come back to stand and face the golden throne knowing that you must be patient and wait. Will the occupant come and speak to you?

Stillness and serenity pervade the temple. You go to the door and look out across the lush valley and you know how easy it would be to be seduced by it and stay here. You have a strong desire to go no farther. Your reveries are broken by the strong smell of sandalwood and cedar. When you look within the temple the throne is now occupied. Standing in the entrance you instinctively bow low. You are beginning to feel more comfortable with your etiquette, which now comes naturally. The king smiles and beckons you to take the small stool that is by his feet and close to him. He takes your hand and sets you down.

He is dressed as the kings you saw in the Kingdom of Tiphereth, save that his purple robe is trimmed with gold and sable. His sceptre and ring are of gold, and in the sceptre is a large square amethyst which also looks familiar. He wears a circlet of gold with four golden spires. You know this gold circlet was on throne in the temple of Tiphereth. He speaks.

'How can this Kingdom help you?'

'I seek the god Pan.'

'Each Kingdom has attributes it can add to the quest and these can be of use in your own place. In the Kingdom of Malkuth and the Moon you required imagination and sensitivity. This is an asset and would help you discover what it is you seek: to find the 'Tree' and its 'fruit,' but even if you find this it is of itself no guarantee of success. The Moon can cast a false light that makes things appear other than what they are. She can give illusion.

'In the Kingdom of Yesod, Mercury is primarily of the mind and the mentality needed for the search. Any imbalance in this Kingdom can give cunning and facile knowledge, without feeling and lacking the understanding of what is known.

'The Kingdom of Hod, in the land of Venus, gives earthly love that often aspires to the spiritual, a love of beauty and refinement with discrimination in your life and what you do with it. If unbalanced it can produce sloth, indolence and a dissolute life lost to hedonism and dissipation. Naturally we do not condemn pleasure. Good is rewarded and what good they do is rewarded in the physical, with little if anything being carried forward to the plane yet to come.

'The Kingdom of Netzach, in the land of Mars, gives impetus and energy to initiate and direct it to the search of higher principles such as this quest. If in unbalance, the excess of misdirected force may destroy the vessel that contains it, in fits of recklessness and uncontrolled energy.

'The Kingdom of Tiphereth gives loyalty and honour, magnanimous governance and the gentle rule of the heart. If unbalanced, there is a haughty pride and the desire for dominance wrought through egotistic and despotic means to gain a favourable outcome, whatever the cost.'

'The Kingdom of Geburah, in the land of Saturn, can give Time to undertake the duty and the search. Temper this with prudence and the patience to bring the crystallization of success, to hold the crystal essence of the matter in your hand free, from all dross. If you have imbalance this Kingdom can bring doubt, apprehension, limitation, depression and finally, loss that turns all to dust.

'Finally we come to this Kingdom. We are no different from the other Kingdoms you have contacted for we too not only give, but receive by contact. At this level of manifestation we take from your kingdom. We do not always receive what we would like, or like what we are given and a gift demands a gift. In this Kingdom we too have dual gifts to offer.

'Some of our gifts are ceremony and tradition, wisdom and dignity, philosophy and all the matters and learning that appertains to the higher and uplifting aspects of life on earth. In any imbalance will be found excess, which gives self-indulgence, complacency, extravagance, sloth and misjudgement with its consequences.

'Balance is the keyword. A simple word that is so hard to achieve. Duality and unity are vitally important factors, but never make anything this or that. People acknowledge and worship Light and tend to despise his equally legitimate brother Darkness, which is also deserving of our deference. Do the trees and plants disdain their dark, unseen roots from which they draw their life and without which they could not live? Therefore, why should you? They cannot grow upwards to the light without growing downwards to the darkness in direct proportion. If they do not grow downwards into the dark earth, they will fall, as they must, and, so will you.

'This is why not all the people who attempt the journey of the Tree complete it. If imbalance or excess is found and not controlled, it will attract that part of the Kingdom at the expense of the rest. They will be lulled into complacency and ease, distracted from their purpose and another quest is lost.

He smiles. 'That you have got this far does not make you a god or even particularly strong. It merely means that your strength of purpose held and, I think you will agree, the journey did not severely test you?

'May I ask about those beautiful gems lying on the path outside the hidden gate, were they a test to see if I could be deterred?'

'Were you tempted?

'To lie to you would be useless when you can so easily read the heart and it is unnecessary; yes, I was sorely tempted. In my place in the scheme of things they would have made life so easy.

He puts his hand in a casket by his side and brings out a clenched hand. It is filled with precious stones that cascade from his hand to the floor, scattering across it when he opens his hand. He takes another handful of gems, this time with both hands. When he lets them fall they are dead leaves and fine dust as they hit the floor which blow across the temple and out of the door. He smiles at your puzzlement, then leaning across he touches your heart and whispers in your ear - 'fairy gold!'

He continues. 'To allow the traveller to go too far before the Kingdoms have been mastered or access gained could bring the personal Tree down with irreparable damage and consequences. We too have laws that have to be obeyed and great responsibility comes with these laws. Usually people want the rewards but not the responsibilities involved. A gift for a gift. Sometimes this is why it is wise not to offer too much.

'You took the Kingdoms in a certain order that, in your particular case, proved to be out of order. You arrived in the Kingdom of Tiphereth without the metals or blessings to place in the Crucible of the Sun, with which to make your personal key.'

'Does this apply to all? Must all follow the path I have taken?'

He replies. 'Each must find their own path. It is not the same for all and it cannot be so, for you are all different.'

'Then I should have collected the blessings of the six Kingdoms, before presenting myself in the Kingdom of Tiphereth?'

'For you this would appear so. Take with you the blessings of this Kingdom in your quest to find him whom you seek. You now seem to have the Blessings of the seven Kingdoms of the seven Sacred Groves and there must be a reason why this is so, but it is not given to me to know why? It may be you are being tested to see if such a reward for your effort will prove a help or a hindrance. Could you handle such a prize or will some unseen weakness from within pull you down? You have already been to the Kingdom of Tiphereth and back to it you must return if you are to make the attempt. At least you have the advantage of knowing the way.

'This much more I can tell you. Once you have presented the metals in the Kingdom of Tiphereth, whether you go on and achieve your goal or be turned back, will depend on the answer you will receive. You must set your feet on the central path that will lead you towards the Sacred Kingdom of the Crown. There is the Kingdom of the Ancient of Days - the *Lux Occulta*. What will happen there, again if you are permitted to go, even I do not know.

'There you must prostrate yourself. Even I go down on my knees with head bowed there, not in fear but in love, reverence and the desire to give service. The source of these Kingdoms lies on the other side of the Abyss. Very few who come here have managed to approach it, let alone get to the other side. What will be your fate there, even I do not know.

'It has existed long before we who are here to serve it. For so long it was alone and we can but do our best; in some respects we stumble there even as you do. Before you reach the end of that path you will traverse the Kingdom of Daath. Because you know of its existence, it will exist even though you may not even see it, but you will know you are in it. There you will be given your answer of success or failure that may cause you to try this long journey again. It may not even appear for you. Perhaps you may have to try repeatedly to attain the success you seek or you may even abandon the quest altogether through failure. Even having got this far is no guarantee of success. We can at least set your feet in the "Kingdom of the Sacrificed God." They who may gather there could put you on the path you seek.'

You thank him and give him your farewell. He touches your forehead with his ring and a deep sleep comes upon you, your eyes close and you know nothing. In a state akin to a dream you find yourself outside the magnificent temple of Tiphereth again, with the doors wide open to let you enter. All is as it was before when you left, save all the seven thrones are occupied. The throne of Pan, for you are sure it is his, still remains empty and a feeling of sadness sweeps over you, threatening to overcome you.

Turning to the altar you become aware that you have something tightly clenched in your right hand. You open your hand to find in the palm seven discs. You notice a small tripod beside each throne on which is a small salver of gold. These were not there before when you visited the temple.

The disc of lead you place on the salver of the Kingdom of Geburah and the Lord Saturn and you bow low to him. The disk of gold and silver you place on the salver of the King of Chesed, the Lord Jupiter, from whom you have just come; again you bow low to him and your eyes linger a little longer for he was so kind and there he is before you in his appointed place as promised. The disc of iron and brass you give to the King of Netzach, the Lord Mars; after bowing you take your leave. You give the disc of pure copper to the Queen of Hod, the Lady Venus and to her you bow low. The shimmering disc of quicksilver you give to the King of Yesod, the Lord Mercury; to him you bow but do not remove your eyes from his for some reason. It is almost as if you fear he will fly away he is so volatile, yet in the eyes there is more than even this. You give the silver disc to the Queen of Malkuth, the Lady Moon and to her you bow low. The final disc of gold you give to the King of Tiphereth himself, the Lord of the Sun. To him you bow your head and then make deep obeisance. You return to the throne of Pan. There too is a salver but you have nothing to place in it and you feel you linger here the longest, which may appear disrespectful.

You are disappointed that the salver and throne seem doomed to remain empty. To each throne and its occupant you bow again and then, with great clarity and surprising audacity you say: 'Mighty Kings and Queens of the great Kingdoms, rulers of the Seven High and Sacred Groves, I present myself to you and ask that I may be permitted to go on with my quest and that the die be cast, if you Will it.

The King of Tiphereth looks to those on his left and then to his right though nothing is said to show what has passed between them. Only Mercury, the King of Yesod, shows that a vote is being cast for he raises his caduceus. They all rise slowly and each takes the disc placed on the salver and casts it into the light of the altar, into which it disappears with a blinding flash and a sound like lightning. At first you think it will be failure as nothing appears to happen. You curse the impatience that did not serve you well in the Kingdom of Geburah with the obsidian mirror, but you will control your impatience now. You feel that what you thought was your secret is known to all here, yet you have tried not to even think about it for that is as plain as speaking it here. When the obsidian mirror shattered in Saturn's Kingdom, you caught a small sliver of the mirror which you are holding. You clench your hand tight with the obsidian sliver in it, there is the slight feel of warm blood as it digs into your palm, and you look to the altar.

You feel that impulsiveness rising that is hard to control in its impatience. You are finding it harder by the second to control it but you are not sure what to do or what it is you are controlling. In desperation for an answer you look straight into the eyes of Hermes. How long this lasts you cannot tell but you know the eyes are different now. The eyes have a horizontal iris instead of the round human iris they had first. There is only one creature you have seen like this. Hermes is smiling and he imperceptibly nods as if telling you to obey your impulse, he looks at your hand and then at the altar. You throw the mirror shard into the light and on contact with it there is a blinding flashing of green and a swirling green mist. Now your resolve falters with doubt, but Hermes nods his approval now the deed is done.

Slowly the light within the temple begins to dim until the temple itself can no longer be seen. The altar is a pool of green light and mist in the Stygian darkness. The seven thrones float like islands of light on a pitch black sea around the altar. You look to the altar and when you look up you find the thrones are gone. Finally the light on the altar dims to extinction.

The darkness around you removes all possibility of seeing anything. You close your eyes and when you open them you are standing on a small crest, which you know is on the 13th path leading to the Kingdom of Kether through Daath. Ahead of you, hanging like a diamond necklace on black velvet, are the seven stars of what you call The Plough that you have seen before, only now they seem even brighter. You know this is where you walked to and stopped when you were going to the Kingdom of Chesed. Your request has been granted. The King, you feel, has kept his promise to you, but then you had expected nothing less and you thank him for it.

The Kingdom of Daath...the Hidden Kingdom...

You are now on the path that will take you to the Abyss and closer to the first Kingdom of Kether. The path rises quite steeply and you are not surprised at this for you are coming to the highest part of the island. You are making your way to the high cliffs you sailed around when you approached the island in your craft. You have long known that the island is wedge-shaped, sweeping down from these enormous heights to the far away Kingdom of Malkuth where you hope your craft is still in the harbour waiting for your return.

The path is undulating and every time you reach the top of a new ridge you think you have come to the end. Only you find another ridge on the path that has to be climbed, then another and another. Excelsior - 'ever upwards.' Suddenly, like many things here, you are faced with the outskirts of what may be an enormous forest. It looks very dark and foreboding in the distance and as you approach the trees seem very high. You stand a while on the edge of the forest and walk some way to your left and then to your right, watching and listening.

You feel there is nothing that gives a feeling of threat or danger, only the complete silence of the place. You wonder why you are being so hesitant as there does not seem any alternative but to enter the forest; the path you have chosen to follow goes through it. The forest extends far into the distance on either side where it curves out of sight. This gives it the appearance of being circular or crescent shaped and covering the top part of the island.

You enter the twilight gloom and walk slowly. There is more light than you expected and you have little trouble seeing your way. You find you are straining your ears to pick up any movement or sound, but there is only the silence. However, you still have the strong feeling you are being watched, more in curiosity than animosity. You decide to adopt the now proven tactic of making no movement that could be taken as unfriendly or threatening and walk ever onwards. The trees appear to be getting thicker but the path is clear and unhindered

You arrive at a small clearing that extends on either side of the path, and you think this would be a good time to have a rest: perhaps to reflect on the many things that have happened and what you have learnt since coming here. You have come far and accept there is more to see and learn for this is probably the most vital part of the island and the most critical point in your journey. Yet you feel you are now nearing the end of this particular attempt, for good or ill. You would not like to spoil the conclusion if it is possible.

For the first time since coming here you are feeling just a little tired. You feel this may be due in no small part to the very unusual power you feel is present in this place, that was not there in the other Kingdoms. The atmosphere feels more powerful. It is hard to define in physical terms, but this part of the island appears to be moving faster. Unlike the other Kingdoms visited, this seems to be a place to visit but not to stay.

You decide to stop on the left-hand side of the glade to take your rest. You look up through the break in the forest's canopy and see the seven stars as if they were your guides, pointing the way onwards and upwards to the place you must go. You must have slept for when you open your eyes again the stars have gone, as has the dark sky that held them. The little glade is filled with a welcome light.

You are feeling hungry and thirsty and wonder where you can get something to eat here and a wash to refresh yourself. You hear a small stream splashing over rocks behind you but would swear it was not there when you closed your eyes. The water is cool to drink. You wonder if you can get something to eat and see a bough of apples hanging over the stream, laden heavy with fruit. You take the bough in your hand and looking at the tree and asking 'by your leave,' you take an apple. Then you notice an even stranger phenomenon. You should no longer be surprised but this is unusual. The bough not only contains apples but hazel nuts for you to take. You step back to see what kind of tree you have found growing in such an unusual way.

On this island you have sought and found the seven trees of the High and Sacred Groves, their Guardians and their temples: those of the birch, willow, holly, hazel, oak, apple and yew tree. They, however, were seven separate and distinct trees, but here you have one tree displaying the leaves, bark, branch and fruits of all the seven on one tree. This, of course, is physically impossible, but you are not in the physical world so it is not impossible here and this tree proves it. It seems that what is wrong for the physical, is quite natural here. The more you see of the island the less you are surprised at what you find. All things seem possible here and it is just possible that thinking makes it so.

You take some more nuts and water and thanking the tree return to your place and go over the new facts you have gathered. First you heard the stream behind you. Turning to check you see it is not there now but you know you did not imagine it. The hazel nuts that you have just taken are in your hands. You decide not to question, but accept for now it's time to go about your business. For the first time since entering the forest you think you hear more sound. It is difficult to describe, like voices in the distance or an offstage chorus, close yet soft. It could be described as the voices of small children at play, enjoying themselves, but the voices seem too mature for the piping voice of early youth.

They are mature voices that are pitched higher than the adult of earth. Mixed in the voices are lower pitched sounds, which are obviously what we would call male. The higher ones have a distinct femininity about them. They seem happy and busy, but there is nothing to show where the voices are coming from and you seem surrounded by them. Sensing no danger you get up and start to walk along the path again which takes you to the top of the island. Then, just as suddenly as they started, the trees end. Again you find yourself on the edge of a forest, but this time leaving it. Stretching out in front of you is a large area of what appears to be waving grass with a path between it and the edge of the forest. It is tall: it would come up to your waist and it is gently undulating as if by some breeze not felt.

The light of this Kingdom, if truly it is a Kingdom you are in, for unlike the others there is nothing to say it is so, is electric blue. This light adds a luminosity to the edge of things and the atmosphere of the place seems charged, that is the word, charged, but with what? It could be this strange light that accounts for the place's colour of turquoise and electric blue, which gives it an appearance of water. It has the appearance of a large lake without any shores. You have a lack of the confidence you gained with the other Kingdoms for nothing here seems certain or solid. You choose to take stock of what you have found here, as nothing appears as it should.

First, there is no temple to fix this Kingdom as there was with the others. There is no Sacred Grove for you to seek out; what Sacred Grove, if any, is here? It is true there were trees containing all the attributes of the trees of the previous Kingdoms like hybrids, a Uranian factor. In the other Kingdoms you assumed the existence of a spiritual centre that, in all cases, had a temple at its heart. There is no guide to say if your presence is acceptable or to advise you what to do. It is true the other Kingdoms helped you to arrive here, but they did not guarantee you would be accepted if you got here. The ruler of the Kingdom of Chesed was clear on this.

Next to the path on the left is a large wedge-shaped rock that is quite high at the end so it overlooks the field. It is not unlike the shape of the island. The top part is separated from the rest by a crack running from side to side, though the split is not wide. Climbing it from the low end and approaching the top you notice the rock face would appear at some time to have had markings on it. They are not markings carved by a craftsman. They are more the sort of markings that have been carved on it crudely because of the opportune shape of the rock.

You have the firm impression they were put there by others who, having reached this point, tried to leave a record of their journey. There is a crude representation of the Tree map, though it is very faint. You only found it because you are familiar with the pattern and so can see it. Seeking where you are on the map you divine it is the circular hole that, like Daath, does not appear to have any bottom. You cannot find a stick long enough to reach the bottom. Is that what was trying to be represented? Nothing tangible! The path scribed on the rock continues on the other side of the Kingdom, but then there is the deep crack in the rock. This you presume represents the Abyss and the path on the other side of it is very faint and peters out quickly.

It has long been thought that there is a secret way to this Kingdom, mentioned by some writers, known as the 'Empty Room.' It is also said that the way is very dangerous, this unmarked path from the Kingdom of Chesed; but although you know of it, you know nothing about it and no clues have been left here by others regarding this. Now, is this what you are being told or did you bring this with you? You step back from the plan and notice faint lines, some broken, meandering around the diagram. Finding a pointed piece of rock you join these up and then you see the meandering 'Path of the Serpent.' It is a long and tortuous path which climbs the Tree by touching each path on it, but it circles the Kingdoms and does not enter them.

The Lightning Flash comes down through the Kingdoms but it does not make contact with the paths. It is sudden, almost total and utterly devastating, as most great falls are. This has been adequately illustrated by the tarot card the Lightning-struck Tower. A strong and substantial tower is struck by lightning from a clear blue sky, the traditional 'bolt from the blue.' It has three windows that may represent the threefold aspects of the physical, mental and spiritual outlook, but they are narrow and limited in their view. Thrown from the tower are people who felt secure within it walls, but they are cast down. One wears a crown that shows that when it's time to 'reap what you have sown,' Fate is no respecter of rank and all are equal in its presence. Now you feel it would be wise, being 'The Fool,' not to add the trappings of a clown.

The way back up the Tree is meandering and slow like the Serpent Path. Most religious teachers tell us to be 'as wise as serpents.' The Serpent Path comes out of the area containing the Kingdom of Chesed, in that it crosses the 19th path, which in its turn is intersected by the 13th. Where is the 'Empty Room'? There is a ubiquitous commentary that says, if a disciple grasps the 'tail of the Serpent Wisdom' it will lead him to the Halls of Wisdom. This Kingdom of Daath is sometimes called the 'Upper Room' and Christ sent two of his disciples ahead of him and the rest to the city, to find the Upper Room, where he and they would celebrate the Feast of the Passover. He told them they would be guided to it by meeting 'a man bearing a pitcher of water.' This Kingdom is often given over, astrologically, to Uranus who has taken over the sign of Aquarius - the Water Carrier - from the old king and god, Saturn, who ruled both Aquarius and Capricorn, the Goat. The Christ is held to herald the beginning of the Aquarian Age, yet it would seem that all the old gods are still here, they have neither been conquered or vanquished. You ponder who, or what, you will meet her?

It is all too much for you, still too many questions and still too few answers. You wonder if previous travellers who obviously arrived at this point fared better or worse than yourself. You go to the top and sit with your legs over the edge and take stock. The forest behind you has the shape of a crescent. It is semicircular, like the horns of a new moon that go to the left and right of the path. You are certain the ends of the horns touch the edge of the Abyss on either side. It might well complete the circle on the other side of the Abyss. This leaves an almost circular area within it which, apart from the field with the mound at the other side, appears empty. How can something that appears so empty feel so full and vibrant? The Kingdom of Daath is said to be Knowledge and its position on the tree puts it about here. Some commentators claim this Kingdom doesn't exist; they say it is a later interpolation. Does knowing and thinking of the Kingdom make it so?

The well-worn mark on the rock behind you has obviously been the subject of much contemplation. You feel, a kinship with those who have been here before. You feel as they did perhaps, that there are no short cuts or short circuiting on the Tree, only the direct approach. Must you act now as the Spiritual Warrior and surrender whatever control you have of your life? Is a direct act of faith being demanded of you, which decrees that you leap like a warrior, empty-handed, into the void? The King of the

Kingdom of Chesed said there were no guarantees in this Kingdom and even he knelt at the Abyss, and you are not there yet. You start to question yourself for the first time on the journey, asking, is what I have enough?

You sit on the rock to think things through because it all appears so insubstantial. You do not feel confident to cross over now unless you know you have to, because there is no other way to cross it. The path enters this field but after that it cannot be seen. A high mound rising far away at the other side is where you think it ends and where you are going to have to make for eventually.

First you decide to skirt the field to the left. That should take you in the general direction of the third Kingdom Binah that lies across the other side of the Abyss. This would also take you to the 17th and 18th path. Of course you want to see where the Abyss fits into the scheme of things, even if you don't understand them. So taking a course just inside the edge of the forest and the field you go to the left. You follow the edge of the forest for quite a long time, even by the standard passing of time for the Island. Then you are suddenly faced with your first look at the Abyss itself.

You are near the edge of the Island for you have found the 17th path. Further over is the 18th path that is the limit of the Island. This 17th path goes back diagonally across the Island and would take you back to the Kingdom of Tiphereth. The 18th would be a straight one leading back to the Kingdom of Geburah. You walk across until you are between the two paths. Both paths end at the Abyss and continue on the other side before being swallowed up by one of the densest forests of trees you have ever seen. It is impenetrable from your side yet you know it covers something: something you feel you must not see, something you are not prepared for and may never be, the reasons are endless.

In the depths of this wide ravine you can hear the roar that you know is the sea disappearing into this bottomless pit. You saw this ravine from your ship when you came around the head of the Island. It was the strong current of water being drawn into this place that started to pull you towards the Island. It caused you to steer well away and give the place as wide a berth as possible.

You now see how wise you were in this: once drawn into there nothing could survive and would probably never be seen again. Mists rise from its depths so thick, the bottom cannot be seen, only heard, which is terrifying enough. You take a large rock and throw it into the Abyss in an attempt to see just how deep it may prove. A useless exercise, for what would you hear over that deafening roar?

The Island on the other side seems a little severe, gloomy and very still. Being completely covered by trees you have no way of knowing if this impression is really so. The opposite side rises into forest covered mountains. There is an odd peak high enough to pierce the clouds and mists that shroud the rest of it. You think it is austere, similar though grander to the fifth Kingdom of Geburah on this side.

It seems not unlike a twin town in appearance, but this is pure speculation. Deciding there is nothing to be seen or little to be gleaned from staying here you retrace your steps back to the path that led you to this place. You return to the rock and then carry on in the opposite direction, though you have already decided it will prove similar.

Remembering the sudden appearance of the stream when you wished for it you think it better to try not to decide anything that could possibly influence the outcome. When you do eventually get there, you find the same high impenetrable mountain on the other side of the Abyss. It does not appear so forbidding because the terrain is less severe under its forest canopy compared to the other side. The rocks are not so jagged and the mist does not seem as thick either but you still can't see through it. Here you find paths 15 and 16. 15 would take you back to the Kingdom of Tiphereth and 16 to the Kingdom of Chesed.

It reminds you of the fourth Kingdom of Chesed. Is the higher Kingdom over the Abyss reflected in the fourth Kingdom below it? It's all too much for you and you let speculation go, dealing only with what you can see. There is the same terrible roar beneath your feet, which suggests that if you had taken a route on this side instead of the other, you would have found the sea still pouring into the Abyss at this point also. It is a wonder the sea is not dry. You retrace your steps and come back to the 13th path that brought you to this point. You decide there seems little choice but to try to cross the field in the hope it will bring to the centre of the Kingdom of Daath.

For this is surely where you are, on the central path from the Abyss that is in line with the first Kingdom of Kether that Crowns it all, through Daath down to Tiphereth. It is there, in the Kingdom of Kether, you think the answers lie, not that you will see that Kingdom, if there are any answers for you at this high level. You climb your rocky perch again and, lie on your stomach contemplating the scene and, as seems customary at certain times in the journey, you fall into a deep sleep.

Awakening refreshed you come down from your rocky perch. Standing in the centre of the path you align yourself with the far mound. You stand for a time contemplating this waving sea of grass and the mound seems farther away than ever at this lower level, the air is still and no sounds are to be heard. A hush of expectancy is in the air as if everything about this place is waiting to see what your decision will be; turn back or take the road ahead. There is just one problem, where is the middle of an 'empty room?' It is the first time since coming here that you feel the 'island' is waiting for your decision. Then you think 'in for a penny, in for a pound' and plunge straight into the field. You are relieved to find your feet on firm ground for it did look so insubstantial. When your first flush of bravado has passed and you are well into the soft grass suddenly you hope it is not like the fields of earth or at any moment you will be confronted with an angry owner, irate at the mess you are making their crops.

You look behind you at the point where you entered the field, shown by the gap in the trees. There is nothing to show your progress at all. You are quite a long way in and there is no broken grass to show the path you have taken. It would appear to have closed behind you. You are standing up to your waist with unbroken grass all around you. Feeling relieved you turn and, making the mound your marker, you walk straight towards it. You have the strong impression, as always, that you are being followed and watched, but you cannot see anyone. You can hear the voices around you that you heard in the woodland glade where you rested, but you still cannot see anything.

Stooping below the top of the grass you are surprised to see it is not as dense as it appears on the surface, though there is nothing to be seen above it or below. You can hear the sound of the voices but not to whom they belong. Your heart jumps a few beats as your hands are taken by smaller hands. Whoever is there, they are touching your legs and clothes as they start to lead you toward the mound. After the initial shock you realize they are not malicious but friendly. The hands are like those of small children who play around an adult, laughing, dancing and inviting them to join in their revels. There is a lilt in their steps as if they were skipping or dancing to some unheard music. Their rhythm is regular, easy enough to follow and you find yourself in step with your unseen company, which they seem to appreciate.

Suddenly something small sits on your left shoulder, though there is nothing there that you can see. Your senses tell you a small figure is sitting there who, when the pace becomes uneven, takes hold of your hair in its small hands to keep its balance. At times you are turned full circle by these unseen hands and, accompanied by their laughter, you go willingly with them, sensing no harm, for laughter is a gift you bring Pan. The pace quickens as you start approaching the high mound that is now quite close and it is shown to be much higher than you thought; it is almost as if they are in hurry to get either you or themselves there.

The sea of grass ends and you are standing at the beginning of a path worn in the rock, which winds its way up the side of the mound. You are faced in the direction you must take, little hands are put in yours while others push gently from behind. You look around your feet but nothing is seen and, in complete obedience, you stop at the beginning of the path but do not tread on it yet. Although you can still hear your little helpers, they are no longer holding your hands or clothes, so they are not on the path with you. You take this to mean that having brought here you must make the remainder of the journey on your own. The path takes a meandering course and instinct tells you that you must tread every inch of it.

Placing both your feet on the beginning of the path itself brings a sound that, in any language, means approval. Smiling in the general direction of the sound, you wave your good-bye and mentally give them thanks. The surface of the field of grass was static until you gave your thanks and asked for a blessing. Now, as if something had been dropped in a pond at your feet, ripples spread from you and your path out to the farthest sides of the field. When the last ripple has disappeared the Sea of Grass is still and silent again; it is as if you had never crossed through it. You wonder if you will ever understand this most mysterious Kingdom.

After much climbing you can see the circular area of grass below. You can see the curved crescent of the forest clearly and the straight 13th path beyond disappearing into the distance towards the Kingdom of Tiphereth. Your path becomes wider and at a high wall of rock, it divides. One section goes to your right and the other to the left. You notice the wall takes the same curve as the forest below around the field. As before you take the left-hand path.

Walking to the left the path starts to curve gently to your right. The top of the wall of rock is gradually getting lower. Eventually you reach the end and then you see the high wall is crescent shaped, not circular as you thought it was. You have arrived at one of its points. Behind the highest part of the wall, hidden from outside eyes, are seven trees. These seven trees are magnificent representatives of the Seven Trees of the High and Sacred Grove. They even surpass the wonderful trees seen in the temples and, for quite some time, all you can do is stand and stare, catching your breath.

The yew is in the centre, with three trees on either side. To the left of the yew are the willow, apple and hazel, to its right are the birch, holly and oak. Rising in the centre of the crescent, like the hub, is a high mound of rock, with a rough-hewn throne at the top. There are well-worn steps leading to it. Here, you know instinctively, like Ratty in *The Wind in the*

Willows, 'this is the place of my song-dream, the place the music played to me,' here is a place where you could find Pan. In this place he could come. Like a temple of Terminus and the Kingdom of Saturn it is rock and open to the sky and the elements. There is no roof or walls to hinder or contain him. The large, curved wall of rock behind the Seven Trees and the throne in the centre makes it resemble a cave without a roof. Knowing all the steps on the Island have numerical significance you count them. There are forty-nine in all or seven times seven.

You walk around the throne which is like the one in the Kingdom of Tiphereth, but more substantial. You return to the steps and, forgetting your past experience, muse upon whether you could call up the four Elements. You wickedly think that if there were wind, rain, thunder and lightning lashing this scene it would be a perfect theatrical set of the Brocken on Walpurgis Night. All you would need would be the 'Prince of Darkness' sitting on his throne. The thought is no sooner in your head than it is happening just as you imagined it. You hold on to the rock to prevent yourself being blown way by the high winds that lash the rain across the scene, in waves of unabated fury.

The skies are heavy and overcast, thunder roars and rolls above and quickly echoes into the distance. Sheet lightning behind the clouds cuts across the sky, casting eerie and grotesque shadows in the crescent of the Throne and Grove. Wiping the water from your eyes you wonder what you have done and raise them to the throne above which, in darkness, you can hardly see. A massive lightning flash, like an angel with a flaming sword, cuts across the sky as if it meant to slice the very heavens in two. You are glad to find in its light that one of your thoughts has not been granted. The throne remains empty.

Clinging to your rock, you realize how easy it would be to take back a wrong report of this place. It fulfils all the descriptive requirements of black magic for the ignorant. The more so if a half-goat, half-man figure, bearded with horned head and cloven hoof had taken its place upon the throne. Would it stand a chance, if a description like that was taken back, and would you? No matter how much you protested to the contrary that all you attempted was a genuine quest to seek the God of Nature, you would be said to be consorting with the Devil, your Master, and indulging in Black Magic. It is true there is no longer the stake. Now the 'stake' uses more subtle means of destroying anyone who is different, marching to drums which others cannot hear.

It was so easy to do. You think the thoughts and the realisation comes pat. This Kingdom of Daath appears to operate on a hair-trigger and if those thoughts are not properly controlled, they go off half-cocked.

Yet for this scene to manifest itself as it did, it had to originate from within you. What chance, therefore, does Pan have if you bring to this or his Kingdom, from the outside, that which is yours and not his? You cling even tighter to your rock and think you have learnt your lesson and 'this too will pass.' The thunder, lightning, wind and rain die away as quickly as they came and when you open your eyes again all is as it was before and you are as dry as a bone. You begin to understand the meaning of the trite saying, usually easily dismissed, that 'thoughts are things.' You know your thoughts must be kept firmly under control, particularly in this volatile Kingdom. You do not want to be called Chaos.

Resolving there will be no more thoughts of such an uncontrolled nature here, even though they were partly in jest, you have learnt your lesson. The distance between the throne and the edge of the Abyss is wide. You go to the edge immediately in line with the front of the throne. On the other side is a little used and overgrown path that you know would take you to the Kingdom of Kether. While contemplating the path, you choose your thoughts carefully. The edge of the Abyss echoes the curve of the rock wall and the trees. Out of a vast cavern below where the path ends on your side pours an immense cataract whose waters crash down the Abyss wall into the depths below.

A fine mist hangs over the Abyss, and hanging between the two sides in the pure blue luminous light of this Kingdom, is a rainbow having the appearance of a multicoloured crystal bridge. It looks substantial enough to cross over to the other side of the Abyss, but dare you attempt to try it? The Bilfrost bridge with no Heimdall, was he away on his daily battle with Loki? Is it the Rainbow Bridge, Crystal Bridge or Pons Periculosus? Which is it, and do you have the nerve to find out? Do you have the nerve to take the chance on crossing and paying the penalty for your presumption if you are wrong? What if Heimdal where here, guarding the bridge, and he took you for a giant on the rampage? Discretion is the better part of valour so you decide against any unpremeditated actions. Common sense far outweighs bravado by now.

You spend some time walking around looking at the Crystal-Rainbow Bridge from all angles. It looks so inviting, shimmering in the pure blue light. At the cliff edge above where the cataract below your feet is falling into the chasm there is a ledge a little way down. You carefully lower yourself to it, by holding on to a small tree to do so. There in the moisture laden air you see some reeds by a small rivulet of water, and you notice some have been cut. You try to see if it is seven or nine; it is seven. You look around you to see if anyone is watching, for you are sure someone is. As it was in the legend of Pan and Syrinx, you gather the bunch of cut reeds together and blow across the top of them. They make a gentle sighing sound like the wind.

Now, were those seven cut reeds there or, again, did your thinking of them put them there? You concentrate and visualize them gone, but they are still there when you open your eyes. You haul yourself back and then you notice you have been holding on to the mountain ash - *the Sorb of Thor* - the tree which saved him from drowning in the swelling waters of the River Vimur, and helped him reach the shore. Looking down, and listening to the raging waters below, the rowan could save you from a similar fate. The edge is not far above and you have no trouble in reaching it, the wind making the same sound as the reeds. It is also filled with the same sounds you heard in the *Sea of Grass* but this time you can see who is making them. Gnomes are walking everywhere, and they are as you would expect them to be. Sylphs, fly on currents of air you cannot feel and like the *Ignis Fatuus*, the Salamanders glide in the breeze. Undines dance wherever there is water and in the mists of the Abyss. A happy swirling crowd takes your hand again and leads you to foot of the steps of the throne, setting you on the bottom step.

You become totally absorbed in the spectacle before you, which is a sheer delight. An old gnome comes forward and points behind you and you see the dryads of the Sacred Trees. They are seven maidens of beauty and grace near, within and sometimes part of, the tree themselves. They smile, bow their heads and raise their hands to acknowledge your presence. These beautiful creatures are accompanied by countless nymphs and you absorb the endless activity going on around you and you want to rush in and join the throng.

The gnomes go in an out of rocks as if they did not exist, with others seeming to come from the bowels of the earth itself. All appear to know exactly what they are doing and it seems that it must go on whether you are there or not. The graceful undines appear in water and mist, diving off the rainbow bridge and rocks into the water, playfully sliding down the cataract, gliding and 'swimming' through the mists of the Abyss as if it was the sea itself. The sylphs and salamanders fly above your head, weaving patterns of endless variety. There is too much to see, too much to take in.

Many gnomes are sitting in a circle, with their knees to their chest, their hands clasped around their knees. They are gently rocking back and forth, intoning a low sound, and to this is added the intonation of the other Elementals. It is so gentle it could be easily mistaken for the wind. In like fashion you bring your knees to your chest and clasp them around with your arms and you also find yourself rocking gently back and forth in time with their rhythm. Then, gently, very gently for you do not wish to spoil the low chant, you mentally intone the words 'Io Pan, Io Pan, Io Pan.'

Rocking forward with 'Io' and backwards with 'Pan,' it is gently and quietly done. Your eyes close with the gentle rhythm, though only for a short time, for as suddenly as it began, the chant stops. Have you interfered or destroyed their harmony, by adding your own strange chant?

They back away from you in an ever widening circle, with backs bent, and you wonder what offence you have committed, for it would appear to be great. Everything is silent and you notice that those who were looking at you, are now looking behind you, their eyes fixed elsewhere. Then your ears catch another sound.

Coming down the steps behind you are footsteps in a measured tread, but they are as no other footsteps you have ever heard before. As they come closer you rack your memory to identify the sound which is a familiar one and then, in a flash, it comes to you. It is not the sounds but their order. When you have heard the sound of hooves before, there were usually four sounds. The association is not made easily when there are only two sounds. This sound is as if an animal was walking on its hind legs on rock - but animals do not usually walk on their hind legs, do they?

The sounds stop and something sits behind you on the steps. You feel a warm contact near your back. It feels warm, strong and friendly with a faint smell of musk pervading the air, sometimes very strong. You feel no fear and close your eyes and wait, remembering it was your impatience that shattered the obsidian mirror in the Kingdom of Geburah. You were still holding on to a small shard of it when you left and it helped to bring you here. A tingling sensation runs down your spine and the animal part of your being tells you that the hair on the nape of your neck is erect. You feel that the end of your Quest is nigh, for good or ill. The strangest thoughts go through your head at times like this and of all things you remember Revelations. 'And when he had opened the seventh seal, there was a silence in heaven about half an hour.' You are no John but you think you know just how John felt while he was waiting. This is it for in your own small way you have attempted to open 'the Book of the Seven Seals (= Kingdoms).' Then a voice asks: 'Do you know who I am, traveller?'

'I believe you are he whom I seek, he for whom I have undertaken this search. My quest was to find the God of Nature, he who is called Pan.'

'Given my usual appearance, do you not mean that abomination, the Devil?'

You find yourself speaking very calmly, considering the way you feel. 'For a great number on the Earth Plane your appearance would mean 'the Devil,' but to others, those who seek you out in love, it does not.'

'Do you really love me? Think carefully before you answer, speak only in the truth that I will love you for. Know no penalty will be exacted if it is the truth that you speak. This is very important. Do you really seek me through love?'

'I do with all my heart.'

'This is more than I had expected.' He puts a hand on your shoulder, saying ,'Do not turn yet, lest my appearance cause you concern. True it is the appearance you all know, but is it not the form evil takes on your level of existence?'

'No, speaking for the many who are not here and think as I do, I dare correct you, Sir. It is not. It is a form convenient for the purpose of the time and time has given the image unwarranted strength over countless centuries, but it is not accepted by all. That is an image placed in the minds of children who cannot shake themselves free of it all their lives. I was the same; however, some do question its validity. It is this questioning that has brought me here.'

You fidget a little and then stammer out, ' Sir, may I see...do you have with you...I wonder.'

He interrupts your embarrassment, saying, 'My pipes! Of course, they are with me constantly. They are the one thing your 'Devil' did not take from me and I have often wondered why. Though my enemies did their work well on my destruction, they are the one thing that separates my image from his. My pipes are among the first things sought by those who seek me out.'

Sound and movement tell you he is taking something from his body. A strong arm comes around your shoulder and there, in an equally strong hand are - *the Pipes*. Seven graduated reeds bound with thin leather thongs that look soft like chamois leather. Each pipe is held in place by the binding and the beeswax that fastens them. The smell of the beeswax fills the air. You hesitate to take them from him as you wish to do, but with a movement of his hand he shows you may do so.

You cannot believe it, and who will believe you? What does it matter who believes you or not? Let them believe what they will, at this moment who cares? In your hands are the Pipes of Pan. Not only do they really exist, now you have them in your hands. You almost feel you could die quite happily now, but a gentle laugh behind tells you, better than any words ever could, that is not necessary. There are seven graduated reeds, seven notes to be called forth, one for each Kingdom on the Tree and the Harmony of the Spheres. All the Kingdoms save this one, yet in this Kingdom you have all seven notes in one place and all sounding together.

He continues. 'These pipes are the one thing all travellers seek.

Even I have not fully understood the fascination they hold for you all but I am pleased it is so. Now, of course, you must try to play them. There will be little else talked of until they are out of the way.'

Your attempts are pathetic in truth and an experienced hand appears again to put them to your lips. It adjusts them as only experience can. Your breath does not go through them like a gentle breeze on its journey through Nature. However, there is no explaining the effects they have even when badly attempted because, as on so many occasions on the Island, words are inadequate; there is nothing you can equate them with in your experience. Although no tune is attempted, the sound is pleasant and beautifully plaintive to the ear.

You open your eyes to find the little people, who had disappeared earlier, sitting around you almost to your feet again. Now they are quiet and attentive, some resting head on hands with others resting against each other. It is a sight of great serenity. The god takes the pipes from your hand and speaks again, 'These are my people and they seem to like you. Now traveller, I think you are ready, turn and behold.'

You slowly turn and behold. Sitting on the steps is the god. First you look into the face. It is a good face by any standards, strong and kind, but you are sure it could be very stern if the occasion demanded it. The head is covered with strong, curly brown hair that is tinged with red and gold at the ends. At times in the light it gives the impression of a soft fire. Rising from the hair above the forehead are two horns, they are deep brown in colour, tending towards black at the ends. They begin somewhere in the centre of the head under a large bush of curly hair, sweeping back low over the head toward the ears. The ends then twist and turn upwards, away from the head. Although they are large and prominent there is a chance, from a distance, that they could be mistaken for large locks of hair because of their colour. The rays of the sun are often portrayed as horns from the head.

The forehead has strength with strongly arched eyebrows over deep brown eyes. While the hazel eyes can be described as pools that reflect Nature because they are so moist, there is a slight twinkle in them nonetheless. They are eyes that have lived long and seen much, and so they reflect back the wisdom of the truly wise. They return your gaze unflinchingly as if they had seen this all before and know they will see it again. They appear to read deep into your being, yet they are filled with the compassion of not judging what they see but accepting, so you do not mind your nakedness, you almost invite it. There is something almost cleansing in their lack of pretence. You feel the mask of the actor has been stripped away and at last, to someone, the actor stands revealed; though you are pleased that you do not have to see what is there. The nose is slightly curved and delicately flattened against the face.

Under this is a full mouth that has strength. The hair is pushed back from the temples revealing ears that have thick lobes. They seem pointed at the top, with a tuft of hair going backwards. There is a constant, though slight, movement of the ears, even when he is at rest. The moustache is full on his lip and the luxurious beard beneath it falls to cover an obviously strong, thickset neck. You notice you keep thinking of strength and using the word strong but these are the only words that seem adequate. The head is magnificent in its strength. The upper torso is partially covered with the pelt of a lynx, spotted like a map of the heavens. It falls from his left shoulder down in front of him and touches the ground.

It is the good, lean muscular, strong body of one who has spent his life in the open, bared to the elements, fending for himself. The hands are large, wide but expressive, the fingers taper and the thumb is strong. From the waist down are the hind legs of an animal that is used to running. The legs are powerful and muscular under the brown fur that covers them. This fur has many subtle hues from deep to light brown with slight touches here and there, at the ends of a red golden colour.

It is very curly and like the hair on the head. In the light this gives the impression of subtle flame: a Creature of Earth and Fire perhaps? The legs come down to a thick but flexible ankle ending in perhaps the most famous 'cloven hoof' of all. Doubly famous now as they are the ones used for that monstrosity and abomination, the Christian Devil and the excuse for the existence of evil. These goat-like feet appear more a token of the stability of the Earth, you cannot stop yourself reaching out and gently touching a hoof.

He sits patiently as you view him: in truth it is probably only a short time but you feel it is an eternity. The Pan Pipes are lying at his feet where he placed them when he took them from you. Still as fascinated with them as you ever were, you know they are the treasure you would run off with if you could. Again you come back to seven: seven pipes, seven reeds for the Music of the Spheres once heard on earth, perhaps, according to the harmony of the heavens that surely must have reigned once.

You start from your reverie and look up again to his face and see the eyes that have been watching you with equal intensity. They break into laughter lines as he smiles. You feel embarrassed at have been so inquisitive, and at having taken so long in your inspection of his person as if he was for sale. In your embarrassment you blurt out part of your meagre vocabulary and, to make matters worse, Latin to a God of ancient Greece - 'Pax vobiscum.'

'Et tibi pax,' he immediately replies, as if sensing your embarrassment. He asks, 'Well, traveller, will you remember me, having found me? Tell me what do you see, Pan or the Devil?'

'I have sought and found the purpose of the quest undertaken. I see only Pan, God of Nature. I shall never see something that does not exist. Otherwise, this seeking could not have been.'

'What!' he roars in good humour, 'no fire, brimstone and sulphur smell, no smell of rank goat?'

'No!' Without thinking, you instinctively put your hands on his arm, 'only that which any lover of animals would know, the smell of the clean fur of a healthy animal, like my cat.'

He looks deep into your eyes, almost searching to see if there is anything he has missed, as if trying to confirm an answer he already knows in them. Leaning over and placing his hand on your shoulder, he gently holds it and speaks low, 'You do not object to touching me or that I should touch you?'

'No, it is what I seek, being bounded so firmly by the five senses we possess. I place the sense of touch highly. To have the conclusion of my quest confirmed by these senses is more than I had hoped for.'

'Traveller, can you now see why I cannot always appear to those who seek out my Kingdom and me? Each time someone renews their faith and love in me, I answer and begin to draw nigh. Sometimes my natural divinity and godhead are doubted and I must withdraw again. Thus people think I am an ungrateful god or even that I am dead. What would be the result of my sudden appearance to many, even those who seek me in earnest love? I would gladly appear because of this love but how would I be received by them and what would they think?

'What would be the result of my presenting myself to their sight in the form they know and expect? Even if all was well with the meeting, what would others comprehend of it if they spoke of it? Could they really convince them it was I and not some Evil they had spoken to, consulted or worshipped? Sadly, so many may have died in the past who, when meeting me, were observed by zealous eyes so narrow in their scope.'

'How could they convince anyone they had really invoked and been dealing with an obedient servant of the All-High God, the All-That-Is, the Concealed of the Concealed? Would they be believed or would they be thought mad and dealing with some figment of their diseased imagination?'

'No, I think they would not be believed,' you reply. 'A precious few may but even some of them may doubt the contact. They would probably remain silent lest it is thought they were unbalanced. You once held such sway in the hearts of man that such a great love had to be challenged and broken if it could not be diverted. The evil that exists in the world could not be attributed to the new God; if his world is perfect and he is perfect, it could not come from him.

'A scapegoat had to be found and sadly your appearance, so beloved by many, proved ideal for their purpose of giving Evil a form that could be recognized and rejected. However, things are changing and more people are seeking a fuller understanding of you and your Kingdom.

'Many want to work more with you and not against you. More are aware of your presence and want to remove this monstrous stigma you have been burdened with these long centuries. If they cannot remove it, then they would like to help you to carry it.'

'I am close to the Earth and if men will call upon me I will be good to them as I was to Athens. My Kingdom will respond if the caller is prepared and ready, but to my great sadness so few are. I had my Eden on earth and unlike many other gods I did not leave it, for it was my charge. I was expelled.'

'Into my Kingdom on Earth came the Serpent of Ignorance that perverted love and distorted my form into some diabolical creation to frighten and control. The inflamed mind of these zealots did their work well. They renamed me and I was exiled from Eden.

'This serpent did not bring wisdom but a subtle poison. My Kingdom is natural but you must trust it and love it. If you place a gentle yoke around its neck it will work in harmony with you. I offered life, life and yet more life, which is my blessing. Perhaps it was too strong a blessing for the unprepared vessels to take?

'It was my blessing you called up at my seat, when you invoked the natural Elements of the Earth, the primordial forces, to declare and show themselves. My pine grove, caves and grottoes are deserted and many are destroyed. If you seek to contact the Old Gods you must seek them out in the places where they were honoured and sought. We are not gone...we are not asked...because...!'

It is almost as if his mind has now gone elsewhere, on to other things. Suddenly he rises like an animal sensing the approach of danger, sniffing the air. His ears move to catch sounds inaudible to you, while his eyes have narrowed in concentration. The little people are up on their feet. There is an air of expectation, as if something is going to happen: something you cannot see or hear, but you can sense their disquiet.

He turns and looks into your eyes. There is an urgency in his own and you know your time is over. So few answers and so many questions that have hardly been touched upon. The important question of his form you know now, more than ever, that there is another and it is one that could not be perverted by zealots. He looks almost Egyptian, not unlike Osiris through a green swirling mist. The form looks familiar but it is gone as quickly as it came; apart from Pan and you the place is empty once more. It now feels more like desolation than emptiness, for you have seen the 'empty room' of the Kingdom of Daath so full of life. You wonder how many before you have wasted their chances on the first meeting.

The time has been spent asking him the same questions he must have answered thousands of times. You asked them thinking, wrongly it would seem, that you had plenty of time. Now it is gone, after finding him it is too late, the time has so quickly passed and he will soon be gone. You think you have too little to return with and already you are thinking, how soon will it be before you can get back? He places his hands on your shoulders, and though the eyes are blazing with urgency they are gentle for you and have a hint of sadness in them. He speaks quickly and you know no further questioning will be brooked.

'Time is getting short and it is dangerous for you to stay. You have already stayed too long in this Kingdom. Now I bestow the Gift of Forgetfulness upon you, one of my greatest gifts.'

'No! That is one gift I do not want to accept from your hands, for you cannot call that a gift.'

'It is, traveller. You will not forget me or what you have undertaken. It will simply have the sharp edge of remembrance dulled. Otherwise, to use your thoughts, you will not be able to live and function 'out there' because of what you will feel you have lost 'in here,' he touches your heart, 'and your place is there.'

'Time is short. I must be brief and take command for your own good. You have succeeded in making the 'out there' and the 'in here' one, for a very short time at least. Could you return 'there' with a heart filled with pain and longing for 'here,' being 'there' but wanting to be 'here?' Where you have come from is your allotted place and it is where you must be, no matter how you may be at loss with it at times. It is there the learning and the responsibilities lie, that you have elected to undertake.

'No matter how hard that may be to accept, I cannot cancel them out for you; only you can do that. I promise that we will meet again for I will make myself known to you in many ways. Seek the trees and groves, the solitude, if you have the eyes to see me and the ears to hear me I will be there. Nature was not made dumb, people no longer listen to what is always there.

'I will take an interest in your affairs from now on. Take with you this word.' He leans over and whispers a word in your ear and shows that you should repeat it back to him. You do, whispering the word gently in his ear so he is satisfied that you have heard correctly. 'Call me with that Key that is personal to you and I will come or be near. You may doubt this at times as you call, but I will be there, watching.

'Now the time has come, the time is short and it is time to part.' His hand is placed in front of your face. He moves it slowly towards you. With his middle finger he touches the centre of your forehead. 'Good-bye for a time, traveller. I promise we will meet again. Call me and I will be near. Love me as I love you, it is a great part of the key. The path to love is one of the worthwhile paths a human being can take, perhaps the most worthwhile.'

His face and form start to swim before your eyes and it is the last thing you see of him. Smoke or incense begins to swirl around you and there is a sweet, heady smell, either of cedar or pine, you do not know or care which it is. You feel the ground being gently cut from under your feet and you seem sliding ever downwards. You see every Kingdom you have seen and in the order you saw them. It is not unlike a film being shown in reverse order without the grotesque speed, and the return journey is like quicksilver.

The Homecoming...

Having climbed the Tree you are now coming down it, back to the place from which you started. Last of all you see your barque lying in the harbour where you left it, in the Kingdom of Malkuth. Finally you feel your whole body supported horizontally, a soft pillow beneath your head, the warmth and comfort of your room that you left when you started your journey. There is no light outside the curtains despite your feeling you have been away so long. You look at the hands of your clock glowing in the dark, but the time shown means nothing to you, in fact the clock has stopped.

You get up and stamp your foot on the floor three times, which sounds surprising like a hoof. You rearrange some things in the room to confirm fully that you are back. Then you have the hot drink in the vacuum flask, sandwiches and the sweet biscuits you left by the bed for your return. You lie back on your bed with half closed eyes. There is a strong smell of pine in the room. You are sure of the perfume and it is one that never quite leaves you. You are now firmly back, but in the back of your mind you have more than a faint recollection of a journey undertaken and from which you have returned. Your greatest treasure and recollections are that you feel it was undertaken with success and you will never feel the same again.

Resting, you spend some time going over the things seen, permitting your mind to run uncontrolled in reverie. Your tape recorder is by your bedside so you record your musing on tape, this being the best way to record fleeting thoughts. Settling down, you quietly place whatever thoughts enter your mind now on the machine, speaking softly so as not to disturb the flow of thought.

You do not judge, assess, criticize or modify. Let them come as they may until the well of thought runs dry; it fills again quickly enough as experience has shown. You also know that the thoughts placed on the tape will sound different to you later. Sometimes they are like a different person talking. Your state of consciousness later will make you think you are listening to a person who was in a foreign land. It will seem to have very little to do with you later, because you do not talk like this. It may even sound like a fairy-tale of your mind's imagination and you may even be embarrassed by it, considering it a made-up thing, a wish fulfilment and what you hoped for. Something doubt will wash away, like a water-colour out in the rain, until only a faint unrecognizable trace is left on the paper. It could be so and others may say it is, but you do not believe it.

Each will undertake the journey in their own way, for their own reasons and each, according to their lights, will see and hear differently. There could be a basic pattern to each journey if someone seeks for it but as in everyday life, no two people will see the same place in the same way. Each will have a different recollection of what was there or what they saw. They will be influenced by their interests to a large extent, and by what they can match with their knowledge and beliefs. It will be 'personalized' in some way and this is how it ought to be. You feel special note should be taken of the prayer by Plato given at the beginning of the first chapter.

It was the prayer you said on setting foot on the island for the very first time. It was then you took some of the soil of the Kingdom of Malkuth and let it run through your fingers. Take note of those all-important words 'and let the outward and inward be one.' You feel this is an important key to Pan, both to his nature and ours. There is absolutely no point in seeking Pan 'out there,' unless you seek and find him 'in here' first. For if he is not 'in here' then you will not find him 'out there.' If there is no Pan in your soul you will seek in vain for him anywhere else, so seek and ask to be given 'beauty in the inward soul.' The fact that myth and legend, in particular the Greek and to some extent the Roman as with Faunus, placed Pan as a supreme God of Nature. The endless interpretations people place on this word Nature is legion. In most of the myths we have, their metaphor and imagery place Pan foursquare in our internal landscape. He belongs there by right. Although you may be a stranger to him he is no stranger to you. He is not unlike your blood, so much a part of you that you only see it when you spill it and you are losing it.

You can deny him but you will not remove him. You can repress him, but acknowledgement is better than repression and ultimately it is more healthy. So many people think that if you deny something it will make a noise like a hoop and roll away, but it doesn't. Physical geography places Pan in his beloved Arcadia, where his beloved goats abound and the landscape it so suited to him, but Arcadia is located within and without: if you can go there you can bring a part of it back. Arcadia is like a candle: it is not diminished by those who take from its flame, it freely and gladly passes on its light so that it can be taken elsewhere and lucky are those who find it. Thus that is where he can be found and usually is, spiritually, mentally and often, physically - 'may the outward and the inward man be one.'

However, part of Nature is human nature and, in keeping with others, you cannot see how the two can be separated to any advantage. If the God of Nature is suppressed within, instinct may well go astray without. After all it is his Kingdom we are worried about and trying to preserve, and in the process we could be saving ourselves into the bargain. Logic alone, deprived of instinct, may not be enough to bring the success we are beginning to work and hope for. You have only to look at the manner in which Pan has been personified over the centuries to see where he belongs. Nothing is more basic or earthy than a goat and this places Pan here on earth with us, haunting 'this place.' He is a god of many contradictions as his more usual form and myth show but it is this that makes him so accessible, for what is more contradictory than the human race?

Because of your study of the Tree of Life you meditate that as the human form of the god is above the waist, this theory places Pan's human half in the higher regions the Tree of Life, above the sixth Kingdom of Tiphereth. This would take in the higher spheres for him, if not for us. It takes Pan up to the Supernal Kingdoms, over the Abyss and beyond, for he was welcome in the Kingdom of the Gods but did not choose to live there. Pan lived here with us although he knew the way up the Tree to the highest Kingdoms. He also knew the way back and elected to use it for his Kingdom. Pan, in my opinion, is one of the few gods who has the full range of the Tree of Life. He appears the least restricted to one specific Kingdom. All the Kingdoms contain him, but they cannot restrain or keep him.

Evolving humanity subjugates their animal nature into a more acceptable social form, though, like any good animal trainer, we should not be foolish enough to break the animal's spirit: training is required, not subjugation. It is the goat half of Pan, going below the Kingdom of Tiphereth down to the Kingdom of Malkuth, which supplies the earthing. In many respects Pan is like an *Adam Kadmon*, the father of the earthly Adam, in the way he is placed on the Tree. Many a lifetime is spent in the lower Kingdoms, living wholly in the thrall of physical life and its attractions. This is necessary for propagation and service to the basic instincts that must be understood and controlled before moving up, for we cannot be permitted to take our bad habits with us. For Nature and the Earth do not awaken all or she would have none to serve her. All have to serve their time below Tiphereth before moving on, which is right, for only those who have served know how to give service.

Further, why should the study and pursuit of religions or occult philosophies deny the flesh, why despise the 'vehicle' you travel in? If you despise your body, you will end up despising yourself. It can't be done really and why should it? We exist here in the flesh and only fully discard it at death when our journey is over. Many spend their entire life below the Sun and are totally unaware of the existence of the upper Kingdoms.

They live quite happily in the lower Kingdoms and their lower half, getting on quite happily with their lives. The 'upper half' remains alert for any period of 'waking' in the lower half in which it can make its presence and influence felt, the theme of so many religious philosophies. Unless you are fulfilled from within, you will need constant stimulation from without. Like many people who cannot be quiet or still, they are suddenly faced with a vast emptiness and the boundaries of their life disappear, which panics them and in this we are back with Pan again.

When a life is lived only in the Kingdoms below the sixth Kingdom of Tiphereth, there is 'little new under the sun' in life. All the Kingdoms must be served in the fullness of time, even the lower ones, and all have done so at some time in their lives. We still do in many ways. Only those with an inflated sense of their own importance would saw off the lower part of the ladder because they deem they no longer require it. Do they think their self-acquired sanctity or esteem will hold them aloft?

The Qliphoth - the *Negative Tree* - and its adverse Sephiroth is filled with those who have broken their spiritual bones in their fall from grace. They must now deal with new circumstances of their own making, circumstances from which they must painfully extricate themselves. Some, possibly, have one slight advantage; at least they have seen the Light and 'the Bright and Morning star.' If you have seen something, even though you may not possess it any more, you know it exists and may make the effort to find it again.

Like the goat, Pan is the wanderer, the lone traveller of the mountain peaks. He may visit the villages, towns and temples, sometimes the cities, but in truth you doubt this. He does not stay unless he is offered somewhere natural or wild, not constructed which would try to confine him. He and his companions prefer woodland grottoes, caves and dells, forests, pastures, water and the lonely peaks. Pan is sought and he is often found in 'caves obscure.'

These 'caves obscure' are also found in the dark recesses of the psyche. Found in these caves, hidden away in the mind, are the secret desires, the dreams, fantasies and the panic that we try so hard to hide. Pan is a god and mixes with the gods, but he seems to like the company of shepherds, fishermen and hunters. He invents musical instruments and is a god of music, yet the Muses are found with Apollo whom he taught and not with him.

He is a god of prophecy and has many oracles but these too in the end are taken over by Apollo, again whom he taught. His home is here 'in this place' for he is the abandoned child who was wrapped in warm animal skins. Pan is 'a loner,' he is an outsider often understood best by 'outsiders' who are almost automatically drawn to him. In certain situations when we are weak, feeling lost or abandoned, we may ponder our Pan-like behaviour. He personifies all that is natural and nature bound in our consciousness deep within us with its wellspring obscure. At these times we often act suddenly and spontaneously, without thinking, often some say 'out of character.'

For he is instinct, the chthonic spirit or deep ever-present shadow that often acts without thought of the consequences or the opinions of others. Many seem to have lost the ability to act spontaneously for often we are not strong enough to do it without being accused of behaving wilfully or being rejected by our peers. Instinct does not have to be wilful if properly used, though we often explain and excuse it by saying 'I don't know what came over me!' Something I have repeated so often in this work. Quite often it is Pan who 'comes over' you when you feel lost and abandoned, he wraps you in warm animal skins and what was 'in there,' comes out. It is then you discover it was there all the time. In a dire emergency it is often instinct that saves your skin and the day, not manners and mores. Instinct was there long before manners came on the scene. Of course you must have manners and mores in an organized society, so perhaps this is just a harping back to an instinctive and natural behaviour. There are so many ways of 'getting back to nature,' but whose nature? In the religions after Pan, the oldest god, the new gods were jealous gods before whom 'you shall have no other gods but me.' The early gods were served by many adherents and most knew their worship was not all-inclusive, before sword, fire and rack arrived to see you did not put any god before the new One God.

Nature, like the rest, could not be tolerated because it was personified by the many. It had to be brought under the One. Trees were trees and stones were stones and nothing more, though such worship at first was permitted. However, when a sacred grove had more worshippers than a church then, even if I do not approve I can see their point, something had to go. Finally all had to serve the One God of the new dispensation. Pan and the Nature Gods were discredited so that Nature could be more effectively controlled. When people severed their connection with a personal, deified Nature and with it their basic instincts, the image of Pan and the Devil could be merged with consummate ease. God transcendent instead of God immanent.

The natural elements of Pan's kingdom lost their qualities in the eyes and thoughts of the people. Nature became soulless, without spirit, for when people abused Nature they heard no voice of protest against it. Nature was just there for the taking and they took. The old gods did not die quickly, conveniently or all at once; it took a long time to get rid of them and this kind of book proves they were not completely successful. Nature fought hard before it appeared to 'die' and it seems the word drugged Hebrew prophets have remonstrated against the nature spirits, sacred trees, groves and natural places in vain.

However, with the enforced exile of the god Pan from his Kingdom, what voice was there raised in protest against the wanton acts of desecration perpetuated against it, many being done that were previously forbidden by the God? None! What did the new God do to protect his presumed creation? Precious little that I can see. Any laws made to protect the land came from enlightened people. When Pan said 'Thou shalt not' regarding Nature it was a direct edict from a God who was protecting his creation. A blasphemy worthy of the name bears repeating - it was an edict from God and the God was Pan - I may as well be hung for a sheep as a lamb.

The new god was strangely quiet on the matter and, with the benefit of hindsight, we know where that has led us. No voice of conscience was raised in the land because the voice of conscience had been effectively silenced. Pan as mediator between the people and Olympus was destroyed, his voice became the voice of the Devil beguiling you. The voice of the Nature Spirits, his maidens and the Nymphs became witches who worked their evil under the trees they once protected, often to their death. You wonder why are you putting this on tape? You are only speaking to yourself and you are converted already so that only leaves the cat, and he's probably wiser in all this than I am...

Here you must have fallen asleep in your meditation. All that is found on the remainder of the tape is the gentle ticking of the clock, which is on the table near the tape recorder. However, there was one good thing to record upon awakening. In your sleep you had seen the Gate of Horn - not the Gate of Ivory.

End of Chapter Three. . .

The
Greek and Roman
Deities of Nature

The
Greek and Roman
Deities of Nature

'Earth's increase, *foison plenty,
Barns and garners never empty;
Vines with clust'ring bunches growing,
Plants with goodly burden bowing;
Spring come to you at the farthest,
In the very end of harvest!
Scarcity and want shall shun you,
Ceres' blessing so is on you.'

The Tempest. **William Shakespeare.** (1564-1616).
*foison= 'harvest'

In this section of the work the reader will find a representative selection of the Greek and Roman deities who are connected with Nature and Pan in some way. The list does not lay claim to being complete, but it contains a fair section of the deities connected with the brief set for the book. Included, for example, are the spirits of forests, woods, glades, streams, rivers and those deities that have under their care the cultivated and uncultivated earth with its produce. This chapter is about those nature deities who are concerned with planting crops, their growth and reaping, the cultivation and care of the vines, animals and their fertility. This may mean some information in the previous section could be repeated here, either in cross-reference or because it is about the deity, deities or legends being discussed. Sometimes this is unavoidable.

MIN - an Egyptian God

As MIN is an Egyptian god, not a Greek or Roman one, it may be considered strange to begin this part of the work with him. However, we find the Greeks identifying Pan with the ithyphallic Min, a very ancient Egyptian god, at Panopolis and Coptos. This appears from the Greek name of the former town and from dedications found at both places. Min is identified strongly with Pan by the Greeks, although he bears no physical resemblance to Pan. Let us first digress to the Egyptian God

Khem, because he has a similar connection with Pan.

Khem, like Ptah, is a personified attribute of a special energy or activity of all life. Khem symbolises the generative force. He is often represented as a figure displaying the ithyphallus or erect penis. This made him correspond with the Greek god Priapus. Khem is a god of generation and reproduction and was also identified with Pan by the Greeks, who called his chief city, Chemmis in Thebes, by the name of Panopolis.

Khem not only merges with Num or Neph - the personification of the primeval waters from which all life began - but he also often usurps the functions of, or is the same as, the garden god Ranno. It is but a short step for a god of reproduction to become a garden god. **Keightley,** *The Mythology of Ancient Greece and Italy* (1868), tells us the god Ranno is depicted as an asp. His figure was placed on wine presses, garden and agricultural equipment. The strong connection should be noted between the productive Khem and his classical counterpart Priapus, the tutelary deity of gardens. Num or Neph is the personification of the primeval waters from which all life began, sometimes interpreted as spirit or breath. He is 'the spirit of God moving on the face of the water.' He is sometimes connected with Woden, the life-giving breath or air of heaven.

Min seems to have been looked upon early as a deity who was the protector of the harvest and crops. His cult dates back to the earliest time. In old times he was identified with Horus; later Amen was confused with him and depicted in his image.

It is thought, by some, that Amen originally represented the cosmic elements of the air and wind that created life amid the inert chaos that prevailed before the earth was given form. Later Amen possessed the characteristics of the god Min. In the time of the oldest kings the earliest statues were colossal statues of the god Min from Coptos. Min was the Egyptian god of virility and generation, also known as Amsu. Some statues of him have been found decorated with sea shells and swordfish from the Red Sea. This has resulted in some commentators considering him the god of a maritime or eastern nation, reaching Egypt by this route.

At Mendes in Egypt, the god Min or Pan was worshipped as a goat - the Goat of Mendes. We are told that *mendes* is a generic name for goats and in that place a goat was kept with ceremonious sanctity. In the Egyptian religion the goat never attained religious significance as a sacrifice of the common people as it did elsewhere. In the town of Mendes the important cult of the goat was the Djedet. The *Ba-neb-Djedet* - 'the billy-goat, the lord of Djedet' - was the sacred goat. The goat being a symbol of fertility, women sacrificed to them to have children. On their death sacred goats were often embalmed.

Min (or Amsu) is depicted standing with his legs placed tightly together like a mummy. A flail is held upright in his right hand that is held stiffly above and behind his head, as if he were about to strike. Min has a skull cap on his head with two high plumes and two streamers hanging down his back, and he always has an erect phallus. Regarding this latter symbolism, we must dismiss the idea that this is little more than a pornographic picture. Meditation is paramount to draw from within the symbol its full significance.

This symbolism shows that Min was considered, by his priests and devotees, primarily as the creator of the world. Min passed from being a lord of fertility in animals, to a god of vegetation. In the *Book of the Dead* he tells us, 'I am Min at his coming forth. I have placed my two plumes upon my head.' At harvest time, the first sheaf of wheat was offered to him by the Pharaoh, as a God of fecundity of the crops. This familiar and ubiquitous theme of the first fruits offering, was to give thanks for the harvest.

His sacred animal was a white bull and, under the period of Greek influence, games were held at Panopolis in his honour. Coptos was a town of caravaneers. Min was guardian of the desert roads and protector of travellers in the desert and some have suggested that these functions were transferred to Pan. Travellers would never leave on any commercial venture in the desert without first invoking the aid and protection of Min. Min was God of the Eastern Desert and Lord of the Foreign Lands. The desert was the centre of his cult. Graffiti addressed to him were found at many points in the deserts, scratched on rocks or walls by travellers and huntsmen. These took their place beside the more formal dedications.

Those who know my method of writing also know of my tendency to digress when a byway appears to be a rich vein. However, I am always being jolted by the past in a way that keeps my feet firmly on the ground, especially if I become too smug about the present, which is not often. This nearly always elicits the same thought - is there really anything new under the sun? Today we have many green issues and activities that seek to put a hold on and redirect the misguided management of the planet, its animal and plant life. To the Egyptians, Osiris was the god of vegetation and resurrection. The colour green, then as now, is the colour of vegetation, of life and of the earth itself. The place of the blest and the eternal was a 'field of malachite.' Osiris bears the epithet 'the great green' and this symbolism is taken from his skin colour. Sometimes his skin is white as a mummy's wrappings, sometimes black that is characteristic of the realm of the dead and sometimes green, representative of resurrection. The appellative 'the great green' was also given to the sea, of which the Egyptians were uncertain and thus they respected it. We usually respect, or should, something of which we are uncertain. To the Egyptians, doing *green things* was to do good things. This is the antithesis of doing *red things*, meaning to do evil.

ARISTAEUS

ARISTAEUS was an ancient divinity worshipped in various parts of Greece, Thessaly, Ceos, Boeotia and the African colony of Cyrene. His worship was particularly strong in the islands of the Aegean, Ionian and Adriatic Seas, which had once been inhabited by the Pelasgians. Every region of Greece possesses a form of Pan and in the places listed above there was thought to be a great, beneficent, primitive deity called Aristaeus. The name means very good and it is a title given to Zeus in Arcadia. Although the worship of Aristaeus was widespread, the myths about him are as obscure as his parentage. He was once mortal and ascended to the dignity of a god because of the great benefits he conferred on mankind. He is described either as the son of Uranus and Gaia, or according to a more general tradition, as the son of Apollo by Cyrene, the daughter of Peneus, a King of Arcadia. Cyrene was averse to feminine occupations and spent her days hunting wild beasts and protecting the cattle of her father. **Pindar** tells us 'Aristaeus was carried off, after his birth, by Hermes to Gaia.'

His mother Cyrene had been carried off by Apollo from Mount Pelion, where he found her boldly fighting with a lion. Apollo was taken by both her beauty and her courage. He called the centaur Cheiron out from his cave who told him he should carry her off to the garden of Zeus, where she would bear him a son.

Apollo took Cyrene to Libya, where the celebrated city of Cyrene derived its name from her. It was here that she gave birth to Aristaeus. Hermes took Aristaeus to the 'well-seated Seasons and Earth.' The Horae fed the child on nectar and ambrosia and rendered him immortal. They transformed him into Zeus, the immortal god and to Apollo the pure, guardian of flocks and pasturage. He was raised by the centaur Cheiron, regarded as the wisest and most just of all the centaurs, who taught him the arts of hunting, medicine, music and prophecy.

Aristaeus had a great civilizing effect throughout Greece. Other, more local stories, call his father Cheiron the centaur. The stories of his youth are quite marvellous and show he was a favourite of the gods. In Theban legend, when he had grown to manhood, the Muses married him to Autonoe, the daughter of Cadmus and Harmonia, who bore him several sons, Charmus, Callicarpus, Polydorus(?) and the ill-fated Actaeon. **Wm. Smith,** *Dictionary of Greek and Roman Biography and Mythology* (1844), tells us 'Autonoe was the wife of Aristaeus, by whom she became the mother of Polydorus (**Hesiod,** *Theog.* 977; **Paus.** x 17). According to **Apollodorus** (iii, 4), Polydorus was a brother of Autonoe and Actaeon was her son.' It was the Muses who taught Aristaeus the art of prophecy and healing. After the death of his unfortunate son Actaeon, he left Thebes.

The Delphic Oracle told him to go to the island of Ceos and end a drought there. To do this he had to propitiate the scorching Dog Star by building a temple to Zeus Icmaeus - *the giver of moisture.* The Dog Days are days of great heat. During the summer the Romans named the six or eight hottest weeks, the *caniculares dies* (3rd July - 11th August). According to their belief the Dog Star (= *Sirius*) rose with the sun and added its own heat to it. Building the temple resulted in Aristaeus being identified with Zeus in Ceos.

From thence he returned to Libya, where his mother prepared for him a fleet with which he entered Sicily, visited several islands in the Mediterranean and, for a time, ruled over Sardinia. From these islands his worship spread over Magna Graecia and the Greek colonies. At last he went to Thrace where he became initiated into the mysteries of Dionysus. He dwelt for some time near Mount Haemus, where he founded the town of Aristaeon.

He taught men much the same precepts as Pan and was regarded as the protector of flocks and agriculture. The myrtle nymphs gave him the names of *Agreus* - 'a hunter' and *Nomius* - 'pastoral, belonging to shepherds.' Aristaeus was also named *Alexeter* - 'one who helps keep off, a helper, a guardian or champion.' The nymphs taught him how to curdle milk to make cheese and to make beehives. They taught him the husbandry of making the oleander yield cultivated olives, and their teaching included the vine and viniculture.

These arts he gave to others. Aristaeus was a beneficent divinity of ancient mythology. He gave his blessing to herds and perfected the art of hunting which had been taught to him by his mother Cyrene. He knew the art of bee keeping, the art of cultivating and using oil, fermenting wine and every kind of husbandry. Aristaeus was gifted with healing and prophecy. **Justin** throws everything into confusion by describing *Nomius* and *Agreus*, which are only epithets of Aristaeus, as his brothers.

The introduction of Aristaeus into the legend of Orpheus and Eurydice, cannot be traced to any writer older than Virgil. Orpheus, after returning from his expedition with the Argonauts, settled in Thrace to use his music to civilize its wild inhabitants. While Aristaeus was staying in Thrace he fell in love with a nymph Eurydice, the wife of Orpheus, to whom he brought disaster. Eurydice was mortally bitten by a serpent when she was fleeing from his amorous advances. The Napean nymphs, the companions of Eurydice, destroyed all the bees of Aristaeus.

From his many wanderings Aristaeus came to the naiads' palace in Arcadia. His mother Cyrene instructed him to raise four altars in the woods to the dryads, who had been Eurydice's companions, where he was to make his sacrifice. Returning nine days later he completed the ritual with offerings that included the Poppies of Forgetfulness. Forgetfulness was a gift of Pan though the poppies were created by Hypnos, the god of sleep.

He propitiated the shade of Orpheus, who by this time had joined Eurydice. On the ninth morning a swarm of bees came out of the rotting carcasses that had been used on the first day of the ritual. The bees settled on a tree and he captured them and put them into a hive. The Arcadians now honour Aristaeus as Zeus for having shown them this method of fostering new swarms of bees. His chief seat of worship is Arcadia.

He is said to be the first who found the use of honey. He used rennet to make cheese, oil and many other things. Aristaeus is usually regarded as a beneficent deity so he is often found identified with Zeus, Apollo and Dionysus. He lived in the town of Aristaeon that he had founded and his departing from earth is a mystery, he vanished without a trace on Mount Haemus, near the town.

PRIAPUS

PRIAPUS was introduced late into Grecian mythology. The Romans adopted him simply as a god of gardens and also called him *Mutinus*. Priapus was a god of fruitfulness and the fertility of nature. Pausanias tells us, 'This god is honoured elsewhere by those who keep sheep and goats, or stocks of bees; but the Lampsacenes regard him more than any of the gods, calling him the son of Dionysus/Bacchus and Venus/Aphrodite.' According to **Theocritus**, the shepherds would set up his statue with those of the nymphs, at a shady fountain. A shepherd prays to him promising him sacrifices if Priapus will free him from love. **Virgil** places bees under his care and fishermen also make offerings to him as the deity presiding over the fisheries. In the Greek Anthology, *Priapus-Of-the-Haven* is introduced, giving a pleasing description of the spring and inviting the mariners to put out to sea. The Priaps are enumerated by **Moschus** among the rural gods.

'And Satyrs wailed and sable-coated Priaps;
And Pans sighed after thy sweet melody.'

In Asia Minor the Pan of Mysia was Priapus, and the more usual accounts make him the son of Dionysus and Aphrodite (or Chione or Nais). Priapus is also said to have been sired by 'a long eared father' that some take to be Pan, a satyr or even his own sacred beast - the ass. To this we can add for good measure Hermes, Adonis and even Zeus himself, as his sire.

Aphrodite, it is said, yielded to the embrace of Dionysus, but during his expedition to India she became faithless to him and lived with Adonis. On the return of Dionysus she did go to meet him, but she soon left him again, going to Lampsacus on the Hellespont to give birth to the child of the god. Hera was displeased with her conduct and 'touched her' and, by her magic powers, caused Aphrodite to give birth to a child of extreme ugliness. Born with unusually large genitals, this child was Priapus.

Like Pan, when Priapus was delivered to Aphrodite at Lampsacus, his limbs were so deformed his mother would have naught to do with him. The goddess of beauty was ashamed at having given birth to such a hideous monster. She ordered him to be exposed on the mountains so he would expire. This story has a familiar ring. The baby was found, as in the story of Pan, and tended by shepherds, receiving the name Priapus.

He was a great favourite among the people of Lampsacus, a city famous for its vineyards. Like Pan he was disliked by his parent and nurse, but loved by the people. He was eventually expelled by the inhabitants because he was a little free with their wives. The town of Priapus is near Lampsacus. Naturally Priapus was the chief deity of the place and it took its name from him when he took refuge there when banished from Lampsacus. Priapus punished the Lampsacenes by inflicting them all with disease. When Priapus was recalled to Lampsacus by the people, they built temples in his honour.

An ass is generally one of his sacrifices because its braying woke the beautiful nymph Lotis or Lotos to whom he was about to offer violence. She implored the assistance of the gods to save her from his importunities and was transfigured into a tree called the Lotus, consecrated to Venus and Apollo. Again we have a nymph, as with Pan and Syrinx, Apollo and Daphne changed into a form of vegetation, with the assistance of the gods, to escape the advances of a god. Syrinx was changed into reeds and Daphne into a bay tree.

Priapus is generally represented with a human face that has the ears of a goat. He holds a stick in his hand that he uses to terrify the birds, a club to chase away thieves, a scythe to prune the trees and cut down the corn. He is crowned with the leaves of the vine, but sometimes laurel leaves or rocket were used. The last of these plants was sacred to him because it was said to excite the passions and love. For those readers unfamiliar with the plant rocket, it is a *colewart*, a name given to various *Crucifarae*, of the genus *Hesperis*, specifically the *Hesperis matronalis*, an Italian species, cultivated since 1597 in English gardens.

In the spring he was offered a crown painted with different colours and in the summer, a garland consisting of ears of corn. His worship was introduced into Rome but they revered him more as a god of orchards and gardens and not as a licentious god. The earliest Greek poets, **Homer**, **Hesiod** and others, do not mention Priapus. **Strabo** expressly states it was only in later times that Priapus was honoured with divine worship. He was principally worshipped in Lampsacus on the Hellespont, from whence he is sometimes called *Hellespontiacus*.

We have every reason to think he was regarded as the promoter of fertility. Like Pan, he was seen as the personification of the fruitfulness of nature. This included the fields and herds, horticulture, vine growing, goats, sheep breeding and bee keeping. Sailors and fishermen prayed to him for success and were under his protection. The Romans identified him with Faunus. The original seat of his worship lay in the towns of Asia Minor situated on the Hellespont, as mentioned above. He was predominantly worshipped at Lampsacus which claims both to be his birthplace and to have been founded by Priapus. The wine of Lampsacus was famous and the city was chosen by Xerxes to supply the table of Themistocles with wine.

From here his cult and worship spread to Lydia and finally, through the islands of Lesbos and Thasos, over the whole of Greece, but especially in the Argolis. It was in the Argolis at Ornea, a town famous for a battle, that the people gave the god the epithet *Priapus Oneates*. His festivals were called *Ornea* and they were celebrated by young maidens at Colophon, in Ionia. Ultimately the cult of Priapus spread throughout Italy, with the cult of Aphrodite. As with the other gods occupied with the pursuits of agriculture, Priapus was believed to be possessed of prophetic powers and he is sometimes mentioned in the plural.

He was a phallic god of fertility, and donkeys, which were considered the embodiment of lust, were sacrificed to him at Lampsacus. He was capricious in granting or withholding sexual potency. Because Priapus had similar characteristics with the other gods of fertility, the Orphics identified him with their mystic Phanes, Dionysus, Hermes, Helios, Pan, etc. The Attic legends connect Priapus with a daemon called Conisaltus who, with Orthanes and Tychon, appeared in his train. Conisaltus is said to have been worshipped in Athens with the same ceremonies given to Priapus and according to **Strabo**, Tychon was a god of chance or accident who was also worshipped there.

Mutunus or Mutinus, a deity among the Romans much the same as the Priapus of the Greeks, was regarded as the phallus. It was believed to be the most powerful averter of demons and all the evil that resulted from pride or boasting and the like. Mutunus is often mentioned with the epithet Tutunus or Tutinus, a deity of Rome who presided over the conjugal duties. The statue of Tutunus was touched by people recently married, to remove sterility. He was the personification of the fructifying power in nature, and women made their offering with their heads covered by a veil. A public Mutunus, the one that was used to avert evil from Rome and the republic, had a sanctuary on a ridge in the city known as Velia. Roman matrons and, in particular, newly married women, disgraced themselves by the obscene ceremonies which custom obliged them to observe before the statue of this 'impure deity.' This resulted in the public Mutunus (= Priapus), which existed up to the time of Tiberius, being removed outside the city.

In time Priapus wrongly became regarded only as a god of sensuality; thus his symbol was a phallus, an emblem of productivity and a protection against the evil eye. He had a great deal of poetry written about him, both Greek and Latin, and one that is extant - *Priapea* - included some 85 short Latin poems addressed to him. Some commentators say poetry about him was written by *Virgil*, *Tibullus* and *Ovid*. The poems describe the phallus of the god and the punishment that will be meted out to those who sin against him.

Among the Romans his statues were generally made of wood, a herm with a phallus stained with vermilion. The herm was set up in gardens, with club and sickle, the phallus being the symbol of the fructifying power of Nature. The idea of representing the productive powers of nature in a god form has great antiquity. Later, however, in more depraved times these representations were misused to express coarse sensuality and sometimes lust. This accounts for the diverse representations of Priapus and such gods, which are still appearing today in modern Greece. However, the true purpose of what is depicted is being brought down to its lowest common factor, as it was in the past.

Because of the red staining applied to the herm he often got the name *ruber* or *rubicundus*. Priapus was occasionally offered a sacrifice of ass's milk. Other sacrifices offered to him included the first fruits of the garden and field, the products of the vineyard, milk, honey, rams and fishes.

When Priapus is represented in carved images, the herm is mostly shown as an old man, sporting a long beard and large genitals. As a god of fecundity he is rarely without his indecent and ever ready symbol of productiveness. Priapus, in keeping with the other rural gods, possesses a ruddy complexion. He is sometimes given a long oriental style robe and a turban, although sometimes the turban is replaced with a garland of vine leaves. In **Ibsen's** *Hedda Gabler* the eponymous heroine is trapped in a dull, scholarly marriage. In the play she asks those who have seen her former, more sensual lover, Eilbert Lovberg, 'Yes, but did he have vine leaves in is hair?'

The cloak of Priapus is filled with all kinds of fruits and usually a horn of plenty is present. He has fruit and bunches of grapes in his lap or carries them in his garment. In his hand he carries a billhook, club or cornucopia, while a reed on his head, shaking in the wind, acts as a scarecrow. He is often shown with the symbols of a drinking cup, a thyrsus and a spear, like those of Dionysus. His image was placed on tombs to symbolise the doctrine of regeneration and a future life. Therefore, his name is often found included in sepulchral inscriptions. According to **Pliny** 'the thyrsus is a spear wrapped about with ivy or bay leaves, which they carried in their hands at Bacchus' feasts.' Ask for an image of Pan in Greece and for the most Priapus is the figure you will be offered in the gift shops. If you are seeking a figure of Priapus, and there is no reason why you should not, this is an excellent statue, if it is bought for the right reasons. If you are seeking an image of Pan it is best to look in the shops that sell museum reproductions, for there you will find him; though sadly most shops will tell you Pan is merely a satyr.

The images of Priapus are often sold to tourists for the wrong reasons and sadly modern Greece has succumbed to Mammon and the lowest common denominator. The tourist gift shops now have modified the statues of Priapus, with additional mechanics, for the titillation of the tourist. They're not for me.

FAUNUS

The name of Faunus may mean the well-wisher or kindly, from *favour*= 'to bear good will, to favour' or perhaps, as some believe, from *fari*= 'the speaker or to speak.' *Fatuor*= 'to be inspired, to prophesy.' Faunus is one of the oldest and most popular of the Roman rural deities who, because of his similarities and attributes, was identified with the Greek Pan. During his reign the Arcadian Evander and Heracles were believed to have arrived in Latium and it was Evander who was thought to have brought the cult of Pan to Italy. In fable Faunus appears as an old king of Latium, son of Picus and grandson of Saturnus. He was the father of Latinus by the nymph Marica. In his reign Faunus, like his predecessors Picus and Saturnus was the bestower of fruitfulness upon the fields and gave fertility to the cattle. He promoted agriculture and the breeding of cattle among his subjects. Faunus was a distinguished hunter. A prayer of **Horace** to Faunus shows he was considered a protector of cattle against disease, particularly the young of sheep and goats.

> 'Across my farm in sunshine bright
> Come gently, and retire from sight
> Kind to my cattle's young.'

As such Faunus is akin to or identical with, Inuus or Incubus - *fructifier* - a name the Romans gave to Pan, Faunus and the satyrs. An old name for nightmare in Latin is Inuus and this name is also identified with Pan. In one legend his father Picus was changed into a bird by Circe, a sorceress, who was smitten by love for him. He remained faithful to his beloved wife and Circe in a rage struck him with her wand and turned him into a bird. From this legend we get *picus*= the woodpecker, which is an oracular bird. Picus was a Latin prophetic divinity, he is described as a son of Saturnus or Sterculus, as the husband of Canens, and the father of Faunus. In some traditions he was called the first king of Italy. He was a famous soothsayer and augur, and, as he made use in these things of a picus (= a woodpecker), he himself is often called Picus. He was represented in a rude and primitive manner as a wooden pillar with a woodpecker on the top, but afterwards as a young man with a woodpecker on his head. The whole legend of Picus is founded on the notion that the woodpecker is a prophetic bird, sacred to Mars. When Circe changed him into a woodpecker he retained the prophetic powers he possessed as a man. Another fable made Circe the mother of Faunus, by the god of the sea.

A goddess with similar attributes called Fauna or Fatua. **Keightley** thinks these are 'the feminine names of his worship,' all names of the earth and associated with his worship. In some works she is regarded as his wife, sometimes his daughter. Some authorities believe Faunus may be the same as Tellumo and Saturnus.

To the still barbarous tribes Faunus gave laws and invented the shawm or rustic pipe. Faunus was a beneficial spirit of the fields, pastures, forests and plains who bestowed fruitfulness on the cattle and fertility on all the wild life. He taught the Latin peoples their agriculture and religion.

Faunus, in later times, was worshipped in two distinct capacities. In the first, he was a god of the fields and shepherds. In the second, he was an oracular and prophetic divinity for he had the power of foretelling the future. This he did under the name Fatuus. What Faunus was for the males, his wife, Fauna was to the females. Because of this Faunus and Fauna often bore the names Fatuus and Fatua, Fatuellus and Fatuella. Fatuus as a rural god is sometimes found being equated with King Oberon, while Fatua as a country goddess, a fairy of the woods, with Queen Mab.

Faunus usually delivered his oracular pronouncements in the sacred groves, using Saturnian verse. One sacred grove was near Tibur, around the well Albunea, another on the Aventine in Rome. Faunus caused the secrets of the future to be revealed with strange sounds, terrifying voices and spectral appearances, which could also be heard in the woods and countryside. The manner used by Faunus resulted in him being called a wanton and voluptuous god, fond of the nymphs. The methods of his manifestation may have suggested the plurality of fauns or fauni with which he is found. These fauni are often described as monsters who were half goat and half man with horns.

The Ritual of Incubation was touched upon in the first chapter and is extended here. The incubare (Gr. *enkoimasthai*) was a special sleeping sanctuary where oracular answers were sought in dreams. The object of the ritual was to conjure up the spirit of someone dead or obtain a dream revelation from the god of the sanctuary. Certain preliminaries were observed: there was the sacrifice of an animal upon whose skin it was customary to sleep. These incubations were in vogue, with the Greeks, from early times. The Romans did not practice them extensively until under the Empire, when they generally took place in the temple of Asclepius, the god of healing. The rites observed near Tibur are described by **Virgil**.

First a priest offered up a sheep and other sacrifices and the pilgrim consulting the oracle had to sleep that night in the incubare, on the skin of the sacrificed animal. This ritual is usually regarded as an extremely old one and there was a similar dream oracle of Pan Luterios at Troezen, which also employed incubation within the temple lying on animal skins. These similar methods increase the parallel between Pan and Faunus significantly.

During this time the god gave his reply to the questions asked by the appellant, either in a dream or by the medium of supernatural voices. Similar rites are described by **Ovid** as having taken place on the Aventine. Fauna similarly delivered oracles, but only to women. The Fariani were 'youths that celebrated Faunus' feast, being only girt with a skin, and all naked besides.'

There is a tradition that Numa, by a stratagem, compelled Picus and Faunus to reveal to him the secret of calling down lightning from the heavens and the art of purifying things struck by lightning. There was an oracle of Faunus in the city founded by Latinus. Faunus raised a temple in honour of Pan where they kept his solemnities, called by the Latins *Lupercus*, at the foot of the Aventine Hill and gave hospitality to strangers with a liberal hand. Lupercal was the name of the grotto where the she-wolf suckled and fostered the twins Romulus and Remus. Lupercus is an ancient Italian divinity who was worshipped by shepherds, as the protector of their flocks against wolves. Simultaneously he was summoned as promoter of fertility among the sheep, whence he was called Inuus or Pan.

On the north side of the Palatine hill there had been, in ancient times, a cave that was the sanctuary of Lupercus. The sanctuary was surrounded by a grove that contained an altar of the god with his figure clad in a goat skin, not unlike his priests, the Luperci. The Romans identified Lupercus with the Arcadian Pan. Luperca, or Lupa, was an ancient Italian divinity, the wife of Lupercus, who in the shape of a she-wolf performed the office of nurse to Romulus and Remus. Luperca and Lupa were also worshipped as the protectors of the flocks from wolves. In some accounts she is identified with Acca Laurentia, the wife of the shepherd Faustulus.

The *Lupercalia* was a ceremony of expiation, purification, solemn sacrifices and plays dedicated to Pan. It was performed yearly to give new life and fruitfulness to fields, flocks and people alike, specially to barren women. Pan was called Lupercus by the Romans because he taught them to employ dogs to protect the herds against wolves. Thus Pan, like Luperca or Lupa, was worshipped as the protector of the flocks from wolves. The Lupercalia was held on the 15th of February, in honour of Pan. Goats were often the sacrifice because Pan had goat's feet; others say a dog was sacrificed because it was the guardian of the flocks and the sheepfold.

As previously mentioned, some authorities think this festival was introduced into Italy by Evander, from Arcadia. They think the name is taken from a Greek name for Pan, *Lyceus* - 'a wolf' - not only because the festivals were similar, but from the rapacity of wolves. **Augustus** forbade anyone over the age of fourteen to appear naked or run through the street, during the festival of Lupercalia. **Cicero** reproached Antony, saying he disgraced the dignity of his consulship by running through the streets naked and armed with a whip. **Lempriere** tells us it was during these celebrations that Antony offered the crown to Caesar, but the indignation of the populace forced him to refuse it.

After the sacrifice at the Lupercalia (or Faunalia) of two goats and dogs, animals remarkable for their strong sexual instinct, which were thought appropriate sacrifices to a god of fertility, they would touch the forehead of 'two illustrious youths' with the bloody knife. A condition was that these youths were obliged to break into laughter when they were touched with the knife, laughter is requested by Pan in his rituals. The blood was then wiped from their foreheads with some soft wool that had been dipped in milk. When the sacrifice was concluded, the Luperci partook of a meal with a plentiful supply of wine.

The Luperci then cut the skins of the sacrificed animals into thongs, from which whips were made. Using these whips, they ran through the city striking freely all whom they met. Married women would deliberately stand in their way to be struck as a stroke from the hallowed thong was said to cause fertility and ease the pain of childbirth. The act of running about with the thongs of goatskin was a symbolic purification of the land; and touching the bystanders with them, the purification of the people. The words by which this act was designated were *februare* and *lustare*. These thongs were called *februa*, from the verb *februare* - 'to purify.' The goatskin itself - *februum*. The day, *dies februatus* - 'the day of purification' and the whole month, *februarius* - 'the month of purification.' Take note of the word for 'goatskin' and the next entry, the god *Februus*.

The Festival of Lupercalia was observed until A.D. 494, in which year Bishop Gelasius changed it to the Feast of Purification - 'as a check to the heathen Festival of Lupercalia.' Transferring the festival from the 15th to the 2nd February was due to the institution of the Festival of Christmas, on the 25th December. In A.D. 386 **Chrysostom** refers to the Festival of Christmas as having been introduced in Antioch about A.D. 375. This is a festival of the Latin Church and forty days of purification led to the Festival of Purification the 2nd of February. It was certainly no accident that the day was called in the North of England the *Wives Feast Day*.

It was sheer inspiration of the Church to consecrate the pagan February festival to the honour of the Virgin. It is called in the English Prayer Book - *The Purification of St. Mary the Virgin*. It commemorates the Purification of Mary when she took the infant Jesus to the Temple, where it was disclosed 'that He would grow up a light to lighten the Gentiles.' As with the Pagan Festival of Lupercalia, the theme of the Christian festival is one of purification. The custom of Jewish mothers presenting themselves at the Temple for purification after childbirth, was translated into the Christian faith as churching or the *Churching of Women*.

The fortieth day was appointed for this purpose. The priests of the college of the *Luperci* (= Pan's priests) at Rome helped in the celebration of the Lupercalia in honour of the god Pan, to whose service they had dedicated their lives. It was a very ancient order that originally had two separate divisions called Fabiani and Quintiliani. These names were taken from two of their original high priests, Fabius and Quintilius. The *Fabiani* were instituted to honour Romulus; while the *Quintilian* were made for Remus. To these divisions Caesar added a third that he named after himself, the *Julii*. This addition did little to endear him to those around him and made him unpopular, for they saw in it his high ambition and aspirations. The officials at the Lupercalia were said to be either naked or half naked while performing their ceremonies and **Ovid** relates an amusing explanation for this nudity.

One day Faunus, or Pan, discovered that Hercules and Omphale were sleeping in a grotto. Faunus wanted to take advantage of the young woman while she slept. However, showing that farce has a long and honourable history, the lovers within the cave had playfully exchanged their garments. In the darkness of the grotto Faunus, unaware of the deception, found Omphale but the skin of the lion convinced him it was Hercules. Deceived by the soft robes Hercules was wearing he slipped into his bed thinking he had found the object of his desire. He was rudely repulsed and found himself booted out of bed for his audacity. Therefore, to avoid any similar embarrassing misadventures in the future, Faunus decreed that his priests should be naked when they celebrated his festivals. At least then he would know who was what!

In those times swapping clothes was not considered odd. It was not unlike the Saturnalia, which was a time when role reversal was not only rife, but accepted. At the time of the Saturnalia it was the slaves who sat at the table first to dine with the master and mistress serving them. In the Armed Forces in the United Kingdom I am pleased to see this ancient practice has survived. The Christmas dinner is served to the lower ranks by the higher, who eat later.

The slaves could say anything they chose and on whatever subject, without fear of retribution, even ridiculing if they so wished. It is from this aspect of the Saturnalia that we get parts of our traditional pantomime with its role reversal where the principal boy is played by a woman and the dame by a man.

This reversal has been carried through to later times, with the Lord of Misrule and the Boy Bishop (= Peurorum). The election of the Boy Bishop is the custom of choosing a boy from the cathedral choir, etc., on St. Nicholas' Day - 6th of December - as a mock bishop. The practice is a very ancient one. The chosen lad had full Episcopal honours for three weeks and the remainder of the choir were his prebendaries. Edward I in 1299 permitted him to say vespers in the royal presence, on the 7th of December. Some authorities say the Santa Claus of today keeps the tradition of the Boy Bishop and the Abbot of Unreason alive.

For those three weeks the Boy Bishop was virtually a bishop. If the Boy Bishop died while 'in office' he was buried *pontificatus* or according to the dignity of his office. It has been suggested that this refers to Jesus sitting in the Temple with the doctors while still a youth. The custom was abolished in the reign of Henry VIII. The Puritans were disturbed by the Saturnalian/Christian revelries and I am sure they were well aware of the Pagan roots from which they sprang. They could smell people enjoying themselves a mile off and that couldn't be tolerated, any more than the new puritans of today can permit it. So Oliver Cromwell abolished Christmas and troops would enter houses to find out if anyone was cooking meat. Like most things it went underground. Telling people they can't have something is a certain way of making them want it.

The Lord of Misrule was prohibited in 1555. He was an official at the Christmastide revelry in the Middle Ages and he directed the festivities of the holiday period. He ruled over his subjects like an autocrat and might command or do almost anything he wished without censure. His period of office is usually given as the twelve days of Christmas to Epiphany, but also from All-hallows (31st of October - 1st of November) to Candlemas or the Feast of the Purification (2nd of February). The Abbas (*abbas*= abbot) Stultorum (*stultus*= foolish, simple, unwise) in France ruled over all at the Feast of Fools (1st of January).

Stow writes, 'At the feast of Christmas, in the king's court, there was always appointed, on All-Hallow's eve, a master of mirth and fun.' This 'lord' kept his office until the Feast of the Purification. A similar 'lord' was once appointed by the lord mayor of London, the sheriffs and the nobility. **Stubbs** again tells us that these mock dignitaries had some twenty or sixty officers under their command and they were furnished with hobby horses, dragons and musicians. Their first task was to go in church 'with a confusion of sound and noise that none could hear their own voices.'

I think these feasts show the wisdom of many ancient customs. The reign of darkness, which people feared, was ending. With the approach of light there was a relaxation of the required normal behaviour expected for the remainder of the year. The donkey had its harness taken off and took full advantage of its freedom. In the feasts there was a parody of what the remainder of the year considered holy or sane. The connections that can be made with the Feast of Light - *the Saturnalia* - are too extensive to be gone into here and would extend the brief of the chapter to breaking point.

Another reason for the nakedness of the Luperci and the feast of the Lupercalia is given in an old book, *Dictionarium, Luculentum Novum* (1693). It tells of the 'Feasts sacred to Pan, the god of Shepherds, in which they sacrificed a dog as the wolf's enemy. The priests ran up and down the streets with only Goat's skins about them. As Pan is pictured with the lappets, of which skins they struck all women they met with, to make them fruitful; they went naked as others say, because when Romulus and Remus kept this solemnity, Thieves stole away their Cattel, and they followed them stark naked and took them again.' *Lappets*= a loose or overlapping part of a garment, a flap, a part of anything that hangs loose, as with a fold or pendant piece of flesh.

As we find Pan accompanied by the *Paniskoi* or little Pans, the existence of Fauni or 'little Fauns' was assumed for Faunus. This, as previously mentioned, was sometimes thought to be because of the way the god manifested himself, seeming to appear everywhere at once. They were deemed misshapen, merry, capricious beings and (in particular) as mischievous goblins of the forests who delighted in frightening people. They had pointed ears, tails and goat's feet and loved to torment sleepers and cause nightmares, so they gradually became associated with the satyrs. They were regarded as virtually identical.

As stated earlier, in fable Faunus appears as an old king of Latium, son of Picus and grandson of Saturnus, father of Latinus by the nymph Marcia. Upon his death Faunus was raised to the position tutelary deity of the land. This acknowledged his services to agriculture, cattle-breeding and introducing the religious system of the country. At Rome there was a round temple of Faunus surrounded by columns, on Mount Caelius. Another temple was built to him, on the island in the Tiber, in 196 B.C. Sacrifices were offered to Faunus on the Ides of February, the day the Fabii had perished on the river Cremera.

The Fabii, a noble and powerful family of Rome, waged war against the Veiientes. The whole family, some 306 males, were slaughtered near the river Cremera in 477 B.C. Only one male, whose young age kept him from the battle, survived in Rome. From him alone came the noble Fabii in the ages that followed. Two festivals were celebrated in honour of Faunus. One festival was held on the 13th of February, in a temple on an island in the Tiber, the other in the country on the 5th of December. These festivals were accompanied by libations of milk and wine, banquets and dancing in the open air at cross-roads and in the meadows. The sacrifice of goats was to implore the god to be propitious to fields and flocks.

In the latter festival the peasants and slaves brought him rustic offerings and amused themselves with dancing in the fields and with the performance of games. The Faunalia was a feast in honour of Faunus, kept on the fifth day of December. Faunus gradually became identified with the Arcadian Pan and the Fauni with the Greek satyrs, whence **Ovid** uses the expression *Fauni et Satyri fratres* - the 'Fauns and Satyrs (are) brothers.'

The *Dictionarium Luculentum Novlum* (1693) tells us of Faunus, 'so that the rude people may be kept in awe of him they pictured him with the feet of horn, and two horns on his head.' The fauns and satyrs are taken, in Ennius, 'for Prophets and Birds, who in the woods uttered their predictions.' Afterwards all the gods of the woods went by this name. Because of the way Faunus gave his oracles he was regarded as the author of spectral appearances and terrifying sounds that caused panic to the listener. Therefore, he is often described as 'a voluptuous and wanton god, found dwelling in the woods and fond of the nymphs.'

Februus

The Lupercalia was a festival of purification undertaken during February and Februus, who presided over purification, was an ancient Italian deity to whom the month of February was sacred. In the latter part of the month great and general purifications and lustrations were celebrated. These were intended to produce fertility in humans, and also in the beasts. The month of February was sacred to Juno, the goddess of marriage, which is why she was called *Februata* or *Februtis*. As mentioned in relation to the Lupercalia, the name Februus is connected with *februare* - 'to purify' - and *februae* - 'purifications.'

Another feature in the character of the god, which is intimately connected with the idea of purification, is that he was also regarded as a god of the lower world. The festival of the dead - *Feralia* - was also celebrated in February. Preparations for the *funus* (= a burial, funeral) of the dead were very important but are too extensive to be entered here. The Greeks regarded the burial of the dead one of their most sacred duties, its neglect involved an offence against the dead and the gods. Any one finding an unburied corpse was expected at least to throw a handful of dust over it. They did not believe that the souls of the dead could enter the Elysian fields until their bodies had been buried. The *obolus* (= 'a small Greek coin, one sixth of a drachma') was placed in the mouth of the dead and was among the first duties to be performed. The obolus was to pay Charon the ferryman to take the dead across the river Styx.

A burial quickly after death was presumed to be pleasing to the dead. The festival of the *Parentalia* was an annual festival observed in Rome for the dead. The friends and relations of the deceased met, sacrifices were offered and a banquet provided for those who attended the festival. Februus in Etruscan signified the god of the lower world - *katachthonios* - 'subterranean, infernal.' Therefore, Februus was identified with Pluto when the expiatory sacrifices were burnt. The people threw the ashes of the sacrifice backwards over their heads into the water.

FAUNA/FATUA

Of similar attributes to Faunus, Fauna or Fatua, was the name of a Roman country goddess of the fields and cattle. Her worship was associated with fertility, and the term fauna is used collectively for all the animals in any given geographical area or geological period, or an enumeration of the same. By the ancients these were thought to exist under the protection of the fauns and Faunus. Flora was the goddess of flowers (see below), and from the name of these two deities we get the term used for life of the regions or countries - the *flora and fauna.*

Sometimes Fauna was regarded as the wife of Faunus, his consort, or sometimes his daughter. At other times she was identified with Cybele. Fauna was invoked under the name of Bona Dea - the 'good goddess.' Bona Dea was an Italian deity who was assumed to preside over the earth and all the blessings that came from it. She was the patron goddess of chastity and fruitfulness in women. The names Fauna, Fatua, Maia, Majesta and Ops were considered no more than appellations give by the priests to Bona Dea. Majesta was a divinity worshipped in Rome with Vulcan.

When Fauna is shown in works of art, she usually has a sceptre in her left hand. On her head she wears a wreath of vine leaves, with a jar of wine at her side. Near her image was a consecrated serpent. Several tame serpents were kept in her temple situated on the slopes of the Aventine, in Rome. She was regarded as a healing goddess, as may be taken from the serpents present in her worship; serpents are healing symbols and are also found on the caduceus of Mercury/Hermes.

In Fauna's sanctuary all kinds of healing plants were preserved and sold, which were bought mainly by the poorer classes. Fauna was regarded by the Roman matrons as an austere, virgin goddess and men were forbidden to enter her temple. It was not lawful for any man to look into her temple, upon pain of death some say. When Fauna lived she was so chaste she never looked upon any other man, other than her husband. She belonged to the circle of deities who were worshipped by the Vestal Virgins.

Bona Dea has the same attributes as Fauna. No man was permitted to be present at her ceremonies, at which women alone worshipped her. They sacrificed to her a sow, which causes some to take her as Proserpina the daughter of Ceres, because the swine destroys corn, which is her gift. On the festival commemorating the foundation of her temple, prayers for averting earthquakes were offered to her on the 1st of May. A secret festival for the goddess and the public welfare was performed during the two nights of the 3rd and 4th May. It was secret in as much as it was a restricted festival. It was held in the house of the officiating Consul or Praetor of the city, by the matrons and the Vestal Virgins. The women who participated had to prepare themselves by abstinence from certain things, in particular intercourse with men.

The house was decorated as a temple, with every kind of flower and foliage save the myrtle, because of its symbolic meaning. At the ceremony the number of participants was limited. All present were of the aristocracy, with the mistress of the house presiding over the proceedings. No man was permitted to be present or hear the name of the goddess. Vines decorated the chamber of the festival as it did the head of the statue of the goddess. A serpent surrounded the feet of the statue and the women decorated themselves with vines and flowers.

No one was allowed to bring wine with them. A vessel filled with wine stood in the room from which the women drank and made their libations. However, the wine was called 'milk' and the vessel containing it was called a *mellarium* (= an apiary, a beehive) and even speaking of 'wine' was avoided during the proceedings. After the sacrifice the women performed Bacchic dances and drank the 'milk' (= wine) prepared for them. The goddess herself was believed to have set the procedure for this while on earth. She was said to have become intoxicated by emptying large vessels of wine, when Faunus killed her with a myrtle staff and afterwards raised her to the rank of a goddess.

Statues of men were tolerated but only if they were veiled. A temple to the Bona Dea stood on the Aventine in Imperial times. Under the Empire the festival degenerated into a mystic performance of a highly extravagant nature, said to have been profaned by the introduction of men and debauchery. This degeneration may have been hastened by the scandal of Publius Clodius, a man known for his ambition, avarice and licentiousness.

Clodius was having an affair with the wife of Caesar and he was caught in Caesar's house. Clodius was dressed as a woman and attending the festival of Bona Dea there, in December 62 B.C. Cicero testified against him at his trial, for the violation of human and divine law, although no known animosity existed between them. However, it seems both judge and jury had been well bribed with money supplied by Marcus Licinius Crassus, who defeated Spartacus in 72 B.C.

Associated with Fauna was Ops, an ancient goddess. Ops was the embodiment of the creative force of agricultural fertility, the personification of the earth's riches. She was venerated in the *Opalia* on the 19th of December, and the *Opeconsiva* on the 25th of August. Her epithet consiva is thought to be connected with the verb *serere* - 'to sow.' Her abode was in the earth, so those who invoked her or made vows to her did so either by sitting and touching the earth with one hand or bending and touching the earth.

She is regarded as the wife of Saturn who is a vine grower and planter - *vitisator*= 'a plant or set of vines.' He is a working god, under the name Stercutius - *stercus*= 'dung, muck, compost.' It was Saturn Stercutius who saw to the manuring of the fields. Both had temples and festivals in common because she was intimately connected with her husband. Ops had a separate sanctuary on the Capital and in the *vicus* (= a district or quarter of a city, a street). Not far from the temple of Saturn, she had an altar common with Ceres.

Fauna or Bona Dea was believed to give human beings their abode and food, with newly born children being recommended to her care. She was closely related to Maia, a Pleiad who, in a grotto of Mount Ceyllene in Arcadia became by Zeus the mother of Hermes, and the grandmother of Pan, if Hermes is accepted as Pan's father. Maia is mentioned with Vulcan, and was regarded by some to be the wife of that god. She was honoured on the 1st of May, with the sacrifice of a pregnant sow, by the flamen of Vulcan. The Romans identified Maia with an old goddess, *Maia Maiesta* (also called Fauna, Bona Dea, Ops) who symbolized the earth's fertility at spring; she is also called Magna Mater. Maia is probably the goddess after whom the month of May is named.

FAUNS

In Roman mythology the fauns or fauni were a class of demigods or rural deities, which were often confused with the satyrs by the Romans themselves. The faun was human with small horns, pointed ears and a goat's tail. Later they were represented with the hind legs of a goat, thus taking the character of the Greek Pan. Just as Pan was accompanied by the *Paniskoi,* or little Pans, the existence of many *Fauni* was assumed besides the chief Faunus. They were called satyrs by the Greeks. According the **Lempriere**, the peasants are said to have offered them a lamb or kid with great solemnity. They were imagined as merry, capricious beings, and in particular as mischievous goblins who caused nightmares. In Roman belief the *incubi* and *succubi* were identified with the fauns and this was seriously discussed by the fathers of the church. In 1484 **Innocent III** set forth the doctrine of lecherous demons as an indisputable fact. In the history of the Inquisition and trials of witchcraft may be found the confessions 'of the many who were said to have borne witness to their reality.' It does not say if these confessions were freely given.

In Greek and Roman mythology we find several woodland deities who are clearly spirits of the woods, that are either wholly or partly in animal form. We appear to have a parallel in European folklore in the Russian wood spirit known as the Leshi. The Leshi is believed to appear partly in human shape with the horns, ears and legs of a goat. Remember the admonition previously given not to confuse the satyrs and paniskoi with Pan. This same admonition holds for the fauns and Faunus.

THE SATYRS

In Greek mythology the satyrs represent the elemental spirits of forest and mountain, and they are inseparably connected with the worship of Dionysus. They represent the luxuriant vital powers of nature. They have been described as 'a kind of paltry Demigods and conversant in woods and deserts. They are like men upwards; only horned heads and hairy bodies, with whisking tails and Goat's feet.' They are spirits, half-man, half-beast, who haunted the mountains and woods, whose sudden appearance would terrify both shepherd and traveller alike. The satyrs were the companions of Pan and Dionysus. They are not mentioned in **Homer**, but in a fragment of **Hesiod** they are called the brothers of the mountain nymphs and the Curetes; the satyrs were regarded as an idle and worthless race, good for nothing. It was the Curetes who hid Zeus from the wiles of Cronos, and they were entrusted with his education. Their knowledge of all the arts was extensive.

The more common statement is that the satyrs were the sons of Hermes and Iphthima. Silenus also calls them his sons. The satyrs are mostly shown as robust and rough, lewd, wanton and cunning, for the most part cowardly creatures. They are nearly always seen fleeing because of this, but they are dangerous to men when in their delirious rage. Satyrs are very fond of wine, women, the nymphs and song. Often they are found hunting, tending the cattle and flocks, or dancing and frolicking with the nymphs, for whom they always seem to be lying in ambush. They are found making music with pipe, flute, cymbals, castanets, bagpipes and revelling with Dionysus. They are usually found holding a shepherd's staff, a thyrsus or wine cup. Their own special dance was called the *Sicinnis*, the wild choral dance of the Greek satyric drama. The only extant example of this drama is said to be **Euripides,** play *Cyclops*.

From the Doric paean, at a very early period, several styles of singing came into being. To these three styles of dance (in scenic productions) are said to correspond - the tragic, the comic and the satyric. The dithyramb (= *dithyrambos* - a choral hymn sung at the festivals of Dionysus), was reduced to a definitive form by **Arion.** He was an ancient Greek bard and the beloved poet of Apollo, master of the cithara (= *a lyre*) and native of Lesbos.

Arion composed regular poems, turned the moving band of worshippers into a standing or 'cyclic' chorus of attendants on Dionysus - a chorus of satyrs, the tragic or goat chorus. He invented a style of music adapted to the character of the chorus and called these songs tragedies or goat-songs. **Arion's** goat chorus may have some connection with an early Arcadian worship of Pan, who was associated permanently with Dionysus. Thus he became the inventor of the lyrical tragedy - which was a transition stage between dithyramb and the regular drama.

The satyrs were considered to be antagonistic to mankind. They played all sorts of roguish pranks on people and frightened them with impish artifice. There was something of the he-goat about them. They were fancied to be strongly built with low foreheads, having puck or flat noses and goat-like pointed ears. There were small horns growing out of their foreheads, their hairy athletic bodies ending in a short tail and cloven hooves.

Later writers, especially Roman authors, confounded them with the Pans and the Fauns and accordingly represented them with larger horns and goat's feet. They dressed in animal skins and they wore wreaths of fir, ivy or vine leaves. Originally they were quite distinctive and in works of art they are easily distinguishable, being sensual and pleasure loving. Usually they are shown as lying around sleeping, playing musical instruments, or joining in the wild dances with the nymphs and thus invariably sexually aroused. Such at least was their primitive aspect.

In early Greek art they were usually portrayed as old and ugly, but in later art and poetry they gained higher significance, especially in the works of the Attic school. The savage character was softened with a more youthful and graceful appearance. Their features took on an expression of gentleness and amiable roguishness. Simply put, they were given more grace.

They specialised in music and the dance and this is possibly due to the festivals of Dionysus. Later only their pointed ears and small horns survived. Representations of them are many but the most famous statue (*Capitoline Museum, Rome*) is presumed to be a copy of a work by **Praxiteles**. This statue represents a graceful satyr leaning against a tree, with a flute in his hand. The original is thought to be the one *Pausanias* saw in the Street of the Tripods, Athens.

In early art they were depicted as bearded, fat, ugly, old and usually very indecorous. The source of their ugliness was thought to be the fat selini, the older satyrs; the younger ones where called satyrisci. The chief archetype of the satyrs was that ancient Falstaff - Silenus - who was credited with being their father (see below). In some districts of modern Greece the spirits know as *Calicantsars* offer many points of resemblance to the ancient satyrs. They too had goat ears with the feet of asses or goats, were covered with hair, and loved women and the dance.

Herdsmen of Parnassus believe in a demon of the mountain who is the lord of hares and goats. These attributes also belong to Pan and the symbol of the shy and timid satyrs, was the hare. Later Roman writers often confused satyrs with their own fauns, giving them (incorrectly many think), the lower half a goat below the waist. With some of these attributes and their appearance, it is easy to see how the unwary could confuse the satyrs with the god Pan.

In the Authorised Version of Isaiah the word 'satyr' is used to render the Hebrew *se'irim* (= 'hairy ones'), a demon or supernatural being of Hebraic folklore that lives in uninhabited places. 'But wild beasts of the desert shall lie there; and their houses shall be full of doleful creatures; and owls shall dwell there, and satyrs shall dance there.' Isa.13:21. 'The wild beasts of the desert shall also meet with the wild beasts of the island, and the satyr shall cry to his fellow'. Isa.34:14. The custom of sacrificing to the *se'irim* is alluded to in Leviticus, 'And they shall no more offer their sacrifice unto devils, after whom they have gone a whoring.' Lev.17:7, the interpretation is 'devils' but the desire implied is undeniably 'satyric' in its nature.

Rhys points out that the name *ferodyree* or *phynnodderee* was found in the 1819 Manx Bible, in place of satyr. The ferodyree was the name for a hairy being or satyr, similar to the dwarves of Nordic myth and the elves, brownies and cluricanes of the Celts.

SILVANUS/SYLVANUS

SILVANUS (Lat. *silva=* wood) is an old Italian divinity related to Faunus who, according to **Aelian** and **Probus**, was the son of Crathis, an Italian shepherd and a goat. **Aelian** tells a similar legend regarding Pan. Though there are other reports as to his parentage, most say he was established in

Italy only. With the circumstances of his birth he is usually represented as half man and half goat. Silvanus is connected with woods - *Sylvestris deus*. He presided over and cared for the plantations and delighted in trees growing in the wild, and was connected with the boundaries, the fields and cattle. Many Latin words connected with this God's name bear witness to his widespread acceptance, for example. *Sylvanicus*= of or belonging to a wood, *Sylvos*= of trees or woods, woody. In the United States there is Pennsylvania, named in 1682, which name is made up from the name of the founder of the state, William Penn and sylvania= 'Penn's forest or wood.'

This deity is sometimes represented as holding the trunk of a cypress, torn out by the roots, in his hand because he became enamoured of a beautiful youth called Cyparissus of Ceos. Cyparissus was also enamoured of the god Apollo, whose favourite stag he accidentally killed. Inconsolable in his grief, he pined away and was changed into a cypress tree. This legend was thought to have been transferred to Silvanus. Originally Silvanus was a god of woods, plantations, and trees in fields and gardens to whom, in the earliest times, the Tyrrhenian Pelasgians are said to have dedicated a grove and a festival. Subsequently he was regarded as protector of the fields and gardens themselves, also the cattle that grazed in the meadows, specially those in or near woods.

He was simultaneously the guardian of the boundaries between field and meadow; the god of untilled land and land not entirely reclaimed outside the recognised boundaries. Because of this he is partly wild and partly civilized, so he was somewhat feared and propitiated every time new ground was broken or new land cleared of trees. He was particularly feared by children and women in labour or pregnancy. We are told that Silvanus would molest those women in labour who were lying-in, so such women were placed under the care of three deities called Intercido, Pilumnus and Deverra.

To protect the pregnant women against Silvanus, at night three men would go around the house to show that these three deities were alert. First they would strike the threshold with an axe, then with a pestle (= *pilum*) and finally sweep it (= '*deverrere*') with brooms. This showed to Silvanus that the house was occupied and he would not enter. Trees are not cut (= '*caeduntur*') or pruned without an axe. Corn is not bruised without a pestle, nor is corn heaped up without brooms. Therefore, one name of the deities who kept the wood god away from pregnant women lying-in and protected them, was *Intercido* - 'to land or fall between without striking and wounding, specially of missiles, spears, etc.' Although he is citing **Varro**, most of the material about the terror of Silvanus regarding postparturient women is quoted by **St. Augustine**, I am sure for his own purpose. 'Therefore the watch of the just would not prevail against the wrath of this malicious god if there were not several against one to repulse him, who is rough, uncultivated and repugnant, as from the woods, with the signs of cultivation which are opposed to his nature.'

There is an equivalent to Silvanus in modern Greece: the goat-shaped *Koutsodaimoas*, who is described as having a very long chin with a goat's beard, eyes set deep in fibrous hair and the voice of a goat. Not only does this creature assault young girls but he is dangerous to pregnant women, in that he butts their abdomen with his horns.

It appears there is another modern Greek demon, thought by some the equivalent of Pan, known as the *Laboma*, who lives on Parnassus according to the shepherds. They say the demon copulates with members of their flock, which causes the animal extreme pain and it dies soon afterwards. He apparently lures the animals to him by imitating the call of the pipes, or the particular call of the herdsmen. Even when the herdsman is aware of the creature he will not use his gun as many of them have exploded on firing, which has been fatal in some cases to the user.

I am not sure how this little monster was conceived but nothing will convince me that it has anything to do with Pan, if that is the intention. The explanation of the Laboma is wholesome only as far as copulating with the flock, but the way it is done and the results are not. As mentioned often, Pan is a god of fertility of the wild and domestic flocks. However, Pan would have no need to imitate any pipes, why should he? His were the original pipes and being natural, therefore, the response of the flocks would have been the same. The fact that the Laboma causes the animal not only extreme pain after copulation but death is the complete antithesis for the reason of Pan's existence. Pan's existence has been longer and more successful than this creature, who is indeed a demon.

Hyginus tells us Silvanus was the first to set up stones to mark the limits of fields and that every estate had three Silvani. This is reflected by the early settlers in Italy. Their descendants took Silvanus to the far corners of their empire. Even in Britain we have many votive inscriptions to Silvanus.

These inscriptions are as friendly as the deity dwelling outside the new clearing, who was benevolent and protective to the new settler in a strange land. This leading characteristic is reflected clearly in Roman literature. **Horace** writes of the '*horridi dumeta Silvane*' (=horrible, rough thorny wood), but he also calls Silvanus '*tutor finium*' (= the watcher, protector (of the) boundaries, or the horizon which bounds our sight), while for Virgil he is '*arvum pecoralis deus.*' (= arable field/cultivated land of, or belonging to (the) cattle god.) **Agrimensors,** a writer on land measurement, tells us that every estate, farmhouse and every possession should have three Silvani, as follows.

Silvanus domesticus= 'belonging to the household or family'. For the possession itself, to protect the house or farmhouse and all that belong to it, the holding itself, in inscriptions called *Silvanus Larum* and *Silvanus Sanctus Sacer Larum. Silvanus agrestis=* 'pertaining to the fields, or belonging to the country'. He is also called *salutarius=* 'a forester, a verderer, a ranger, a keeper of forest, park or wood,' into whose care the shepherd and his flocks were commended, of the wilder, uncultivated pasture land. *Silvanus orientalis=* 'Eastern, belonging to the East. He that watches over boundaries, the point at which the estate starts.' In this last capacity Silvanus often had groves dedicated to him, on the boundary of the different estates. Therefore Silvani are often spoken of as in the plural. The passage is obscure and is usually taken to mean that Silvanus was worshipped under three different titles, as protector of the family, the cattle and public pastures, boundaries and the possessions.

There is little doubt, as his widespread popularity shows, that the Italians regarded him as one of their most useful deities. This is shown by the extraordinary number of inscriptions regarding him. He is described as the divinity protecting the flocks of cattle, warding off wolves and promoting their fertility. He is described as fond of music; the syrinx was sacred to him and he is mentioned along with the pans and nymphs. Later speculation identified Silvanus with Pan, Faunus, Inuus and Aegipan. He has been called Mars Silvanus (see below), from which it is clear he must have been connected with the Italian Mars. It is further stated that his connection with agriculture referred only to labour performed by men; females were excluded from his worship.

Unlike Mars, from whom he is probably an offshoot, and like Pan, Silvanus never made his way into the towns. Silvanus is almost the only Roman deity who retained his perfectly defined rustic characteristics. Mars is a great god of nature who has been overshadowed by only one aspect of his nature, his warlike attributes. In the hymn of the *Fratres Arvales* he is the 'fierce Mars' (= *jere Mars*). In the prayer of Cato's farmer, directed to be made for the health of oxen, he is named *Father Mars*, the dweller in the woodland that surrounded the agricultural clearing. He was termed Pater like the other gods.

These attributes are strengthened by the artistic representations of Silvanus that show clearly his double nature as deity of both the woodlands and cultivated land. In one hand he carries a young tree (= woodland), and in the other a pruning hook (= cultivated land). In the Latin poets and in works of art, Silvanus always appears as an old man: cheerful, bearing a cypress plucked up by the roots and in love with Pomona, the Latin goddess of fruit trees. During the harvest festivals, farmers, vinedressers and those who had plantations of trees, offer to him on their rustic altars, corn ears, grapes, wine, fruits, milk, pigs and rams.

As with Faunus, Silvanus was identified with Pan and to him, like Pan, the sudden terror caused by the solitude of the woods, groves and the lonely places was ascribed. It was believed there were many Silvani. They were later rather freely identified with the Greek satyrs and selini.

Regarding Aegipan, the Goat-Pan mentioned above: according to some Aegipan is quite distinct from Pan, while others naturally regard him as identical. Although the story is thought late, some make Aegipan the father of Pan and state he was 'like his son in the legend of Typhon, half goat and half fish.' Old works say Pan is so called 'because he is shaped like a Goat, only with a Fishes tail for inventing the trump-marine, the blowing of which caused panic fear. As to shape, he is much the same with Capricorn, a sign of the zodiac. From him were called Aegipane, i.e. Panes Capripedes (Pliny). Beasts like men, having their feet and lower part like Goats. Satyrs, in truth, Devils.' Alternatively they are 'naked people light and nimble, have Goat's feet, with long whisking tails. The Ancients worshipped these Monsters, or Baboons for demigods, or the gods of the woods.' Pliny said they were 'a sort of people in Afrik.' *Dictionarium - Luculentum Novum* (1693).

Zeus was captured in his fight with Typhon and the sinews removed from his hands and feet to prevent him escaping. Some think it was Hermes and Aegipan who secretly restored them to him and fitted them in their proper place, rather than Hermes and Pan (see above). Sometimes Aegipan is thought to be a different name for Silvanus.

SILENUS

Silenus is always prominent in the retinue of Dionysus, whom he brought up and instructed and from whom he is inseparable. Silenus and his sons were held to be primitive mountain people of northern Greece by **Graves**. Like the other satyrs he is given as a son of Hermes by a nymph or Gaia. **Nonnus** calls him a son of Pan and an autochthon. Silenus is a primitive deity in the legends of Asia Minor.

Silenus being a constant companion of Dionysus he is, like the god, said to have been born at Nysa. Hermes 'mingled in love with the nymphs in pleasing caverns,' according to **Homer**. **Diodorus** even represents him as a king of Nysa. He is a divinity of woodland, spring, fountain, a forest god who possessed the gift of prophesying. He was an inspired prophet who knew all the past and the most distant future but, like Proteus, would only impart information under compulsion. People were always trying to catch him to make him prophesy and sing to them, when he would give an account of the creation of the world. This could be done by surprising him in a drunken sleep for then he could be bound with chains of flowers.

He is the reputed inventor of music and he is often mentioned with Marsyas and Olympus as the inventor of the flute, which he is often found playing. Despite the almost constant drunkenness mentioned later, he was said to be extraordinarily wise and regarded as a revered prophet - *In vino veritas*? **Plato** displayed great reverence for his teacher **Socrates** who was likened to Silenus, because of his wisdom, irony and ugliness. Thus Silenus came to represent wisdom that conceals itself behind a rough and uncouth external appearance. This is why he is likened to **Socrates**. Today perhaps we would use the term 'a rough diamond.'

King Midas of Phrygia managed to get him into his power by mixing wine with the spring water where Silenus was accustomed to drinking. Some say Midas found Silenus lying drunk in his rose garden and plied him with more wine and many questions. The king was said to have received some astounding answers, but sadly we can't discover what Silenus told Midas apart from one brief part of the conversation. The question was, 'What is best for men?'

It is said that Silenus paused a long time before answering and then he said 'Ephemeral seed of a toilsome fate and hard fortune, why do ye oblige me to tell ye what it were better for you not to know? Life is most free from pain when one is ignorant of future evils. It is best of all for a man never to have been born...the second is, for those who are born, to die as soon as possible.' Perhaps Midas would have agreed with him after he had been given the gift he requested from Dionysus for the safe return of his old tutor. Midas asked that everything he touched should turn into gold. This was fine up to a point, but it included all his food and drink. Finally he touched his daughter, with the inevitable results. Dionysus was greatly amused by the fate of Midas when he pleaded with him to remove the gift that had become a curse. Dionysus agreed to rid Midas of the requested 'blessing.' He told Midas to wash himself in the source of the river Pactolus near Mount Tmolus. The river became auriferous and the sands are said to be bright gold to this day as the result of freeing Midas of his 'golden touch.'

Silenus often spoke with the great gravity of a philosopher, concerning the nature of things and the formation of the world. Hercules was entertained by the centaur Pholus, on his way to his fourth labour, with wine laid down by Dionysus four generations earlier. Pholus was the offspring of Silenus and an ash nymph. In his work on the *Greek Myths*, **Graves** writes 'Centaurs were often represented as half goat, rather than half horse.' One local tradition tells us Silenus was born at Malea. He was added to the train of Dionysus where he took the role of foster-father, teacher, trainer and constant companion.

He attended the wild army of satyrs and maenads, whose weapons consisted of a staff entwined with ivy and tipped with a pine cone called the thyrsus, swords, serpents and a fearsome bull-roarer. The bull-roarer known to anthropology is a small piece of thin, flat wood shaped like a fish. This is tied to a thong and whirled in the air around the head to produce a loud roaring noise, which is why it is called the *bull-roarer*. The bull-roarer is used by the natives of Australia and other countries, to call the men and to frighten away the women from the religious mysteries; it is known as a turndun. In the Mysteries of Dionysus the Greeks used a kind of turndun, which was called a *rhombos*, Lat. *rhombus*. Gr. *rhombos* - 'spinning wheel,' *rhembo* - 'to revolve.'

Silenus claimed it was he who slew Enceladus during the giants' revolt, when he was fighting at the side of Dionysus. He said he spread panic among the hosts of the giants, with the braying of his old pack-ass but, not unlike Shakespeare's Falstaff, most think he was too drunk, as usual, to know. He is held to have been the one who prompted the god Dionysus to invent the cultivation of the vine, wine making and keeping of bees.

In art he is generally shown as a little, pot-bellied man, with bald head and a snub nose. His whole body is very hairy, though this is not born out, for example, by the beautiful statue of Silenus and the infant Dionysus at the Vatican, a most beautiful work of art. He is inseparable from his skin of wine. With his brethren Silenus is often depicted lying asleep on his wine skin, or sometimes he is bestriding it. He has a great love of music and a special kind of dance is called after Silenus, while he himself is designated as the dancer. Perhaps it is from his skin container and the habits of Silenus we get the common vernacular, said of someone who has drunk rather a lot, 'they've had skinful.'

Silenus is nearly always drunk and so is usually shown being carted around on the back of an ass, because he cannot trust his legs, led and supported by the satyrs or selini. He spends much time educating the child Bacchus, as many statues represent him doing. Later art takes a kinder view of him than given in parts of the above. In Athens, figures of Silenus, standing or reclining, were used as caskets for keeping within them precious pieces of carved work. There were also the Sileni, the plural form which is applied to a group of woodland spirits or semi-deities often confused with the satyrs, to whom they bore a resemblance. However, the selini were older and were differentiated from the goat-like satyrs by their horse-like characteristics. Some say they had the ears of horses, not goats.

In Asia they were regarded as the inventors of native music on the flute and syrinx, being wonderful musicians. They were frequently characterised as wise, drunk and prophetic. This ubiquitous combination of 'wise, drunk and prophetic' must have something going for it for somehow its potential has lasted, even if the results are dubious at times. Their father was Papposilenus, lit. '*Daddy Silenus.*' Papposilenus is represented as completely covered with hair and bestial in form. Silenus had a temple at Elis where Methe - drunkenness personified - stood by his side offering him a cup of wine. With the orderly mind of the Romans we looked to see if Methe, who represented '*personified drunkenness,*' had a companion. He did. It is Kraipale - '*drink and its after effects.*' I think they're still both alive and well!

IBER AND THE LIBERALIA

With so much wine in evidence, perhaps we should mention the ancient Roman festival of the *Liberalia* and the ancient Italian God Liber or Liber Pater. Pater was usually attached to the name and it is rare to meet Liber alone. We will find it is usually the poets who use the name Liber Pater for this deity. The Italians would commonly add the word *pater* (= 'father, sire') to the names of their gods. Although a god of wine, Liber played no part in either of the great wine festivals of the *Vinalia* which were celebrated biannually. Some authorities distinguish clearly between Liber and Dionysus, his Greek equivalent. **Cicero** makes the distinction that Liber was worshipped by the early Italians, with Ceres and Libera.

Liber and the feminine Libera were ancient Italian divinities presiding over the cultivation of the vine and the fertility of the fields. Libera was identified by the Romans with Core or Proserpina, the daughter of Ceres (= Demeter) These three divinities had a temple dedicated to them near the Circus Flaminius, maintained by later rulers. Cicero speaks of Liber and Libera as the children of Ceres, to whom the Romans gave their adoration. They were worshipped under their native name but with Greek rites in a temple on the Aventine and, like Dionysus, they had an urban and country festival. Core means lit. the maiden. Her festival was held under the name *Coreia* in Greece.

The most probable etymology of the name Liber is considered to be from *libere*= 'freely, without let or hindrance.' Some authorities give the name *Liber* as a epithet of Bacchus saying it was symbolic of freedom. *Libo=* 'to pour out in honour of a deity, the make a libation.' Bacchus is said to have received it because he delivered some citizens of Boeotia from slavery, or because wine delivers mankind from the slavery of their cares. The word *liber* is often used as a name for the wine itself.

The festival of *Liberalia* was much the same as the Greek *Dionysia*. Country festivals were held, with unrestrained merriment, at the time of gathering the grapes and straining off the wine. The urban ceremony was celebrated annually. The festival was performed on the 17th of March, in honour of the god Liber in Italian mythology. It was celebrated in honour of Bacchus among the Greeks. These festivals were observed in Athens with greater splendour than anywhere else in Greece. Side by side with the public celebrations, a secret worship of Bacchus (= *Liber*), was performed in the Bacchanalia, which found its way into Rome and into the whole of Italy. The *Bacchanalia* were celebrated by men and women in Italy, outside the cities, and in Rome in the sacred enclosures of Stimula or Semele. They were accompanied by such shameless excesses that in 186 B.C. they were put down, with unsparing severity, by a decree of the senate. Sometimes, with these festivals having so much in common, it is hard to know which of them you are writing about.

The Dionysia was a festival that contained many parts. At first the festival was quite simple. First came a vessel of wine, adorned by a vine branch. After this followed a goat, a basket of figs and *the phallus*. The phallus was borne in solemn procession in the Bacchic festivals and orgies, as an emblem of the generative power of nature. The worshippers would clothe themselves in the skin of fauns, fine linen and mitres and carry a thyrsus with drums, pipes and flutes. They crowned themselves with garlands of ivy, fir and the vine. Some would imitate Pan, Silenus or the satyrs by the manner of their dress, behaviour and mannerisms. Some would ride on the backs of asses, while others would drive goats. Both sexes joined in the solemnity and ran around the countryside crying in a loud voice, '*Evoe Bacche! Io! Io! Evoe! Iacche! Io Bacche! Evoe!*' It was unlawful and forbidden to reveal what was seen or done during the celebration.

All the celebrations of the Greek god of wine were said to be done with great licentiousness that, it was claimed, corrupted the morals of both sexes and people of all ranks. Finally the state intervened and when the festival was reinstated, it was with more control and gravity. This is only a brief summary of the proceedings, which were extensive.

The *Oschophoria* was celebrated during Pyanepsion (October-November), when the grapes were ripe. It was named after the vine with grapes on them. These grapes were carried in a race from the temple of Dionysus, in a southern suburb of Athens, Limnae, to the sanctuary of Athene Sciras, in the harbour town of Phalerum. The bearers and runners were twenty youths (= epheboi) of noble descent whose parents were still living. The victor received a goblet containing wine. He also received cheese, meal, honey and an honorary position in the procession. They had a great feast and sacrifice when the race was over, moving from the temple of Athene to the temple of Dionysus.

The smaller or *Rustic Dionysia* was held during Poseideon (December-January) at the tasting of the new wine. It was celebrated with much rustic merriment throughout the country districts. They sacrificed a goat to the god followed by feasting and revelry, with the festival lasting many days. The *Haloa, Harvest-home* or - *the feast of the threshing floors* - was celebrated at Athens to Demeter and Persephone during the same month. As mentioned earlier, the country festivities were held with unrestrained merriment at the time of the grape gathering. The priestesses of Liber, in the Liberalia, were old women crowned with ivy, who made cheap cakes of meal (= *libeis*) ar d sold them in the streets with honey and oil. There they cooked them on little pans or portable fireplaces, for the purchasers.

In Rome, the boys took their *toga virilis* or *toga libera* on this day. This was assumed by a youth in his 16th year and involved sacrifice on the Capital. Slaves were permitted to speak with complete freedom, not unlike the Saturnalia. At this time they introduced the ivy of Dionysus. Everything had the appearance of freedom and they offered sacrifices on the mountains.

According to **Varro**, on the festival days of this god, the Phallus was carried in procession on a carriage. It was taken through the fields and lanes about Rome, then into the city itself. He adds that in Lavinium, where the festival lasted a month, the most indecent language was used while the Phallus was carried through the market. Then, one of the most respectable matrons was obliged to place a garland on it in public. This, most likely, was a practice derived from earlier times. The emblem of fructification was supposed to exert a beneficial influence on the fields and promote the production of the fruits of the earth. It is thought the name Liber or Liberius signifies 'to pour out, in honour of a deity, to make a libation, to offer, dedicate, consecrate' - from libo. He was probably a god of productiveness by moisture.

In Athens, during Gamelion (January-February), the *Lenaea - the feast of the vats* - was held at the oldest and most venerated sanctuary of Dionysus in the city. A banquet of meat was provided at public expense, with the usual processions and revelry. The *Anthesteria* was celebrated for three days. On the first day, the *Pithaegia - the opening of the vats*, the casks were opened and master and servant alike tasted the new wine.

On the second day - the feast of the beakers - a public banquet was held during which a beaker of new wine was set before each guest. One most important part of the ceremony was the marriage of the Basilissa, or wife of the Archon Basileus (the chief magistrate), with Dionysus. The *Basilissa* was regarded as representing the country. This took place in the older of the two temples in the Lenaeon, which was never opened save for this occasion.

The last day of the festival was called Chytroi - the feast of the pots. On this day they made offerings of cooked pulses in pots to Hermes, in his office as Psychopomp (= '*the guide of the dead*'); the pulse was also offered to the souls of the departed. In particular the offering was for those who had perished in the flood of Deucalion. The great urban Dionysia was held in Athens for six days during Elaphebolion (March-April) with great ceremony and was similar to the festival described above.

THE HORAE

Pan was often found in the company of the Horae. Zeus' second wife, after Metis, was Themis, until she was replaced by Hera. Themis was especially honoured in Athens, Delphi, Thebes, Olympia and Troezen. With Zeus, Themis was the Law that regulated physical and moral order. She represents divine justice in all its relationships to mankind. In works of art Themis is represented as a woman of commanding and awe-inspiring presence. She holds a pair of scales and a cornucopia, and sometimes a sword, the symbols of the blessings of order.

She protected the just and the oppressed and punished the guilty. Her name was Soteria - *the protectress* - and as such she was honoured in many towns. Themis presided over public assemblies and was called Euboulos - *the good counsellor*. She had the power of foretelling the future and consequently the Delphic Oracle was in her possession for a time before it passed into the hands of Apollo. It is no surprise, therefore, that her children should be the Horae or Seasons, the goddesses of order in nature because they caused the various seasons to change in their regular course, which is symbolically described as 'the Dance of the Horae.' With the Charites, Hebe, Harmonia and Aphrodite, they accompany the songs of the Muses and they dance to Apollo playing on the lyre.

They saw to it that all things blossomed and ripened at their appointed times, especially at spring and autumn. Sometimes they were regarded as an abstraction rather than a concrete personification. In **Homer**, who gives them neither genealogy nor names, they are mentioned as the handmaidens of Zeus. **Hesiod** notes them briefly as 'the children of Zeus and Themis,' entrusted with being the custodians and guardians of the gates of Olympus, which they open and close by scattering or condensing the clouds. They are weather goddesses sending down or withholding the fertilizing dew and rain, and yoking the horses of Pheobus at the approach of morning.

Hesiod describes the Horae as giving to a state and its people good laws, justice and peace. He calls them Eunomia (= *Order*), Dike (= *Justice*) and Eirene (= *Peace*) who, he tells us, watch over the works of mortal men. By an unknown poet the Horae are called the daughters of Chronos (= Time), and by later poets they were named the children of the year, and their number increased to twelve. Some made them seven or ten in number. The Horae seem to have been originally regarded as the presidents of the three seasons in which the ancient Greeks divided their year, spring, summer and winter. Some think the choice of three is probably another instance of Greek partiality for that particular number and its multiples, as with the three Horae, Moerae (= Fates), Charites (= Graces), the nine Muses, etc.

The number of the Horae is different in different writers. The most ancient number at Athens seems to be two, elsewhere in Greece it was three, like that of the Moerae and Charites. They were also worshipped at Argos, Corinth and Olympia. At Athens two Horae, Thallo (= the Hora of Spring) and Carpo (= the Hora of autumn), were worshipped from very early times, their temple at Athens contained an altar of Dionysus Orthus. Thallo is the 'goddess of the flowers of spring or Bloom-giver,' it is she who accompanies Persephone every year on her ascent back from the lower regions. Therefore the expression 'The chamber of the Horae opens' could be the equivalent of our phrase, 'spring is coming.' The second Hora is Carpo, 'the Fructifier, the goddess of the fruits of autumn.'

They were thought to promote the prosperity of everything that grows and they appear as the protectresses of youth and new born gods. On being admitted to the epheboi the youth of Athens took a solemn oath in the temple of Agraulos at which they swore by the Hora Thallo and the other gods. At this time they received their first suit of armour and took the oath to defend their country to the last. In a long protracted war, Athens was told by an oracle, the conflict would cease if someone would sacrifice themselves for the good of their country. Agraulos came forward and threw herself from the Acropolis. In gratitude the Athenians built her a temple with a festival and mysteries in honour.

To the two Horae of Athens was sometimes added Auxo (=*'increase'*) who is the goddess of the growth of plants, although Auxo is one of the two Charites at Athens; this might have been done to make the number agree with the tripartite year. When an Athenian youth took his civil oath, he invoked Hegemone (= *'queen'*), the leader or ruler of the Athenian Charites.

Under Alexandrian influence and in later mythology, the Horae were recognized as four in number, distinguished by the attributes of the seasons we recognize, those of spring, summer, autumn and winter. Order and regularity being indispensable conditions of beauty it was easy to conceive the Horae as beautiful young females with lovely hair and golden diadems. Because they were thought to be inseparable from the idea of springtime, they were light, moving creatures. According the Hesiod, 'They mellowed the behaviour of men.' The Horae were the companions of the Graces and nymphs, with whom they are often confused. They were the companions of the superior deities that were connected with the spring growth of the vegetation, such as Demeter and Dionysus.

An annual festival was celebrated in honour of the Horae at which their protection was sought against drought and the scorching heat. Offerings were given of boiled meat, thought to be less insipid and more nutritious than roast meat. They are frequently represented as the daughters of Zeus and Themis who watch over the field operations of mankind. When their sphere of influence was extended, from presiding over the order of nature, to the events in human life, this invested them with moral attributes and order.

The attributes of spring, the flowers, fragrance and graceful freshness were transferred to the Horae. Thus they adorned Aphrodite as she rose from the sea. They made a garland of blossoms for Pandora and their influence was even transferred to inanimate objects that were said to derive their innate charm and beauty from the Horae. Hence they bear a resemblance to the Charites and they are frequently mentioned with them. Often the two groups were confounded.

The Moerae (= Fates) and the Horae regulated the destinies of man and watched over the new born. They secured good laws and saw to the administration of justice. Dike, like her mother, presided over legal order and was found enthroned with her mother at the side of Zeus. The Fates or Moerae were said to be the children of Themis, as were the Hesperides. The Greek word from which the Horae take their name, signifies time, (Lat. *hora*, hour), which term can be applied to a year, a season, even an hour.

'Universal Pan,
Knit with the Graces and the Hours (= Horae) in dance,
Led on the eternal spring.' **Milton.**

When the day was divided into twelve equal parts, each part took the name of Hora. **Ovid** describes them as placed at equal intervals on the throne of Phoebus (= a special name for Apollo, as god of light), with whom are also associated the four seasons. The Greek poet Nonnus, a native of Panopolis, in the Dionysiaca, unites the twelve Horae representing the day with the four Horae as the seasons, in the palace of Helios (= the Greek Sun-god).

DEMETER/CERES

Demeter is one of the great divinities of the Greeks. The name is usually thought to derive from be the same as the Greek for 'Mother Earth.' Her name implies that she is a giver of barley or food, the gift of Demeter. She was the daughter of Cronos and Rhea, sister to Hestia, Hera, Hades, Poseidon and Zeus. As with all the children of Cronos she was devoured by her father, but he 'gave her forth' after taking an emetic that was administered by Metis. At the wedding of Harmonia Demeter fell in love with her brother Iasion. 'In a thrice ploughed field' she became by him the mother of Pluton or Plutus in Crete, according to **Homer.** Zeus killed Iasion with a lightning bolt because of this, although there are other contenders for his death. By Zeus she gave birth to Persephone and by Poseidon, Despoena (= 'the ruling goddess or the mistress'). This name appears as an epithet of several divinities, such as Aphrodite, Demeter and Persephone in one version.

Plutus (= the god of riches) was regarded by the Greeks as a fickle divinity, never there when you wanted him. They portrayed him as blind because he distributed his bounty indiscriminately. He was lame because he was slow in coming and only came gradually. He was given wings to intimate he flew away faster than he came. If you can tell me a better description of wealth or money, I would like to hear it.

Demeter and her daughter Persephone are so closely connected that it would be difficult to write of one without the other. The most prominent part of the Demeter/Ceres story is the abduction of her daughter Persephone/Proserpina by Hades/Pluto to his underworld kingdom. Unknown to Demeter, Zeus had promised her daughter to Hades. The unsuspecting maiden was out on the Nysian plain with the Oceanid nymphs, gathering flowers which Zeus had created to tempt her and to aid the scheme of Hades. Persephone had plucked a rose, a violet, a crocus and a hyacinth when she beheld a narcissus of surpassing size and beauty.

To 'all immortal gods and mortal men' this narcissus was an object of amazement. There were one hundred flowers growing from a single root. Unconscious of the danger she was in, the maiden stretched forth her hand to collect the wondrous flower. When she took it, the earth gaped wide and Hades in his golden chariot caught the terrified goddess and carried her off shrieking for help. She was not heard or seen by gods or mortals, save two. Hecate heard her cry as she sat in her cave and Helios, whose eye nothing on earth escapes, saw what happened. Hades came out of the bowels of the earth and took her.

With a flaming torch in her hand Demeter wanders nine days over the earth. She tastes neither nectar or ambrosia nor enters the bath, while she seeks her daughter. **Cicero** tells us that Ceres meets a youth who ridicules her because she drinks so avidly when tired and afflicted in her vain pursuit, and she turns him into an elf for his taunts. On the tenth day she meets Hecate, but she cannot say who took her, for she heard but did not see. Together the two goddesses travel to Helios who sees all that happens on earth. They both stand in front of his horses and she learns the truth as the god of the sun tells her what she wants to know. Not only had her daughter been taken by the god of the underworld, it had been with the consent and connivance of Zeus. She avoided all contact with Olympus in her wrath, leaving the Gods there in little doubt of her anger. She abandons the society of the gods and wanders about among men as an old woman.

The absence of the goddess causes the general failure of the crops and the people of the Earth are in danger of slow death by famine, but none know of the place of her retreat. In one popular legend it is while Pan is out hunting that he chances to see her and passes on the information to Zeus who sends the Fates to her. They persuade her to remit her anger and cease her mourning. She was worshipped at this cave under the name - Black. Her statue was clad in black with the head and mane of a horse, says **Pausanias**.

In another version, under the name of Deo or *The Seeker*, she receives kindness and comfort in Eleusis. In one tale she meets a mythical woman called Baubo, who is sometimes called 'the nurse of Demeter.' This version says that while searching for her daughter Demeter was received with great kindness and hospitality by Baubo, who offered her something to drink, but this was refused because of her great grief. Baubo 'made such a strange gesture that the goddess laughed and accepted the draught.' It has been said that Baubo raised her clothes over her head and exposed her genitals, perhaps reminding Demeter, like Pan, of her purpose which is the fecundity of life or simply rustic and baudy humour. I think Victorian probity may have Bowdlerised such a passage in many earlier works of myth and legend. In a fragment of an Orphic hymn there is added a boy named Iacchus who made an indecent gesture at her grief. These later stories, concerning the reception of Demeter at Eleusis are thought to be inventions to give mythical context to the jokes in which the women indulged at the festival of this goddess.

Another, to me more plausible account, is that of Iambe who is a serving maid. She is the daughter of Pan and, with her rustic humour, manages to get Demeter to smile, then laugh. The Queen of Attica discovers Demeter in the act of anointing and putting her son Demophoon (Triptolemos in some versions) in the flames to make him immortal. The gift is prevented by the mother's fear, but Demeter says he will be famous for his having been held and nursed by her.

She had been anointing the baby with ambrosia and holding him to her breast, and at night placing him in the fire. Because she had lost her daughter she had taken great comfort in tending the new-born child. She revealed her true nature and the blessing she had intended for the child 'who throve like a god,' but the natural concern and interference of the mother stopped her completing the process. The parents built a temple in honour of the goddess. This story has been dealt with in the section on Pan.

Zeus acceded to the demands of Demeter that her daughter be permitted to spend two-thirds of the year with her, above the earth. This was during spring and summer. During the transition of autumn and then in winter, Persephone had to return to spend her time under the earth with Hades. This was because she had eaten some pomegranate seeds while there, or because Hades had secretly placed the seeds under Persephone's tongue in full knowledge of what he had done and why.

There is a very old and traditional admonition never to eat anything in a place you are uncertain of, specially salt and bread. Salt has many meanings attached to it, the main one being its incorruptibility that preserves from decay. Salt typifies friendship and wisdom. To eat another man's salt was to establish a mystical bond between the giver and the receiver. This pact, if accepted, was regarded as an inviolate bond that could not be broken with impunity or safety. To eat the salt of the king was to owe him the utmost fidelity. Eating salt and bread together was to make an unbreakable bond of friendship.

Once it was the salt-cellar that told you in what esteem, if any, you were held by your host. To sit *above the salt* was a place of distinction. Formerly the family *saler* (= salt-cellar) was an impressive mass of silver and was placed in the centre of the table. Those of distinction were set above the saler, that is between the saler and the head of the table. The 'dependants and inferior guests,' sat 'below the salt.' This gave us the expression 'to sit above the salt.' Despite this bond of friendship, to help someone to salt was to 'help one to sorrow' and this was once a firmly accredited belief. When a witch cursed land, making fruitful land barren, she would sprinkle it with salt as did the armies of some nations to the land of their enemies. 'And Abimlech fought against the city all that day; and he took the city, and slew the people that was therein, and beat down the city, and sowed it with salt.' Judges.9:45.

With the agreement that Persephone was to spend the better part of her time on earth, Demeter permitted the earth to be fruitful again. Although Demeter was a goddess of the earth it was, more accurately, 'the earth in fruitfulness.' These ideas were extended to all aspects of fertility in both natural and human affairs and accordingly Demeter was looked upon as the goddess of marriage and worshipped, especially by women. Her priestesses initiated young, married people into the duties of their new situation and responsibilities.

On her return to Olympus she left the gift of corn and agriculture. Demeter left her holy mysteries with her hosts, the king, the queen and the people who befriended her in her time of need at Eleusis, in Attica. She sent Triptolemos, the Eleusinian, around the world on her chariot drawn by serpents. He was to diffuse the knowledge of agriculture and the other blessings that accompany it, such as the settlement of fixed places of abode. The most ancient seats of her worship were Athens and Eleusis, where the Rharian plain was solemnly ploughed every year in memory of the first sowing of wheat. *Rharius* was an epithet of Demeter from this plain in Eleusis, the prime seat of her worship. It was here that Rhea descended to gain conciliation with Demeter, and where she first let the fruits of the fields grow again. Cakes of barley, grown on the Rharian plain, were used on the third day of the Eleusinia. The Eleusinia was one of the greatest festivals and Mysteries to be held in Greece. It is too extensive to be gone into here. Worth noting is the seventh day of the festival, when the initiated were returning to Athens. There would be outrageous raillery and jests, specially when they rested on the bridge over the Cephisus. Here they would pour forth their ridicule on those who passed by. This was to honour Iambe and her service to the goddess when she gave Demeter the gift of healing laughter.

The myths of Demeter and her daughter Persephone embody the idea of the productive powers of the earth and nature resting or being concealed in the earth during the winter season. Persephone ate, or was given, pomegranate seeds under the earth. The pomegranate is an abundant seed fruit that she takes into herself during her time under the earth. In the fullness of time, the vivifying seeds germinate and strive ever upwards from the darkness into the animating light, which nourishes all living creatures with its fruits.

Statues of Demeter are always in full attire; she is never found partially clothed. Her attributes are ears of corn (= a symbol of fruitfulness), a basket of fruit and a little pig. Emblems of mystic significance were the torch and the serpent, living in the earth. It symbolises the renewal of life by shedding its skin, or giving up the old to take on the new. Demeter is represented as the friend of peace and a law-giving goddess. Sometimes in her hands she has some poppies, which now enter folklore.

An ancient Greek legend tells us the poppy was created by Hypnos, the personification and god of sleep. The ancients described the Greek god Hypnos as the brother of Death and a son of Night. In works of art Sleep and Death are represented alike as two youths sleeping in the arms of their mother, or holding inverted torches in their hands. Hypnos gave Demeter the flower of sleep and oblivion because of its narcotic qualities. The qualities of the flowers relieved her of her weariness during her nine day search for her lost daughter. The Roman god of sleep, Somnus, is depicted by Ovid dressed in black but with his robe scattered with stars, wearing a crown of poppies and holding a goblet of opium juice.

On the tenth day she learned of her daughter's fate and was angry with Zeus for permitting the act of violence, in which state she could not make the corn to grow. Hypnos gave her poppies to help her sleep and, with renewed strength, she made the corn grow again. Although modern farmers would not agree, the presence of poppies growing among the cornfields to the farmers of old was considered beneficial to the welfare of the corn, and a blessing of Demeter.

Poppies were associated with fertility, as were most of the many seeded plants. The seeds were used to flavour foods; for example they were given, with honey, to the athletes training for the Olympic Games. However, they are still considered plants of ill-omen and it is thought best to leave them and not to bring the blossoms into the house.

The Romans received the worship of Demeter to whom they applied the name of Ceres. The first temple of Ceres in Rome was built to avert a famine due to war and, with the introduction of this foreign divinity, the Romans responded in their usual efficient manner. According to **Wm. Smith**, 'In introducing this foreign divinity they instituted a festival with games in honour her (= Cerealia), and gave the management of the sacred rites and ceremonies to a Greek priestess, who was usually taken from Naples or Velia, and received the Roman fanchise, in order that the sacrifices on behalf of the Roman people might be offered up by a Roman citizen. In all other respects Ceres was looked upon very much in the same light as Tellus. Pigs were sacrificed to both divinities during the sowing season, harvest time and the burial of the dead. Smith also thinks it was strange to find that the Romans, in adopting the worship of Demeter from the Greeks, did not at the same time adopt the Greek name of Demeter, saying, the name Ceres can scarcely be explained from the Latin language.

Carphori was a name given to Demeter and Persephone in Tegea from the influence that they possessed over the fertility and produce of the earth. *Demeter Proerosia* or *Prerosia* was an epithet of Demeter at her festivals that were celebrated in Athens and Eleusis before the sowing of the corn. At the temple of Megara, the name given to Demeter was *Demeter Mallophora*, because she taught the inhabitants the usefulness of wool and the advantages to be gained from tending sheep. This temple was very old at the time of **Pausanias**, when it was already falling into decay. Megara was a city of Megaris and was situated equidistant from Corinth and Athens.

The festival of Ceres, the date of which is doubtful but is thought to be the ides or the 13th of April, was the Cerealia. Another festival to Ceres was held in August. The Cerealia was celebrated by the women to honour the search and eventual reunion of Ceres with Proserpina. Fasting for nine days, the women, clothed in white and adorned with crowns of ripe corn ears, ran about the city with lighted torches. Then they offered to the goddess the first fruits of the harvest. After 191 B.C., a fast (= *ieiunium Cereis*) was introduced by command of the Sibylline Books. This was originally kept every fourth year, but in later times was kept annually on the 4th of October. I have given more information regarding the Sibylline books at the end of this section as an short addendum, see 'Notes on the Sibylline Books.'

The native Italian worship of Ceres was probably maintained in its purest form in the country where she was offered a sow and the first cuttings of corn. The *Lityerses* were the songs of the reapers, either in honour of Ceres who presided over the corn or in remembrance of Lityerses the son of Midas who was killed by Hercules. These songs were later borrowed by the Greeks and applied to the songs that the reapers sang when harvesting.

Another festival of Demeter/Ceres was the *Mysia* celebrated by the inhabitants of Pellene in Achia. This was held to honour Demeter Mysia. It lasted seven days in a temple surrounded by a beautiful grove. On the first two days the men and women celebrated together, on the third day the men left the sanctuary leaving the women to ceremonies held at night. During this period not even male dogs were permitted to remain within the sacred enclosure. On the fourth day the men returned to the temple to be greeted with shouts of laughter and assailed each other with various railleries. This is reminiscent of Iambe and Demeter. The many epithets of Demeter here were thought to be derived from the Greek to '*cloy*' or '*to satisfy*' because, of the Gods, the goddess was among the first to satisfy the needs of men by giving them corn.

An important festival of Demeter/Ceres was the *Thesmophoria*, which was also a epithet of Demeter. This was given in honour of the goddess, and has been mentioned earlier. The festival was observed with great solemnity by all the major cities of Greece, especially Athens. The worshippers were freeborn women whose husbands were obliged to defray the expenses of the festival. These women had to be of genuine Attic birth and of spotless reputation, though some ceremonies were performed by maidens. They were helped by a priest who carried a crown on his head and the priestess who conducted the festival had to be a married woman. They had to dress in spotless white robes to intimate similar purity and observed the strictest chastity.

During the period of the festival they had to scatter their beds with agnus castus and fleabane and any such herbs that would 'have the power of expelling libidinous propensities.' They were solemnly charged not to eat pomegranates nor to wear garlands on their heads, because they had to conduct themselves with the greatest solemnity. However, it was usual for them to jest with one another as Demeter was made to laugh by the jesting of Pan's daughter Iambe. It was held from the 9th to the 13th of Pyanepsion (October-November) with some authorities saying from the 11th. Some particulars mentioned by the ancient writers regarding the Thesmophoria are not possible to put in place, as to how they were connected with the festival or on what day they took place.

As the goddess of fertility Demeter was in many regions associated with Poseidon, the god of the fertilising water. This was particularly the case in Pan's Arcadia, where Poseidon was regarded as the father of Persephone. She was joined with Dionysus, the god of wine. Demeter is connected with the lower world under the name of Chthonia. It was to her care that people committed the seed of life and the dead.

Addendum: Notes on the Sibylline Books

N.B. Those readers already familiar with the subject of the Sibylline books could, without detriment, omit this section and move directly to the next section, the Nymphs/Dryads/etc.

In Roman history the Sibylline Books are often met with. Sibyllae, in the singular, Lat. *sibylla*. Gr. *sibulla*, from the Doric *sio-bolla=theoboule*, 'the will of God.' The name was given in antiquity to inspired prophetesses of some deity, often Apollo. The Sibylae were women who were inspired by heaven with the knowledge of futurity, although sometimes they were young maidens. Dwelling in lonely caves or by inspiring springs they were possessed with a spirit of divination, and gave forth prophetic utterances while under the influence of enthusiastic frenzy. They existed in different parts of the world and there is no certain record of their names, country or date. The first Sibyl, from whom the rest are claimed to have derived their name, is said to be a daughter of Dardanus and Neso.

Some authors mention only four Sibyls, however, it is more commonly believed that their number was ten. The Sibylline Books were a collection of oracular utterances composed in the time of Solon and Cyrus, at Gergis on Mount Ida. They are ascribed to the Hellespontic Sibyl, who was buried in the temple of Apollo at Gergis. These eventually found their way to Rome during the reign of the last king.

According to legend, the Cumaean Sibyl, the most famous of their number, offered to Tarquinius Superbus nine books of prophecy. When the king declined to buy them, because of the exorbitant price she solicited, she left and burnt three of them. Then she returned with the remaining six and demanded the same asking price. Again the monarch disregarded her and she left, taking the six books with her. She burnt another three and returned yet again, persisting with the asking price for the original nine books, even though only three were left. The monarch was astounded at her behaviour and this time he bought the last three for the original price. The Sibyl vanished and she was never seen again. A college of priests was created called the Decemviri (= a commission of ten) and later the Quindecemviri (= a college of fifteen men in commission) to take possession of the works and care for them.

Tarquinius had them preserved in a vault, a stone chest, under the Capitoline temple of Jupiter. The use of these oracles was from the outset reserved for the State and they were consulted when it was in imminent danger. They were not consulted for the foretelling of future events, but only when singular calamities took place, such as pestilence, or earthquake, as a way of expiating portents. It was only the rites of expiation prescribed in the Sibylline Books that were passed on to the public, not the oracles themselves. The Books were recognised as sacred and worshipped with due ceremony.

As mentioned above, Tarquinus entrusted the care of the volumes to a special college. At first these were two men of patrician rank. After 367 B.C., their number was increased to ten, five patricians and five plebeians. Subsequently their number was still further increased to fifteen (= quindecemviri); but at what time is uncertain. We read of the quindecemviri in the time of Cicero (ad Fam. viii. 4), it appears probable that their number was increased from ten to fifteen by Sulla, especially as we know that he increased the numbers of several other ecclesiastical corporations. Julius Caesar added one more to their number; but this precedent was not followed, as the collegium appears to have consisted afterwards of only fifteen. They were, in fact, considered priests of Apollo, whence each of them had in his house a bronze tripod dedicated to that deity.

They held their office for life and were exempt from all other public duties. Their sole responsibility was the safety and secrecy of the books, consulting them at the expressed command of the Senate and interpreting the utterances found in their pages.

The Sibylline Books were destroyed in the burning of the Capitol in 83 B.C. The Senate sent envoys to make a collection of similar oracular sayings from divine places. particularly from Ilium, Erythrae and Samos. This new collection was placed in the restored temple, with similar sayings of native origin.

There is a collection of poetical utterances in Greek which was compiled between A.D.138-167. The collection is said to comprise of eight or twelve books and pertains to the later empire, and included the sayings of Jesus Christ. It was entitled *Oracula Sibyllina* - which has no connection with the original Sibylline Books. The authenticity of these later works is questionable. They are said to have been composed partly by Alexandrian Jews and partly by Christians in the interests of their respective religions. They contain a medley of pretended prophecies. Some of these describe, in greater detail than any chapter of the Bible, the coming of the Saviour, his teaching, suffering and death. The manner of writing makes most commentators consider them the work of the followers of Christianity, desirous of showing the heathens the error of their ways, by helping the truth along with unalloyed artifice.

NYMPHS/DRYADS/ETC.

In Greek mythology the name nymph is the generic name of many female divinities sometimes described as a being of *inferior rank*. I dislike the use of the word 'inferior' for the nymphs as much as I do for Pan. They are frequently designated by the title Olympian and were called to the meetings of the gods of Olympus. They are described as the daughters of Zeus. The nymphs are the personification of the creative and fostering activities of nature, dwelling on earth within groves, on the summits of mountains, besides and within rivers and streams, in glens and grottoes. All regions of the earth and water were peopled by these beautiful female forms. They each had their allotted places of abode and specific charges.

The Mountain-nymphs were the *Oreiades*; the Dale-nymphs who haunted the valleys were the *Napaeae*; the Mead-nymphs who took the meadows were the *Leimoniades*; the Water-nymphs of the rivers, brooks and springs were the *Naides/Naiades*; the Lake-nymphs of lakes and pools, were the *Limniades*. We find the Tree-nymphs, the *Hamadryads* who were born with and died with their trees. The Wood-nymphs were the *Dryads* who looked after woods, glades and the trees, especially oak trees. The Fruit tree-nymphs were the *Meliades*, especially the ash tree, they also watched over the gardens. The Flock-nymphs who looked after the flocks, particularly the sheep, were the *Epimelides*.

Early in the history of Southern Italy the Epimelides nymphs were dancing on the Sacred Rocks in Messapia. Not knowing who they were some young shepherds said they could dance better; of course they could not and they were vanquished. The nymphs told them, 'O youths, you have been contending with the Epimelides nymphs! You shall therefore be punished.' The shepherds instantly became trees where they stood at the temple of the nymphs and to this day, writes **Nicander**, 'a voice as of lamentation is heard at night from the grove.' The place is called the place of the Nymphs and Youths.

The nymphs loved Terambus the son of Euseirus and Eidothea, and grandson of Poseidon. He dwelt at the foot of Mount Othrys in Thessaly. Terambus tended his flocks on the mountain under the protection of the nymphs whom he delighted with his songs. Perhaps these nymphs were of the order *Perimelides*, the name given to those nymphs who presided over the sheepfolds in the country. Pan loved Terambus also and warned him to drive his flocks down into the plain as a severe winter was coming. Terambus, elated with the confidence of youth and lacking the experience of age, ignored the advice of the friendly deity and even went as far as to mock the gentle nymphs. He even said they were not the daughters of Zeus. Soon the presage of Pan came to pass. The winter came and all the streams and torrents were frozen. The snow fell in great quantity and Terambus and his flocks disappeared with all the paths and trees.

We read the nymphs changed Terambus into the animal (insect?) called by the Thessalians - *kerambyx* - or a cockchafer 'of which the boys make a plaything, and cutting off the head carry it about; and the head with the horns is as the lyre made from the tortoise.' So says **Antoninus Liberalis**. Ovid tells us of Cerambus on Mount Othrys, who escaped the Deucalionian flood by means of wings that had been given to him by the nymphs. Other authorities give the same story, sometimes saying he is changed into a bird, but they place it on Mount Parnassus before the deluge. Others writers say Terambus and Cerambus are the same.

Deucalion, in Greek mythology, was the son of Prometheus and Clymene. Zeus decided that mankind had become degenerate and they should be destroyed. This destruction would be achieved by a great flood. Deucalion, on the advice of his father, built a wooden chest in some accounts and a ship in others, in which he saved himself and his wife Pyrrha. After nine days they finally landed on Mount Parnassus and made sacrifices to *Zeus Phyxius* (= 'the god who protects fugitives'), who sends help by flight. In some versions others also escaped and made to safety on other mountains. Any differences in the story are usually attributed to local traditions. For example, the inhabitants of Delphi were said to have been saved by the howling of wolves that led them to the summit of Parnassus.

Deucalion asked the oracle of Themis at Delphi how the human race could be renewed. He received the answer that Pyrrha and he should veil their heads and throw behind them the bones of their mother. They had some misgivings regarding this, thinking they had misunderstood the priestess. Eventually, they agreed that the priestess was referring to stones, which they accordingly threw behind them. The stones of Deucalion turned into men and those of Pyrrha into women. A later version places animals in the story. Dangerous and tame animals lived in perfect harmony on the ship during the journey, before being let loose. The world's deluge myths have remarkable similarity, as will have been already noted by the reader I am sure.

The word nymph signifies 'a bride, a mistress' derived from 'to cover or veil.' It was gradually applied to married or marriageable young women, with the idea of youth always included. The nymphs are found in various relationships with both gods and men, and their liaisons are many. They were given the task of rearing both gods and heroes and they were nurses to Dionysus, Pan and even the great Zeus, Aristaeus and Aeneas. The tended to the needs of the goddesses, waiting upon Hera and Aphrodite and, in the attire of huntresses, they were found in the company of Artemis.

The nymphs were of divine nature and they were present when Zeus called his councils. Despite their divine origins they frequently 'blessed the bed' of heroes and many a warrior who fought before Troy could boast descent from a Naiad or a Nereid.

The homes of the nymphs were found on mountains, in groves, by rivers and springs, in valleys and in cool shaded grottoes. Among the many graceless and brutal divinities were found the nymphae, properly 'the young maidens,' who were distinguished by the special appeal of their beauty and youth. They were frequently found in the retinue of some divinity of higher rank, particularly Apollo, Artemis, Dionysus, Hermes and Pan. The nymphs of Dionysus' retinue were in all points similar to their sisters who peopled the rivers and springs.

The nymphs appeared as the benevolent spirits of these sites and led a carefree life of liberty. Sometimes they were found weaving in grottoes, dancing, singing and watching kindly over the fate of mortals. Like the nymphs in the retinue of Artemis and Apollo they were tutelary deities of the forests and mountains. The nymphs are usually well disposed towards mortals and ready to help them. They are regarded as a beneficial and protective influence. The *Homeric Hymns* tell us,

'They rank neither with mortals nor with immortals; long indeed do they live, eating heavenly food and treading the lovely dance among the immortals, and with them the Sileni and the sharp-eyed Slayer of Argus mate in the depths of pleasant caves; but at their birth pines or high-topped oaks spring up with them upon the fruitful earth, beautiful, flourishing trees, towering high upon the lofty mountains (and men call them holy places of the immortals and never mortal lops them with the axe); but when the fate of death is near at hand, first those lovely trees wither where they stand, and the bark shrivels away about them, and the twigs fall down, and at the last the life of the Nymph and of the tree leave the light of the sun together.'

After the introduction of their cult into Latium, the Greek nymphs were gradually absorbed into the ranks of the indigenous Italian divinities of springs and stream. Among these was Juturna, an old Latin goddess of fountains who, as beloved of Jupiter from whom she received her immortality, received dominion over all the rivers and waters of Latium. There was a well at Latium that was famous for its healing and its water was used in nearly all sacrifices, a chapel being dedicated to its nymph at Rome in the Campus Martius. Juturna being a goddess who ruled water, she was, with Vulcan, often invoked at any outbreak of fire. A pond in the forum, between the temples of Castor and Vesta was called *Lacus* (= any hollow, hence a basin, tank, tub, especially a wine vat). She was sometimes called the wife of Janus and by him was the mother of Fons or Fontus, the god of springs. The *Juturnalia* was celebrated on the 11th of January, by the state and private citizens. Egeria, a goddess of fountains, who was also a goddess of childbirth, possessed the gift of prophecy.

Fons or Fontus, had an altar on the Janiculum, which derived its name from his father Janus and on which Numa is believed to be buried. The name of this divinity is connected with *fons*= 'a well,' and he was connected with flowing waters. Fontus is the Latin god of springs and at the festival of the Fontinalia garlands of flowers were laid around the springs and wells, some being thrown into them. This festival was held in his honour on the 13th of October.

The Lymphae, Lat. *lympha*= 'water, especially, pure or spring water' originally Lumpae, were Italian water-goddesses who, owing to the accidental similarity of the name, were identified with the Greek *nymphae*. Among the Romans their sphere of influence was restricted and they appear almost exclusively as divinities of the element of water. The number of nymphs is infinite and they are divided into two great classes. The first class embraces those who are regarded as the lesser divinities of nature and were worshipped as such.

In all aspects of nature the early Greeks thought there was some visible manifestation of the deity. Therefore, caves, grottoes, springs, trees and mountains to them were fraught with life, the embodiment of the divine agents of the deity. The powers of nature, and the emotions engendered by the contemplation of nature, awe, delight, joy, reverence and terror, were personified and ascribed to the direct agency of these many divinities. Those nymphs that comprised the second class were the personifications and guardians of tribes, races and states, etc.

As indicated at the beginning, the various forms of the nymphs, the oreads, dryads, nereids, naiads, etc., owe their origin to the animism that believes that every natural object is endowed with a living spirit. This remains a pleasing and endearing trait of old Paganism. It loved to trace every *modus operandi* in nature directly to the influence of a specific deity or group of deities.

The unfettered imagination of the Greeks peopled the earth, sea and sky with deities to whose agency it was thought the laws of Nature responded. When we are feeling philosophical and reflective we may conclude, with some regret, that the lost feeling of the heart was too great a price to pay for the cold intellect of the head. It is foolish, in the writer's belief, to think Pan and the nymphs have been banished. They are a part of our psyche that we may neglect but we cannot destroy them. Although we may not know it at the time any loss is ours, not theirs, and we are throwing out the proverbial baby with the bath water.

When we respond to Nature, no matter how slightly, listening to rain instead of cursing its inconvenience, hearing the wind through leaves, reacting to or tending a special tree or garden, watching the cycle of Nature through her manifold creations, becoming concerned about conservation and pollution or wanting to save a tree or a wood in the way of a road, have no doubt that Pan and the nymphs are working within us. Not unlike the yeast that makes bread rise, Pan and the nymphs make us rise and try to do something, and suddenly you find out they always were there, patiently waiting.

You cannot invoke Pan without invoking the nymphs and if you invoke the nymphs, Pan will be there somewhere on the periphery, watching and taking note. In one legend he was born of a nymph, so the nymphs are a part of him and he is part of them. Many nymphs are found fleeing from Pan but do not read too much into this as so many do. Pan is *active* and the nymphs are *passive*. Flight is an essential part of the inherent behaviour of the nymphs. Not only did they flee from Pan - *they flew from practically everyone*. We can find them in flight from Apollo, Hermes and Zeus, which is only a very short list showing this behaviour. There is, of course, the playful aspect of love often expressed as 'chase me, chase me!'

With Pan the flight may be caused by the panic he excites within people and nature, for he is all-embracing and very few of us can respond to this form of ecstasy. The measure of love is said to be what we are prepared to give up for it. Many seek this 'great love' thinking it would be divinely sent, which it would be, if it was granted. Frequently it is too powerful and overwhelming an emotion and very few are strong enough to handle it. This is why great loves and lovers are so few, and often end in tragedy. It is something the participants usually cannot sustain when they are given it, and something the world cannot understand because they are not. People who are in the grip of this most powerful of all the emotions will often sacrifice all on its altar. Again, this is something the majority cannot understand. The enthusiasm of love is balanced in its intensity only by its opposites of hate and revenge, the dark side of the coin. An intense all-consuming love has long been considered akin to madness by most of humanity who do not understand it, and nor do the majority want to. It fascinates them in the extreme, but I think it frightens them the same way, it demands too much which they are not prepared to give.

There has long been a belief the nymphs and deities could be contacted and persuaded to help the suppliants in their aspirations and their life. People offered up sacrifice and honour to them, individually or with the other, greater gods. For example, for Hermes and Pan the sacrifices usually consisted of goats, lambs, milk and oil. However, wine was never offered to the nymphs, this was often left for Pan. The nymphs and Pan are the powers of nature personified: make contact with them and you make contact with Nature - or vice versa.

In time the spirit separated from its environment. The dryad for example inhabits its sacred oak tree but only so long as the oak itself is animated. The indwelling spirit has not yet become immortal for the dryad or hamadryad cannot outlive the oak. Popular belief assigns to the nymphs an exceedingly long life but they do not possess immortality.

The nymphs of the first classification can again be divided according to the various areas of nature they represented. Now let us deal with some nymphs of the watery element. The sea-nymphs were the daughters of Oceanus and so they were the oceanids. Oceanus is the god of rivers, but not in the modern sense. In the notion of the ancient Greeks the whole world was surrounded by the river Oceanus. In **Homer**, Oceanus appears as a mighty god who yields to none but Zeus. **Hesiod** calls him a son of Uranus and Gaia and the oldest of the Titans. From his marriage with Tethys sprang some three thousand rivers and an equal number of oceanids. Rivers were represented by the Potameides who, as local divinities, were often named after their rivers, for example the Acheloides, Pactolides, etc. Even the rivers and waters of the infernal regions were accredited with having their own nymphs. Therefore, we find *Nymphae inferiae paludus* (lit. 'the nymphs who offer sacrifices to the dead in the country full of marshes, fens or lakes') or *Avernalis* (= of or pertaining to Lake Avernus: *Sibylla*, dwelling by the lake). Avernus is the name of lake in Campania, which the Latin poets describe as the entrance to the lower world, or as the lower world itself.

Perseus, collecting the items needed to cut off Medusa's head, had to obtain them from the Stygian nymphs and only the Graeae knew where to find them. These three sisters of the Gorgon had only one eye and one tooth that they had to share among them. Perseus stole the solitary eye as they were passing it from one to the other, and he would not return it to them until they had told him the whereabouts of the nymphs.

Many of these nymphs presided over water or springs that were thought to inspire those who drank from them. Because the nymphs were deemed to have prophetic powers, it was thought they inspired people and gave them the gift of poetic arts. Inspired priests, priestesses and soothsayers were often said to be possessed by the nymphs, which meant they were rapt or entranced.

The nereids were the nymphs of the Mediterranean, which was

often called the 'inner sea.' These nymphs were born from the union of Doris, a goddess of the sea whose name is sometimes used for the sea itself, with her brother Nereus, from whom they got their name. From their marriage came their daughters, some fifty in all, attendants of the sea-goddess.

Nereus is usually represented as an old man with a long flowing beard and long hair that is azure in colour. Though his realm was the Mediterranean, his main home was the Aegean Sea so he is sometimes called *Aegeus*. He lived surrounded by his loving daughters, who could be found dancing around him, singing their chorus. Nereus had the gift of prophecy to a remarkable degree and to those who consulted him he revealed what fate was imminent for them. As with his wife Doris the name of Nereus was used as a name for the sea itself. He was often called 'the most ancient of gods.'

The naiads were the nymphs of fresh water, of springs, streams, wells and fountains. They were deities of the nourishing and fructifying water. They were rich in their favours, giving increase and fruitfulness to plants, herds and mortals alike. In art they are often depicted as drawing water or carrying water in an urn. The names of some nymphs have been handed down to us. We have Daphne for the laurel, Philyra for the linden, Rhoea for the pomegranate and Helike for the willow. It was assumed that the existence of the dryads was closely bound up with the growth and decay of the tree in which they dwelt. When the nymphs were stationed in trees and forming part of it, they were deemed to be hamadryads. The dryads, crowned with oak leaves and sometimes armed with an axe to punish any outrage against the tree(s) they guarded, could be found dancing around the oaks sacred to them.

It is the dryad who decides whether the cuttings we take from the trees are 'deadwood' or 'livewood.' If the wood is taken incorrectly it most certainly will be 'deadwood' and definitely so if taken without the dryad having first giving her permission, or if it is not taken at the correct time. Therefore, the wood will have little worth, as a wand for example, to a practitioner of Nature, an Occultist or Magician. It will have had the life-force withdrawn from it when it was cut, and will have become deadwood.

This is why it is often quite pointless to touch wood for luck or protection, particularly as most of the wood touched is deadwood. The dryad is not there, so if possible always touch living, growing wood or wood taken with permission. In passing, the woods used to 'touch wood' should be the sacred trees such as oak, ash, hazel, hawthorn, apple or willow for the Pagans. For the Christians it is the 'woods from the four quarters of the globe' that traditionally made up the Cross - *Ligna crucis palma, cedrus, cupressus, oliva* - palm, cedar, cypress and olive.

An old master carpenter told me that wood had to be 'put up properly' when putting in doors, windows or making anything of wood, particularly in the days before carpenters had ready made windows and standard sizes from a factory as now. He was called in to fit doors and windows into the holes the builder left him, as my grandfather did, as a master carpenter. Each window was tailor-made to the builder's or client's requirements.

He, like my grandsire, said you had always to make sure the wood was the right way up, particularly if it was a front door that governed your going out and coming in. The wood had to be the right way up and not be installed upside down or it would be an unhappy house, with everything and everyone in it equally upside down. The grain of the wood had to be as it was when the tree was growing in the wild, otherwise you were insulting the spirit of the tree every time you entered the house and if you did do this he said - 'be sure that no good would come of it!' If I were making a wand of wood, first choice hazel, I would attempt to know the correct way of the grain and that would be symbolized on the wand to show me the grain direction. The grain of the hazel wand pointing away from the operator is for *repelling operations*; the grain pointing toward the operator, for *operations of attraction*. One is bringing to and the other is taking from.

The nymphae enjoyed divine honours from early times, originally at the places where they had power: the fountains, groves and grottoes. As their influence was exercised in all departments of nature, they frequently appeared in the company of higher divinities, for example with Apollo, the prophetic god and protector of the herds and flocks. The nymphs were also found with Artemis; the huntress and protectress of game. Finally they were found with the Sileni and the satyrs, with whom they join in their Bacchic dances and revels. The nymphs of forests, groves and glens were also thought, like Pan, to appear and frighten solitary travellers.

In later times they had their own shrines built to them, even in the cities, called *Nymphaea*. These were eventually enlarged and became magnificent buildings in which it was customary to celebrate marriages. Goats, lambs, oil and milk were offered to them. Works of art show the dryads as charming maidens, naked or lightly clad, bearing flowers and garlands.

As said earlier, hamadryad wood nymphs lived and died with the tree to which they were attached. The hamadryad is the presiding deity of the tree and shares its joy and sorrows; whatever wounds the tree wounds the hamadryad, whatever kills the tree kills the nymph. The hamadryad was implanted in the tree and part of it. They were often shown as female down to the waist with their lower extremities as trunks and/or roots. The hamadryads were esteemed by both the gods and men. They possessed the power to reward or punish those who prolonged or abridged the existence of their associated tree.

In the famous *Homeric Hymn* to Aphrodite, they are spoken of as neither mortal nor divine. The nymphs tasted immortal food and mated with the sileni and the sons of Zeus. This is one of the most accurate descriptions of them. Aphrodite, when she tells Anchises that she is pregnant and of her shame at having it known among the gods, says of the child:

> But him, when first he sees the sun's clear light,
> The Nymphs shall rear, the mountain-haunting Nymphs,
> Deep-bosomed, who on this mountain great
> And holy dwell, who neither goddess
> Nor woman are. Their life is long; they eat
> Ambrosial food, and with the Deathless frame
> The beauteous dance. With them, in the recess
> Of lovely caves, well-spying Argos-slayer
> And the Sileni mix in love. Straight pines
> Or oaks high-headed spring with them upon
> The earth man-feeding, soon as they are born;
> Trees fair and flourishing; on the high hills
> Lofty they stand; the Deathless' sacred grove
> Men call them, and with iron never cut. But when the Fate of death is
> drawing near,
> First wither on the earth the beauteous trees,
> The bark around them wastes, the branches fall,
> And the Nymph's soul at the same moment leaves
> The sun's fair light.

Aphrodite entrusted her infant Aeneas to the care of the hamadryad of the wooded Ida. While tending her father's flocks on Mount Oeta in the company of the hamadryads, the nymph Dryope was seduced Apollo. He approached her as a tortoise that Dryope put to her bosom, then changed into a hissing serpent to chase away the hamadryads; after that, he 'enjoyed her.' Dryope bore him a son Amphissus who founded the city of Oeta and there, in the temple of his father, his mother served as priestess, until one day the hamadryads stole her away and left a poplar in her place.

The dryads are the nymphs least taken with human beings, keeping themselves rather aloof from our affairs. As previously mentioned, the nymphs were wooed, won, bedded and wedded by gods and mortals alike. From these unions sprang many heroes and unusual people. If they display antipathy it is not because they are openly hostile. They are merely uninterested and so they tend to disregard us. It is not unheard of, however, for them to take an interest in individuals or communities and if they do, they will grant considerable help and benefits. The ancients often called the nature spirits the Hooded Ones because frequently their faces were hidden beneath the shadow of a cowl, not unlike that of a monk. It is discourteous to try to see their faces, unless they offer you the privilege. This is why they are often reported as standing just behind the person, who can turn and see the figure, but not beneath the cowl.

VERTUMNUS

Vertumnus, or Vortumnus according to some authorities, is a god like Mercurius, a deity presiding over merchandise. He had a temple in the vicus Tuscus and originally he was worshipped in the form of a rough wooden post, until a beautiful bronze statue was made of him that stood in the vicus Jugarius near the altar of Ops, where considerable trade went on. He was, on this account, regarded as the protector of business and exchange.

Sacrifice was offered to him in his chapel on the Aventine, on the 13th of August. **Varro** in one place says he is a Tuscan god and therefore his statue was in the Tuscan street in Rome. In another he places him among the gods worshipped by the Sabine king Tatius. **Horace** uses Vertumni in the plural, and the scholiast observes that his statues were in almost all of the municipal towns in Italy. Vertumnus - possibly from *verto*= 'the turner, the changer, the god who changes or metamorphoses himself' - is thought to be the translation of a Tuscan name. The most likely hypothesis, apropos this god, is related to all the occurrences to which the verb *verto* applies.

He is the deity presiding over such matters as the changing seasons, purchase and sale, the return of rivers to their proper beds, etc. In reality the god was connected with the transformation of plants and their development, from blossoming to bearing fruit. He presided over the changing year, in particular over the fruits of the earth whether in orchards or gardens. This metamorphosis is shown in the story of Vertumnus and his love for Pomona. She was not very enamoured of him and he changed himself into many forms to gain her favour. He finally gained his objective by turning himself into an old woman who extolled the virtues of marriage, especially marriage to Vertumnus, with whom she then fell in love.

Gardeners offer him the first produce of the gardens and garlands of budding flowers. The general populace celebrated the Vortumnalia on the 23rd of August, which denoted the transition from the beautiful season of autumn to a much less agreeable one. Many authorities give the date of October as his annual festival, somewhat resembling the harvest festival. He is often presented like Saturn, as a gardener and a cultivator of the soil, a wreath composed of ears of corn on his head, fruits in his lap and a pruning knife in his hand. His worship was important in Rome and this is borne out by the fact that he was attended by his own *flamen* - the *Flamen Vortumnalis*.

POMONA

Pomona is the Roman divinity presiding over fruit trees - from *pomun=* 'fruit of any kind, apples, cherries, nuts, berries, figs, dates, etc.' - therefore *Pomorum Patrona*. She was initially a hamadryad before she yielded her affections to Vertumnus. Pomona was dedicated to the cultivation of gardens and orchards to which she confined herself, shunning all forms of society with the male deities. She is represented by the poets as have been beloved by several rustic divinities, such as Silvanus, Picus, Vertumnus, the Pans and Satyrs, Priapus and others. It was Vertumnus who eventually won her.

Sometimes he came to her as a reaper, a hay maker, a ploughman or a vine dresser. As mentioned above, at length he chose the guise of an old woman who won the confidence of the goddess. 'She' enlarged on the evils of a single life and the blessings of wedded bliss, launching into the praises of Vertumnus in particular. By telling the tale of the punishment for female cruelty to a lover, 'she' moved the heart of Pomona. When 'she' weakened her resolve he resumed his real form and clasped her to him for Pomona was no longer the reluctant nymph.

Her worship was a long-standing one in Rome where she had a *Flamen Pomonalis* who sacrificed to her every year for the preservation of the fruit. Pomona's worship, like that of her husband Vertumnus, was of great importance. It is possible that Pomona may have been a personification of Ops. Art represented her as a fair damsel with fruits in her bosom and a pruning knife in her hand. At times she has a horn of plenty filled with fruits of the earth, and a dog at her side.

FLORA

Flora is the goddess of flowers and a very ancient Italian deity who was honoured by the title *Mater*. Flora, the goddess of spring, was also worshipped under the title of Chloris, the goddess of buds and flowers. Chloris was loved by both Boreas, the north winter wind, and Zephyrus, the west spring wind; she chose Zephyrus and became his faithful wife. For those interested the other two winds are Eurus the East wind and Notus the South. In one account they are all committed by Zeus to the charge of Aeolus. Elsewhere they appear as independent personalities. They carry out their activities at the command of Zeus and the other gods, and are invoked by men with prayer and sacrifice. In works of art the winds are usually represented with winged head and shoulders, open mouth and inflated cheeks.

Those writers whose object was to bring the Roman religion into contempt, tell us that Flora, like Acca Laurentia, was a courtesan who accumulated a large property and bequeathed it to the Roman people. She did this in return for being honoured by the annual festival of the Floralia. However, Flora's worship was established at Rome from very early times. A temple was given to her by king Tatius and Numa appointed a flamen to serve her, which is usually the mark of a respected worship. The resemblance between Flora and Chloris led the later Romans to identify the two deities. Chloris was also a goddess flowers and the personification of the spring season. By Zephyrus she was mother of Carpos (=*fruit*) and she is connected with the lower world under the name of Chthonia. Her temple in Rome was situated near the Circus Maximus.

The *Floralia* or *Florales Ludi* was the festival to honour both Flora and Chloris. It was solemnized during five days starting on the 28th of April and ending on the 2nd of May. The festival was begun at Rome in 238 B.C., at the command of an oracle in the Sibylline Books, to obtain the protection of the goddess Flora for the blossoms. The Floralia was ended for a time but was reinstated by command of the senate in a year when the blossom suffered severely from hail, rain and winds. It was often conducted, some thought, with excessive revelry, drinking and lascivious games. The Floralia was originally a festival of the country people that was later, in Italy and Greece, introduced into the towns, where it assumed a more dissolute and licentious reputation. The country people continued to celebrate them in their own happy, more sober way.

ACHELOUS/ACHELOOS and the Sirens

Rivers, springs and wells have been mentioned frequently throughout the work. It would be difficult to write of the Kingdom of Nature, fertility and growth without mentioning that most precious element of life for us all - water. Representative of this is Achelous, the god of the river Achelous which was the greatest and, according to tradition, the most ancient of the rivers of Greece. He, with three thousand brother rivers, is variously described as the eldest son of Oceanus and Tethys, Oceanus and Gaia or of Helios and Gaia. There are also other versions of his origins. When Achelous lost his daughters - the Sirens - in his great grief he invoked Gaia and she received him to her bosom. At the place where she received him, Gaia caused a river to gush forth bearing his name. Some say his daughters sprang from the blood that ran from the horn that was torn off his head by Heracles, as will be recounted later.

The Sirens are described by **Homer** as dwelling between Circe's island and that of Scylla, on an island where they sit in a flowery meadow, surrounded by mouldering bones on men. With their sweet song the allure and infatuate those who sail, 'their voice stilled the wind,' according to **Hesiod**. **Plato** places one of them on each of the eight celestial spheres where their voices form what is called the music of the spheres. Whoever listens to their song and draws near them never again beholds wife and child. They know everything that happens on earth. They were only to live until someone passed their island unmoved by their song. Odysseus did this and Orpheus protected the Argonauts, with the result that they cast themselves into the sea and were changed into sunken rocks. They are represented as great birds with the heads of women or the upper part of the body like that of a woman, with the leg of a bird; with or without wings. Later they were regarded as keeping their original character of fair but cruel temptresses and deceivers. They are generally represented as singers of the dirge for the dead, and they often appear as ornaments on tombs, or as symbols of the magic of beauty and eloquence. On this account they could be seen on the funeral monuments of fair women and girls, orators and poets, for example, **Sophocles**.

Achelous was a competitor with Heracles to win the hand of Deianeira. She was a daughter of Althaea by Oeneus, Dionysus or Dexamenus. Achelous fought with Heracles but he was conquered in the contest though he had the power to metamorphose. He took the form of a serpent, a bull-faced man and then a bull and it was in the latter form that Heracles beat him. As a bull he was deprived of one of his horns which, however, he recovered by giving up the Horn of Amalthea. According to **Ovid** the Naiads changed the horn that Heracles took from Achelous into the horn of plenty.

Strabo proposes a highly ingenious interpretation of the legends about Achelous that, according to him, arose from the nature of the river itself. The noise of the river resembles a bull's voice. The winding and reaches of the river produced the story about his forming himself into a serpent. **Ovid** says about the horns that the formation of the islands at the mouth of the river provided the explanation. His conquest by Heracles lastly refers to the embankments by which Heracles confined the river to it bed. Thus he gained large tracts of land for cultivation that are expressed by the horn of plenty. **Strabo** explains the fable by describing the frequent inundations of the river. He tells of the disputes between the neighbouring nations of Aetolia and Acarnania concerning the compass of their borders. These continued until the causes of their quarrel were removed by the labours of the hero, who constrained, by strong dykes and solid banks, the waters in their proper channel.

Others derive the legends about Achelous from Egypt and describe him as a second Nilus. Nilus, the god of the river Nile is said to have been a son of Oceanus and Tethys and father of Memphis and Chione. **Pindar** calls Nilus a son of Cronos.

However, Achelous was from very early times considered a great divinity and was invoked in prayers, sacrifices and on taking oaths, etc. As the oldest and most venerable of river gods, he was worshipped throughout Greece and her colonies, especially at Rhodes, Italy and Sicily. The oracle of Dodonean Zeus, in every answer it gave, added the injunction to offer sacrifice to Achelous. The wide extent of the worship of Achelous accounts for his being regarded as the personification of *sweet water*, that is, *the source of all nourishment.* In religious usage Achelous stood for any stream or running water.

GAIA/GAEA/GE

The Greeks, when they considered the creation of the world, generally appeared to be satisfied with the explanation and Theogony as given by the poet *Hesiod.* In similar fashion to the story in the Bible, their world began from Chaos, a shapeless mass, that was also 'without form and void.' The first to be created were the spirit of love, Eros, and the personification of the earth, Gaea, Gaia or Ge - 'the broad chested.' There are some who say she came first. She gave birth to Uranus and Pontus. To Gaia black sheep were sacrificed and she was invoked along with Zeus, the Sun, Heaven and Hell, by people taking oaths. Next followed Erebus who was the primeval darkness. The word Erebus is commonly used of the lower world filled with impenetrable darkness. Nyx, Nox or Night is night personified, and she was born next. According to the Orphics she was the daughter of Eros, though sometimes she is said to be without any husband. **Hesiod** places the abode of Night in Tartarus, behind where Atlas supports the heavens. Night and Day, he says are there by turns; when one goes in the other goes out. Day bears light to mortals. Night 'wrapt in a sable cloud carries Sleep in her arms.' The union of Day and Night gave us Aethyr who is the clear sky.

Gaia married her son Uranus, and was the mother of many beings, but her children were hated by their father. Therefore, Gaia concealed them from him in the bowels of the earth. Grieving at the fate of her offspring, she made a huge flint sickle and gave it to her sons, desiring them to take vengeance on their father. It was Cronos who undertook the task of mutilating Uranus.

Those drops of blood from Uranus that fell upon the earth (= Gaia) became the seeds of the Erinyes or Eumenides (= *the angry goddesses or curses*), the Gigantes (= giants) and the Melian nymphs (= *the nymphs of the ash from which the shafts used in war were fashioned*). Thus it was that Spirit (= *heaven/Uranus*) and Matter (= *earth/Gaia*) were 'divorced' or separated and the period of evolution started, because the time of involution had ceased. Matter was impregnated with the qualities and forms later to be evolved, and this is world-wide symbolism.

Later Gaia became the mother of other children by Pontus (= *the personification of the sea*). Various other divinities and monsters sprang from her, such as Typhon and Cecrops. As Gaia was the source from which arose the vapours that produced divine inspiration, she herself was regarded as an oracular divinity. She was held to be the first to possess the Oracle of Delphi and in early times, an oracle at Olympia.

Gaia belonged to the *Deoi Chthonioi*= 'the gods of the earth,' which requires no explanation. Therefore, she is frequently mentioned when they are invoked. The many surnames and epithets given to Gaia are a reference to her character as the all-producing and all-nourishing mother - *mater omniparens et alma*. She was predominantly honoured as the mother of all, who nourished her creatures and poured rich blessing upon them.

She is often found presiding over marriages. Her worship was almost universal among the Greeks and she had altars and temples at Athens, Bura, Delphi, Olympia, Phylus, Sparta, Tegea and many other places. We know statues of her existed, for example at Athens where

Servius tells us she was represented by a key, according to the records. However, none of them seem to have survived or come down to us. We know that at Patrea, in the Temple of Demeter, she was represented in a sitting position. In Athens in particular, she was worshipped as *Kourotrophos* or 'the nourisher of children.' Simultaneously she was the goddess of death. It was she who summoned all her creatures back to her and hid them in her bosom.

At Rome the earth was worshipped under the name of Tellus - a variation of Terra. In Rome she was regarded as an infernal deity mentioned with Dis and the Manes; see the next entry. As Uranus was eventually superseded by Cronos, so Gaia the primitive mother of the earth finally gave way to Rhea.

TELLUS MATER

The deity Tellus, another form of terra, is the name under which the earth was personified among the Romans, as Gaia was among the Greeks. Often she is called Tellus Mater and she is the most ancient of all the gods after Chaos. She is often mentioned in contrast to Jupiter, the god of the heavens, and connected with Dis and the Manes. When an oath was taken by Tellus or the gods of the nether world, people stretched their arms out with the palms down. When swearing by Jupiter and the gods of the heavens, they stretched arms out with the palms up.

While we are the subject of ritual it may not be remiss to digress a little at this point to discuss the subject, the better to aid our understanding. It was the custom of the Greeks to raise their hands and face the East, while the Romans turned to the North. A suppliant who is praying to or invoking any sea deity would stretch their hands towards the sea. Sometimes those suppliants who were invoking the gods of the lower worlds would beat the earth with their hands. This was sound practice, with no pun intended. If the prayers were given in a temple the suppliant would naturally turn to face the image of the deity. Any other stance would be regarded as disrespect that could result in rejection or punishment. If the suppliant was in great suffering, they would come carrying an olive branch or rod around which they had entwined some wool, not unlike the original caduceus. They would then throw themselves on the ground before the sacred image and embrace the feet.

Offerings typically were fruits, cakes and wine, while others could be animal sacrifices that would be led to the altar decked with ribbons and garlands. After due ceremony had been observed, the animals would be slain and a part of the flesh placed on the altar fire. It is not quite certain how the gods took their share of the sacrifice, like the libations of wine, though with burnt offerings the smell of the sacrifice was presumed to be agreeable to the gods, not unlike the incense and burnt offerings of the Hebrew altars.

When an animal was selected for this purpose it was a healthy one with the age, colour and sex appropriate to the deity for whom it was intended. The time of the day was important. If the ceremony was for the gods of the heavens then the morning was chosen but if it was for a deity of the lower world, the evening would be used. To the chthonic deities the victim was always offered in its entirety for it was not regarded possible 'to share the feast with the company of men.' The wood for the fire was carefully chosen as the fire was regarded as holy. It was fed with wood appropriate to the god, that would give a pure flame.

Regarding the pure flame of fire the Romans would never extinguish a lamp, but would 'suffer it to die out of itself.' This, whenever it is practicable, is my own rule. One of the reasons for this was that it was thought that all flame was of kindred stock: the fire of Prometheus stolen from heaven for which the Titan had to pay so dear. That same divine fire had been lit in the human breast. It was regarded as symbolic of the Gods, and so one should not injure it, nor harm or destroy anything that lives unless it harms us first. Fire was regarded as a living creature. It had need of nourishment as we did, without which, it perished. It was self-moving and, when it was extinguished, it uttered a voice as if it had been slain.

The custom was also taught that neither fire, water or any other necessary thing should be injured after it had served its turn or purpose. Others that needed it were allowed to make use of it and it was relinquished to them when no longer needed. You never stirred a fire with a sword. The augury lamp had its rules, for the lamp was an emblem of the body that holds the soul. The soul within is as a light and the intelligent and reasonable part of it should always be open, so no cover was put on the lamp, nor was it enclosed or blown out. These were some of the practices they taught their augurs when they went out for observation: not to go out when the winds were blowing, but to go in calm weather, when they were able to use their augury lamps open and uncovered.

Sacrifices could be performed spontaneously apart from the regular occasions, particularly when it was felt some blessing had been bestowed by the gods, or if the person performing the sacrifice was atoning for some sin of which they were conscious. Usually sacrifices were made at some given time, as with the sowing of the fields or the time of harvest, the beginning of a venture or a battle, to sanctify a treaty or seek purification for a crime. The herdsman would sacrifice the first born of his flock, the merchant part of his profits, the soldier part of his booty, the farmer part of his crop, etc. As the gods were considered the source of all blessings and prosperity so it was thought that they expected their due of these benefits, while punishing instances of disrespect and neglect.

For those sacrifices performed by people to the gods of the underworld, there was the belief that if the blood of the victim was poured into a hole in the ground it would sink down to them and be accepted. In the same hole or another, the ashes from the sacrificial altar were buried. If the deities being invoked were of the sea or rivers, their portion was sunk in deep water.

The Greeks and Romans combined a beautiful practicality with their prayers to the gods, even to the extent of having an altar 'to an unknown God,' not 'to the unknown God.' After all, there might be more than one who had been missed out: no fools the Ancients, this was just in case anyone had been glossed over. One of the more usual forms, which admirably shows this, is a favourite of mine - 'Zeus, our Lord, give unto us whatever is good, whether we ask it of thee or not; whatever is evil keep from us even if we ask it of thee.'

Let us remain with the last lines given above regarding methods of worship and prayers a mite longer. All religions of the past took great pains to address their gods correctly, as we all do today; in the Lord's Prayer we say 'hallowed by thy name.' A recent report tells us the Methodist Church has given permission for God to be called 'Mother.' This, in part, is probably an attempt to make female worshippers feel happier and more comfortable. However, this would have been a baffling solution to what would have been a simple problem for the Ancients. Now the One God of the Methodists has become the 'Two Gods' - one sex for the males and one sex for the females - with each praying to their individual god. This is likely to satisfy some form of correctness or to deal with what may be thought of as an old prejudice, though it appears to be done more for the sake of the congregation, not for God. It seems to be a modern method of attempting to *degender* God, along with everything else. It would appear more to separate than unite for it gives them one god apiece - most egalitarian.

I feel, however, **Aeschylus** did the job much better with, 'Zeus, whoever thou art, and by what ever name it pleases thee to be named, I call upon thee and pray.' This could be simply modified to read - 'God, whoever thou art, and by whatever gender it pleases thee to be named, I call upon thee and pray.' After this all-embracing and genderless introduction, you got on with your praying whatever your gender. I feel this would have satisfied the Ancients because I believe they would have understood it better. The Methodists have used the either/or solution and not the sometimes more satisfactory either/and alternative. I write 'sometimes' for obviously it does not always work, but I think it more satisfactory on the whole than - this or that!

The either/or concept attempts to solve most of its problems by replacing one stereotype or imbalance with another, usually its direct opposite; assuming, I think, with equal simplicity that one automatically cancels the other, thus automatically solving the problem. I have written 'I think' because any book is largely a combination of facts, theories and interpretation of what the writer thinks. This makes the writer popular with some and an idiot to the others - either/or!

This problem was adequately covered in Greece, according to **Lempriere**, by holding the festival of the *Theoxenia*, which was celebrated in honour of *all the gods, in every city in Greece,* particularly in Athens. Games were observed and the winner received a large sum of money. The Romans had the *Pandiculares*, days on which sacrifices were made to *all the gods* in common. However, this is yet another digression, as if that has ever stopped me; now let us quickly return to the subject of the chapter.

A festival in honour of Tellus was held on the 15th of April, which was called the Fordicidia or Hordicidia, from fordus or hordus - 'a bearing cow.' At the time of sowing and harvest, in private life, sacrifices were offered to Tellus. Another occasion was when a member of the family had died without due honour having been given to them. The sacrifice was made to Tellus, for it was she who received the departed into her bosom. At the festival of Tellus, and when sacrifices were offered to her, the priests also prayed to a male divinity of the earth called Tellumo, who was also worshipped.

When the temple of Tellus was dedicated at Rome in 268 B.C. an earthquake occurred, so it is no surprise to find her invoked on such occasions. She is a goddess by whom, as the common grave of all things, solemn oaths were sworn with the Manes of Jupiter. As with the Greek Demeter, Tellus was worshipped as a goddess of marriage. She was highly revered in her conjunction with the earth mothers. Tellus is the same divinity who is honoured under the several names of Cybele, Rhea, Vesta, Ceres, Tithes, Bona Dea, Proserpina, etc.

Tellus is usually represented as a woman with many breasts, distended and flowing with milk to express the fecundity of the earth. She appears crowned with turrets, holding a sceptre in one hand and a key in the other, expressive of her sovereignty and of the treasures that she (= the earth) contains. At her feet lies a tame lion without chains, to intimate that every part of the earth can be tamed and made fruitful by means of cultivation. As a goddess of fruitfulness of the fields and cattle, festivals were held to ensure fruitful harvests and fertility among the cattle and other livestock.

In her honour was held the festival of sowing - *feriae sementivae* - celebrated during January at the end of winter seed time and held on two consecutive market days. The dates were fixed by the Pontifex - *pontifex*= 'bridge' - a member of the highest priestly college in Rome to which belonged the supervision of all sacred observances, whether performed by the state or the individual. The *Paganalia* was a movable festival held simultaneously by the Pagus (= the scattered, small, old village communities of the country), when a pregnant sow was sacrificed to Tellus and Ceres. Besides these there was the feast of Fordicidia or Hordicidia (mentioned above) at which cows in calf (= fordae) were sacrificed to the goddess.

This was held on the 15th of April to ensure a time of plenty during the year and was celebrated under the management of the pontifices and the Vestal Virgins, partly on the Capitol in the thirty curiae - the thirty parts into which Romulus divided the Roman people - and partly out of town. The ashes of the unborn calves were kept by the Vestal Virgins. These ashes were used later at the feast of the Palilia or Parilia on the 21st of April, during the purification rites to honour the Italian goddess Pales.

The *Palilia* or *Parilia* was properly a herdsman's festival to promote the fruitfulness of the flocks, to purify the sacred groves and fountains from all unintentional injury or pollution caused by the herds. It was believed to be the anniversary of the founding of Rome, 'the former abode of shepherds,' and was celebrated in Rome and the villages by all the inhabitants. Pales, the god(dess) of shepherds is described by some as a male and by others as a female; some writers consider Pales was a combination of both sexes. Some of the rites observed at the festival of Pales make some think the divinity was female. Others point out there are reasons for assuming a male divinity. The god was, with the Romans, the embodiment of the same idea as Pan among the Greeks. The date of the festival was chosen because it was the birthday of the city of Rome, on the 21st of April. Early tradition has it that this was the day Romulus commenced the building of Rome; therefore, this date is the *dies natalius* of Rome. Some of the rites customary in later times were said to have been first performed when he fixed the *pomoerium* or *pomerium*. The Pomoerium is an interesting conception. It is the name given by the Romans to the space, along the city wall, within and without. This space was left vacant, free of all buildings, and reckoned holy. It was marked off by stones (= *cippi* or *termini*) and in respect to the auspices formed the limit between city and country. An extension of the Pomoerium was only admissible on the ground of an extension to the legal boundaries of the Empire.

The name Parilia is thought to be derived from *pario* (= 'to bring forth, to bear; of animals, to drop, lay, spawn etc.'), because the sacrifices offered on that day were *pro* (= 'before') *parturio* (= 'bringing forth, producing young') *pecoris* (= 'cattle') or - pregnant! The festival itself was quite extensive and celebrated differently in Rome to the rural areas. It was customary to purify the house, the steading and sheep with sulphur, rosemary, fir-wood and incense. As expiation they offered incense with a mixture of the blood of the October horse. This was a horse sacrificed to Mars, the blood of which was collected and preserved in the temple of Vesta to be used at the Palilia for the purposes of purification.

The ashes of an unborn calf, which was burnt at the feast of Tellus at the Fordicidia or Hordicidia, were kept by the Vestal Virgins. These ashes were used for purification at the feast of Parilia when they were used with bean straw, also obtained from the Vestals. When the solemn act of purification was over, the lighter part of the festival began. Bonfires were lit comprising of straw and hay and the shepherds leapt across them three times with the livestock being driven through three times. Cakes of millet were offered to the goddess Pales and the festival concluded by a feast in the open air. This is similar to the Celtic Need Fires lit at the festivals of the agricultural communities, at their fertility rites and rites of the dead. After A.D. 2, the festival of Parilia was combined with that of the Dea Roma and the date used to celebrate her birthday. Like many other earth deities she was associated with rites of the dead.

SATURNUS

Saturnus is 'the sower' and a being the sickle or scythe. He was the husband of Ops and father of Picus. Saturn and Ops must not be regarded only as protectors of all that was agricultural: all vegetation was under their care and everything that promoted its growth. In later times Saturn was identified with the Greek Cronos who, thrust out by Zeus, came across the sea to Latium. He was received by Janus and settled as king on the Capitoline Hill, which was called the Saturnian Hill.

He made the people acquainted with agriculture, suppressed their savage mode of life, and led them to order, peaceful occupations, and morality. The result was that the whole country was called Saturnia or the land of plenty. Saturn, like many other mythical kings, suddenly disappeared, being removed from earth to the abode of the gods

At the foot of the Capitoline Hill a temple was dedicated to him and to his wife Ops. Under his temple was the Roman treasury, no fools the Romans for Saturn was renowned for his practical use of money and getting value for any money spent. His temple not only contained the public treasury but many laws were deposited in it. His statue was hollow and filled with oil, probably to show the fertility of Latium in olives. In common with all the gods of this nature, in his hand he held a pruning knife. The pediment of the statue of Saturn had two figures resembling Tritons, with horns, whose lower extremities grew out of the ground. The statue was wound around the feet with woollen fillets, but not at the time of his own festival, which the ancients called the Saturnalia and we call Christmas.

Sacrifices were offered to Saturnus in the open air around the 17th of December, in front of the temple; the sacrifices were presented to him with bared head, from a conviction that no ill-omened sight would interrupt the rites of such a happy day. They started at a period when the agricultural labours of the year were complete. It was enjoyed by the rustic population as a joyous harvest home, when the harvest was safely gathered in. The Saturnalia originally began on the 19th of December, but with the reform of the calendar by Caesar, on the 17 December. The 17th and 18th December formed the Saturnalia, the 19th and 20th December the Opalia. Under Caligula a fifth day was added, the *dies juvenales*. Eventually a week of festivity was observed from the 17th to the 23rd of December. These dates do vary a little and the above agrees with a consensus.

All the things that were usual and accepted were suspended with the Saturnalia and the unusual prevailed for the time of the festival. It was a happy occasion enjoyed by all classes of society, a period of absolute relaxation and unrestrained merriment. In this period of five days, all forms of fantastic amusements were devised, the more outlandish the better. At the time of Saturnalia the senators and nobles laid aside the toga, the symbol of their rank and put on the *synthesis*= 'a loose, easy garment worn at the table.' After all had feasted and they could eat and drink no more, they would separate with the cry *Io Saturnalia!* This was termed the *clamare Saturnalis*. The festival was as much a private practice as a public one.

Schools had holidays, the law courts closed and all work ceased. War was deferred and no punishment was administered to criminals for seven days. Every householder kept an open house and invited to his table as many guests as he could find. Garlands of ivy were assumed and mirth and revel indulged in without restraint.

The festival was symbolic of the time of the Golden Age, when men were thought perfect and laws unnecessary. As mentioned elsewhere, it was a time of role-reversal. Special indulgences were granted and every freedom was given to slaves. They were relieved of all domestic duties and ordinary toil. Slaves sat at the table first and were served by their masters. They were permitted to wear the *pileus*= a small, felt skull cap that was the badge of freedom, also mentioned elsewhere. This freedom also meant they could speak on any subject they chose and in any manner. They could ridicule and castigate, in theory at least, without repercussions, in remembrance of the fact under the rule of Saturnus, there had been no differences in social rank.

There was a series of observances during the festival that places the Saturnalia firmly in line with the fertility rites; everything inclined towards increasing the fruitfulness of people and nature. People gave presents to each other, played social games and gambled for nuts. They gave presents of wax tapers (= cerei) symbolizing the making of new fire that was customary almost world-wide at the solstices with the Need Fires and new light created; such gifts were an acknowledgement of the sun returning on its path to the northern hemisphere. The sun was reversing its course, preparing for its return journey and, for a while, people did the same. The usual was dispensed with and the unusual was encouraged. The waxen or imitative fruit was given, apparently connected with growth and increase.

Varro suggests that small dolls (= *sigillaria*) were thought to be the remnant of the human sacrifice once practised in the past. The giving of clay dolls in the later days of the Saturnalia came about because the *Sigillarii*= 'the doll-makers,' who made the figurines held a festival at this time. This festival was the Sigillaria and was celebrated in Rome at the close of the Saturnalia, for the last two days. Small human figures of paste, wood or wax were presented to Pluto and given to friends. Hercules was believed to have been the first to begin this ceremony as a surrogate for human victims that earlier were sacrificed to Pluto and Saturn.

During the Saturnalia public gambling and games of chance were permitted by the aedilie, just as our ancestors permitted card playing on Christmas Eve. *Aedilis*= a magistrate in Rome who had the suprintendence of public and private buildings, public worship, theatres and dramatic performances, the duties of the police, etc. *Firmianus Symposius Caelius* was the author of a work of 'one hundred insipid riddles' each comprising three hexameter lines, collected for promoting the festivities of the Saturnalia. Perhaps these are the origin of the mottoes we find in Christmas crackers and, as some of them appear ancient and 'insipid,' perhaps the same ones? Many customs of the Saturnalia will be seen to bear more than a passing resemblance to our own traditional Christmas and to the Italian Carnivals, which were taken from the older festival. The loose garments with the pileus are reminiscent of the mummers, masques and fancy dress. The pointed hat that was worn at this time, originally the hat of the free man, was now known as the Fool's Cap.

There was universal teasing and mockery, not unlike Iambe's raillery at the festival of Eleusina. Once confetti, originally grains of wheat or barley, was thrown. It is true that Christmas inherited the general merriment in a more restrained form, mainly in eating, drinking and the giving of gifts, in particular to children. There was an abundance of sweetmeats and, as a more ceremonious element, the burning of candles. The Christmas trees I saw when I was a child were lit with candles, not electricity, and Christmas had a certain smell lacking today. There was once traditional bathing before the festival, which is in keeping with most rites. Christmas, like the Saturnalia, lasted seven days.

The policy of the early Church was to divert the people from their pagan customs by consecrating them to possible Christian use. It is possible that the Mithraic Festival of the *Natalis Invictus*, on the 25th of December, may have had more influence in fixing the actual date of Christmas than the Saturnalia in the Western Church. However, there can be little doubt that the merriment and relaxation of the Saturnalia were transferred to Christmas, even though the pagan festival was a little earlier than our present day festival.

At this time there was the election in private society and public of a mock king, which is still to be seen in the Lord of Misrule and the Boy Bishop, (see Faunus above). Not all the customs have been mentioned here. Saturnus had a festival in his honour at Athens called the Cronia and the Rhodians observed the same festival in honour of Cronos - perhaps the Phoenician Moloch - to whom human sacrifices, generally consisting of criminals were offered.

OPS

Ops was a female Roman divinity of plenty and fertility, as suggested by her name which is connected with *opinus* (= thinking, expecting), *opulentus* (= rich, wealthy, opulent), and *copia* (= abundance, ample store, plenty). The name Ops or *Opis*= 'power, might, help, assistance,' is reasonably connected with *opes*= 'rich, helpful, wealth,' of which the earth is the bestower. She was also named Bona Dea, or 'Good Goddess,' Maia, Fauna and Fatua. There was also the masculine aspect named Tellumo, Tellurus, Altor - *Alitor*= 'he that nourishes, feeds and keeps one, the cherisher, maintainer,' and Rusor, connected with *rus* or *ruris*= 'The country, or a place without the city, a country house or farm where husbandry is exercised.' Under the name of Ops she was regarded as the wife or the partner of Saturnus and accordingly the protectress of everything connected with agriculture. Her abode was the earth and therefore everyone who invoked her or made vows to her touched the ground. She was believed to give to human beings their place of abode and their food. Newly born children were commended to her care.

Her worship was intimately connected with Saturnus and she had temples and festivals in common with him. However, she did have a separate sanctuary on the Capitol. In the *vicus* (= a district or quarter of a city, a street) Jugarius, not far from the temple of Saturnus, she had an altar in common with Ceres. The festivals of Ops were called the *Opalia* and *Opiconsivia*, the latter from her epithet Consiva, connected with the verb *serere* - 'to sow.' The Opalia was celebrated during the Saturnalia, on the 14th day before the Calends of January (19th of December) being the third day of the Saturnalia. A consensus of most authorities seems to indicate that Ops and Bona Dea are the same.

FORNAX

Fornax is a Roman goddess who, it is said, was worshipped so that she would ripen the corn. In particular Fornax tended to the baking of the bread and prevented it being burnt in the oven. Oven =*fornax* from *fornus* = *furnus*, a furnace, kiln, oven. By some authorities she is considered identical with Vesta. The *Fornacalia* was a festival in honour of her, held so that the corn might be properly baked. This ancient festival is said to have been instituted by Numa. The time of the festival and its celebrations was proclaimed every year by a priest called the Curio Maximus. He announced the time of the festival in tablets which were placed in the forum, laying down the different part that each curia had to take part in the celebration.

It was held in February and it was said to have been inaugurated to give thanks for the 'earliest enjoyment of the corn.' Corn was baked in ovens in the ancient fashion. Those who missed the festival were thought fools (= *stulti*), if they did not know which was their curia (see below). They had to make an offering at the so-called Feast of Fools (= *Stultorum feriae*) on the 17th of February, the day of the *Quirinalia*, which fell on the last day of the Fornacalia.

The curia, in this abridged explanation, was the name of the thirty divisions into which the three tribus of the Roman patricians were divided for political and religious objects. Every curia contained a number of gentes, supposed to be exactly ten and a president, curio, whose duty it was to look after its secular and religious business. At the head of all the curiae stood the Curio Maximus, who was charged with the notification of the common festivals. The term *curia* was also applied to certain houses intended for holding meetings, as, for instance, the official residence of the Salii on the Palatine, and especially the senate house, Curia Hostilia, built by king Hostilius on the *comitium* (= 'a place in or near the forum, where assemblies were held') and burnt down in 52 B.C. The senate met in the *Curia Pompei*, in the entrance hall of Pompey's theatre, where Caesar was murdered.

FERONIA

Feronia is an old goddess of the Italians, who originally belonged to the Sabines and Faliscans and was introduced by them among the Romans. Roman writers, as usual, describe her as of Roman origin. It seems she was originally regarded in much the same light as Flora, Libera and Venus, but it is difficult to form a definite notion as to the nature of this goddess. **Dionysus** (ii.49) thus relates, that the Lacedaemonians who emigrated at the time of Lycurgus, after long wanderings, at length landed in Italy, where they founded a town of Feronia, and built a temple to the goddess Feronia. However this may be it is extremely difficult to form a definite notion of the nature of the goddess. She had a temple, grove and fount near Anxur. It was usual to make yearly sacrifices to her and to wash the face and hands of the votaries Romans called her a goddess of flowers and represented her as a young girl with flowers in her hair. Her festivals and shrines were well attended and she was offered flowers and the first fruits of the fields. The interpretation of her name is - *flower-bearing or garland-loving* - but some render it as Proserpina. She was also called Juno Virgo.

Some regarded Feronia as the goddess of commerce and traffic, because these things were carried on during the festival at Mt. Soracte. However, commerce was carried on at all festivals at which many people met, and must be looked upon as a natural result of such meetings rather than their cause. To others, Feronia was regarded a goddess of liberty, because at Terracina slaves were emancipated in her temple, and because on one occasion the freedmen of Rome collected a sum of money for the purpose of offering it to her as a donation. Emancipated slaves received the pileus and their freedom in her temple.

As mentioned elsewhere the pileus was a felt cap or hat, made to fit close and shaped like half an egg: a skullcap. It was worn by the Romans at festivals, when a slave stood equal and the master served as in the Saturnalia. The pileus was given to a slave at this enfranchisement as a sign of freedom. Those freeborn people who fell into captivity wore the pileus for a time after the recovery of their freedom, to signify their regained status.

Others again look upon her as a goddess of the earth or the lower world, akin to Mania and Tellus: partly because she is said to have given her son three souls, so that Evander had to kill him three times before he would die; partly because of her connection with Soranus, whose worship strongly resembled the worship of Feronia. As well as her sanctuaries at Terracina and near Mount Soracte, she had others at Trebula in the country of the Sabines, and at Luna in Etruria. Soranus was a god worshipped on Mount Soracte. He was similar to the Roman Dis or Orcus (= Hades). His priests, called Hirpi or Hirpini, would walk barefoot over heaps of burning coals of pine wood, carrying the entrails of the sacrifice. There is a legend connecting wolves with his worship that is thought to account for the name of his priests, *hirpus* being Sabine for wolf. This led to his identification with the Grecian Apollo.

THE LARES

The Lares, by some authorities, were held to be the deified spirits of men and developed into a beautiful conception of the family Lares being the souls of the ancestors who watched over and protected their descendants. In Etruscan the word Lasa or Larth signified lord, equivalent to the Greek concept of the hero. Old Latin - *lases*= 'household deities'. *Lar*= 'the chimney, fireside, a hearth, a dwelling house, one's home.' This is thought to show that the Roman Lares were of Etruscan origin. The old Latins, we are told by **Apuleius**, called the soul, when it left the body, a Lemur. If the Lemur was good they believed it became *a family-Lar*. If it was bad, it became *a Larva* to haunt the house and the occupants. Because it was not known to which class a departed soul belonged, the general term Dii Manes - *the Good Gods* - was used when speaking of the dead.

The name of the mother of the Lares was Acca Larentia to whom the *Larentilia* was celebrated on the 10th of December. The sacrifice was performed in the Velabrum which led to the Via Nova, outside the city, near the porta Romanula. At this place Acca was said to have been buried. The festival was not confined to Acca Larentia, but to have been sacred to all the Lares. The *Compitalia* (or the feast of the Lares) *compitalis*= 'pertaining to cross-roads' - was a festival annually celebrated at cross-roads in honour of the Lares Compitales. The sacrifice was honey cakes given to the inhabitants of each house, especially the slaves or those not free, because the Lares took pleasure in the service of slaves. It was quite an extensive festival. It was celebrated a few days after the Saturnalia. The days were appointed by the magistrates, often at the Calends of January. Although it varied it was always during the winter months.

This goddess was also called Lara or Larunda. A legend says she was a nymph, the daughter of Almon. Because of her tattling her tongue was cut out by Jupiter and she was sent, under the conduct of Mercurius, to the Nether World. Her keeper violated her on the journey and she became the mother of two Lares. Perhaps this is why the Lares were usually represented in pairs, of course Mercury, astrologically, rules Gemini, the Twins. Her name is also given as *Genita Mana*. It was the custom to sacrifice a dog to her and to pray to her that a good house slave would stay.

The statues of the household Lares were set by the fireplace, arrayed in dog skins and with a figure of a dog beside them, for this was an animal sacrificed to their mother. Offerings of food, wine and incense were made to them with garlands hung on the statues. The ancient Roman and his children saluted them daily with a morning prayer and an offering from the table. When the chief meal was over, a portion of the meal was laid on the fire on the hearth.

In the streets (= *compita*) of Rome there was a niche for the street Lares, not unlike those of the saints today who, in very old buildings, may simply have replaced them. At the Compitalia cakes were offered to them by the slaves who lived in the street, the Lares being regarded as presiding or guardian powers (= *praestes*). It was not unnatural that there were Lares of heaven, the sea, the roads, the villages, streets, towns and the whole city - *lares praestites* - as well as of private houses. They were invoked with the mother of the Lares, also called Lara, Larunda, Mania or Muta (= *the dumb*). To this goddess, instead of the early sacrifice of boys, heads of poppies and garlic were offered to her. Woollen dolls (= *maniae*), called after her, were suspended on the doors as protection. For those interested in the Roman domestic deities the following list may help their search.

Marriage: Jugatinus, Domiduca and Domiducus, Domitius, Manturnia, Subigus, Prema and Partunda. Childbirth and the rearing of children: Natio, Vagitanus, Cunina, Rumina, Edusa, Potina, Statilinus, Fabulinus, Adeona, Abeona, Volumnus and Volumna. Sacrifices were made to these when the act over which they presided began. When a child first began to speak, the sacrifice of the parents was to Fabulinus.

When a husband brought home his bride he invoked Domiduca and Domiducus, the Roman surnames for Jupiter and Juno who, as gods of marriage, were believed to conduct the bride to the house of the bridegroom. Those bereft of their children sought the help of Orbona, a female divinity of Rome whose temple was near that of the Lares. She was invoked by parents who had been deprived of their children and who craved to have others. She was also invoked for dangerous maladies in children. When death came it was Nenia who looked after the performance of the dirges and funeral rites.

ACCA LARENTIA

Acca Larentia or Laurentia, according to common legend in early Roman history, was the wife of the herdsman Faustulus and nurse to Romulus and Remus after they had been taken from the she-wolf. According to another legend she was a favourite of Hercules and the wife of a rich Etruscan whose possessions she bequeathed to Romulus and the Roman people. Finally, she was not the wife of Faustulus, but a prostitute who, because of her mode of life, was called *lupa* (= she wolf) by the shepherds. She left the property she gained by way her calling to the Roman people. Whatever may be thought of the contrary statements respecting Acca Larentia, this much seems clear. She was of Etruscan origin and connected with the worship of the Lares, from which her name Larentia may be derived. This appears from the number of her sons which answers to the twelve country Lares and, from these circumstances, the day sacred to her was followed by a day sacred to Lares. As written above, the worship of the Lares at Rome was closely connected with that of the Manes and both were analogous to the hero worship of the Greeks. The Lares may be divided into two classes, the *Lares domestici* and the *Lares publici* with their worship being part public and part private.

Acca Larentia is said to have had twelve sons with whom she made sacrifice for the fertilizing of the Roman fields (= *arva*), her sons were thence named Arval Brothers (=*fratres arvales)*, one of them having died Romulus took his place and founded the priesthood so called. It was to the rural Lares whom the Arval brethren invoked their songs.

The pontiffs and flamen of Quirinus sacrificed to her on the spot where she disappeared at the feast of Larentalia, on the 23rd of December, while invoking Jupiter. All this, with her name meaning 'mother of Lares,' shows that she was originally a goddess of the earth, to whose care men entrusted their seed corn and their dead. Probably she is the Dea Dia worshipped by the Arval Brothers. The Dea Dia - a Roman goddess, probably identical with Acca Larentia, the ancient Roman goddess of the country, her worship was provided for by the priestly collegium of the Fratres Arvales.

ARVAL BROTHERS

The Arval Fratres are of great antiquity and that is determined by the legend which refers their institution to Romulus, of whom it is said, that when his nurse Acca Laurentia lost one of her twelve sons, he let himself to be adopted by her in his place, and called himself and the remaining eleven 'Fratres Arvales.' The office of the Fratres Arvales was for life, and was not taken away even from an exile or captive. Their badge of office was a white fillet, used to fasten to the head a corona of corn spikes (= *spicea corona*). The Arvales held a three days' festival annually in honour of Dea Dia, supposed to be Ceres, sometimes held on the 17th, 19th and 20th, or the 27th, 29th and 30th of May. Of this the master of the college, appointed annually, gave public notice from the temple of Concord on the Capitol. On the first and last of these days, the college met at the house of their president, to make offerings to the Dea Dia; on the second day they assembled in the grove of the same goddess, about five miles south of Rome, and there offered sacrifices for the fertility of the earth.

Besides this festival of the Dea Dia, the Fratres Arvales were required on various occasions, under the emperors, to make vows and offer up thanks-giving. **Strabo** informs us that, in the reign of Tiberius, these priests performed sacrifices called the Ambarvalia at various places on the borders of the ager Romanus, or original territory of Rome, (*ager=* 'the territory of any particular community'); and amongst others, at Festi, a place between five or six miles from the city, in the direction of Alba.

The Arval brothers had to offer solemn vows for the Imperial House on extraordinary occasions and, on the 3rd of January, they were honour bound to fulfil them. Among the other priestly duties they performed were the expiatory sacrifices in the groves. These were performed if any damage had been done to the grove, through the breaking of a bough, if any damage had been caused by a stoke of lightning, or if any labour had been performed in the grove, even if necessary, and particularly so if iron tools had been used. They had to perform sacrifices at various places to invoke a blessing on the whole territory of Rome.

The private Ambarvalia were certainly of a different nature from those mentioned by **Strabo**, and were so called from the victim (= *hostia ambarvalis*) that was slain on the occasion of being led three times round the cornfields, before the sickle was put to the corn. The most common animal sacrifices at Rome were the *suovetaurilia* or *solitaurilia* consisting of a pig, a sheep, and an ox, from *sus* (= a swine, hog, pig), *ovis* (= a sheep), and *taurus*(= a bull, bullock, an ox). They were performed in all cases of a lustration, and the victims were carried around the thing to be lustrated, whether it was a city, a people, or a piece of land. The Ambarvalia ceremony was a *lustratio* = 'a purification by sacrifice, a lustration.'

After prayers, originally addressed to Mars, they offered them to Ceres and other deities of agriculture, that the fruits of the fields may thrive. The victims were accompanied by a crowd of merrymakers (= *chorus et socii*), the reapers and farm workers dancing and singing, as they marched along, the praises of Ceres, and praying for her favour and attendance, while they offered her the libations of milk, honey and wine. It bears a strong resemblance to the ceremonies of rogation (*rogatio*= 'an asking, an entreaty, request') or gang week of the Latin church that followed a similar pattern, but without the sacrifice. There was the perambulation, the blessing of the fields and the fruits of the earth with prayers. This was also carried out for three days during Whitsuntide. The custom was abolished during the Reformation in consequence, it is said, of its abuse. The perambulation of the parish boundaries were substituted in its place.

The great god Mars, through the excessive emphasising of one of his attributes, became regarded only as a god of war. This was done at the expense of his other excellent attributes, which were relegated almost out of existence. Originally he was a mighty god of nature, who accorded fertility and protection to fields and herds. This imbalance regarding Mars should really be redressed by now. The first month of the old Roman year, March, was dedicated to him as the fertilising god of spring. Mars was an ancient Roman god who was, at an early period, identified with the Greek god Ares or the god *delighting in war*, although there are indications that the Italian Mars was originally a divinity of a very different nature.

First, Mars had the epithet Silvanus and sacrifices were offered to him for the prosperity of the fields and flocks. Secondly, a lance was honoured as a symbol of Mars at Rome, as also at Praeneste, so that Mars resembles more the Greek Pallas Athene than Ares. The transition from the idea of Mars as an agricultural god to that of a warlike being was not too difficult for the early Latins as the two occupations were intimately connected. The name of the god in Sabine and Oscan was Mamers, and Mars itself is a contraction of Mavers or Mavors. Next to Jupiter, Mars enjoyed the highest honours in Rome. He is frequently designated Father Mars, under the forms Marspiter and Maspiter, analogous to Jupiter. He had a very ancient sanctuary on the Quirinal hill from which he derived his name *Quirinus* and was regarded as the father of the Roman people.

Mars was, therefore, the protector of agriculture and invoked to be propitious to the household of the rustic Roman. Under the name Silvanus, he was worshipped to take care of the cattle. Mars appeared in three principle aspects: to the rustics he was Silvanus; as the warlike Mars he was *Gradivus* (*gradus*= 'a step, pace; *pleno gradus*= 'at double time'); and to the state he was Quirinus (*quiris* or *curis*= '(a Sabine word) spear'). Concerning the first it is to be observed that females were excluded from his worship and he presided particularly over those occupations of the country that belonged to males only. So it cannot be an automatic conclusion that all aspects of agriculture and the earth were the exclusive province of the Goddess, see further example at the end of the next paragraph.

Mars was often mentioned in the company of female divinities and that is natural. One of them was Nerio, Neriene or Nerienus, though little is known about her. The ancients themselves seemed uncertain about her correct name, though Nerio appears to be the one mainly used, according to **Gellius**. Her names are said to be Sabine in origin and synonymous with *virtus* = 'manhood' - and *fortitudo* = 'strength.' Sometimes she was described as the wife of Mars. Mars was possessed of prophetic powers and near Reate he had an ancient oracle with the future being revealed through his sacred bird, the woodpecker (= *picus*). In an earlier time he was invoked at the hallowing of the fields, at the Ambarvalia. He was asked to bless the family, the fields and the cattle and to keep off sickness and bad weather. Mars was asked for protection against all that did the fields and livestock harm - a defensive Mars, not an aggressive Mars. The cult of Mars was entrusted to the college of the Salii. In the Egyptian model of Heliopolis, Geb was male and earth and Nut, the female, the sky or heavens. Ra ordered Shu, the god of air and the atmosphere to thrust himself between their constant embrace. Standing on Geg, Shu pushed Nut upwards and she was forced on high to become the vault of the heavens and the Milky Way; she is often shown arched over Geb resting on her toes and fingers. While the ithyphallic Geb was thrown down, his sprawling limbs became the hilly earth, Geb is an interesting exception to the rule that the earth is always female.

The goddess Fecunditas first made an appearance in A.D. 63 when the senate gave orders for a temple to be built in her honour in gratitude for the successful delivery of Nero's favourite, Poppea in childbirth. From this time it is probable that the Arvales made sacrifice to her. She is thought to be the personification of good fortune among the Romans.

Fecunditas was worshipped in various sanctuaries in Rome. She is represented as either carrying a child in one arm and a sceptre (or herald's staff) in the other. Sometimes she has a child in both arms. Under the name *Fecunditas Temporum* she appeared on some coins

There was an old custom in the North of England, at funerals in particular, when the Arval Bread was distributed to the poor. Arval Bread has been described as being 'a thin, light, sweet cake.' The reason for the origin of the bread is lost but it is said that 'the custom may be borrowed from the ancients.' An Arval Dinner was given at the death of a person of great possessions when friends and neighbours were invited and the corpse was put on public display. This was done to exonerate the heirs from any accusation that the person did not die fairly and to show that they did not suffer personal injury from the beneficiaries for personal gain.

It is thought that the custom was introduced here by the Romans as it is of very old date. In Wales it was written *ardell* which is said to signify *asserere* - 'to avouch.' These funeral customs 'were thought to have originated with Cecrops for renewing decayed friendships among old friends, etc.' Whether there is any actual connection with the Fratres Arvales, as suggested by the similarity of the names, I cannot find. It could simply be no more than coincidence.

CECROPS

Cecrops is generally held to be the first to rule over the country which was called Crecropia after him; more commonly know as Attica from its peninsular form. Some say that he was a monster, half human and half serpent. Cecrops was a king of Athens and he divided the rude inhabitants into twelve communities, founded the stronghold of Athens, which was called Cecropia after him, and introduced the elements of civilization. The laws of marriage and property, to cultivate corn for their substance and he is believed to be the first to bury the dead, the earliest political arrangements, teaching the cultivation of the olive and to accept Athene as the patroness of the city, the earliest religious services, notably those of Zeus and Athene. He changed the old mode of worship inasmuch he abolished the bloody sacrifices which had until then been offered to Zeus and substituted barley cakes in their stead; the abolition of the blood sacrifice is to his credit.

It was during the reign of Cecrops that Poseidon struck the rock on the Acropolis, causing a spring to arise which was known in later times as the Erechthian well, from it being enclosed in the temple of Erechtheus; according to another story a horse sprang forth. Poseidon wanted to take possession of the country; he lost many countries to others and I think perhaps, that the sea, which he rules, has been trying to take back the land ever since. However, Athene entertained the same desire and in a contest for the country her gift to the human race was deemed the more acceptable by the gods: the olive tree - the treasure of Attica. Thus the city is called Athens. Athene had taken Cecrops as her witness while she planted her olive tree and he added his vote in her favour. Poseidon had no witness to attest that he had created the well. To show his annoyance at their choice Poseidon inundated the land.

It was, therefore, natural that the names of his family all related to agriculture and worship of the tutelary deity of Athens. There were temples of both Agraulos and Pandrosos at Athens and Athene herself was called by these names. Cecrops married Agraulos (= *field-dwelling*) the daughter of Actaeos, who gave him a son Erysichthon (= *mildew*) and three daughters, Agraulos (=*field-dwelling*), Herse (= *dew*) and Pandrosos (= *all-dew*). Pandrosos was the first priestess of Athene, honoured together with her in a sanctuary of her own, the Pandroseion, on the Acropolis of Athens. She was invoked in times of drought with the Attic Horae, Thallo and Carpo, in her temple stood the sacred olive which Athene had created.

Erysichthon died without children. Agraulos had by Ares a daughter named Alcippe (= *strong-mare*) appropriate to a god of war. Herse bore a son called Cephalos (= *shady*) by Hermes. Like the Athenian Graces and Seasons, the *Cecropides* (= offspring of Cecrops) were originally only two.

Naturally, others dissent from this 'imperfect fragment of Diodorus' and the Scholia, in which the Egyptian Cecrops occurs, maintain it is a sophism and no myth. Later Greek writers described Cecrops as having immigrated into Greece with a band of colonists, from Sais in Egypt. They were thought to have arrived in Attica around 1556 B.C. In the time of the Ptolemies it became the fashion to regard the Egyptians as the colonisers of half the world. This is rejected, not only by the ancients themselves, but by the most able commentators of modern times.

Plato intimates it, when he says that the priests of Sais informed Solon, from their temple archives, that the goddess Neith or Athene was found in both their cities. Athens was the older by one thousand years. Neith is the Egyptian war goddess and patroness of Sais who is equated with Pallas Athene, *Net* is an alternative spelling. Cecrops is often missing from the lists of the Athenian kings, for example Socrates, which speaks of a pure Athenian autochthony. 'Neither a Pelops nor a Danaos, nor a Cadmos, nor an Aegyptos, nor any other, being originally a Barbarian, has been naturalised among the Hellenes, has settled among us. We are of pure Hellenic blood, no mixed people, and thence the hatred of foreign manners and customs is especially implanted in our city.' so says **Socrates** in **Plato's** *Menexenus*. This is the genuine Athenian creed of his day.

Cecrops, in the Attic legends, is represented as the teacher of civilised life to the rude aboriginals. **Keightley** suggests the names Cecrops or Cercops may be explained by the golden tettiges the ancient Athenians were said to wear in their hair to denote their autochthony. Tettiges (*tettigonia*= a type of small grasshopper or cricket, a tree-hopper); this species of insect was named *kerkoph* and this is an explanation offered regarding the name of Cecrops. After a reign which lasted fifty years he died.

BONUS EVENTUS

Closely connected with Fortuna is the Roman deity Eventus or, more correctly, Bonus Eventus - lucky or happy event - who was thought to have been introduced into Italy by the peasants. Initially in the Roman religion he was the god of rural prosperity and he appears as a type of masculine parallel to Felicitas (= 'the personification of happiness'). In this he was like the Greek Agathodaemon, whose image in later times was transferred to the Italian deity. Originally his powers extended only over these rural events but eventually Bonus Eventus acquired the more general meaning of the friendly fortune that secures a lucky issue to undertakings, for the whole human race. Bonus Eventus acquired attributes similar to those of the goddess Fortuna.

He is one of the gods addressed by **Varro**, one of the most learned of the Romans. In the commencement of his work on agriculture he joins Bonus Eventus with Lympha. He prays to this deity, for without his aid nothing could come to a happy conclusion. Bonus Eventus is included in **Varro's** famous list of twelve deities of the farmers. The twelve, which he calls the *Consentian Gods* of the country are: Jovis and Tellus, Sol and Luna, Ceres and Libera, Robigus and Flora, Minerva and Venus, Bonus Eventus and Lympha.

Bonus Eventus is credited with a statue made by Praxiteles that was placed in the Capitol. There is evidence showing an active private worship. However, as the head of the god appeared on the denarii in Caesar's time and frequently on the coins of the empire, this shows a state religion. The god had a temple of his own on the Campus Martius in the neighbourhood of the Pantheon. Bonus Eventus in statuary is represented as a youth making a libation at an altar. He has a patera or cup in one hand, and ears of corn in the other.

The Greek Agathodaemon - *good daemon* - in mythology was a good spirit of the cornfields and vineyards to whom a libation of unmixed wine was made at meal times. In the world of art he is represented as a youth holding in the right hand a horn of plenty and a bowl, in the other a poppy and ears of corn.

Fortuna seems to have begun as an agricultural goddess but she developed into the personification of blind chance that seems to characterize a farmer's life, even today. Her cult in later times grew to tremendous proportions. With typical logic the Romans had an opposing goddess to Fortuna. She is Mala Fortuna and she is the goddess of evil fortune. She was worshipped in Rome.

TARAXIPPUS

The Greeks had a little nightmare demon who made horses restive and timid. He was called Taraxippus, a son of Poseidon, who was worshipped at Elis. Sometimes he has been associated with Pan, though the link is not always a satisfactory one. His station was near race courses and his protection was implored that no harm should come to the horses while racing. This little demon had a circular altar on the Olympia race course, at the far end of the centre division from the starting area. The drivers had to pass around this after going down the first of the long sides, going around the altar to come back down the other to the start again. This spot on the Olympic race course was named after him because horses often became frightened, shied or panicked when they reached it.

Pausanias writes, 'Here was the horror of horses, the Taraxippus. It has the form of a round altar and, when the horses pass it, they are struck, without a visible cause, with great fear which produces great restiveness and confusion; the reason why chariots often break and the charioteers are wounded.' The Taraxippus was the first goal of the race, the point where the chariots turned to come down the other side. The second was at the other end of the course, where there was a statue of Hippodameia, and her statue marked the spot the chariots had to reach to gain the victory. I think it was the great fear 'without a visible cause' that produced 'restiveness and confusion' that has allied Taraxippus with Pan and with *panikos*= 'panic' in the minds of some.

Some account for this panic by saying the altar of Taraxippus was the burial place of Myrtilus who sabotaged the chariot of Oenomaus, in which his master was slain. Myrtilus was bribed by Pelops so he could win the race, for otherwise he had to die. This was the condition set for all who wished to gain the hand of the king's daughter, Hippodameia. **Pausanias** considers Taraxippus to be a epithet of Poseidon Hippius. As said, none have been able to identify Taraxippus and Pan satisfactorily, though I think there are many who would like to.

COPIA

Copia was the goddess of plenty among the Romans. She is represented with the figure of a young virgin of tall stature, with her head covered with flowers. The horn of plenty - *the cornucopia* - she holds was the horn of the goat Amalthea that was presented to the nymphs that nursed Jupiter. This favourite animal was placed in the constellations of the heavens by a grateful god. From the cornucopia fall fruits, raisins, flowers, pearls and pieces of gold and silver. In her other hand she holds a bundle of different ears of corn. Many statues of the deities, for example, Bacchus, Hercules, Apollo, Ceres, etc., and some heroes of antiquity, are shown with this celebrated symbol. It often alludes to the services they are supposed to have rendered to mankind.

As **Hastings** writes, some authorities think she is simply the personification of the *copia* or *cornu copia* and denies her existence in actual worship. However, she appears to have been the subject of public worship because an inscription to her has been found at Avignon and the fact that two Roman deities, one at Thurii in 193 B.C., and another in Lugdunun in 43 B.C., were named Copia, which seems to point to a real cult. If there was a public cult then a private one is almost certain. As well as Copia, there were other deities who presided over the various operations of agriculture and the various parts of the country. Some of these deities are only known by name. Rusina presided over the whole country. Collina ruled over the hills and Vallonia over the valleys. The Romans had two divinities said to be the protectors of the stables, Bubona and Epona. Bubona was the protectress of the oxen and cows. Epona, the better known, was the protectress of the horses. Epona is said to have been the daughter of Fulvius Stellus by a mare. Small figures of these divinities were placed in niches (*aediculae*= a shrine, a place to set images in), or in the pillar supporting the roof. Sometimes they were painted over the manger only.

Segetia was a Roman divinity who, with Setia or Seja and Semonia, was invoked by the early Italians at seed time and the spring corn. Segetia, like the other two names, is connected with *sero*= 'to put in a row, to connect, to join' and *seges*= 'a cornfield, standing corn, a crop.' Runcina was invoked by the people of Italy to prevent the growth of weeds between the corn and promote the harvest; she is thought to be a epithet of Ops. The deity Occator was the god of harrowing, invoked when the soil went under the harrow for levelling the soil and covering the seed. Sator was a sower, a planter, a begetter, who presided over the sowing and raking.

Robigo was the female deity among the Romans who protected the corn from the blight. Her male counterpart was Robigus. The Robigalia, instituted by Numa, was held in their honour. It was celebrated on the 25th of April, just before the festival of the Floralia. This was in a grove some five miles from Rome. The citizens, dressed in white festal attire, marched there under the supervision of the *Flamen Quirinalis Robigus*. First the people presented themselves to Mars or Quirinalis, and invoked Mars 'as the protector of arable land' - please note, *not* as the God of War. At the Robigalia, in the grove of the ancient deity, prayers were offered to Robigus accompanied by offerings of incense (= *frankincense*) and wine. The prayer was for the preservation of the ripening seed from mildew. The flamen offered the entrails of a young sorrel dog and a sheep. Races were also held.

Stercutius, Sterculius or Sterquilinus, were epithets of Saturnus, the god of dunging or fertilising the ground. These epithets of the god were derived from *stercus*= manure, because he had promoted agriculture by teaching the people the use of manure. This would seem to be the original meaning. However, some Romans said that Sterculius was the epithet of Picumnus, the son of Faunus, to whom these improvements in agriculture were also ascribed.

The rustic religion of the ancient Romans possessed the two deities Picumnus and Pilumnus, who were regarded as brothers and beneficial gods of matrimony. It was these two divinities that presided over the auspices required before the celebration of the nuptials. In a house when there was a new born child a special couch was prepared for them. Pilumnus was thought to protect the infant from the sufferings of childhood with his *pilum* (= 'pestle, or pounder'). He is said to be the first to teach people to pound the grain. Therefore he was invoked as the god of millers and bakers. Picumnus, under the name of Sterquilinius, was thought to have discovered the use of manure for the fields. He conferred upon the infant strength and prosperity. Hence both gods were looked upon as the gods of good deeds and, as such, were identified with Castor and Pollux.

Spinensis or Spiniensis was a god of the Romans whose power was invoked to clear the fields from brambles and thorns, hence the name. *Spinetum*= 'a place where thorns and briars grow, a bush of thorns.' The *Feriae Sementivae* or *Sementina dies* were the festivals observed in Rome at the time of sowing the corn and praying for a good crop. The holiday lasted only one day and this day was appointed by the high priest or chief magistrate. Nodotus or Nodutus is the divinity attending the joints or knots of the stems of plants producing grain. Some think it probable this was originally a epithet of Saturnus.

The Vergiltae, the seven stars - the Pleiades - have already been mentioned in the section devoted to Pan. When the Pleiades set the ancients would begin their corn sowing.

Patella or Petallana was described as having charge of the unfolding or opening of the stems of the corn plants when they first made their appearance, so the ears may shoot forth. Some believe these to be epithets of Ops. Volusia was the goddess of the folding of the blade. Lactans, Lacturnus or Lacturcia, 'minded it when milky' or these divinities were thought to protect the young fruits in the field. Some believe that Lactans and Lacturcia are merely epithets of Ops, while Lacturnus is a epithet for Saturnus.

Volutrina was the goddess invoked by the countrymen to give prosperity to the crops and not leave the ears of corn exposed, but to surround them with a protective integument. Lat. *integumentum*= 'a covering - as with our skin or the outer covering of a seed.'

Matura brought the seed to ripeness. Tutelina or Tutulina was described as the Roman agricultural goddess who was invoked to protect the harvest once it had been brought in, though some consider her an attribute of Ops. Tutelina, Secia and Messia had three pillars with altars before them in the Circus. Mellona or Mellonia was the goddess who presided over honey but she is otherwise unknown. Fornax was the goddess of baking the corn with the festival of the Fornacalia celebrated in February. From the above it will be seen it is possible to take a sequence of natural events and call upon the deities for their support, at almost every stage of it.

This short introduction is not sufficient to do justice to the extensive subject in hand but I hope there is enough to encourage the reader to look further for themselves. We have looked at Pan and the other wonderful deities and heroes of the natural world. We have touched upon some of their festivals, feasts, folklore and myth, most of which involve the earth, animals and all that is fertile and growing. The history of man's religious ideas is an important part of the human mind and soul. You cannot touch myth without myth touching you.

We have touched upon only a small part of this great heritage in this work and only the beauties and philosophy of Greece and Italy. We have ventured very little into other countries including our own. Science has tried for a long time to extinguish these poetic feelings and to make this beauty and elegance no more than museum pieces, saying this is where they belong, the object of contempt and neglect; intimating that they are no more than stories and fairy tales for children. Sad the lot of a country or a people that agrees with this jaundiced point of view.

Anyone who thinks the god of the Bible is the only 'jealous god' demanding there will be 'no other god before me' is mistaken. Science has my admiration for what it has given me to make my life easier in so many areas, but it does not have the exclusive worship it so arrogantly demands in return for these gifts. I do not take kindly to being told that everything I own or think must be brought to the Altar of Science to ask for its stamp of approval and blessing. The fiat decrees that what is brought will be weighed in the balance of Science. If it is found wanting, it must be discarded and I must go away and try again until I bring something that merits approval. Science should be afforded its rightful portion, that to which it is entitled, but no more and no less!

I condense a conversation from the novel quoted at the beginning of the work. The lines are given to the doctor in the story. 'You may not like it but it is the majority who are the arbiters of sanity at any given time, there was a time when the majority thought the sun went around the earth, one man said it didn't and he was deemed mad.' The next are taken from the character 'Mr Stanger' in the novel. 'I am no lover of convention, but we live in a conventional world. You must adapt yourself to your surroundings or your surroundings to yourself. And the second is a laborious and lengthy process...because society cannot allow exceptions to its fundamentals...we must submit or go into exile...anyone who shares that view, however, is a pioneer; and the way of the pioneer is hard.' *The Oldest God*, **Stephen McKenna**.

Even today, in a world that now eschews the mores of the time when the above work was written, considering them old fashioned, nothing has really changed. We have new sets of rules to replace the old. You must subscribe to a manner of dress, particularly if you wish to belong to a specific group, and take up their approved manner of speaking, thinking and reading. Certain books, or anything disapproved of, are removed from the public by a minority because it is thought an improvement on what went before; though how the tail wagging the dog is equated with improvement I have yet to work out. The actors and scenery may have changed and the script may use a different set of values, but I do not think today's script is as refined and erudite as it used to be. The play, however, is the same.

Any time given by the reader to the subject of this work will, in the opinion of the writer, repay any effort expended - seven times seven. I hope this introduction will prove of help to those readers who may not be familiar with these wondrous myths and legends, the neglect of which would impoverish the world beyond measure.

A Gallimaufry of the Semones and Festivals.

First - the Semones the Lesser or Inferior gods ...

OSCILLUM, a diminutive through *osculum* from *os*, meaning a 'little head.' These were faces or heads of Bacchus, the god who gave Pan his name when Hermes took the babe to Mt. Olympus, which were suspended in the vineyards to be turned in every direction by the wind. Whatever way they looked, they were supposed to make the vines in that quarter be fruitful and prosper. The head on the left represents the countenance of Bacchus, with a beautiful, mild expression. The pupils of the eyes and mouth are perforated. The other figure is from an ancient gem, representing a tree with four *oscilla* hung upon its branches. Pan, as God of Nature, is symbolized by the syrinx and pedum (= a shepherd's crook) placed at the roots of the tree. From this noun came the verb *oscillo*, meaning 'to swing.' Swinging (= *oscilatio*) was among the bodily exercises practised by the Romans

Semones
the Lesser or Inferior gods ...

Semones are those deities termed the inferior deities who were not included in the number of the Twelve Great Gods. Among these semones will be found Janus, Pan, Bona Dea, Priapus, Luna, Vertumnus, Pomona, Silenus, etc., and many illustrious heroes who received divine honours after their death. Most people with only a slight knowledge of myth and legend can give the names of some major gods and have some idea who they were. The lesser gods usually elicit no recognition. 'Semones' has the 'classical' meaning of being inferior or lesser than *the supreme gods*, but *superior to men*, it really does not mean inferior in a derogatory sense used today. Perhaps a better word to keep in mind is 'lesser,' as the Classical dictionary definition, given above, suggests.

It became obvious over the years that these deities were to be found in the various encyclopaedias and dictionaries owned and consulted. However, unless you know their names, it defeats your full use of this type of work and deprives you of many delightful aspects of the Greek and Roman deities. They are listed in most of these works and once you know them, they are obvious and easily found. If you do not know them you can miss so much. As I progressed in my reading over the years I started to list these deities as I found them.

I thought it could prove to advantage, although it does go beyond the brief of the subject of the work. However, when has that ever stopped me? This brief has already been broken often enough before reaching these last few pages. With my great love of the deities of Greece and Italy I have often thought the great gods are not unlike beautiful swans swimming serenely and gracefully on the Lake of Legend. However, if we were to look under the water we would see this lot paddling away for all they're worth to keep the whole thing moving.

These are the deities who are more concerned with the everyday working of life here on earth and they are necessary to this place and us, just as the great gods naturally are. It is true many of them are not involved with the glamorous, grand design of things but perhaps they are a little closer to us because of that, a little more accessible? I have always called them 'the mediators' for they seem to be between the Gods of High Olympus and the People of the Earth.

The descriptions have been kept brief but they should prove

sufficient to advise the reader of the deities and their attributes so they can take the matter further should they wish to. There may be some duplication, in that a deity may have already been mentioned in the main text, naturally it is not a long list. The purpose of the list is to start the reader off, to begin to compile their own.

ACHLYS
According to some ancient cosmogonies, the eternal night, and the first created being, which existed even before Chaos. **Hesiod** tells us that she was the personification of misery and sadness, and as such she was represented on the shield of Heracles; pale, emaciated, and weeping, with chattering teeth, swollen knees, long nails on her fingers, bloody cheeks, and her shoulders thickly covered with dust.

ACMON
Lempriere tells us, according to some Greek mythologists the oldest of the gods who is said to have existed from eternity and produced Chaos.

AEOLUS
Favourite of the gods whom Zeus appointed king of storms and keeper of the winds which, in one legend, he kept enclosed in a mountain so he could use them to excite or soothe at his pleasure. In another, he lived on his Aeolian island floating to the far West. Its steep cliff was encircled by a brazen wall within which dwelt in unbroken bliss with his wife and his six sons and daughters. He gave hospitality to Odysseus and gave him the unfavourable winds in a leather bag with a kindly breeze to take him on his way. The hero's comrades opened the leather bag and the winds broke out and took them back to Aeolus, who drove them away as those hateful to the gods. It was to him that Hera applied when she wished to destroy the Trojan fleet.

AGENORIA or AGERONIA
A goddess among the Romans who presided over industry.

ANNONA
This is a Latin word meaning 'the year's produce', especially wheat, the staple food of the city population. It was afterwards applied to the corn provided by the State to feed the population. The annona, like so many other things, was personified by the Romans and became the goddess of the importation of corn, whose attributes were a bushel, ears of wheat and the horn of plenty.

ANTEVORTA, PORRIMA or PRORSA

Antevorta together with Postvorta are either two sisters or companions of Carmenta. Some think they are two aspects of the same goddess, Carmenta, with the former giving knowledge of the future and the latter the past. They did have two separate altars and were invoked by pregnant women to avert the dangers of childbirth.

ANTIAS

A goddess of fortune, chiefly worshipped at Antium.

ATE

The goddess of all evil who was a daughter of Zeus or Eris. Zeus hurled her from Olympus to earth and she was banished by him forever. As said, she came to dwell on earth with us. She pursues her mission by walking lightly over men's heads and never touches the ground. Behind her follow the Litae - '*the prayers of the penitent*'- who are sweet-natured goddesses, the daughters of Zeus. The Litae if called upon can heal the hurt inflicted by Ate for that is their express duty, to relieve the distress and mischief brought about by her. In the Homeric poems they are described as lame, wrinkled and squinting, these malformations being brought about in the trouble they have suffered by making good the harm of Ate. To the stubborn they bring yet more trouble. Those who disdain to receive them have themselves to atone for the crime that has been committed, according to some. It was the Litae who were considered as placing before their father the prayers of those who have asked for his assistance.

ATHELII

The gods at Athens whose statues were constantly exposed to the sun.

AUTOMATIA

A epithet of Tyche or Fortuna that seems to characterize her as the goddess of fortune. She is a goddess who manages things in her own way without any regard to the merit of people.

AVERRUNCUS

A divinity of Rome who averted all evil.

AZONES

The name given to those divinities who had no fixed habitation assigned to them and were worshipped by all nations promiscuously.

BELLONA
The goddess of war, called by the Greeks Enyo, companion of Mars though sometimes his sister or wife. She was highly respected among the Romans. The main object for which she was worshipped was to grant a warlike spirit and an enthusiasm which no enemy could resist. It was her temple where the senate met the ambassadors of foreign nations and where their generals proclaimed their triumph. The pillar of war - *Columna Bellica* - stood hard by.

BONUS EVENTUS
A Roman deity whose powers were not unlike Fortuna.

BUBONA
A Roman goddess who presided over oxen and cows.

CACA
A goddess of the Romans who presided over the excrement of the body. The Vestals offered her sacrifice in her temple.

CARMENTA or CARMENTIS
A prophetess and healing divinity of Arcadia who came as a fugitive to Italy. She had a temple in Rome. The Greeks offered sacrifices to her under the name of Themis. **Hyginus** relates that she changed fifteen characters of the Greek alphabet, which Evander had introduced into Latium, into Roman ones. She protected women in childbirth.

CARNA, CARNEA
(**Wm. Smith**) or Cardinea (**Lempriere**)= A Roman goddess whose name is probably connected with caro= flesh, who presided over hinges, entrails and the secret parts of the body. She was regarded as the protector of the physical well-being of man, especially the chief organs of the body without which we cannot live, such as the heart, liver and lungs. She warded off evil influences especially the Strigae, who were believed to suck the blood of children by night. A sanctuary was dedicated to her on the Caelian Hill, and a festival was celebrated to her on the 1st of June, which was called *fabrariae calendae*, from beans (= *fabae*) and bacon offered to her.

CENSUS
Roman god, the same as Consus.

COLLINA
A goddess of Rome who presided over hills.

CONCORDIA
A goddess who was the personification of peace and concord among Roman citizens who was worshipped at Rome. She was represented with cornucopia and olive branch. She was sometimes invoked with Janus, Salus and Pax.

CONSALUS
A god worshipped at Athens with the same ceremonies as Priapus.

CONSUS
A Roman god who presided over counsels. He was a god of secret deliberations, probably a god of earth and crops. He is often thought of as an infernal god, for very little is known of him. Romulus claimed to have found his altar under the earth, apparently as a sign of the deity's activity in the bosom of the earth. He is a secret and mysterious god.

COPIA
A goddess of plenty among the Romans.

COTYS or COTYTTO
A Thracian goddess of debauchery and wantonness. Her festivals were celebrated in the hills with riotous proceedings and licentious frivolity.

CUNINA or CUNARIA
A Roman divinity who presided over children when sleeping in their cradle. The three genii who were worshipped as protectresses of infants sleeping in their cradles were Cuba, Cunina and Rumina.

DEATH
In the **Homeric** poems Death is called the twin brother of Sleep. In **Hesiod** he is born of Night without father, with Cer or Ker (= 'the goddess of mortal destiny') Moros (= 'the mortal stroke of death) Hypnos (=sleep) and the Dreams. **Hesiod** represents Death, the hardhearted one, hated by the immortal gods, as dwelling with his brother Sleep in the darkness of Tartarus, 'wither the sun never penetrates either at his rising or his setting.' Euripides introduces Death on the stage in his Alcestis. He has a black garment and black wings with a knife to cut off a lock of hair as an offering to the gods below.

EDUSA or EDULICA
A Roman goddess whose office was looking after young children after they had been weaned by their mother. She blessed their food just as Potina and Cuba blessed their drinking and sleep.

EILEITHYIA
She was regarded by the Greeks as a goddess of 'coming and helping.' She was a goddess of birth who came to the assistance of women in labour. If she was kindly disposed she furthered the birth, but when she was angry, she protracted the labour and delayed the birth.

EMPANDA or PANDA
Her temple was an asylum which was always open and the suppliants who came to her were provided with food from the funds of the temple. The name Panda is connected with *pandere*= 'to open' and she is accordingly the Roman goddess who is open to and admits anyone who needs protection.

ELEGEIA
The goddess of elegiac poetry invoked, among others, by **Ovid.**

EPIDOTAE
Certain deities who presided over birth and growth of children, who were known among the Romans by the name *Dii Averunci.* They were also worshipped by the Lacedaemonians, being invoked by those who were persecuted by the ghosts of the dead.

EREBUS
A deity of hell, son of Chaos and Caligo. The name signifies darkness and it is, therefore, applied to the dark and gloomy place under the earth through which the shades pass into Hades. The poets often used his name for Hades itself.

EGERIA or AEGERIA
A Roman goddess who was regarded as a prophetic divinity and the giver of life, she was invoked and given sacrifices at the approach of childbirth.

FABULINUS
A god of the Romans who considered him as presiding over the first articulation of children.

FASCINUS
An early Roman deity, identical with Mutinus or **Tutinus**, who was worshipped as a protector against sorcery, witchcraft and evil demons; and represented in the form of a phallus - *fascinum* - an image of which was hung around the neck of children as a preventative against witchcraft. He was especially invoked to protect women in the childbed and their offspring; women wrapt in the *toga praetexta* (= a toga worn by boys until they attained manhood, and by girls until marriage) used to offer up sacrifices in the chapel of Fascinus. His worship was under the care of the Vestals, and generals who entered the city in triumph, had the symbol of Fascinus fastened under their chariots, that he might protect them from envy (= *medicus invidiae* - 'to cure or heal grudges, envies or jealousies'). Envy was believed to exercise an injurious influence on those who were envied, it was a custom with the Romans, when they praised any body, to add the word *praefiscine* or *praefiscini* (= 'meaning no evil, without offence, without vanity'), which seems to have been an invocation of Fascinus, to prevent the praise turning out injurious to the person to whom it was given.

FESSONIA
A goddess of Rome who aided the weary, especially soldiers. (Lat. *fessus*= 'wearied, tired, exhausted').

FIDES
A Roman goddess who was the personification of faith, faithfulness, honesty and oaths.

FIDIUS DIUS
A divinity of the Romans, the god of faith and truth by whom they generally swore. He was also called Sanctus Sabus and Semipater solemnly addressed with prayers on the 5th of June, a day annually consecrated to his service.

FONTUS
Belived to be a son of Janus and brother of Volturnus. He had an altar on the Janicultus, which derived its name from his father. he is connected with *fons*= a well, and he is the personification of wells and flowing water. On the 13th of October the Romans celebrated the festival of wells, called Fontinalia, at which the wells were adorned with garlands, and flowers thrown into them.

FORNAX
A goddess of Rome who presided over the ripening of the corn and prevented it being burnt while baking the bread in the oven. Her festival, the Fornacalia, was announced by the *curio maximus*. She is sometimes though identical with Vesta.

FORTUNA
A most powerful goddess who was worshipped from remote antiquity by all the ancients. The goddess of fortune, chance and good luck. The Romans placed great confidence in her and some of her epithets are: *Fortuna liberum=* of children; *muliebris=* of women; *patricia, plebia, equestris=* of the different orders, classes and families of the population; *primigenia=* who determines the destiny of the child at its birth; *privata=* of the family; *redux=* who brings safely home; *tranquilla=* the giver of prosperous voyages; *victrix=* giver of victory; *virginalis=* worshipped by newly married women, who dedicated their maiden garments and girdle in her temple, while boys and youths would dedicate to her the first cuttings of their beard and from this - *Fortuna barbata*, etc.

FRAUS
A divinity worshipped among the Romans. She was represented as a beautiful woman whose deformities were concealed in the extremities of her body, which terminated in a serpent spotted with various colours. She was said to preside over treachery, etc.

FRENATRIX or FENATRIX
A epithet of Pallas-Athene because she was said to have been the first to have tamed the horse and rendered it useful to mankind.

GELASINUS
A god of laughter.

HIPPONA
A goddess who presided over horses whose statues were placed in the horse's stables, better know as Epona.

HYGIA or HYGIEA
The daughter of Asclepius, the goddess of health who was held in great veneration among the ancients. She is sometimes conceived as the giver or protectress of mental health - the *mens sana* - lit. 'sane judgement or intellect.' She was identified by the Romans with Salus. She is often

represented giving a serpent a drink from a saucer.

HYMEN or HYMENAEUS
The Greek god of marriage who carries a bridal torch and the nuptial veil. His legend makes him a champion of all women and damsels.

ICELUS
The son of Somnus, brother of Morpheus, was believed to shape the dreams which came, whence he derived his name. The gods, according to **Ovid**, called him Icelus, but men called him Phobetor.

IRIS
Her office was as the messenger from god to god and from the gods to men, just as, for a time, the rainbow connects the heavens with the earth. Some say she cuts the thread that holds the soul in the body of those dying. She is the Greek goddess of the rainbow, with others thinking she is the rainbow itself, and so she is represented with variegated coloured wings. The rainbow is thought to be the road Iris travels, which she dispenses with when not required; it was thought this is why the appearance of the rainbow is so fleeting.

JUVENTAS or JUVENTUS
The Roman goddess of youth and vigour. She is the same as Hebe of the Greeks, a beautiful nymph who was the personification of youth. The chapel of Juventus existed on the Capitol before the temple of Jupiter was built there. She and Terminus, are said to have opposed the consecration of the temple of Jupiter.

KER
The necessity of death personified. Ker is the goddess of death or of fate, doom and destruction. The goddess of mischief or evil, so of bane, evil itself, moral evil or disgrace. The plural form seems to allude to the various ways of dying. The *Keres* (= the plural, not the goddess Ceres), are described as formidable, dark and hateful because they carry off men to the joyless house of Hades. None living can escape them yet they have no absolute power over the life of a human being. They are under Zeus and the gods, who can stay them in their course or hasten them in their task. Even mortals may, for a time, evade them to prevent their purpose by flight and such like. During battle the Keres wander about with Eris (= the goddess who calls forth war and discord) and Cydoimos in bloody vestments, quarrelling over the wounded and the dead, dragging them

away by the feet. They avenge the crimes of men. The Keres are described as raging in fight and glutting themselves with the blood of the wounded.

LARES
Gods at Rome, the good spirits of the departed who even after death continued to be active in bringing blessing on their posterity, closely connected with the Manes, who presided over the houses and families. Every house had a lar familiaris who was the 'lord' or tutelary spirit of the family and its chief care was to prevent the family dying out. There are two classes: the *Lares domestici* and *Lares publici*. The Lares were invoked as protectors on journeys in the country, in war and while on the sea.

LARVAE
In Roman belief the Larvae were in direct contrast to the Lares - the good spirits of the departed. The Larvae were the souls of dead people who could not find rest, due to their having met a violent death, their own guilt or having met with some indignity. It was thought they wandered abroad in the form of spectres who would strike the living with madness. The expiatory rites to expel them from a house were held on three days of the year, the 9th, 11th and 13th of May, the *Lemuria*, when all temples were closed and marriage avoided. Now you know why the month of May, in the West, is considered unlucky for marriages.

LEVANA
A goddess of Rome who presided over the action of the person who took up from the ground a new-born babe after it had been put there by the midwife. This ceremony was generally performed by the father and was so religiously observed and binding that the legitimacy of a child could be disputed without it. In picking up the child the father declared his intention not to kill it but to bring it up.

LIBERA
A Roman goddess who was regarded as the same as Proserpina. Liber and Libera were regarded as the children of Ceres. Libera was a name give by St. Augustine to the divinity who presided over the union of the sexes.

LIBITINA
The Roman goddess who presided over funerals. Some think she is the same as Venus or, more properly, Proserpina/Persephone because of the connection with death and burial. Her temple in Rome was the repository for everything necessary for burial which could be bought or hired.

Sometimes poets would used her name for death itself, because of this connection an undertaker was called *libitinarius*, and his business *libitina*, the beds on which the corpses were burnt were also called *libitina*.

LITAE
The personification of the prayers offered up in repentance. They are described as the daughters of Zeus who follow closely behind crime and endeavour to make amends for what has been done. Those who disdain to receive them have to atone themselves for the crime that has been committed. (see Ate).

LUA
The goddess of Rome who presided over things that were purified by lustration. She is called sometimes *Lua Saturni*, and she is thought of as being the same as Ops, or Rhea of the Greeks. Sometimes the arms of the defeated enemy which were taken in battle were dedicated to her and burnt as a sacrifice, to avert punishment or further calamity.

LUCINA
The goddess of light, or rather the goddess that brings things to light, and hence she presides over the birth of children. It was a epithet used for Juno and Diana and the two are sometimes called *Lucinae*. When women of rank gave birth to a son, a lectisternium was prepared for Juno Lucina in the atrium of the house. *Lectisternium*= 'the feast of the gods, an offering in which the images of the gods, lying on pillows were placed in the streets, and food of all kinds set before them; these banquets were prepared by the Epulones (= a college of priests who superintended the sacrificial banquets to the gods), and consumed by them.'

LUNA
The moon. The sun and moon were worshipped by Greeks and Romans and among the latter the worship of Luna is said to have been introduced in the time of Romulus. However this may be, it is certain, despite the assertions of **Varro** that Sol and Luna were reckoned among the great gods, their worship never occupied a prominent place in the worship of the Romans. The two divinities only had a small chapel in the Via Sacra. As Helios and Selene were distinct from Apollo and Artemis, so Sol and Luna seem to have been very early distinguished from Dianus (= Janus) and Diana. **Tatius** worshipped both Diana and Luna. We can also find Luna Mater. Selene, the sister of Helios, drove her chariot through the sky while he was reposing after the toils of the day. This is why we sometimes

find the moon called 'the chariot or car of the sun' for, having no light of her own, she carries the light of the sun; we can also find the Chariot of the Sun used as an old name for the eighteenth card of the tarot - The Moon. In some reports Selene is represented as the sister of Helios, but in another view she is made his daughter, he being 'the source of her light.' The later poets give steers or heifers as the draught-cattle of Selene; this notion had its very natural origin in the contemplation of the horned moon. Luna, on account of her greater influence upon the Roman mode of calculating time, seems to have been revered even more highly than Sol, for there was a major temple of her on the Aventine, the building of which was ascribed to Servius Tulius. A second sanctuary of Luna existed on the Capitol and a third on the Palatine, where she was worshipped under the name of *Noctiluca*= 'lamp of the night,' and her temple was lit up each night. Not a great deal is known regarding her worship. On the Aventine, as goddess of the month, she received worship on the last day of March, which was the first month of the Roman year.

MALA FORTUNA
The goddess of evil fortune as worshipped by the Romans.

MANES
A name given by the Romans to the spirits of the dead, which were held to be immortal like the gods and hence designated as such: *manes*= 'the good' - *dii manes*. They dwell below the earth and only come forth at certain seasons of the year. Mania is an old Italian goddess of the Manes: she was loved on her way to the nether world by the messenger of Jupiter, who was Mercury, and the Lares were their offspring. She had two children by Mercury which is why, it is thought, there are two statues of the Lares. At a later date the heads of poppies and garlic were offered to her and woollen dolls; these latter were suspended on doors for protection.

MATURNA
One of the Roman deities who presided over marriage.

MATUTA
A deity among the Romans, commonly called Mater Matuta. She is usually considered as the goddess of the dawn of morning, identical with Aurora, and her name is considered to be connected with *maturus* (= 'ripe, seasonable, timely, etc.) or *matutinus*(= 'belonging to the morning, morning, matutine). Her ceremonies, observed at her festival to Matralia (*matralis*= 'pertaining to a mother'), which took place on the 11th of June,

were intended to enjoin that people should take care of the children of deceased brothers and sisters, as if they were their own, and that they should not be left to the mercy of slaves and hirelings, who were in fact so odious to the goddess, that she delighted in their chastisement. A certain resemblance between her ceremonies and those of the Greek deity Leuchothea (= the name of the deified Ino) led the Romans to identify Matuta and Leucothea. Because Leucothea (= Ino) had been unfortunate with her own children the people did not entreat Matuta/Leucothea to protect their own children. No female slaves were permitted to enter her temple and if they transgressed, they were severely beaten; one slave was admitted to the Matralia festival, but this was only so she could be struck in humiliation by one of the matrons and sent away. Because Leucothea/ Ino was saved by dolphins when she threw herself and her child into the sea, she was regarded as a marine deity. She was worshipped by sailors in Neptune's temple who implored her to protect them against storms and the perils of the sea.

MEDITRINA
The Roman goddess who dealt with the arts of healing, in whose honour the festival, the *Meditinalia*, was celebrated in October. She presided over curing disorders. The Meditrinalia was one of the festivals connected with the cultivation of vineyards. It took place on the 11th of October, on which day the people of Latium began to taste their wine (= *mustum*), and offer libations to the gods. **Varro** derives the name of the festival from the healing power of the new wine, but **Festus** speaks of a goddess Meditrina.

MEPHITIS
A goddess said by some to preside over the public *cloacae* (= sewers) and all infected places. She had a grove and temple in the Equilliae on a spot that was thought fatal to enter. Who Mephitis was is very obscure. It is thought she was invoked against the influence of mephitic exhalations of the earth in the grove of Albunea. Lat. *mephitis*= 'a noxious, pestilential exhalation, malaria.' **Servius** mentions a male divinity of this name that was connected with Leucothia in the same manner as Adonis with Aphrodite, and that others identified her with Juno.

MORPHEUS
The son of Hypnos and the god and watchman of dreams. The name signifies the fashioner or moulder of dreams, because he shaped or

formed the dreams which appeared to the dreamer, Morpheus only appears in human form, he imitated the grimaces, gestures, words and manners of mankind. He is generally represented as a sleeping child with wings. He holds a vase in one hand, and in the other are some poppies. He is best known from the description of the Caves of Sleep by **Ovid.**

MYIAGRUS or MYIODES
The fly-catcher, is the name of a hero, who was invoked at Aliphera, a town in Arcadia situated on a hill, at the festival of Athene, as a protector against flies according to **Pausanias.**

NASCIO or NATIO
A Roman goddess who watched over the birth of children. Accordingly a goddess assisting Lucina in her functions and analogous to the Greek Eileithyia. She had a sanctuary in the neighbourhood of Ardea.

NEMESIS
She is one of the infernal deities and the goddess of vengeance and retribution. Prepared to punish impiety and, at the same time, liberally reward the good and virtuous. She is a kind of fatal divinity for she directs human affairs in such a manner as to restore the right proportions or equilibrium wherever it has been disturbed. She measures out happiness and unhappiness. He who is blessed with too many or too frequent gifts of fortune is visited by her with losses and sufferings, in order that he may become humble, and feel that there are bounds beyond which human happiness cannot proceed with safety. This notion arose from a belief that the gods were envious of excessive human happiness. Nemesis is thus a check upon the sometimes extravagant favours conferred by Tyche or Fortuna.

NEMESTRINUS
The god who presided over the feasts celebrated in Rome under the name Nemora.

NENIA or NAENIA
The goddess of funerals at Rome. Nenia is a dirge or lamentation uttered quietly or sung with flutes at funerals either by the relatives or the hired mourners (= *praeficae*). At Rome Nenia was personified and worshipped as a goddess with a chapel; so many of the gods connected with the dead, it was outside the city. Nenia was often regarded as a lullaby, because they were sung with a soft voice, by which the dead where lulled to sleep.

NEREUS
God of the sea, son of Pontus and Gaia, and husband to Doris by whom
he was the father of the fifty (according to a later account, two hundred),
beautiful Sea-nymphs, the Nereids. He is described as a wise and unerring
old man of the sea, at the bottom of which he dwelt. His empire is the
Mediterranean or in a resplendent cave in the Aegean. Like other marine
divinities he was believed to have the gift of prophecy regarding the
future and of appearing to mortals in and shape he chooses to assume. He
is represented as an old man with leaves of seaweed for hair and a sceptre
or trident. **Virgil** mentions the trident as his attribute, and the epithets
given him by the poets refer to his old age, his kindliness to mortals, and
his trustworthy knowledge of the future. His daughters were especially
worshipped on the islands on the coasts, and the mouths of rivers; often
seen riding dolphins and Tritons. Triton was the son of Poseidon and
Amphitrite, represented as a man in his upper parts, terminating in the
dolphin's tail; his special attribute is a twisted seashell, on which he
blows, now violently, now gently, to raise or calm the billows. In the
course of time, like Pan and Faunus, there grew up the notion of a large
number of Tritons, regarded as attendants on other sea-gods.

NICE or NIKE
The goddess of victory. She is usually represented as winged with a
wreath and a palm branch. As a herald of victory she had the wand of
Hermes. This representation was especially revered by the Romans under
the name Victoria, called earlier Vica Pota= *'victorious issue.'* She was
adored as the guardian goddess of the senate, where her statue permanently
stood, until Christianity became the religion of the empire. When Zeus
fought the Titans, he called upon the gods for assistance Nice and her two
sisters - Zelus (= *zeal*) and Cratos (= *strength*) - were the first to come
forward and Zeus asked them to come to Olympus to live.

NIXI DII
The general term and name given by the Romans to those deities who
watched over the delivery of women. There were three statues sacred to
them in the Capitol, in a bending posture.

NOCTURNUS
A god assumed to be the same as Vesper and Nox, who were said to
preside over the night.

NODINUS
The divinity who presided over the knots that are found the stems of plants producing grain as it ripens. It is probable that originally it was a epithet of Saturnus.

NOMIUS
A epithet of divinities protecting the pastures and shepherds, such as Apollo, Pan, Hermes and Aristaeus.

NOMOS
The personification of law, described as the ruler of gods and men.

NONDINA
A goddess who presided over the lustrations made for children before they received their name, which was generally nine days after their birth for boys and eight days for a girl. The ceremony of lustration was performed by carrying the child around the divinity's altar fire then sprinkling it with the lustration.

NOVENSILES
This is a name applied to those divinities whose worship was introduced into Rome from foreign countries.

NUMENIA or NEOMENIA
A festival observed by the Greeks at the beginning of every lunar month in honour of the gods, but especially Apollo or the sun. Apollo was justly deemed the author of light and the stated divisions of time, namely, the days and nights, the months and the seasons. Solemn prayers were offered at Athens during the festival for the prosperity of the republic. The demigods, as well as the heroes of the ancients, were honoured and invoked.

ONEIROS
A personification of dream, and in the plural of dreams. According to **Homer**, Dreams dwell on the dark shores of the western Oceanus. The deceitful dreams come through the ivory gate, while the true dreams issue from a gate made of horn. **Hesiod** calls dreams the children of the night, and **Ovid** calls them the children of Sleep and mentions three of them by name: Morpheus, Icelus or Phobetor and Phantasus. **Euripides** called them sons of Gaia and conceived them as genii with wings.

ORBONA

A goddess of Rome who was supplicated not to deprive parents of their children of their parents and she was invoked by those who had been deprived of their children and wanted more. She was the protectress of orphans for she took care of those who were deprived of their parents. She was also invoked in the serious maladies of children. The difficulty with Orbona is twofold. Did she make the children die for she was, 'supplicated not to deprive parents of their children' or, she 'took care of those who were deprived of their parents' ? Is it one, the other or both? My Latin Lexicon gives: Orbona - 'The tutelary goddess of parents bereft of their children.'

ORCUS

Hades, one of the names of the god of hell, the same as Pluto, often confounded with Charon. He carried men off to the lower world and kept them imprisoned there. The name Orcus is often used to signify the infernal regions, Hades.

PANACEA

The 'All-healing.' One of the daughters of Asclepius, who presided over health. She had a temple at Oropus. The word was afterwards applied to salt which was presumed to remove pain. It is the name given to a preparation extracted from herbs thought to possess the power of healing.

PANDEMOS

This is a epithet of Aphrodite and describes one of her two aspects. Pandemos describes her as the goddess of low sensual pleasure, Venus vulgivaga or popularis in opposition to Venus (Aphrodite) Urania or the heavenly Aphrodite. She was worshipped in Athens along with Peitho= *persuasion.* Aphrodite Pandemos was worshipped in Arcadia at Megalopolis, where her sacrifice was white goats. The name is also applied as a epithet to Eros.

PARTUNDA

A Roman deity who presided over childbirth, she was invoked by women in labour.

PAVENTIA

A Roman goddess who was invoked to protect her votaries from the effects of terror.

PAX
The personification of peace, an ancient divinity among the Romans. Her festival, and that of Salus, was celebrated on the 30th of April. She was often found holding Plutus to indicate that peace gives rise to prosperity and opulence.

PEITHO
In Greek mythology the personification of persuasion; she usually appears in the train of Aphrodite with Eros and the Graces. As the goddess of persuasion she is also connected with Hermes who becomes the god of persuasive eloquence. Peitho also occurs as the epithet of other divinities.

PELLONIA
A goddess of Rome whose power was used to assist mortals in repelling the attacks of enemies.

PENATES
The household gods of the Romans with regard to the family and the state as a great family of citizens. Strictly the guardians of the storeroom (= *penus*) which in old Roman houses stood next to the atrium, in later times near the back of the building (= *penetralia*). The penates were two in number. They presided over the well-being and domestic affairs of families and houses which a full storehouse indicated, hence this chamber was sacred to them and holy. It was not to be entered by those defiled. The hearth of the house was their altar. They were called *Penates* because their images were generally placed in the central, innermost and most secret part of the house, the penetralia, and thus protected the whole household.

PERTUNDA
A Roman goddess who presided over the consummation of the marriage. Her statue was usually placed in the bridal chamber.

PETA
The goddess who presided over the petitions that were to be offered to the gods. She was consulted to know whether they would prove acceptable.

PHANTASUS
One of the dreams of Sleep. The son of Somnus, brother of Morpheus and Phobetor. Phobetor is man's name for this son but he is called Icelus by the gods. Phantasus generally changed himself into rocks, rivers, mountains and towns in dreams, while Morpheus assumed the shape of human

beings and Phobetor that of animals. Sleep has a beautiful cave and Phantasus is in his cortege.

PHORCUS or PHORCYS
A sea deity presumably invoked in marine affairs. Acording to the **Homeric** poems 'an old man of the sea' to whom the harbour of Ithaca was dedicated. Father of the Gorgons and the Hesperian dragon which protected the apples of the Hesperides.

PIETAS
The personification of faithful attachment, love, veneration and tenderness among the Romans. This virtue was given divine honours and was made a goddess of domestic affection. Her legend says she supported the life of one of her parents with the milk of her breast, when they were condemned to death by starvation. She is seem on Roman coins, as a matron throwing incense upon an altar, and her attributes are a stork and children. Pietas is sometimes represented as a female figure offering her breast to an aged parent.

POSTVERTA or POSTVORTA
This is thought to be a epithet of Carmenta, describing her as looking backward and looking to the past, which she revealed to poets and other mortals. In like manner the prophetic power with which she looked into the future, is indicated by the surnames Antevorta, Prorsa and Porrima. Poets have personified these attributes of Carmenta, and describe them as companions of the goddess.

POTINA or PONUA
A goddess of Rome who presided over children's potions.

PRAXIDICE
A Greek goddess who presided over the execution of enterprises and who punished evil actions. She is the goddess who carries out the objects of justice or watches that justice is done to men. In Boeotia we find the Praxidicae, in the plural, who were called the daughters of Ogyges, with the names Alalcomenia, Aulis and Thelxinoea. Their images consisted merely of heads and their sacrifices where the heads of animals.

PREMA
A Roman goddess who presided over the consummation of marriage.

PUDICITIA

A goddess of modesty who, as her name implies, presided over chastity. Lat. *pudicitia*= 'chastity, modesty, purity (in a more limited application than *pudor*). She was worshipped both in Greece and in Rome where she had two sanctuaries dedicated to her, the *Pudicitia patricia* and the *Pudicitia plebia*. No woman who had married twice was permitted to touch her statue. She was considered by many to be the same as *Fortuna Muliebris*, a epithet of Fortuna. The cult died with the decay of morals.

PUTA

A divinity of Rome who presided over the pruning of trees.

QUIETIS FANUM

A temple outside the walls of Rome. Quies was the goddess of rest and the personification of tranquillity who, some say, the Romans refused to permit within the city walls. It is suggested this was because the glory of Rome and the Empire rested on activity of which Quies was the antithesis. Other authorities tell us there was a chapel to her that stood on the via Lavicana, probably as a resting place for the weary traveller. Some think Quies means death or Proserpina.

REDICULUS

A deity whose name is derived from the word *redito*= 'a returning.' This deity was held responsible for having induced Hannibal, when he was close to the gates of the city, to retire or return southwards. A place on the Appian road, near the second milestone from the city was called Campus Rediculi. It is thought he may have been one of the Lares of the city of Rome. **Varro** tells us he calls himself Tutanus= 'the god who keeps us safe.'

RUMILIA, RUMIA or RUMINA

A Roman goddess who presided over the female breasts and infants while still at the breast, the protectress of infants in general. Suckling cattle were also under her protection. The sacrifices offered to Rumina consisted of libations of milk and not wine. Some think it signifies breast or milk and the fig tree under which Romulus and Remus were found bore the name of *Ruminal ficus*. This epithet, *Ruminus* - 'the nourishing' - was also a epithet of Jupiter.

RUNCIA

This is possibly a epithet of Ops by which he was invoked by the people of Italy to prevent the growth of weeds among the corn and to promote the harvest.

SALUS

The personification of health, prosperity and the public welfare, among the Romans. In the first of these three senses she answers very closely to the Greek goddess Hygia, and was accordingly represented in works of art with the same attributes as the Greek goddess. In the second sense she represents prosperity in general, and was invoked by husbandmen at seed-time. In the third sense Salus is the goddess of the public welfare - Salus publica or Romana. She had a temple on the Quirinal Hill, she was worshipped publicly on the 30th of April in conjunction with Pax, Concordia and Janus. She was consulted every year to observe the signs for the purpose of ascertaining the fortunes of the republic during the coming year; this observation of the signs was called the augurium Salutis. Salus was represented, like Fortuna, with a rudder, a globe at her feet, and sometimes in a sitting posture, pouring from a *patera* (= a broad flat dish or saucer) a libation upon an altar around which a serpent is winding itself.

SIGALION

The name of the god of silence honoured by the Egyptians under the appellation Harpocrates.

SLEEP

The son of Night and twin-brother of Death. With his brother Death, according to **Hesiod**, he dwells in the eternal darkness of Tartarus, from where he sweeps over the land bringing sleep to men and Gods, since he has power over all alike. He could even lull Zeus himself to sleep. Sleep is depicted in various forms and situations, frequently with the wings of an eagle or a butterfly on his forehead, a poppy stalk and a horn from which he dropped slumber upon those he lulls to rest. Hermes was also a god of sleep. Somnus is the personification of the god of sleep, the Greek Hypnos is described by the ancients as a brother of Death and as a son of Night. In works of art Sleep and Death are represented alike as two youths sleeping in each others arms or holding inverted torches in their hands. (Gr. *Hypnos*; Lat. *Somnus*).

SPINENSIS or SPINIENSIS

A god of the Romans whose power was invoked to clear fields from thorns and briars, hence the name.

STIMULA

A Roman goddess who roused and animated the indolent, though others say she presided over excess of all kinds and patronised debauchery.

SUADA or SUADELA
A goddess of persuasion, called Peitho by the Greeks. She is also called by the diminutive Suadela.

TACITA
A goddess of silence - 'the silent one.' One of the Camenae, whose worship was thought to have been introduced by Numa. He was said to have paid particular veneration to her and recommended that others do the same, as she was the most important of the Camenae, the prophetic nymphs.

TARAXIPPUS
A deity placed near racecourses whose protection was invoked so no danger or harm might come to the horses during the races.

THEMIS
She personifies the order of things established by law, custom and equity, whence she is described as reigning in the assembles of men and, at the command of Zeus, convening the assembly of the gods. She presided over the petitions that were to be presented to the gods, being vigilant that nothing improper or unreasonable was asked of the divinities. She was an ancient prophetic divinity and it said she had possession of Delphi as the successor of Ge, and prior to Apollo. She is often represented on coins resembling Athene, with a cornucopia and scales.

TIMOR
A divinity among the Romans worshipped by the Greeks under the name of Phobos. Lat. *timor*= 'fear, dread, apprehension and alarm.'

TUTELINA or TUTULINA
A goddess of Rome, most likely an attribute of Ops, invoked to protect the fruits which at harvest time had been brought in from the fields. Tutelina, Secia and Messia had three pillars with altars before them in the Circus.

TUTINUS or TUTUNUS
A deity of Rome who presided over conjugal duties, whose statue people lately married touched to remove sterility. Women made their offerings with their head veiled.

TYCHE

The personification of chance or luck, the Fortuna of the Romans. In time she came to be extensively worshipped as the goddess of prosperity. She is represnted with different attributes, with a rudder she was conceived to be the divinity guiding and conducting the affairs of the world; in this respect she is called one of the Moerae. With a ball she represents the unsteadiness of fortune, with Plutus or the cornucopia as plenty and so forth. She is usually found with symbols that express her variability.

VEJOVIS or VEDIUS

A deity of ill-omen in Rome where he had a temple raised by Romulus which stood in the hollow between the Arx and the Capitol. Some think he was similar to Jupiter in the cradle, as he was without thunder or sceptre. The only thing by his side was the goat Amalthea and the Cretan nymph who fed him while an infant. Some viewed him as the 'Little Jupiter or Young Jupiter,' others call him the 'destructive Jupiter' while others saw in him the avenging Apollo of the Greeks, and identify him with Pluo, his nane sig .fies *Injurious Gcd*. The Etruscan divinity had lightning that produced deafness in those wl o were struck by them, even before they were actually hurled. His templc at Rome stood between the Capitol and the Tarpeian rock.

VERTUMNUS or VORTUMNUS

A deity at Rome who presided over spring and orchards, the change of the seasons, purchase or sale, the return of the rivers to their proper beds, etc., though some authorities say he is actually only concerned with the transformation of plants and their progress from being in blossom to that of bearing fruit. His name signifies 'the god who changes or metamorphoses himself.' Thus the Romans connected him with anything of this nature and to which the verb *verto*= 'to turn, to turn around, about, esp. to turn, to change, to alter' refers.

VICAPOTA or VICA POTA

A deity of Rome - 'the Victor and Conqueror' - who presided over victory, whose temple was situated at the foot of the hill Velia.

VITULA

A goddess of Rome who presided over festivals and their rejoicing.

VITUMNUS

A Roman deity who was invoked by women after conception that he may preserve the foetus and bring it to maturity.

VOLTUMNA or VULTURNA
A goddess in Rome who presided over kindness and good will. She is the same as Volumna.

VOLUMNUS and VOLUMNA
The two deities who presided over the will. They were chiefly invoked at marriage to preserve concord between husband and wife.

VOLUPIA or VOLUPTAS
A goddess, the personification of sensual pleasure who was worshipped at Rome, she was honoured with a temple near the Porta Romanula. She was represented as a young and beautiful women, well dressed and elegantly adorned, seated on a throne, and having Virtue under her feet.

The Festivals

The following list are the 'festivals' mentioned in the title at the head of this chapter. A few festivals have been introduced in the main text and some could be repeated in part here. Like the semones, it was thought it might be of interest to the reader to introduce some of the lesser known festivals. They are concerned, generally, with birth, growth, life and death in the human world and the world of nature, or of general interest regarding Athens and Rome and their respective countries. With some entries only the significant information is given.

AGRAULIA
This is a festival celebrated by the Athenians in honour of Agraulos, the daughter of Cecrops. We have no details regarding the time or manner of its celebration. It is thought to be connected with the solemn oath, which all Athenians, when they reached manhood, were obliged to take in the temple of Agraulos, that they would defend their country, and always obey its laws.

ALOA
An Attic festival, but observed primarily at Eleusis, in honour of Demeter and Dionysus, the originators of the plough and protectors of the fruits of the earth. Ceres has also been called Aloas and Alois. It took place every year after the harvest was over, as a grateful acknowledgement for the benefits the husbandman had received, and partly that the next harvest might be bountiful. We learn from **Demosthenes**, that it was illegal to tender any bloody sacrifice on the day of this festival, and that the priests alone had the privilege to offer the fruits.

AMBROSIA and the BRUMALIA
These were festivals observed in Greece, in honour of Dionysus, which is the same as the Brumalia of the Romans. They may have their name from the luxuries of the table, or from the indulgence of drinking. *Ambrosia*= 'the food of the gods; as nectar is their drink.' These festivals were solemnized in the month of Lenaeon (= January or February), during the vintage. The Brumalia were celebrated in Rome during December, they were first instituted by Romulus. They are thought to have derived their name either from *Bromius* (= 'the noisy one' - on account of the

tumultuous celebration of his festivals), one of the surnames of Dionysus, or from an allusion to the cold season (*bruma*= the shortest day of the year or winter), the time at which they were celebrated.

AMPHIDROMIA
A family festival of the Athenians at which the newly born child was introduced into the family, and received its name. No particular day was fixed for the solemnity; but it did not take place too soon after the birth of the child, for it was believed that most children died before the seventh day. The solemnity was generally deferred until after that period, that there might be at least some probability of the child remaining alive. The house was decorated outside with olive branches when the child was a boy, or with garlands of wool if a girl. The child was carried by the nurse who ran around the fire and thus, as it were, presented the baby to the gods of the house and the family, at the same time the child received its name to which the guests were witness.

ANTHESPHORIA
A flower festival, primarily celebrated in Sicily, in honour of Demeter and Persephone, in commemoration of the return of Persephone to her mother at the beginning of spring. It consisted of gathering flowers and twining garlands, because Persephone had been carried off by Pluto while doing this. The women gathered flowers for the garlands which they wore on the occasion, it would have been a disgrace to buy flowers for that purpose. The Anthesphoria were also solemnized in honour of other deities especially Hera at Argos where maidens carrying baskets filled with flowers, went in procession, while a special tune was played on the flute. Aphrodite too was worshipped at Cnossus, under the name of   and has therefore been compared with Flora, the Roman deity, as the Anthesphoria have been with the Roman festival of the *Florifertum*, or *Floralia* (= 'a flower garden').

ARTEMESIA
One of the great festivals celebrated in honour of Artemis in various parts of Greece, in the spring of the year. It is mentioned at Syracuse in honour of Artemis Potamia and Soteria It lasted three days, which were principally spent in feasting and amusements. Bread was offered to her as the 'goddess of childbirth.' Artemis is the protectress of youth, especially those of her own sex. The Ionians, at their Arpaturia, presented her with some hair of the boys. Almost everywhere young girls revered the virgin goddess as the guardian of their maiden years, and before marriage they offered up to her a lock of their hair, their girdle, and their maiden garment.

These festivals occur in many other places in Greece, as at Delphi, where, according to **Hegesander,** they offered to the goddess a mullet on this occasion; because it appeared to hunt and kill the sea-hare, and thus bore some resemblance to Artemis, the goddess of hunting. *Soteria*= 'the saving goddess' occurs as the epithet of several female divinities in Greece; just as *Soter*= 'the saviour' (Latin: *Servator*= 'one who gives attention, watcher, saviour' or *Sospes*= 'saving, delivering') occurs as the epithet of several male divinities.

CARMENTALIA
An old Roman festival celebrated in honour of the nymph Carmenta or Carmentis and she is supposed to be the divinity to whom the Greeks offered sacrifice under the name Themis, who was worshipped at Athens. This festival was observed annually on the 11th and 15th of January, and no other particulars of it are recorded except that Carmenta was invoked in it as *Postvorta* and *Antevorta*, epithets which had reference to her power of protecting women in childbirth, and the power of looking back into the past and forward into the future. *Postvorta*= 'a goddess presiding over childbirth, who was invoked when the child made the wrong presentation.' This goddess was entreated to render the Roman matrons prolific, and their labours easy. *Antevorta*= 'The name of a goddess who reminds men of things past.' The festival was chiefly observed by women. In Rome, Carmenta, had a priest attached to her service, the *Flamen Carmentalis*, and at her festival of the Carmentalia, the flamen and pontifex assisted at a shrine near the gate under the Capitol, named after her, the Porta Carmentalis.

CERERALIA
A festival celebrated at Rome in honour of Ceres, whose wanderings in search of her lost daughter Proserpina, were portrayed by women clothed in white, who ran about with lighted torches and they were adorned with crowns of ripe ears of corn, they offered to the goddess the firstfruits of the harvest. During the festival, games were celebrated in the Circus Maximus, the spectators of which were dressed in white, However, on any occasion of public mourning the games and festivals were not celebrated, as the matrons could not appear at them except in white. The day of the Cereralia is doubtful; some think it was the ides or 13th of April, others the 7th of that month.

CHARISTIA
The name of the festival comes from the Greek meaning - 'to grant favour

or pardon,' *charisticum*= 'a gift, present.' A Roman feast, to which none but relations and members of the same family were invited, in order that any quarrel or disagreement which had arisen among them might be made up, and reconciliation affected. It was celebrated every year on the 19th of February.

CHLOEIA or CHLOIA

A festival celebrated at Athens in honour of Demeter Chloe, or simply Chloe, whose temple stood near the Acropolis. A epithet of Demeter, the protectress of the green fields, who had a sanctuary at Athens together with Ge Curotrophas. Chloe - 'the blooming.' The name Chloe is supposed to have the same significance as Flava, so often applied to the goddesses of corn. The Chloeia was solmenized in spring, on the sixth of Thargelion (May-June), when the blossoms began to appear, with the sacrifice of a goat and much mirth and rejoicing; a ram was often sacrificed to her.

COMPITALIA

This is also called *Ludi Compitalicii*, a festival celebrated once a year in honour of the *lares compitales*, to whom sacrifices were offered at the places were two or more ways met. Small images of men and women were placed on tables on public roads, to represent the protecting gods, lamps were burned in their honour, and the doors of houses were decked with the branches of trees. Within the master offered sacrifices at the feet of his Lares. **Dionysius** tells us the sacrifices consisted of honey-cakes which were presented by the inhabitants of each house, and the persons, who assisted as ministering servants at the festival, were not freemen, but slaves because the Lares took pleasure in the service of slaves; he further adds that the Compitalia were celebrated a few days after the Saturnalia with great splendour, and that the slaves on this occasion had full liberty given them to do what they pleased. The Lares were invoked with the mother of the Lares, also called *Lara, Larunda* or *Mania*, and had an ancient altar and temple to themselves in Rome. The Lares were invoked as protectors on a journey, in the country, in war and on the sea. In contrast to these good spirits we have the Larvae. The exact day on which this festival was celebrated appears to have varied, though it was always during the winter. **Lempriere** gives the 12th of January and the 6th of March.

CONSUALIA

A festival with games, celebrated by the Romans in honour on Consus, an ancient god presiding over councils and secret deliberations or, according the Livy, of Neptunus Equester. **Plutarch**, among others, say that Neptunus Equester and Consus were only different names for one and the same deity. Neptunus had a temple in the Circus Flaminius, whilst in the Circus Maximus, the old Italian god Consus had an altar in a similar capacity. The Consualia was solemnized twice every year, on the 21st of August, after the harvest, and the 15th of December, after the sowing was ended. The Consualia was symbolically celebrated, in the Circus with the ceremony of uncovering an altar dedicated to the god, which was buried in the earth. For Romulus, who was considered as the founder of the festival, was said to have discovered an altar in the earth on that spot, this altar was always covered except for this festival. This solemnity took place on the 21st of August with horse and chariot races, and libations were poured into the flames which consumed the sacrifices. During these festive games, horses and mules were not allowed to do any work, and were crowned and adorned with garlands of flowers and led through the streets. Consequently the god Consus was afterwards identified with *Poseidon Hippios* or *Neptunus Equester.*

ELLOTIA or HELLOTIA
A festival with a torch race celebrated at Corinth in honour of Athene as goddess of fire. Hellotia or Hellotis, a epithet of Athene at Corinth, the name is said to be derived from the fertile marsh near Marathon, where Athene had a sanctuary or from Hellotia, one of the daughters of Timander. She fled to the temple of Athene when Corinth was burned down, both she and her sister perished when the temple was destroyed by fire. A plague broke out in Corinth and the oracle said it would not cease until a sanctuary of Athene Hellotis was built and the souls of the sister propitiated. According to **Seleucus**, a myrtle garland twenty yards in circumference, which was carried about in the procession of the festival of Ellotia.

HILARIA
This seems originally to have been a name which was given to any day or season of rejoicing, *hilaris*= 'cheerful, merry, jovial.' The *Hilaria* were, therefore, according to **Maximus Monachus** either private or public. Among the former he reckons the day on which a person married, and on which a son was born; among the latter, those of public rejoicing appointed by a new emperor. Such days were devoted to general rejoicing and public sacrifices, and no one was allowed to show any symptoms of grief or sorrow. The Romans also celebrated Hilaria, as *feria* (= 'days of rest, holidays, festivals') *stativa*(= 'abiding still in one place'), on the 25th

of March, in honour of Cybele, the mother of the gods; and it is probably to distinguish these Hilaria from those mentioned earlier, that **Lampridius** calls them *Hilaria Matris Deum*. The day of its celebration was the first day after the vernal equinox, or the first day of the year which was longer than the night. The winter with its gloom had passed away, and the first day of a better season was spent in rejoicing. The exact form the festival took is not known, but the statue of the goddess was carried through the streets in procession, preceded by her votaries carrying their finest possessions. The city was filled with laughter and pleasure for several days and individuals could dress as they saw fit, even in the robes of a magistrate.

INOA
Festivals celebrated in several parts of Greece in honour of the ancient heroine Ino. At Megara she was honoured with an annual sacrifice, because the Megarians believed that her body had been cast up by the waves upon their coast, and that it had been found and buried there by Cleso and Tauropolis. Another festival of Ino was celebrated at Epidaurus Limera, in Laconia. In the neighbourhood of this town there was a small but very deep lake, called the *Water of Ino*, and at the festival of the heroine people threw barley-cakes into the water. When the cakes sank it was considered a propitious sign, but if they floated on the surface it was an evil sign. An annual festival with contests and sacrifices, in honour of Ino, was also held on the Corinthian Isthmus.

MATRALIA
A festival celebrated at Rome every on the 11th of June, in honour of goddess Mater Matuta, whose temple stood in the Forum Boarium. It was celebrated only by Roman matrons, only freeborn matrons were allowed to attend, and sacrifices offered to the goddess consisted of cakes baked in pots of earthenware. Slaves were not allowed to take part in the solemnities, or to enter the temple of the goddess. One slave, however, was admitted by the matrons, but only to be exposed to humiliating treatment, for one of the matrons gave her a blow on the cheek and then sent her away from the temple. The matrons on this occasion took with them the children of their sisters, but not their own, held them in their arms, and prayed for their welfare. This was done in remembrance of the history of Ino and Melicerta, her son, a custom which indirectly tended to introduce harmony and friendship into private families. The statue of the goddess was then crowned with a garland by a matron who had not

yet lost a husband. The real import of the worship of the Mater Matuta appears to have been to inculcate upon mothers the principle that they ought to take care of the children of their sisters as much as their own, and that they should not leave them to careless slaves. The contempt for whom was symbolically signified by the infliction of a blow on the cheek, and the dismissal of the solitary slave admitted to the temple for the ceremony.

MATRONALIA, also MATRONALES FERIAE
A festival celebrated by the Roman matrons on the 1st of March in honour of Juno Lucina on the Esquiline hill. In the temple of the goddess women and girls prayed to her, and her son Mars, and brought pious offerings. Juno was intimately concerned with the affairs of women and on their birthday the women would offer sacrifices to Juno surnamed Natalis; just as the men sacrificed to their Genius Natalis. Juno was further, like Saturn, the guardian of the finances and protectress of money, under the name Moneta, she had a temple on the Capitoline Hill to which the mint was attached. In the houses sacrifices and prayers were offered for a prosperous wedlock. At this festival wives used to receive presents from their husbands an at a later time, girls from their lovers; the women were accustomed to feast with their female slaves and waited on them as the men did at the Saturnalia. Hence we find the festival called by **Martial** the Saturnalia of women.

MYSIA
A festival celebrated by the inhabitants of Pellene in Achaia in honour of Demeter Mysia. The worship of this goddess was introduced at Pellene from a place called Mysia in the neighbourhood of Argos. Mysia is a epithet of Demeter, it is said to have been derived from an Argive Mysius who received her kindly during her wanderings, and build a sanctuary to her. The festival lasted seven days, and the religious solemnities took place in a temple surrounded by a beautiful grove. The first two days men and women took part in the celebration together; on the third day the men left the sanctuary, and the women remaining in it performed during the night certain mysterious rites, during which not even male dogs were allowed to remain within the sacred precincts. On the fourth day the men returned to the temple, and men and women received each other with shouts of laughter and assailed each other with various raileries. This latter part is reminiscent of Iambe's part in the Demeter myth and the later mysteries and festivals.

PALILIA

This is an extensive festival which has been mentioned earlier. Briefly, it is a festival celebrated in Rome annually on the 21st of April, in honour of Pales, the tutelary divinity of shepherds and cattle. Some of the ancient writers called this festival *Parilia,* deriving the name from *pario,* (= 'to produce, bring forth') because sacrifices were offered that day *pro partu percoris* (= 'before bearing cattle'). The date of the festival was, according to early tradition, the date on which Romulus had commenced the building of Rome, so at the same time the festival was solemnised as the *dies natalitius* (= natal day) of Rome. The October-horse has already been mentioned. When towards the evening the shepherds had fed their flocks, laurel branches were used as brooms for cleaning the stables, and for sprinkling water through them, and lastly the stables were adorned with laurel boughs. The shepherds then burnt sulphur, laurel, rosemary, pine-wood, olive- wood and incense, and made the smoke pass through the stables to purify them; the flocks themselves were also purified with the smoke. The sacrifices which were offered on this day consisted of cakes, millet, milk, and other kinds of provender. The shepherds then offered a prayer to Pales and after the solemn rites of the festival were over, the relaxed part began. First, bonfires were made of hay and straw and lit, through these fires, to the sounds of flutes and cymbals, the sheep were driven three times, quickly followed three times by the shepherds. The festival ended for all in the open air with a feast, at which people sat or lay upon benches of turf and drank their fill.

PLYNTERIA

From *pluno= to wash, of* or *for washing.* Was a festival celebrated at Athens every year, on the 22nd of Thargelion (May-June), in honour of Athene goddess of the city, surnamed Aglauros, whose temple stood on the Acropolis. The day of this festival was at Athens among the *apophorades* or *dies nefasti* (= 'd*ays on which judgement could not be pronounced or assemblies of the people be held*'); for the temple of the goddess was cordoned off by a rope to preclude all communion with it. Her statue was stripped of its garments and ornaments for the purpose of cleaning them, and was in the meantime covered over to hide it from the sight of man. The city was, therefore, so to speak, on this day without its protecting divinity, and any undertaking commenced on it would be unsuccessful. A procession was also held on the day of the festival in which a quantity of dried figs was carried about, because figs were the 'leaders of humanity,' and intimated the progress of civilization among the first peoples of the earth, as they served them as food when they developed a dislike for acorns.

PROMETHEIA

A festival celebrated at Athens in honour of Prometheus, the time it was solemnized is not known, but it is one of the Attic festivals, which were held with a torch-race in the Ceramicus, for which the gymnasiarchs had to supply the youths from the gymnasia. Prometheus himself was believed to have instituted this torch-race, whence he was called the 'torch-bearer.' The torch-race of the *Prometheia* commenced at the altar of Prometheus in the academia, or in the Ceramicus, from where the youths with their torches raced to the city and, he who carried the torch without extinguishing it, won the prize.

SEPTERION

A festival celebrated every nine years at Delphi, in memory of the slaying of the serpent Python by Apollo.

SEPTIMONTIUM

A Roman festival which was held in the month of December. It lasted only for one day (*dies Septimontium*= the circuit of the Seven Hills, *dies Septimontalis*= of or belonging to the feast of the Seven Hills'). The date of the festival is disputed, but the consensus is that it took place on one of the last days of December. The day of the Septimontium was a *dies feriatus* (= 'day of rest from work, to keep a holiday') for the montani, or the inhabitants of the seven ancient hills or rather districts of Rome, who offered on this day sacrifices to the gods of their respective districts. These *sacra* (= 'holy, solemnities') were, like Paganalia, not *sacra publico* (= 'to show or tell the public'), but *privata* (= 'apart from State affairs, for oneself, private'). They were believed to have been instituted to commemorate the enclosure of the Seven Hills of Rome within the walls of the city; on this occasion the sacrifices were offered, as mentioned, in seven different places.

TERMINALIA

A festival to honour the god Terminus, who presided over boundaries. His statue was a stone or post stuck in the ground to indicate the boundary between properties. On the festival the neighbours of the adjoining properties gathered around the landmark, with their wives, children and servants, they crowned the statue with garlands and raised a rude altar, on which they offered up some corn, honeycombs, and wine, they sacrificed a lamb or a sucking pig. They ended the festival with singing the praises of the god. The public festival in honour of this god was observed between the fifth and sixth milestone on the road near the ancient borders of the town of Laurentum at a place called Festi, and at that ancient boundary of the ager Romanus continued to be revered with the same ceremonies as the boundaries of private estates. Here they sacrificed a lamb at the grove of Terminus. On the Capitol there was a stone dedicated to Terminus, which had originally stood in the open air, but when the temple of Jupiter was founded by Tarquin Superbus, it was enclosed within the building, as the augurs would not allow it to be moved. The festival of the Terminalia was celebrated on the last day of the old Roman year, from which some infer its name. February was the last month of the Roman year and the festival is usually set on the 23rd of February. On the day before the *Regifugium* or *Fugalia* (*regi-fugium = rex-fuga* - 'the king's flight' - 'A festival celebrated on the 24th of February, to commemorate the expulsion of the kings'). The Regifugium was a festival at Rome, to celebrate the flight into exile of the Tarquin family. On that occasion, after sacrifices were offered to the goddess of liberty, the chief or king of the priests was obliged to flee from the temple, and to take refuge in the country for a few days.

Terminalis is also a epithet of Jupiter, because he presided over boundaries and lands of individuals before the worship of the god Terminus. Some, and particularly Dionysius suppose that Jupiter and Terminus are the same divinity; remember when the new temple of Jupiter was being built, the removal of the Terminus was not permitted, and was incorporated into Jupiter's temple.

THALYSIA

A festival celebrated in honour of Dionysus and Demeter, or according to others, to Demeter alone as described by Theocritus. It was held in the autumn, after the harvest, to thank the gods for the benefits they had given upon men.

TITHENIDIA

A festival celebrated at Sparta by the nurses who had the care of the male children of the citizens. On this occasion the nurses carried the little boys out of the city to the temple of Artemis surnamed *Corythallia*, which was situated on the bank of the stream Tiassus in the district of Cleta. Here the nurses sacrifice sucking pigs on behalf of the children, and had a feast, there were tents erected near the temple. Each had a separate portion allotted him, together with a small loaf, a piece of new cheese, part of the entrails of the victim and figs, beans and green vetches, instead of sweetmeats.

VINALIA

There were two festivals of this name celebrated by the Romans: the *Vinalia* (= of or belonging to wine) *urbana* (= belonging to the city, town) or *prioria* (= priority, preference), and the *Vinalia rustica* (= of or belonging to the country, rural) or *altera*. (= the one, the other of two). The *Vinalia urbana* was celebrated on the 23rd of April. The festival answered to the Greek *pithoigia* (= the cask opening), as on this occasion the casks which had been filled the preceding autumn were opened for the first time, and the wine tasted. Before the men actually tasted the new wine, a libation was offered to Jupiter, which was called *calpar* (= a vessel for liquids, especially for wine, a wine-cask, a wine-pitcher).

The *Vinalia rustica*, fell on the 19th of August and was celebrated by the inhabitants of Latium, this was the day on which the vintage was opened. On this occasion the *flamen dialis* (= a priest of one particular deity) offered lambs to Jupiter and poured the wine upon the earth, and while the flesh of the victims lay on the altar, he broke with his own hands a bunch of grapes from a vine, and with this act he opened the vintage, no *must* (= 'wine from grapes not fermented') was allowed to be conveyed into the city until this solemnity was performed. This day was sacred to Jupiter, and Venus too appears to have had a share in it, for she was the goddess of gardens and also had vineyards under her protection.

VULCANALIA

A great festival in honour of Vulcan, celebrated in Rome on the 23rd if March and the 23rd of August, with games in the Circus Flaminius. Among his shrines in Rome the most noteworthy is called Vulcanal, a level space raised above the surface of the *Comitium* (= the place for the assembling of the Romans voting by the curiae), serving as a hearth. The sacrifice on this occasion consisted of fishes which the people threw into the fire on the hearth. It was also customary on this day to commence working by candlelight, which was probably considered as an auspicious beginning of the use of fire, as the day was sacred to the god of this element. Sacrifices were also offered to Vulcan as the god of metal working, he also bears the name Mulciber (*mulceo*= the softener or smelter of metal), on the 23rd of May, the day appointed for the purifying and cleansing of the trumpets used in the worship and sacrifice (*dies tubilustrium*= the feast of the trumpets). As lord of fire he was also the god of conflagrations; hence his temples were built outside the city, while this temple at Rome was situated on the Campus Martius. Stata Mater, who caused fires to cease, was worshipped with him as the goddess who protected from fires, and a public sacrifice was offered to her and him at the festival of the *Vulcanalia*. The Roman poets transferred all the stories which are related to the Greek Hephaestus to their own Vulcan, the divinities having, in the course of time, been completely identified with each other. Stata Mater is a Roman divinity, who image at one time stood in the forum, where fires were lit every night, she is probably identical to Vesta.

Finis.

APPENDIX ONE

Throughout the text we have used some of the Attic months,
but not all; again it might be helpful to the reader to
complete the list:

The Attic Months

Hekatombaion (July-August)
Metageitnion (August-September)
Boedromion (September- October)
Pydnepsion (October-November)
Maimakterion (November-December)
Poseideon (December-January)
Gamelion (January-February)
Anthesterion (February-March)
Elaphebolion (March-April)
Munychion (April-May)
Thargelion (May-June)
Skeirophorion (June-July).

APPENDIX TWO

Table of Planetary Hours

After Sunrise	SUN.	MON.	TUES.	WED.
1st	Sun	Moon	Mars	Mercury
2nd	Venus	Saturn	Sun	Moon
3rd	Mercury	Jupiter	Venus	Saturn
4th	Moon	Mars	Mercury	Jupiter
5th	Saturn	Sun	Moon	Mars
6th	Jupiter	Venus	Saturn	Sun
7th	Mars	Mercury	Jupiter	Venus
8th	Sun	Moon	Mars	Mercury
9th	Venus	Saturn	Sun	Moon
10th	Mercury	Jupiter	Venus	Saturn
11th	Moon	Mars	Mercury	Jupiter
12th	Saturn	Sun	Moon	Mars

After Sunrise	SUN.	MON.	TUES.	WED.
13th	Jupiter	Venus	Saturn	Sun
14th	Mars	Mercury	Jupiter	Venus
15th	Sun	Moon	Mars	Mercury
16th	Venus	Saturn	Sun	Moon
17th	Mercury	Jupiter	Venus	Saturn
18th	Moon	Mars	Mercury	Jupiter
19th	Saturn	Sun	Moon	Mars
20th	Jupiter	Venus	Saturn	Sun
21st	Mars	Mercury	Jupiter	Venus
22nd	Sun	Moon	Mars	Mercury
23rd	Venus	Saturn	Sun	Moon
24th	Mercury	Jupiter	Venus	Saturn

THURS.	FRI.	SAT.	From Midnight
Jupiter	Venus	Saturn	12-1 a.m.
Mars	Mercury	Jupiter	1-2 a.m.
Sun	Moon	Mars	2-3 a.m.
Venus	Saturn	Sun	3-4 a.m.
Mercury	Jupiter	Venus	4-5 a.m.
Moon	Mars	Mercury	5-6 a.m.
Saturn	Sun	Moon	6-7 a.m.
Jupiter	Venus	Saturn	7-8 a.m.
Mars	Mercury	Jupiter	8-9 a.m.
Sun	Moon	Mars	9-10 a.m.
Venus	Saturn	Sun	10-11 a.m.
Mercury	Jupiter	Venus	11-12p.m.

THURS.	FRI.	SAT.	Noon
Moon	Mars	Mercury	12-1 p.m.
Saturn	Sun	Moon	1-2 p.m.
Jupiter	Venus	Saturn	2-3 p.m.
Mars	Mercury	Jupiter	3-4 p.m.
Sun	Moon	Mars	4-5 p.m.
Venus	Saturn	Sun	5-6 p.m.
Mercury	Jupiter	Venus	6-7 p.m.
Moon	Mars	Mercury	7-8 p.m.
Saturn	Sun	Moon	8- 9 p.m
Jupiter	Venus	Saturn	9-10 p.m
Mars	Mercury	Jupiter	10-11 p.m.
Sun	Moon	Mars	11-12 a.m.